C0-AUM-854

BEING AND PREDICATION

**STUDIES IN PHILOSOPHY
AND THE HISTORY OF PHILOSOPHY**

General editor: Jude P. Dougherty

Studies in Philosophy
and the History of Philosophy   Volume 16

Being and Predication
Thomistic Interpretations

by Ralph McInerny

THE CATHOLIC UNIVERSITY OF AMERICA PRESS
Washington, D.C.

To Otto Bird

B
765
.T54
M34
1986

Copyright © 1986
The Catholic University of America Press

All rights reserved

Printed in the United States of America

Library of Congress Cataloging in Publication Data
McInerny, Ralph M.
  Being and predication.
  (Studies in philosophy and the history of
philosophy ; v. 16)
    1. Thomas, Aquinas, Saint, 1225?–1274—Contributions
in metaphysics—Addresses, essays, lectures.
  2. Metaphysics—Addresses, essays, lectures.   I.   Title.
  II. Series.
B21.S78   vol. 16 [B765.T54]   100 s [110′.92′4]   85-16603
ISBN 0-8132-0612-X

Contents

Preface

This book brings together previously published articles bearing on issues which have defined my scholarly efforts for some years. Such a collection cannot, of course, have the cohesion of a planned book, but there is a not too fanciful sense in which these studies can be thought of as chapters of a book I was half-consciously composing.

Every student of St. Thomas Aquinas is impressed by the distinction the Angelic Doctor draws between the way things are and the way we think and speak of them. The identification of the two is what Thomas means by Platonism; their distinction lies at the basis of his epistemological realism. It is this distinction that I have in mind in giving these studies the title *Being and Predication*.

With certain noble exceptions, the kind of research I bring together here has not characterized the work of Catholic philosophers in North America over the last twenty years. When I entered the profession three decades ago, great intramural battles were in progress: the quarrel between transcendental and more traditional Thomists; the skirmishes betweeen those who had been trained at Louvain and those who had been trained in North America and, among the latter, the disagreements between those who had studied at Toronto and those of us who had studied at Laval. But this does not begin to capture the ferment of the time. After all, many studied in Germany, Switzerland, and France, to say nothing of Rome. Moreover, a James Collins was a product of the Catholic University of America.

Nowadays those past dissensions turning on degrees and accuracy of Thomisticity can seem quaint. Certainly erstwhile foes have long since become allies in the battle against the dying of the light. Undeniably, there has been a great flight from the Catholic philosophical tradition on the part of American Catholic philosophers. As editor of *The New Scholasticism*, I have seen our common effort fragment into dozens of apparently unrelated efforts. Nor has the need and purpose of such an entity as the American Catholic Philosophical Association gone unquestioned. Were the days of Gilson, Maritain, De Koninck, Owens, Weisheipl, Klubertanz, Vincent Smith, James Collins, Leo Ward, Maréchal, Fabro, Vernon Bourke, Van Steenberghen, Garrigou-

Lagrange, Chenu, on and on, simply a phase happily surpassed in the intellectual life of the Church?

Along with the level of work evoked by those names there was also the level of required courses in Thomistic philosophy and the text-books that were their favored instrument. When the Council came, and with it salutary reminders of what it was that the great Leonine revival of Thomism had in view, one did not imagine that criticisms of the workaday classroom implementation of the revival would be turned on Thomas himself. The Council Fathers accorded St. Thomas Aquinas the deference one had come to expect from the Magisterium; indeed, Thomas is mentioned twice by name in conciliar documents, an extraordinary thing. But in that creeping miasma that dared call itself the spirit of Vatican II it became fashionable to say that the Council had demoted Thomas, set him aside, even somehow repudiated his role as the Common Doctor of the Church.

When I wrote *Thomism in An Age of Renewal* in 1966 I still thought the Council would bring a strengthening of Thomism and that some of the more trivial nostrums being proposed for Catholic colleges and universities would be seen for what they were. Who at that time could have foreseen how bad things would become in the intellectual life of the Church, particularly in theology? God is merciful. A new dark ages was about to descend upon us and we did not know it.

Signs are all about us now that the shadows are lifting. The old essential work has been going on during these decades, of course. Books and essays have appeared which have not yet received the attention they deserve. The all but abandonment of Thomas Aquinas by Catholics has had the effect of releasing him into the public domain, and one now has the sense of addressing a wider, more ecumenical audience. While too many Catholic theologians seem engaged in a reprise of a discredited Modernism, more and more Catholic thinkers wish to recapture, renew, and extend the intellectual capital that is our inheritance. Attending to the true voice of Vatican II and taking note of the reiterated endorsements of St. Thomas Aquinas by John XXIII, Paul VI, and John Paul II, we can take up again the great task associated with those heroes and giants mentioned above.

The first essay in this volume provides an overview of the life and work of Thomas. There follows a series of studies which put him into relation with Aristotle, Boethius, Albertus Magnus, Bonaventure, and Scotus. The heart of this volume is a group of studies which interpret the metaphysics of Thomas in a way that differs markedly from the so-called existential interpretation associated with Gilson, Owens, and

Fabro—needless to say, there are noteworthy differences among these three.

I owe to Charles De Koninck's inspiration my conviction that *sine Aristotele Thomas mutus esset*, to reverse the judgment of Pico della Mirandola. An appreciation of the fundamental Aristotelianism of Thomas Aquinas affects one's interpretation of his metaphysics and, above all, of his doctrine on how we can know and talk about God. The views expressed in *The Logic of Analogy* in 1961 are still my views, and I am more convinced than ever of their Thomisticity.

I end with a discussion of judgment by connaturality and a study of Maritain's employment and extension of it to talk about poetic knowledge. Apart from the intrinsic interest of the topic, this is meant as a tribute to Jacques Maritain, the Thomist to whom so many owe so much.

Acknowledgments

I would like to thank the publishers, editors, and journals who first published the research that makes up this book and to acknowledge their kind permission to reprint it here. Credit is given according to the chapters of this book.

1. First appeared as "St. Thomas Aquinas" in vol. 1 of the *Dictionary of the Middle Ages*, Joseph R. Strayer, editor-in-chief, Charles Scribner's Sons, New York, 1982, pp. 353–66.

2. "Beyond the Liberal Arts" appeared as chap. 10 in *The Seven Liberal Arts in the Middle Ages*, ed. David. L. Wagner, Indiana University Press, 1983, pp. 248–72.

3. "The Prime Mover and the Order of Learning" first appeared in the *Proceedings of the American Catholic Philosophical Association*, Washington, D.C., 1956, pp. 129–37.

4. "Ontology and Theology in Aristotle's Metaphysics" was my contribution to the *Melanges à la mémoire de Charles De Koninck*, Les Presses Universitaires Laval, Quebec, 1968, pp. 233–40.

5. "The Nature of Book Delta of the *Metaphysics* according to the Commentary of Saint Thomas Aquinas" appeared in *Graceful Reason: Essays in Ancient and Modern Philosophy Presented to Joseph Owens, CSSR*, ed. Lloyd Gerson, Pontifical Institute of Mediaeval Studies, Toronto, 1983, pp. 331–43.

6. "Ultimate End in Aristotle" appeared in *Vérité et Ethos: Recueil commemoratif dedié à Alphonse-Marie Parent*, Les Presses Universitaires Laval, Quebec, 1982, pp. 43–55.

7. "Boethius and Saint Thomas Aquinas" was published in *Rivista de Filosofia Neo-Scolastica*, Anno 66, fasc. 2–4, 1974, pp. 219–45.

8. "Albert on Universals" appeared in *The Southwestern Journal of Philosophy* 10/3, 1980, pp. 3–18.

9. "Albert and Thomas on Theology" appeared in *Miscellanea Mediaevalia*, Veröffentlichungen des Thomas-Instituts der Universität zu Köln, herausgegeben von Albert Zimmermann, Band 14, *Albert der Grosse*, Walter de Gruyter, Berlin, 1981, pp. 50–60.

10. "The Contemporary Significance of St. Bonaventure and St. Thomas" appeared in *The Southwestern Journal of Philosophy* 5/2, 1974, pp. 11–26.

11. "Scotus and Univocity" appeared in *De Doctrina Ioannis Duns Scoti*, Acta Congressus Scotistici Internationalis, vol. 2, *Problemata Philosophica*, Rome, 1968, pp. 115–21.

12. "A Note on 'Thomistic Existentialism'" appeared in *Sapientia Aquinatis*, Proceedings of the International Thomistic Congress, Rome, 1955, pp. 509–17.

13. This chapter includes both "Some Notes on Being and Predication," *The Thomist* 22/3, 1959, pp. 315–35, and "Notes on Being and Predication," *Laval théologique et philosophique* 15, 1959, pp. 236–74.

14. "*Esse ut actus intensivus* in the Writings of Cornelio Fabro" appeared in the *Proceedings of the American Catholic Philosophical Association* 38, 1964, pp. 137–42.

15. "Philosophizing in Faith" is my presidential address to the American Catholic Philosophical Association which appeared in the *Proceedings* for 1972, vol. 46, pp. 1–9.

16. "On Behalf of Natural Theology" appeared in the *Proceedings of the American Catholic Philosophical Association* 54, 1980, pp. 63–73.

17. "Can God Be Named by Us? Prolegomena to Thomistic Philosophy of Religion" appeared in *The Review of Metaphysics* 32, 1978, pp. 53–73.

18. "The Analogy of Names Is a Logical Doctrine" appeared in the *Atti del Congresso Internazionale*, vol. 6, *Essere*, Edizione Dominicane Italiane, Naples, 1974, pp. 647–53.

19. "Apropos of Art and Connaturality" appeared in *The Modern Schoolman* 35, March 1958, pp. 173–89.

20. "Maritain and Poetic Knowledge" appeared in *Renascence* 34/4, 1982, pp. 203–14.

1

ST. THOMAS AQUINAS: AN OVERVIEW

St. Thomas Aquinas (1224–1274), was born Thomas d'Aquino at Roccasecca Italy, into a family of minor nobility. At the age of five, he was presented as an oblate to the monastery of Monte Cassino, where he remained from 1230 to 1239 and where he began his studies. When the monastery became unsafe because of war, Thomas was sent to Naples, where he continued his studies (1239–1244). During this period he met his first Dominicans and felt drawn to this new order, which, like that founded by St. Francis, embraced poverty and represented reform. Thomas's family, seeing in a vocation to the Order of Preachers the loss of family benefits from his religious profession, was violently opposed to his becoming a Dominican. But Thomas prevailed, and in 1245 he set off for the north in the company of Dominican confreres.

Thomas continued his studies in Paris, then was sent to Cologne (1248), where he studied under Albert the Great, famous for his openness to Aristotle. Doubtless Thomas had already been introduced to the writings of Aristotle at Naples, but Albert's enthusiasm for the new learning was an important influence. Thomas prepared Albert's commentary on the *Nicomachean Ethics* for publication and, perhaps with the exception of some minor logical works written during the year his family detained him in the hope of dampening his desire to become a Dominican, this is the first product of his pen.

After his stay in Cologne, Thomas returned to Paris, where he remained from 1252 to 1259. For four years he lectured on the *Sentences* of Peter Lombard, the twelfth-century bishop of Paris whose collection and arrangement of fundamental theological topics provided the material that, along with Holy Scripture, the apprentice theologian had to discuss. In 1256, Thomas became master of theology, and he and St. Bonaventure, his great contemporary, were appointed to chairs reserved for mendicant friars. There was opposition from secular masters, and it was only in 1257 that Thomas became *magister re-*

gens. (By that time Bonaventure had been called to high office in the Franciscan Order.)

It was during this time in Paris that Thomas began his first great summary of theology, the *Summa contra gentiles* (1258–1264). Thomas spent the years 1259–1268 in Italy, where, after being attached to the papal court for several years, he taught in Dominican houses at Rome, Viterbo, and Bologna. He then returned to Paris, where he remained from 1269 to 1272, resuming his chair and continuing work on the *Summa theologiae*, which he had begun to write in Italy. The final period of Thomas's life (1272–1274) was spent in Naples. He was on his way to the Council of Lyons when he fell ill and was taken to the Cistercian monastery at Fossanova, south of Rome, where he died on 7 March 1274.

Thomas was a Christian, a Dominican, and a theologian; this meant, among other things, that he believed God had revealed himself to men in the scriptures and in his son Jesus. Owing to original sin, man's will has been weakened and his mind clouded, but grace and revelation both restore the natural destiny and elevate men to a new and supernatural one. While men can by their natural powers arrive at some knowledge of God, revelation puts them in possession of truths about God that could never be achieved by natural reason. Truths that can be achieved by natural reason are known in the sense that they are derivable from self-evident truths by way of an argument such that if one accepts the premises as true, one must accept the conclusion as true. Believed truths are held to be such on the basis of the authority of God's say-so. The distinction is one between faith and reason, belief and knowledge, and it gives rise to a distinction between philosophy and theology. Thomas Aquinas is of peculiar importance in the Middle Ages for the carefulness, subtlety, and precision with which he handled this question. The following passage provides what may be called the motto of his intellectual effort:

On this matter I want first to warn you that in arguing with nonbelievers about articles of faith, you should not try to devise necessary arguments on behalf of faith, since this would derogate from the sublimity of faith, whose truth exceeds the capacity not only of human but also of angelic minds. These things are believed by us as revealed by God. However, because what comes from the highest truth cannot be false, nor can what is not false be impugned by necessary arguments, our faith can neither be proved by necessary arguments, because it exceeds the human mind, nor, being true, can it be impugned by necessary argument. (*De rationibus fidei*, 2)

Thomas's receptivity to pagan thought, his serene confidence that known truth cannot be in conflict with believed truth, his conviction that faith is the culmination and perfection of intellectual inquiry, led to what has fittingly been called the Thomistic synthesis, a breathtaking effort to show the continuity and compatibility of philosophy and theology, and to use what he took to be the achievements of natural reason to cast light on revealed truths.

THEOLOGY AND PHILOSOPHY

In the prologue to his exposition of the *Sentences* of Peter Lombard, Thomas, as had many expositors before him (notably his mentor Albert the Great), discussed the nature of theology. He returned to this subject in his two great theological summaries, the *Summa contra gentiles* and the *Summa theologiae*, as well as in other works. Because of its central importance to his teaching, it is useful to consider closely his abiding thought on this matter. (It is of great historical interest to compare this preliminary discussion with the corresponding expositions of Lombard made by Albert the Great and St. Bonaventure.) Since Thomas's definitive position is to be found in the *Summa theologiae*, we will be guided principally by that work.

The first question that arises is why there should be need for any doctrine beyond that contained in philosophy. This question assumes two things: that philosophy is the name of any and all knowledge acquired by man's natural faculties, and that the classical Greek concept of philosophy as comprising knowledge of God, as well as of man and the world, is the correct one. Thus, Thomas is asking: If philosophy includes all knowledge of anything whatsoever, what need is there for any cognitive discipline or science over and above philosophy? In reply, Thomas says that man requires a special teaching in order to be apprised of the end beyond the reach of reason to which he has been called. Man is called to a supernatural happiness, but this had to be made known to him by divine revelation. Furthermore, Thomas holds that the human mind needs faith and revelation even concerning things we can naturally know, "because only a few men come to rationally acquired truth about God, and this after a long time and with the admixture of error" (*ST*, Ia, q. 1, a. 1).

Theology as a discipline over and above philosophy is necessary because faith and revelation put us in possession of truths that could not be arrived at by natural reason. As a discipline or science, theology, accepting as true whatever God has revealed, uses argumentation to see, for example, what might be implied by the conjunction of belief A and belief B. The characteristic note of Scholastic theology is its employment of philosophical truths and method in reflecting on revelation. Thus, when he speaks about the subject of theology, when he asks if theology is a practical or a speculative science, when he speaks of theology as a subalternate science, Thomas is developing a concept of theology that depends on a whole series of features of Aristotle's thought. Whether this should be done is a question Thomas put to himself. This is his answer:

Just as sacred doctrine is founded on faith, so philosophy is founded on the natural light of reason; hence it is impossible that those things which are of philosophy should be contrary to the things of faith, but they do fall short of them. Nonetheless, they contain similitudes and preambles, just as nature is the preamble to grace. If something contrary to faith should be found in philosophy, this is not philosophy but an abuse of it due to a defect of reason. Therefore one can, employing the principles of philosophy, refute an error of that sort either by showing it to be in every way impossible or at least not necessary. Just as the things of faith cannot be demonstratively proved, so too some things contrary to them cannot be demonstrated to be false, but they can be shown not to be necessary. Therefore philosophy can be used in three ways in sacred doctrine. First, to demonstrate the preambles of faith, . . . (what things in faith it is necessary to know), those things about God which can be proved by natural argument, such as that God exists, that God is one, and the like (as well as other truths about God and man proved in philosophy which faith presupposes). Second, for making known by way of similitudes those things which are of faith, as Augustine in his work *On the Trinity* uses many similitudes taken from philosophical doctrines to manifest the Trinity. Third, for resisting things said against faith either by showing them to be false or by showing them not to be necessary. (*In Boethii de trin.*, q. 2, a. 3)

FAITH AND REASON

The conception of preambles of faith is of great importance to Thomas's doctrine on the compatibility of faith and reason. If we believe a proposition to be true, we accept its truth on the basis of an authority, someone's say-so. Thus, if we think of a proposition as minimally the ascription of a property to a subject—S is P—the link between predicate and subject, when the proposition is believed, is initially supplied by an authority. For example, I first take someone's word for the fact that the Seine is a more beautiful river than the Tiber. Then I look at the two and assert the truth of this comparison on my own.

Thomas interprets knowing a proposition to be true as either immediately seeing that S is P or deriving this from truths already held, and ultimately from self-evident or immediate truths. To know mediately that S is P is to have a middle term that connects them. In short, Thomas's conception of knowing is connected with syllogism. Propositions immediately known to be true function as principles or starting points. "The whole is greater than its part" and "Equals added to equals give equal results" are examples of immediately known truths. To know what a whole is and what a part is is to know the truth of the first claim, just as knowing what equality and addition are suffices for the second.

Something first taken on authority can subsequently be accepted or rejected on the basis of knowledge, but religious faith is different. If I accept a proposition as true because God reveals it, I am accepting something I cannot know. To hold that Jesus Christ is a single person, human and divine in nature, is not to hold a self-evident truth or one that could be proved by appeal to known things. The believer must always in this life hold such a truth on the basis of revelation. Thus, religious belief is not seen as something replaceable by knowledge in this life.

Although the realms of knowledge and faith thus seem quite distinct, with no overlap possible, the concept of preambles of faith seems to blur the sharp distinction. Preambles of faith are exemplified by "There is a God" and "God is one." These are truths that Thomas believed as a child but that as an adult he felt he could prove to be true. Some of the things God has revealed are knowable. The revealed truths that can be known are not so much matters of faith as preambles of faith. Matters of faith, what is *de fide*, are mysteries. The sharp distinction between religious belief and knowledge applies only to the mysteries.

Thomas finds it significant that God has revealed to us truths we can in principle know. That we need special help even to grasp knowable truths indicates how the human mind has been weakened by sin. But one can also say that if some of the things God has revealed can be known to be true, it is reasonable to accept as true the rest of what he has revealed. This argument on behalf of the reasonableness of religious faith is not, of course, an argument on behalf of a particular datum of revelation, as if one were proving its truth.

In a famous passage Thomas (*ST*, Ia, q. 2, a. 3) describes five ways in which the existence of God can be demonstrated: from an analysis of motion, from an analysis of efficient causality, from an analysis of the possible and the necessary, from the grades of nature, and from the governance of things. In some of these arguments it is clear that Thomas is simply taking over an earlier philosophical position. For instance, the proof from motion is taken from Aristotle. For Thomas it was simply a fact that some philosophers had arrived at truths about God of the sort he calls preambles. Once more we are confronted with Thomas's conviction that philosophy and theology are compatible, that the latter depends in various ways on the former.

ARISTOTLE

Faith preceded the study of philosophy for Thomas, but he held that the study of philosophy must precede theology. When Thomas speaks of philosophy, he means the thought of Aristotle. Although, in the early Middle Ages, Aristotle was known only through a few of his logical writings, namely the *Categories*, and *On Interpretation*, toward the end of the twelfth century, a flood of Aristotelian works translated into Latin came onto the scene from centers in Spain, Sicily, and elsewhere. The influx of so impressive an amount of pagan thought, accompanied by Muslim commentaries and interpretations—Avicenna and Averroes playing an important if subsidiary role—presented problems of digestion for the Christian West.

The traditional educational system, grounded on the seven liberal arts—grammar, rhetoric, logic, arithmetic, geometry, astronomy, and music—with the standard *auctores* to be read, could scarcely be unaffected by a system that divided intellectual labor differently and was conveyed in works of overwhelming mastery. The natural works of Aristotle—the *Physics*, the *Parts of Animals*, *On Heaven and Earth*—when accompanied by Arabic works on medicine and mathematics, represented a veritable earthquake. But such works were only part of the vast Aristotelian system. Knowledge, Aristotle held, is either speculative or practical, and that is the first division of philosophy. Practical philosophy contains three basic divisions: ethics, economics, and politics. Speculative philosophy is first divided into natural science, mathematics, and metaphysics. How does one go about acquiring all this?

The intention of philosophers was chiefly this: that they might arrive at knowledge of first causes from consideration of all other things. So they put the science of first causes last and devoted the final part of their lives to its consideration. Beginning first with logic, which provides the method of the sciences; moving second to mathematics, of which even children are capable; third to natural philosophy, which requires time and experience; fourth to moral philosophy, of which the young are not appropriate students, they came finally to divine science which considers the first causes of beings. (St. Thomas, *On the Book of Causes*, proemium)

LATIN AVERROISM

Thomas studied Aristotle at Naples, Paris, and Cologne, but as a master of theology he would not have lectured on the writings of Aristotle as such. It is, therefore, a matter of great significance that he commented on so many Aristotelian works. One reason may well have been the use to which some masters of arts at Paris put Aristotle. Two extremely polemical works by Thomas, *On the Eternity of the World* and *On the Unicity of Intellect against the Averroists*, were aimed at what he took to be misunderstandings of Aristotle and/or the implications of Aristotelianism.

Aristotle, in proving the existence of the Prime Mover, assumes that the world is eternal. The clear teaching of scripture is that the world had a beginning and is not eternal. Thomas's views, as we have already seen, will not allow that a philosophical truth can be in conflict with a truth of faith. Since he believes the world is not eternal, he knows that "The world is eternal" is false. Can he show it to be false? He doesn't think so. He thinks that, from a purely philosophical standpoint, the matter is undecidable. Furthermore, he argues that Aristotle himself regarded the matter as debatable.

In the work on the unicity of the intellect, Thomas argues that Averroes' interpretation of Aristotle to the effect that there is but a single mind through which all men think, a sort of satellite in the ontological skies that survives the coming and going of individual men, is wrong. Thomas does not simply assert this. The little work is a textual analysis meant to show that Aristotle held that each man has a soul that will continue to exist after his death. The Latin Averroists maintained the following, according to Thomas: "By argument I conclude necessarily that there is numerically one intellect; however, I firmly hold the opposite on faith." What is one to make of such a position?

He [the Latin Averroist] therefore thinks that faith bears on things whose contrary can be proved with necessity. Since only what is necessarily true can be proved with necessity and its opposite is the false and impossible, it follows from the above remark that faith bears on the impossible, which not even God can make be, nor can the ears of the faithful tolerate it. (*The Unicity of Intellect*, ch. 5, n. 123)

Clearly, this sort of response to the influx of Greek and Muslim thought had to be countered. Holding that what Aristotle taught is compatible with Christian faith was not simply an abstract policy for Thomas. His commentaries on Aristotle exhibit this in detail. This is not to say that there is any overt reconciling of knowledge and faith in the commentaries; rather, there is the painstaking effort to clarify precisely what Aristotle means.

COMMENTARIES ON ARISTOTLE

Thomas commented on the following works of Aristotle: *On Interpretation* (incomplete), *Posterior Analytics*, *Physics*, *On the Soul*, *On Heaven and Earth*, *Nicomachean Ethics*, *Politics* (incomplete), *Metaphysics*, and some minor works. There has been discussion as to the significance of this vast output for the evaluation of Thomas's own teaching. When Albert the Great embarked on the gigantic task of paraphrasing the whole work of Aristotle, he said that that was all he was doing, setting forth Aristotle's views, not his own. Some have felt that the same motto can be put over Thomas's commentaries on Aristotle. Given the two little polemical works—*On the Eternity of the World* and *On the Unicity of Intellect*—this seems unlikely. Indeed, Thomas's statements about philosophy indicate that what he is interested in is the truth of propositions, not just historical accuracy.

Perhaps he finds truths in Aristotle that are not there? Some students of Aristotle contest Thomas's rejection of Averroes' interpretation of Aristotle on the human mind. It is sometimes said that Thomas baptized Aristotle—that is, that he read the great Greek philosopher with Christian eyes and found compatibilities the text will not support. Those who maintain this do not suggest that Thomas deliberately distorted Aristotle. Obviously there is no way in which such claims can be assessed other than by the careful study of the commentaries and the texts of Aristotle. When this is done, it becomes impossible to take Thomas as simply setting forth things he does not himself accept. When he says an argument is sound and cogent, he clearly means that without qualification; he does not mean Aristotle thought it sound and cogent. Nor are there any major instances of misunderstanding and distortion. Thomas called Aristotle *the* philosopher, and it would be impossible to understand his writings without knowing Aristotle. That his interpretations differ from others is true enough, but we have the text of Aristotle as the basis for deciding on their accuracy.

THOMAS AND PLATONISM

If Aristotle was *the* philosopher, he was not the only philosopher. In recent times increasing attention has been paid to the Platonic and Neoplatonic elements in the thought of Thomas Aquinas. Thomas commented on two works of Boethius, *On the Trinity* (incomplete) and the so-called *De hebdomadibus*. He also commented on the *Book of Causes*, proving that it was compiled of selections from Proclus. He also commented on the *On the Divine Names* of Pseudo-Dionysius, whom he took to be Dionysius the Areopagite, converted by St. Paul. It has been held that such concepts as that of participation and such signal teachings as the composition of essence and existence in every being other than God are indications of the Platonism of St. Thomas. Some have gone so far as to say that Thomas is more a Platonist than he is an Aristotelian. Surely that is an exaggeration. No one can read the commentary on the *Book of Causes* and fail to be struck by the way in which Aristotle serves as the measure in assessments of the basic claims of the work. Furthermore, insofar as Platonism and Aristotelianism are distinguished on the basis of differing positions on the problem of universals, there is little doubt where Thomas stands.

The problem of universals, so much discussed in the early Middle Ages, consisted of three questions formulated by Porphyry in his *Introduction* (*Isagoge*) to the *Categories* of Aristotle. Do common nouns like "man" refer to something real or to a figment of the imagination? Is the real thing they refer to corporeal or incorporeal? Is the real, incorporeal thing they refer to associated with bodies, or separate from them? It can be seen that the sequence of questions incorporates certain answers and suggests a solution to the problem. Plato can be said to have held that "man," while a common noun with respect to Plato and Socrates and Alcibiades, is the proper name of an entity distinct from these changing, evanescent individuals. The Ideas or Forms exist apart from particulars, and are their ontological ground as well as the possibility of knowledge.

In *On Being and Essence*, a youthful work, Thomas develops his own position by distinguishing the following propositions: Man is rational; Man is seated; and Man is a species. The first is true essentially; to be human is to be rational; rationality is part of the definition of man, part of his essence. The second is true because it happens that one or more men are seated. To be human and to be seated are only accidentally conjoined. The third is true because the human mind forms a concept of humanity and refers that concept to a variety of individu-

als. "Species" is one of the five predicables Porphyry discusses in his
Introduction; the others are "genus," "difference," "property," and "accident." These are five instances of universals. A universal is some one
thing that is said of or predicated of many. Species is a universal predicated of many numerically distinct things.

Thomas holds that the unit predicated is a consequence of human
understanding. To-be-said-of or to-be-predicated is not part of man's
essence. But insofar as we formulate a concept of the nature, there is
some one thing that can be predicated of many. If being seated is an
accident of the nature or essence thanks to material individuals, then
to be a species is an accident of essence thanks to the character of human knowing. There is a real similarity between individual men, and
this is the basis in reality for the formation of the concept "man." But
it is only as conceived that the nature or essence is something one-
over-many. Thomas's position on universals is called moderate realism. He does not think that natures exist apart from individuals (realism) or that there is no basis in individuals for the formation of the
concept (nominalism).

On this basic point, then, Thomas opts for Aristotle as against Plato.
But in the following passage he states what may be taken to be his
basic policy toward Platonism. Having summarized Platonic realism,
Thomas remarks:

This argument of the Platonists agrees with neither truth nor the faith with
respect to separated natural species, but, with respect to what it says concerning the First Principle of things, their opinion is most true and is consonant
with Christian faith. (*On the Divine Names*, proemium)

That is, Thomas wishes to distinguish between the view that there is a
separate entity Man over and above men, a separate entity Horse over
and above horses, and so with all natural species, which he rejects, and
the claim that there is a separate Being, Goodness, One on whom all
other things depend. Platonism is a bad way to interpret the import of
the common nouns with which we speak of creatures, but it is a most
fitting way to speak about God.

In somewhat the same way, Thomas compares Aristotle and Plato
on separated substances or angels. Aristotle's talk about immaterial
beings other than God has the great merit of being grounded on sound
argument. Plato's argument for immaterial being is deficient. But
what is appealing in Plato is the vast number of immaterial beings he
speaks of, whereas Aristotle, rightly bound by experience, can formulate arguments for only a small number of separated substances.

HYLOMORPHISM

Since Plato did not regard the things of this world as really real or as adequate objects of knowledge, he did not develop a natural science. The *Timaeus* can hardly be compared with the sequence of natural writings that came from Aristotle. One of the oddities of the transmission of classical texts is that in the twelfth century, Plato was known as the physicist. By the time of Thomas there was no longer any confusion as to which of the great pagan philosophers had devoted himself to natural science. Thomas's understanding of the nature of physical objects is derived from Aristotle.

His treatment of the constitution of physical objects—that is, objects that come to be as the result of a change—can be found in his commentary on the *Physics* and in the opusculum *On the Principles of Nature*. Besides these formal treatments there are many other works in which Thomas recalls the basic doctrine; it is safe to say that the bulk of what he says would be unintelligible without an understanding of this conception of the constitution of physical objects.

One of the consequences of the Aristotelian maxim that art imitates nature is that one can look to art to cast light on nature. So too in analyzing change, Aristotle first refers to changes wrought by the human artisan, as opposed to those brought about by nature, using the former as a way to understand the latter. And he can look at the change involved in a human being's acquiring a skill or art. Thus, he says, consider the following statements: (1) A man becomes skilled; (2) An unskilled man becomes skilled; (3) The unskilled becomes skilled. These are meant to be three different expressions of the same change. The artifact of language too may, when analyzed, cast light on what language is about.

There are two basic ways in which we can express a change: "A becomes B" or "From A, B comes to be." (1), (2), and (3) are all stated in the "A becomes B" form. Could each of them be reexpressed as "From A, B comes to be"? Thomas suggests that we would feel comfortable doing that with (2) and (3), but not with (1). The grammatical subjects of (2) and (3) do not express the subject of the change except accidentally; but the grammatical subject of (1) directly expresses the subject of the change. What is meant by "the subject of the change"? That to which the change is attributed and which survives the change.

This analysis leads to the claim that in any change there must be a subject, and that the subject acquires a characteristic it did not have earlier. It is because of an example Aristotle used that the subject came to be called "matter" and the acquired characteristic "form." If wood is taken and shaped into boards, a material has acquired a new form. The Greek words here are *hylē* and *morphē*. Thus, the theory that whatever has come to be as the result of a change is a complex of matter and form—that is, the subject and its acquired characteristic— is dubbed the hylomorphic theory.

When this analysis is applied to natural changes, it yields the view that things, from not being in such-and-such a place, come to be in such-and-such a place; from not having quality, come to have that quality; from being small, become large; and so on. The analysis, in short, provides a first way of interpreting changes in place, quality, and quantity. The subject to which such changes are attributed seems to be an entity of a more important kind than are the qualities, places, and quantities it loses and acquires. The Greek word for that subject is *ousia*, which becomes the Latin *substantia*, the latter term retaining the context of the analysis of change; the substance "stands under" the forms acquired in change, not unlike the way the subject of a sentence stands under the predicate. Thus, the application of this analysis of change to natural things comes down to saying that it explains the way substances can take on new accidents (things that befall or inhere in substances).

For Aristotle, the great problem confronting natural science in the fourth century B.C. was whether substances themselves come to be as the result of a change. He felt this had been denied because of the influence of Parmenides. Being cannot come to be: what is, is; what is not, is not. This should have stopped all talk of accidental change, but the line was drawn by saying that nothing really real, no substance, comes to be. Talk of change is all right as long as it does not suggest real novelty, that new being comes to be. Aristotle opted for substantial change—that is, for the view that substances, too, come into being as the result of change.

Thomas accepts the view that there are substances and that they come to be as the result of a change. Both these are givens, not a matter of theory. There are basic units in the world, things like Socrates and Plato and an olive tree. Once these things were not, and now they are; and it was by a process of change that they came to be. The problem, therefore, is not to prove that substantial change occurs—only a theory would lead one to deny it—but to ask how the analysis and terminology of accidental change can be adapted to talking about it. If the subject to which a substantial change is attributed (for example, "Xanthippe is born") were itself a substance, it would not be a substantial change, the coming into being of a new substance, but merely the modification of a substance that survives the change. The subject of substantial change cannot be a substance. If we call it the matter of the change, we must set it off from the subject of accidental change. "Prime Matter" is the term devised to name the subject of substantial change. The form it takes on is called a substantial form. Thus, not only is the product of the change whereby the Green Knight becomes tan describable as a complex of matter and form, but substances themselves are compounds of matter and form, of Prime Matter and substantial form.

ANALOGY

Words like "matter" and "form" and "nature" pervade the writings of Thomas Aquinas. The contexts of their use make it difficult to think that they are meant to be understood in the same way all the time. Thus there seems to be a constant threat of equivocation. This is a difficulty we ought to have when reading Thomas, if only because it makes his justification for so limited a vocabulary more interesting.

Already in the discussion of accidental and substantial change, words like "matter" and "form" have several meanings. When he wished to speak of the matter of substantial change, Aristotle said we should think of it on an analogy with the subject of accidental change. Thomas is going to put the matter-form dyad to a variety of uses, as in his analysis of knowing, but the retention of these terms is meant to incorporate similarities as well as differences in the things talked about. If there are connections among the things talked about, if our knowledge of one is dependent on our knowledge of another, then the use of the same terminology to speak of these various things can itself reflect these epistemological and ontological connections.

Thomas distinguishes three major ways in which things can share a name. If I say that Socrates is a person and Xanthippe is a person and Cyrus is a person, the recurring predicate here is shared, and presumably we would give the same account of "person" in these three occurrences of the word. Thomas calls such a shared term "univocal." On the other hand, the Latin *volo* means both "I wish" and "I fly" and *liber* means both "book" and "free." Thus, *volo* in "*Volo hodie*" can receive quite different and unrelated accounts. Thomas calls such a shared term "equivocal." Of course there is nothing about "*volo*" and "person" as such that makes them equivocal or univocal; we could easily find uses of "person" in which it would be equivocal and uses of "*volo*" that would be univocal.

There is another way in which a term can be shared, which Thomas says is midway between univocation and equivocation. He calls it "analogy," and he exemplifies it by "healthy" in the following situation. We say that Fido is healthy, that exercise is healthy, and that a sleek coat is healthy. Here we are unlikely to say either that "healthy" has exactly the same account in all these occurrences or that it has entirely different and unrelated accounts.

An analogous term is one that has a variety of accounts or meanings, and these accounts are partly the same and partly different. In what does the sameness and in what does the difference consist? The adjective "healthy" may be defined as "that which has health," and this may be made yet more abstract as "——— health." Then we can say that any account of "healthy" will include the abstract term "health" (that is, the element of sameness), but that the accounts differ because what fills in the blank differs. What can fill in the blank? Subject of; preservative of; sign of. Fido is the subject of the quality "health," exercise is preservative of it, and a sleek coat is a sign of it. In sum, the many meanings of the analogous term are partly the same—all include health—and partly different—each expresses a different mode or way of referring to health.

There is more to Thomas's theory of analogous names. One account takes precedence over the others, is prior to them, is the primary analogate. The primary analogate of "healthy" is "subject of health" because that is understood when we say "preservative of health" (in the subject of health) and "sign of health" (in the subject of health). The analogous name not only has a variety of accounts that are partly the same and partly different; one of those accounts is primary in the way just described.

When he commented on the fifth book of Aristotle's *Metaphysics*, a work often referred to nowadays as a philosophical lexicon, as if it merely set down a technical vocabulary, Thomas Aquinas saw it as a basic manifestation of the way in which words whose natural habitat was the physical world become analogous, as accounts for them are fashioned that enable us to use them to speak of immaterial things. After we have seen how Thomas uses the language of hylomorphism to analyze knowledge, we will return to that metaphysical use of analogy, particularly as it enters into his discussion of how we can speak meaningfully about God.

KNOWLEDGE

In his analysis of what knowing is, Thomas emphasizes such statements as "Socrates came to know such-and-such." To possess knowledge, in short, is to be in a condition that is the result of a change. This is why he can apply the language of change to knowing.

To be a thing is to be a kind of thing, and while there are many things of the same kind, there are also different kinds; thus A, being the kind of thing it is, does not have what B, a different kind of thing, has. If a thing comes to be as the result of a change, it is the completion or perfection of the process of change. Thanks to its kind, a thing has the perfection it does, and of course it does not have the perfections of other kinds of thing. Thus, in a certain way, though a thing is perfect of its kind, it is imperfect, only a part of the total perfection of the universe.

Hence, in order that there might be a remedy for this imperfection, another mode of perfection is found in created things, thanks to which the perfection proper to one thing is found in another. This is the perfection of the knower as such, for thus it is that something is known by the knower, that what is known is in some way within the knower. That is why Aristotle says in *On the Soul*, book three, that the soul is in a certain way all things, because it is fashioned to know all things. (*Q. D. de ver.*, q. 2, a. 2)

If coming to know is thought of as a kind of change, a way of coming to be, then knowledge will be thought of as taking on the form of another. Now, in natural change, to take on a kind of form is to become a thing of a certain kind. In acquiring the form of redness, a thing becomes a red thing. Furthermore, it ceases to be the kind of thing it was before the change occurred. Thomas wants to speak of knowing as having-the-form-of-another-as-other—that is, having another's form without the knower's ceasing to be himself. Seeing red, as a species of knowing, is to have the form of the red thing; it is not to become another red thing.

The change that knowing is thought to be is an intentional rather than an entitative change. The form acquired by the knower is a means whereby the known thing is present to it. Thus, the form stands for (intends) the thing whose form it is. Furthermore, though knowing is a change, it is not to be thought of as passive, as something that happens to the knower. The knowing powers are faculties of the soul that enable the living thing to initiate activity. There is, however, a passive element in knowledge. For example, when our sensory apparatus comes into contact with things, an entitative change occurs.

When I touch something warm, the temperature of my hand alters. That change is not cognition.

"There is nothing in the mind that was not first in sensation." This maxim incorporates the empiricism of Thomas Aquinas. The human soul is man's substantial form; its faculties or powers belong to a form actuating matter. The proper object of the human intellect is the quiddity or essence of the material object. Sensation is the indispensable condition for intellectual knowing. The ideas that the mind forms are ideas of physical objects, of sensible things. Thomas's theory of concept formation is Aristotle's. The agent intellect, a faculty of the soul, abstracts a form from sense data, and it is this form that actuates the passive intellect and permits the activity of knowing to take place. The concept is as form and the passive intellect is as matter.

This analysis of knowing permits Thomas to make use of terminology already fashioned in speaking of natural changes, but of course knowing is a change of a special kind. Thus there is continuity as well as variation in the use to which Thomas puts an amazingly small basic vocabulary, and it is his theory of analogous signification that saves him from the charge of equivocation.

METAPHYSICS

Being is the first thing grasped by the intellect. Being as being is the subject of metaphysics. Understanding the relationship between these two fundamental Thomistic tenets is of the utmost importance. Their conjunction would seem to suggest that a man can become a metaphysician without difficulty. Yet for Thomas, as we have seen, metaphysics is the last of the philosophical sciences to be studied.

Thomas's theory of knowledge, according to which it is the nature or essence of physical objects that is the proper object of the human mind, entails that, until proved otherwise, to be and to be material are identical. If there is immaterial being, we do not have direct access to it, because of the nature of human knowing, and its existence will have to be knowable through what is known of physical objects. The ways of proving God's existence formulated by Thomas all employ as premises truths about material things.

When Thomas speaks of a science, he has in mind an argument or syllogism of a certain kind. The subject of a science will be the subject of the conclusion of such a demonstration; the object of a science is the conclusion. There can be a network of demonstrations making up a single science if their subjects are all defined in the same way. That is, sciences will differ formally insofar as their modes of defining differ.

The notion of demonstrative syllogism that Thomas takes from Aristotle involves two notes: necessity and immateriality. Necessity, because really to know is to know that something is true and that it could not be otherwise. Immateriality, because of the nature of the faculty of knowing. The intentional reception of a form is different from the entitative; it is unlike the reception of a form in matter. If the object of theoretical knowing is necessary and immaterial, there can be different speculative or theoretical sciences insofar as there are formally distinct removals from matter and motion. What has matter can be otherwise, since matter is precisely the potentiality for forms other than the one currently actuating matter.

Some things require matter both in order to be and in order to be defined. Physical objects are by definition composed of matter and form, and their appropriate definition will express this fact. Natural science is concerned with things of this kind. Other things require matter in order to exist, but they can be thought of without thinking of matter. For example, line and circle and square can be defined without mentioning sensible matter, but this does not commit us to the claim that lines and circles and squares exist apart from material things. Mathematics is concerned with things of this kind.

Yet other things are such that they require matter neither in order to be nor in order to be defined, either because they never exist in matter (such as God and angels) or because they sometimes exist in matter and sometimes do not (such as being, act, potency, cause, and such). Just as, from a philosophical point of view, that there is a God or that there are angels must be proved, so it must be proved that some beings are immaterial. In order for metaphysics to be a possibility, what Thomas calls a judgment of separation must be made—that is, a judgment that something exists apart from matter and motion— and such a judgment must be the conclusion of an argument. Such arguments are found in natural science. The proof of the Prime Mover and the argument that the human soul does not cease to exist at death, the first found in the *Physics* and the second in *On the Soul*, are, for Thomas, the warrant for commencing a science whose subject is being as being.

THEOLOGY

If there is a philosophical theology, there is also a theology based on Sacred Scripture:

Theology or divine science is twofold: one in which divine things are considered not as the subject of the science but as principles of the subject, and this is the theology pursued by philosophers, which by another name is known as metaphysics; another, which considers divine things themselves as the subject of the science, is the theology which is treated in Sacred Scripture. (*In Boethii de trin.*, q. 5, a. 4)

Either sort of theology, and Sacred Scripture itself, will speak of God, and the question arises as to how this is possible. Human language is the expression of human knowledge, and human knowledge bears on physical things as its commensurate object. Our language is fashioned to talk about things so different from God that it seems to be an inadequate, even a misleading, instrument for the task of revelation and theology.

Since God's essence is not the essence of a material thing, he is not an appropriate object of human cognition. Such knowledge of him as we have will be indirect, grounded in our knowledge of other things; and words fashioned to speak of those other things will have to be extended by way of analogy to express, however inadequately, what God is.

It was shown above that God cannot be known by us in this life in his essence, but He is known by us from creatures, because of the relation of principle and by way of excellence and remotion. (*ST*, Ia, q. 13, a. 1)

God can be known by us through his effects and by the concept of a perfection found in creatures but considered in a mode excelling the creaturely by removing from it the limitations that attend it in creatures. At the root of this is a proof of God's existence, and it is in the proof that our language is extended to refer to him. Consider the bare bones of the proof from motion.

It is certain and evident to the senses that in this world some things are moved. Whatever is moved, however, is moved by another. But nothing is moved if it is not in potency to that to which it is moved: something moves to the degree that it is actual. To move is nothing else than to lead something from potency to act; but something can be reduced from potency to act only by a being already in act, as the actually warm fire makes wood that is potentially warm to be actually warm, and in this way moves and alters it. It is impossible that a thing be simultaneously in act and in potency in the same respect, but only in respect to different things. What is actually warm cannot be at the same time potentially warm, but it can be potentially cold at the same

time. Therefore it is impossible for something to be in one and the same respect moving and moved, or that it move itself. Whatever is moved, therefore,
must be moved by another. If, then, that by which it is moved should itself be
moved, it must be moved by something else, and that something else by something further. But this cannot go back infinitely, for then there would be no
first mover, and consequently no other mover, because secondary movers
move only insofar as they are moved, as the stick is moved only when it
is moved by the hand. Therefore one must come to some first mover, itself
unmoved, and this all understand God to be. (*ST*, Ia, q. 2, a. 3)

What justifies the extension of the term "mover" to God is the truths
adduced about moved and moving things in the world. That God is
not a mover like any other is captured by adding "prime." The whole
sense of the term "prime mover" is read off the world, and the proof
is what grounds the denotation of the phrase.

Thomas analyzes the meaning of terms applied to God by taking
them to be shared terms, common to God and creature. Furthermore,
he assumes that while we can more or less easily explain what a term
means as applied to creatures, the difficulty arises in extending it to
God. Thus "God is wise" and "Socrates is wise" exhibit the shared
term "wise." When we say "Socrates is wise," we mean he has acquired
the ability to assess all things with reference to what is first and best.
Clearly the term cannot be shared univocally by God and Socrates;
nor does it seem to be an equivocal term.

In taking the shared term to be analogous, Thomas finds the primary analogate in creatures. He does not take "God is wise" to mean
only that God is the cause of wisdom in creatures, but rather that
wisdom, found in creatures in a limited and incomplete way, is found
in God fully and excellently. Thomas sees three stages in such talk
about God: God is wise, God is not wise, God is wise in a manner that
exceeds our ability to understand. The affirmation bears on the quality
"wisdom," the negation bears on the created way of being wise, and
the final way of putting it admits that we can have no idea of the divine
mode of wisdom.

One sign of the inadequacy of our knowledge of God's possession of
wisdom is that in him wisdom is identical with Himself and with the
other attributes. In God, wisdom and justice and mercy and unity are
one simple reality. This does not mean that "wise" and "just" and so
forth, when affirmed of God, mean the same thing, as if we would
give the same account of each, but they refer to the same entity. For
every creature, to be is to be in a limited and restricted way; God is
unlimited perfection. Furthermore, there is no necessity that any
creature be, whereas God is such that he cannot not be. It is these and
other things that Thomas has in mind when he says that the least in-

adequate way of referring to God is as subsisting existence: *Ipsum esse subsistens*. Any creature has existence; God, so to speak, is existence.

Thomas's remarks on the reach of our knowledge and language in the matter of God make it clear that we are here at the very limit of our capacity. Finally, he wrote, what we know of God is that we do not know what God is. Human knowledge is always imperfect and inadequate in its attempt to think about God. This does not mean either that it is unimportant to seek precisions or that it matters little what we say of God. But, in the phrase of Nicholas of Cusa, man's knowledge of God seems to be a learned ignorance.

THOMAS AND SCRIPTURE

It would be misleading to view Thomas's work as a theologian solely in terms of the *Summa theologiae* and the *Summa contra gentiles*. These justly famous efforts to produce systematic summaries of theology were not products of Thomas's teaching, but were undertaken by him independently of his academic tasks. The three academic tasks of the theologian were *praedicare, legere, disputare*: to preach, to lecture, to dispute. The *Quaestiones quodlibetales* are records of the free-for-all disputes Thomas conducted at specified times in Advent and in Lent. The *Quaestiones disputatae* of Thomas contain some of his most important treatments of various subjects. His *Disputed Questions on Evil*, those *On Truth* and *On the Power of God*, are indispensable sources for his thought. The literary form of the recorded disputation clearly provides the model for the *Summa theologiae*: A question, a proposed answer with a number of arguments on behalf of it, followed by the citation of an authority indicating that the opposite of the proposed answer is true. Then a magisterial resolution of the question, after which the arguments offered on behalf of the first solution are dealt with singly. The *Summa theologiae* thus appears a closet drama when compared with the records of university disputations, however edited these may be.

Legere means literally to read. What texts was the theologian held to read and explicate? Chiefly the books of the Bible. The medieval Master of Theology was first of all a *Magister Sacrae Paginae*, one who had mastered Holy Writ. We have seen how Thomas, in his systematic description of theology, states that its starting points are to be found in what God has revealed. Thomas's lectures on Scripture were given throughout his academic career. In the Parisian custom, he probably alternated a work of the Old Testament and a work of the New. These are the biblical works for which we have Thomistic commentaries: Isaiah, Matthew, Canticle of Canticles, Lamentations (*In threnos Jeremiae*), Jeremiah, Paul's Epistles, Job, John, the Psalms. A distinction is made among these between those which are *reportationes* and those which are *ordinationes*. The difference is that the former were taken down by others and not checked by Thomas, whereas the latter were checked by Thomas. Sometimes a *reportatio* is called a *lectura* and an *ordinatio* an *expositio*.

Thomas learned from Augustine the various "senses of Scripture" (cf. *ST*, Ia, q. 1, a. 10). A human author can make the word for one thing mean another thing, but God can make the thing meant by a word another thing. Thus, in reading Scripture, we first attend to the things meant by the words: this is the historical or literal sense. The sense according to which those things refer to other things is the spiritual sense of the text. The spiritual sense is subdivided into the allegorical (the way the Old Testament prefigures the New), the moral (the way Christ's deeds indicate how we should behave) and the anagogical (the way the text signifies what will be in eternal glory).

The preeminent commentary on Job was Gregory the Great's *Moralia*. St. Gregory emphasizes the spiritual and moral senses of the book. Indeed, it came to be thought that it was impossible to find a literal sense for some passages in Job. In any case, the tradition of interpretation was heavily allegorical. Thomas, as the editors of the Leonine edition point out, explicitly breaks with this tradition.

We intend to give an exposition of that book said to be *Of Blessed Job* as compendious as we can and according to its literal sense, trusting in divine aid; for its mysteries have been laid open for us so subtly and fully by Blessed Pope Gregory that he seems to have left nothing further to say of them. (*In Iob*, prologue)

It should be noted that Thomas will include the figurative or metaphorical sense under the literal. "And although spiritual things are proposed under the figures of corporeal things, what is intended of spiritual things through the corporeal figures should not be assigned to the mystical sense but to the literal, because the literal sense is what is first intended by the words, whether it is expressed properly or figuratively" (*In Iob*, chap. 1, ll. 229–234).

MORALITY

If speculative philosophy is divided into three sciences on the basis of different modes of defining, practical philosophy is divided into three sciences on the basis of the difference between the goods or ends aimed at. Ethics is concerned with the perfection of the individual; economics is concerned with the good shared by the members of a domestic community; politics is concerned with the good shared by the members of a state.

Thomas's views on morality may be described as both eudaemonistic and incorporating the theory of natural law. Man's happiness consists in achieving the end or good that is perfective of his nature. There are some things that are good for men but that are not peculiarly human goods. Thus, simply to be and to survive are good; food and sex are good; but these are goods pursued by beings other than man. The good for man is to be found in the perfection of his distinctive activity, rational activity. Other creatures pursue goals, but man alone consciously directs himself to goals he judges are perfective of him.

But "rational activity" is a phrase that covers a wide variety of types; consequently, doing it well will be various and man's perfection or happiness is made up of a plurality of virtues. Rational activity can mean mental activity as such whose end is truth, and the perfections of it in this sense are called intellectual virtues. Some human acts are rational because desires and activities other than reasoning come under the sway of reason. To feel anger or sexual desire is neither good nor bad as such; it is the way man conducts himself when he feels such passions or emotions that determines the moral good or evil. Acting well in this way is productive of moral virtue. Constituents of the human good are the cardinal virtues—temperance, courage, justice, and prudence—as well as intellectual virtues. Thomas recognizes a vast number of subsidiary moral virtues as well.

Natural law is the peculiarly human participation in God's eternal law, whereby man directs himself to the end perfective of the kind of agent he is. Thomas held that it is comparatively easy for any person to recognize the basic values constitutive of human perfection and to formulate judgments that these are to be pursued and their opposites avoided.

Because the good has the note of a goal and evil the contrary note, all those things to which man has a natural inclination, reason naturally apprehends as goods, and consequently to be striven for, while their opposites are seen as evils to be avoided. Therefore, according to the order of natural inclinations, there is an order in the precepts of natural law. First, there is an inclination in man toward the good of the nature he shares with all other substances, since any substance seeks to preserve itself in existence as the kind of thing it is. On the basis of this inclination there pertain to natural law all those things through which man's life is preserved and its opposite impeded. Second, there is in man an inclination to more special things because of the nature he shares with other animals. According to this inclination those things "which nature teaches all animals" are of natural law, such as the union of man and woman, the rearing of children, and the like. Third, there is in man an inclination to the good of reason that is peculiar to him; thus men have a natural inclination to know the truth about God and to live in society. Things that look to this inclination pertain to natural law, for example, that man avoid ignorance, that he not harm those with whom he must live, and other like things. (*ST*, IaIIae, q. 94, a. 2)

Natural law precepts are the starting points of moral reasoning; the moral task is to pursue the goods they incorporate in the fluctuating and altering conditions of our lives.

Unlike Abelard, who maintained that any action is morally neutral and becomes good or bad only because of the intention with which we perform it, Thomas held that there are objectively good and bad actions. Indeed, if there were not, he felt it would be difficult to know what a good or bad intention would be. Intention is the soul of morality, but good intentions are those that aim at performing good acts.

CONCLUSION

Thomas Aquinas was principally a theologian, and the vast majority of his writings consists of commentaries on scripture and discussion of the mysteries of the Christian faith, as well as sermons. Many of his writings arose naturally out of his duties as master of theology; besides the kinds just mentioned there are a great number of *Disputed Questions* and a volume of *Quodlibetal Questions*. Among his writings we find a goodly number of responses to requests made to him for the discussion and solution of vexing theological and ecclesiastical questions. His theory about the propaedeutic necessity of philosophy for theology is everywhere evident in his vast literary output. But Thomas was not merely an intellectual; he was also a saint. His biographers tell us of the time he spent in prayer, begging for the light with which to see his way in his studies. In the last year of his life, as the result of a mystical experience, Thomas stopped dictating, telling his intimates that after what he had been shown, his writings seemed as mere straw. And yet, on his deathbed, at the request of the Cistercians at Fossanova, he undertook a commentary on the Canticle of Canticles.

Thomas's thought came under censure after his death. Several teachings associated with him found their way onto lists of condemned propositions. But this was a momentary, and indeed local, setback. Thomas quickly became the preferred author of Dominicans engaged in the study of theology, and over the centuries his teaching has attained an authority among Roman Catholics all but unequaled by any other author. Pope Leo XIII, in 1880, established a commission to edit and publish a definitive edition of Thomas's work. This (Leonine) edition is still incomplete. Whether he is regarded simply historically as one of the most important medieval theologians or is taken as a personal guide, Thomas Aquinas continues to be read and written about. In 1974, the seven-hundredth anniversary of his death, there were meetings, conferences, special editions of journals, and volumes of studies devoted to his thought. If few have read everything Thomas wrote, it is becoming humanly impossible to read everything written about him. By the same token, one who has spent over a quarter of a century studying Thomas finds it impossible not to add to those writings. The chapters that follow contain interpretations of the thought of Thomas made over the course of the past several decades.

2

BEYOND THE LIBERAL ARTS

"Non est consenescendum in artibus."[1]

Once upon a time—in the early Middle Ages, to be less inexact—the liberal arts tradition reigned supreme and education consisted or could consist largely in the pursuit of these arts for their own sake. Yeats said of Anne Gregory that only God could love her for herself alone and not her yellow hair. In the godly times of which we speak, students loved a liberal art for herself alone and not for any ladder that might be plaited of her yellow hair and used for ascent or descent to other windows. This golden age was not to last. It was succeeded by another in which the arts, while not ignored, were pursued in interested ways, as stepping stones to other matters. The liberal arts became enslaved and were made subservient to allegedly higher disciplines. This sad story can be summed up by saying that the liberal arts tradition was replaced by Scholasticism.

That is the story. History, of course, is a good deal more complex, as I hope to show here. Nonetheless, it is well to start with an assumption that is widely made, even though no one would embrace it in the simplistic form I have given it. What can be accurately said is this: there was a time when the liberal arts were preeminent in education, and this was followed by a time when they were not preeminent but subsumed within a vision of knowledge wider in scope. This simple statement is historical. There is in it no suggestion of a fall from grace, as if scholars of the period following the preeminence of the liberal arts had weakened and succumbed to a temptation that those of the preceding age had manfully resisted. It may be well to set down at the very outset a sort of *syllabus errorum* on the topic assigned me.

---

1. Cf. Fernand Van Steenberghen, *Maître Siger de Brabant* (Louvain: 1977), p. 31 and note 2.

1. There was a time when the liberal arts were studied for their own sake.

2. There was a time when the trivium and quadrivium were studied uniformly everywhere.

3. We need not worry too much about the difference between the monastic and cathedral liberal arts schools.

4. Scholasticism is something that can be opposed to the liberal arts tradition.

All of these propositions are false. As the terms *trivium* and *quadrivium* suggest (and the latter goes back to Boethius), the liberal arts were grouped in terms of a threefold way and a fourfold way—they were stepping stones, means to an end beyond themselves.[2] Prior to the thirteenth century, different schools could be distinguished not only in terms of an emphasis on the trivium to the virtual exclusion of the quadrivium, but, among those that emphasized the trivium, differences obtained because of an emphasis on dialectic in one place and on grammar in another. Further, the very character of grammar differed from school to school depending on whether study focused on grammarians or on the reading of classical texts.[3] The time when the liberal arts were preeminent in education was not a time when schooling was uniform. The third and fourth errors will be seen to be such after we rephrase our task with greater sensitivity to historical fact.

Something happens between the twelfth and thirteenth centuries with respect to the organization of secular learning. In the twelfth century, the traditional liberal arts could still seem to provide sufficient categories to contain the full range of secular knowledge. In the thirteenth century this is no longer so. It is not so only because the arts school, formerly associated with the cathedral or monastery, has now become a faculty of the university, a faculty through which one must go if one would enter the faculty of theology or law or medicine. The great reason for the replacement of the liberal arts as an adequate division of secular learning is the flood of literature that comes in from the Arabic world. More simply, it is the introduction of the complete Aristotelian corpus, with the result that one of the divisions of philoso-

---

2. Cf. Boethius, *De arithmetica*, Liber primus, caput 1, in Migne, *PL* 63 : 1079D–1083A.

3. Cf. Heinrich Roos, "Le *Trivium* à l'Université au XIIIe Siècle," *Arts Liberaux et Philosophie au Moyen Age*, Actes du Quatrième Congrès International de Philosophie Médiévale (Montreal: 1969), pp. 192–93. Hereafter this collection will be cited as ALPAMA.

phy that had been known all along is suddenly made concrete in a library of hitherto unknown works.[4]

The second chapter of the *De trinitate* of Boethius had acquainted the early Middle Ages with the Aristotelian division of theoretical philosophy into natural science, mathematics, and theology, but for all practical purposes this triad of speculative sciences enjoyed only a nominal existence. What was natural science other than that portion of the *Timaeus* that had been translated into Latin plus reflections generated by Genesis? Like the Stoic division of philosophy into physics, ethics, and logic, the Aristotelian division was known but for the most part as labels without the labeled. Only after the introduction of the whole Aristotle could it be asked whether the liberal arts provided an adequate division of secular knowledge.

This claim needs qualification, but let us seek initial support for it by comparing several reactions to the Boethian mention of the three-fold division of speculative philosophy, that of Thomas Aquinas in the thirteenth century and those of Gilbert of la Porée and Thierry of Chartres in the twelfth. First the text of Boethius:

Speculative Science may be divided into three kinds: Physics, Mathematics and Theology. Physics deals with motion and is not abstract or separable. . . . Mathematics does not deal with motion and is not abstract. . . . Theology does not deal with motion and is abstract and separable.[5]

Thomas began a commentary on this work that he did not complete; indeed it breaks off just slightly beyond the passage quoted from the second chapter of Boethius's *De trinitate*. The work has six chapters and Thomas's commentary covers approximately one-fourth of the text. It is not an interlinear or line-by-line commentary, like his commentaries on Scripture and on the works of Aristotle; rather, as is the case with his comments on the *Sentences* of Peter Lombard, he first gives a *divisio textus* and then discusses its content in a fairly independent series of questions in the style of a *Quaestio disputata* or of an article in the *Summa theologiae*. Furthermore, Thomas wrote his commentaries on Boethius early in his career.[6] The fifth question of his

4. Fernand Van Steenberghen, *Aristotle in the West* (Louvain: 1955); *La philosophie au XIIIe siècle* (Louvain: 1966), pp. 72–117.

5. "Nam cum tres sint speculativae partes, *naturalis*, in motu inabstracta anupexairetos . . . *mathematica*, sine motu inabstracta . . . *theologica*, sine motu abstracta atque *separabilis*." *De trinitate*, cap. 2, in *Boethius*, Loeb Classical Library, ed. H. F. Stewart and E. K. Rand (London & New York: 1918), p. 8.5–15.

6. In 1948 Paul Wyser published a partial edition, the commentary on chapter 2, so far as Thomas got, comprising questions 5 and 6. *Thomas von Aquin In Librum Boethii De Trinitate Quaestiones Quinta et Sexta* (Fribourg & Louvain). Bruno Decker published a complete edition a decade later: *Sancti Thomae de Aquino Expositio Super Librum Boethii de*

commentary bears on the passage quoted and is divided into four articles, the first of which asks whether the division of the speculative into three parts as Boethius has done is a good one. Among the considerations suggesting that it is not, we find this:

Objection 3. Again, philosophy is commonly divided into seven liberal arts, which include neither natural nor divine science, but only rational and mathematical science. Hence natural and divine should not be called parts of speculative science.[7]

Here is Thomas's resolution of the difficulty.

Reply to obj. 3. The seven liberal arts do not adequately divide theoretical philosophy; but, as Hugh of St. Victor says, seven arts are grouped together, leaving out certain other ones, because those who wanted to learn philosophy were first instructed in them. And the reason why they are divided into the trivium and quadrivium is that 'they are as paths introducing the eager mind to the secrets of philosophy.' This is also in harmony with what the Philosopher says in the *Metaphysics*, that we must investigate the method of scientific thinking before the sciences themselves. And the Commentator says in the same place that before all the other sciences a person should learn logic, which teaches the method of all the sciences; and the trivium belongs to the domain of logic. The Philosopher further says in the *Ethics* that the young can know mathematics, but not physics, which requires experience. So we are given to understand that we should learn mathematics, to whose domain the quadrivium belongs, immediately after logic. And so these are as paths preparing the mind for the other philosophic disciplines.[8]

The ambience of the discussion is Aristotelian—we notice the now familiar epithets: Aristotle is *the* philosopher and Averroes is *the* commentator (contrast this with earlier identifications of Aristotle as *logicus* and Plato as *physicus*!)—but the reference to Hugh of St. Victor displays Thomas's penchant for ligature rather than rupture with the tradition. The liberal arts are neatly fed into the order of learning the

---

Trinitate (Leiden: 1959); Wyser, in his Einleitung, gives the correct title: "Der in vielen, auch ältesten Werkkatalogen angeführte Titel *Expositio in librum Boethii de Trinitate* entspricht daher dem Inhalte nur teilweise. Die mittelalterliche Expositio literalis ist eine Form des sog. Commentums oder Commentariums, die—zum Unterschiede von der zweiten scholastischen Kommentarform der Glossen und Paraphrasen—den zu erklärenden Text in ein logisches Einteilungsschema bringt und sodann Wort für Wort, Satz für Satz erklärt. Der Thomaskommentar in librum Boethii de Trinitate ist aber nur zum kleinsten Teile Literalkommentar des Boethiustextes. Er verbindet nämlich die Divisio und Expositio textus mit der Quaestio, die aber in Umfang und Inhalt die Expositio literalis bei weitem übertrifft." Wyser, p. 4.

7. Translation from Armand Maurer, *St. Thomas Aquinas: The Division and Method of the Sciences* (Toronto: 1958), p. 4: "Praeterea, communiter dividitur philosophia in septem artes liberales, inter quas neque naturalis neque divina continetur, sed sola rationalis et mathematica. Ergo naturalis et divina non debuerunt poni partes speculativae."

8. Maurer, pp. 10–11.

philosophical sciences, an order gleaned from various passages in Aristotle, just as it is his authority that establishes what are the philosophical sciences. In his *expositio* of the *Liber de causis*, Thomas gives this statement of the *ordo addiscendi*:

Thus the chief intention of philosophers was that they should come to knowledge of the first causes by way of all the things they learned about other things. That is why they put the science of first causes last, devoting the final period of life to its consideration, beginning first with logic, which teaches the method of the sciences, proceeding next to mathematics of which even boys are capable, then to natural philosophy which requires time for experience, fourth to moral philosophy, of which a youth is not an appropriate student, and coming finally to divine science which considers the first causes of beings.[9]

The terminology of the liberal arts tradition is taken to point to *paideia*, the introduction to learning, and the arts are thus seen to be instrumental, prerequisites for what is to follow. That the study or studies beyond themselves to which the arts point is/are diversely identified by a Hugh of St. Victor or a Thomas Aquinas goes without saying, but Thomas himself says nothing of this difference with the tradition because his tendency is to reconcile rather than to underline differences.[10]

In the continuation of the text, Thomas takes up a question that is at least as old as Cassiodorus:[11] why are some studies called both arts and sciences?

9. "Et inde est quod philosophorum intentio ad hoc principaliter erat ut, per omnia quae in rebus considerabant, ad cognitionem primarum causarum pervenirent. Unde scientiam de primis causis ultimo ordinabant, cuius considerationi ultimum tempus suae vitae deputarent: primo quidem incipientes a logica quae modum scientiarum tradit, secundo procedentes ad mathematicam cuius etiam pueri possunt esse capaces, tertio ad naturalem philosophiam quae propter experientiam tempore indiget, quarto autem ad moralem philosophiam cuius iuvenis esse conveniens auditor non potest, ultimo autem scientiae divinae insistebant quae considerat primas entium causas."—*Sancti Thomae de Aquino Super Librum De Causis Expositio*, ed. H. D. Saffrey (Fribourg & Louvain: 1954), p. 2.15−24. It was Thomas who saw that the *Liber de causis* had been compiled from Proclus's *Elements of Theology*. See Saffrey's introduction, p. xxiv. Perhaps the most striking thing about Thomas's exposition of this Neoplatonic work is the fact that he reads it through an Aristotelian lens. It is Aristotle who provides standards of acceptance, rejection, interpretation. Much interest has recently been shown in the Platonism of Thomas by Geiger, Fabro, Klaus Kremer. This is a large subject, but the conclusion that Thomas remains basically an Aristotelian seems inescapable. This is true not only of his reading of Boethius's *De hebdomadibus* early in his career, but also of his exposition of the *Liber de causis* in the last years of his life. In short, there is nothing unusual about his reduction of the liberal arts to Aristotelianism.

10. On Hugh of St. Victor, see the introduction to Jerome Taylor's *The Didascalicon of Hugh of St. Victor* (New York: 1961).

11. See Ralph McInerny, *A History of Philosophy*, vol. 2, *Philosophy From Augustine to Ockham* (Notre Dame: 1970), p. 77.

We may add, too, that these are called arts among the other sciences because they involve not only knowledge but a certain work which is directly a product of reason itself; for example, producing a composition, syllogism or discourse, numbering, measuring, composing melodies and reckoning the course of the stars. Other sciences, like divine and natural sciences, either do not involve a work produced, but only knowledge, and so we cannot call them arts, because, according to the *Metaphysics*, art is called 'productive reason'; or they involve a material product, as in the case of medicine, alchemy and other sciences of this sort. These latter, then, cannot be called liberal arts because such actions belong to man on the side of his nature in which he is not free, namely, on the side of his body.[12]

This is an ingenious passage. In it, Thomas provides a reason why some of the philosophical sciences recognized by Aristotle are called arts while others are not, and he distinguishes the liberal arts from the mechanical arts which, according to Hugh of St. Victor, are also seven in number.[13] Taking the Aristotelian conception of art as *recta ratio factibilium*,[14] an intellectual skill in making, Thomas suggests that, in its obvious sense, making is a transitive activity involving corporeal effort and resulting in a product that differs from, and is distinct from, the activity itself. Thus, art in its primary sense is servile or mechanical, and its result is a spatio-temporal entity, an artificial object taking up room among natural objects. Art therefore involves the natural as its material in the way that a statue is shaped marble that continues to take up space just as it did in its purely natural condition. If some of the sciences are called arts, this must be because, on an analogy with arts in the usual or primary sense, they have an opus, a product. The products Thomas lists proceed through the arts that make up the traditional liberal arts: grammar aims at syntax or construction; logic at the forming of syllogisms; rhetoric at the making of speeches; arithmetic at enumeration; geometry at measuring; music at the forming of melodies; and astronomy at the charting of the courses of heavenly bodies. The suggestion is that the works or products of the liberal arts are more spiritual, products of that in us which is the root of freedom, namely, mind.[15] Sciences that have such *opera* or products are called arts by way of analogy. Sciences that have no such products are not called arts. We notice that moral science is still unaccounted for. "And although moral science is directed to action, still that action is not the

---

12. See Maurer, op. cit., p. 11. This is the continuation of q. 5, a. 1, ad 3.

13. See McInerny, pp. 190–94. I use *Didascalicon*, ed. Buttimer (Washington: 1939).

14. Thomas must have had in mind *Metaphysics*, E.1.1025b22, but he could equally as well have cited *Nicomachean Ethics*, 1140a8–10.

15. The sciences not called liberal arts are nonetheless liberal and may be more so than the sciences that are called liberal arts.

act of the science but rather of virtue, as is clear in the *Ethics*. So we cannot call moral science an art; but rather in these actions virtue takes the place of art."[16] The virtuous action with which moral science is concerned is neither a matter of knowledge alone nor, as such, a transitive activity producing a spatio-temporal object as its effect.

In this remarkable discussion, then, the liberal arts have entered the universe of Aristotelian philosophy. Rather than see the latter as replacing the former, as if they were rivals, Thomas interprets the liberal arts tradition as a *partial* and *inadequate* division of philosophical labor. Traditionally, the liberal arts had been regarded as propaedeutic—the terms trivium and quadrivium indicate this—but, if they were instrumental, they were more or less directly *ancillae theologiae*, that is, ways to the wisdom contained in Scripture. We will return to this. With Thomas, they are seen as propaedeutic and ancillary *to other philosophical sciences*, which for different reasons must be learned later than the trivium and quadrivium. Of course, philosophy taken as a whole, the sum of the liberal arts and the sciences that are not arts, continues to be regarded as *ancilla theologiae*.[17] The difference is that philosophy is a larger whole than it was when philosophy could be equated with the liberal arts.[18]

What do commentators writing prior to the influx of the integral Aristotle make of the text of Boethius? Gilbert of la Porée's commentary is included in the volume of Migne that contains the theological tractates of Boethius.[19] It is a running commentary. Having cited the Boethian remark *Nam cum tres sint speculativae partes*, et cetera, Gilbert explains it thus:

> There are many kinds of science. For some are theoretical, that is, speculative, namely those whereby we see whether and what and how and why each created thing is; others are practical, that is, active, namely those whereby we know how to act rather than see, like medicine, magic, and the like. Putting the practical aside, the speculative lay claim to that appellation because through them we see, and some are called physical, that is, natural, others ethical, that is, moral, and others logical, that is, rational. If we now set aside the moral and rational, those which are called by the one term natural, and by common usage speculative, have three parts. . . .[20]

16. Maurer, pp. 11–12 = *In Boethii de trin.*, q. 5, a. 1, ad 3.

17. *ST*, Ia, q. 1, a. 5.

18. Thomas discusses the different senses the theoretical/practical contrast has applied to philosophy as a whole, to the arts, and even to different aspects of a practical art like medicine. *In Boethii de trin.*, q. 5, a. 1, ad 4.

19. Migne, *PL* 64. The commentary on *De trinitate* runs from 1255B to 1300C.

20. Ibid., 1265B–C: "Scientiae multorum sunt generum. Aliae namque sunt theoricae, id est speculativae, ut illae quibus intuemur an sint et quid sint et qualia sint, et cur sint singula creata; alia vero sunt practicae, id est activae, ut illae quibus potius in-

Gilbert identifies the practical by citing medicine, magic, and the like, and sets it to one side; he then invokes the Stoic threefold division of philosophy (physics, logic, and ethics), and presents it as a division of *speculative* philosophy. The threefold division of the text is then discussed as a subdivision of one of the parts of speculative philosophy, an oddity justified by appealing to common usage. The passage gives evidence of acquaintance with the *Posterior Analytics* in its listing of the four questions that the theoretical sciences put to created things.[21] In the sequel, some display is made of Greek and it may be that Gilbert has *akhōristos* (unseparated) for *anupexairetos* (inseparable). The discussion of the criteria for distinguishing the three speculative sciences is quaint. The matter-form couplet is discussed with references to Plato and indeed there is something Platonic in the presentation of the objects of these sciences.[22] Insofar as the text of Boethius refers to the Aristotelian natural writings and the *Metaphysics*, and not to the *Timaeus*, it cannot be unpacked by Gilbert.

If we glance at the various commentaries on the *De trinitate* attributed to Thierry of Chartres by Häring,[23] we find a similar Platonizing explanation, one that makes explicit reference to the *Timaeus* but that also employs[24] other passages from Boethius. The threefold division of philosophy into physics, ethics, and logic is altered to *logica, ethica et speculativa*, these being distinguished as concerned, respectively, with arguments, actions, and causes.

Now what is noteworthy about these twelfth-century commentaries on the *De trinitate* of Boethius, that of Gilbert of la Porée, and all those attributed to Thierry of Chartres by Häring, is that, in the supposed heyday of the liberal arts tradition, they exhibit no interest whatsoever

---

spectionem scimus operari: ut medici, magi, et hujusmodi. Ut autem de practicis taceamus, speculativae ex his quae per ipsas inspicimus contrahunt appellationem, et vocantur aliae quidem physicae, id est naturales; aliae vero ethicae, id est morales; aliae autem logicae, id est rationales: et ut item morales atque rationales praetereamus, illarum quae uno nomine naturales dicuntur, quae etiam usu majore speculativae vocantur, tres partes sunt. . . ."

21. Cf. *Posterior Analytics*, II.1.89b24–25.

22. Etienne Gilson, *History of Christian Philosophy in the Middle Ages* (New York: 1955), pp. 140–44.

23. See Nikolaus Häring, "A Commentary on Boethius' *De trinitate* by Thierry of Chartres (Anonymus Berolinensis)," AHDL (1956), pp. 257–325; "The Lectures of Thierry of Chartres on Boethius' *De trinitate*," AHDL (1958), pp. 113–226; "Two Commentaries on Boethius (*De trinitate* and *De hebdomadibus*) by Thierry of Chartres," AHDL (1960), pp. 65–136. L. J. Bataillon has disputed some of these attributions to Thierry. See his "Bulletin d'histoire des doctrines médiévales: Le douzième siècle," *Revue des Sciences Philosophiques et Théologiques* 62/2 (1978), p. 245, and his "Sur quelques éditions de textes platoniciens médiévaux," in the same journal, 61/2 (1977), pp. 253–60.

24. For example, AHDL (1960), p. 93, note 7.

in comparing the division of intellectual labor given in the texts with that embodied in the liberal arts. Insofar as arts are alluded to, they are immediately excluded from consideration. In the case of Gilbert, the arts mentioned are not liberal (medicine and magic *et hujusmodi alii*), but one can still be surprised at the failure to mention the liberal arts.

On the basis of the twelfth-century commentaries on Boethius of Gilbert and Thierry and the thirteenth-century one of Thomas Aquinas, we would have to say that it is the earlier writers who, confronted by a division of intellectual labor apparently different from the liberal arts, gloss the text with reference to Plato and the *Timaeus* only, whereas Thomas is concerned to relate the Aristotelian division of speculative science to the liberal arts tradition. Let this serve as caveat, then, and a check to the tendency, if we feel it, to say that it is in the thirteenth century, with the rise of the universities and the introduction of the complete Aristotle, that the liberal arts are rudely cast aside or made subservient to other and alien ends. We have seen at least two twelfth-century figures who completely ignore the liberal arts tradition when commenting on a text that invites mention of it.

But perhaps we have simply come up with bad or unrepresentative samples of these two centuries. Surely, as we have acknowledged, there is something to be said for the claim that there was a time when the liberal arts were considered an adequate division of secular learning and there was a subsequent time when the liberal arts were no longer so considered. Let us take a swift look at that earlier period, having in mind as we do so the first item on our *syllabus errorum*.

In recalling the tradition of the liberal arts, we could do worse than begin with St. Augustine. Having left his native Africa to take a post as teacher in the imperial rhetorical school in Milan, he listened to the sermons of St. Ambrose and then, one day, in his garden, he heard from over the wall the voices of children at play. *Tolle et lege*, take and read, and he picked up St. Paul and read the passage on which his eye fell.[25] Its application to himself seemed incontestable; he decided to prepare himself for baptism. Now how did he do this? He went into retreat at Cassiciacum and began to write works on the liberal arts! His *De musica* dates from this time and is one proof that he kept his intention. He also wrote (more accurately, dictated) the *De ordine* and the *De magistro*, the latter a dialogue with his son, Adeodatus, in whom

25. Augustine, *Confessions*, VIII.9, ed. Pierre de Labriolle (Paris: 1956), p. 200. See the *Retractationes*, I.6.

Augustine took much justified paternal pride. We can see in these works some traces of what Augustine must have been like as a teacher and what the education of his time was like. In any case, he speaks of the liberal arts as a preparation for philosophy, the latter having as its two great concerns the soul and God.[26] The arts give one the skills necessary to discuss these great questions. And what are the liberal arts? Grammar, rhetoric, logic, arithmetic, geometry, music, and astronomy. With Augustine, the number of the liberal arts is fixed at seven, under the influence of Martianus Capella, whose allegorical work, *De nuptiis Mercurii et Philologiae* lopped off the medicine and architecture that Varro had included along with the arts that were to become the traditional seven. Augustine himself sometimes and confusingly replaces astronomy with philosophy,[27] apparently because of his distaste for astrology which catered to superstition. Notice that, for Augustine, the liberal arts are taught and learned in order that, given them, something else, namely philosophy, might be done. Although it is not the case that we find in Augustine a clear-cut and consistent distinction between philosophy as an activity in which a pagan might engage and philosophy as a reflection on Christian belief, to study the soul and God is to employ the liberal arts but to engage in something else.

Cassiodorus Senator, a contemporary of Boethius who survived, as Boethius did not, his association with the Ostrogoths, founded a monastery at Vivarium and wrote for its inhabitants a work called the *Institutiones*.[28] It is divided into two parts and may originally have been two works, the first of which deals with the liberal arts, the second with Scripture. Here we have what will become a commonplace, namely, that the study of the liberal arts is a preparation for the reading of Scripture. The arts are seen as secular, even pagan attainments that the believer can redeem and put to a higher purpose.

We have already seen how the threefold Stoic division of philosophy was employed by two men in the twelfth century. This division of philosophy into logic, physics, and ethics could have been known by the medievals from Book VIII of Augustine's *City of God*. Alcuin, the teacher of Charlemagne, knows that the seven liberal arts are studied as preparations for the study of Scripture. If the trivium and quadrivium are ways to something, that something is wisdom and wisdom is to be found in Scripture; thus the arts are viewed as the seven pillars

26. *Soliloquies*, I.ii.7. See McInerny, pp. 12–15.
27. *Retractationes*, I.6.
28. *An Introduction to Divine and Human Readings*, trans. L. W. Jones (New York: 1946).

of wisdom. But if the pursuit of wisdom, i.e., philosophy, comprises three parts, these parts must be found in Scripture. They must be linked to books of the Bible. Where is physics to be found? In Genesis. Where is ethics to be found? In the sapiential books. Where is logic to be found? Alcuin's answer boggles the mind. Logic is contained in the Song of Songs.[29] Of course Alcuin's theory poses many difficulties. Is not logic one of the liberal arts that are presupposed by the pursuit of wisdom, one of whose parts is logic, improbably located in the Song of Songs?

It is tempting to consider Hugh of St. Victor in the twelfth century as the apotheosis of the liberal arts tradition. In his *Didascalicon*, he balances the liberal arts with a list of servile or mechanical arts, on the one hand, and with the wisdom contained in Scripture, on the other. Hugh knows the traditional divisions of philosophy; for him philosophy is not equated with the liberal arts but includes the mechanical arts and the wisdom of the word of God. He takes seriously the commodious traditional definition: *philosophia est disciplina omnium rerum humanarum atque divinarum rationes plene investigans* (philosophy is a discipline that seeks understanding of all things both human and divine).[30] But philosophy is a whole within which the arts serve as stepping stones to the fullness of the Christian life. This can be seen as a reiteration of the views of Cassiodorus and of Alcuin and of other earlier figures in the liberal arts tradition, a reiteration intended to oppose what Hugh regarded as the growing secularization of the schools. That is, Hugh saw the move toward the autonomy of the liberal arts as a threat to their true value.

We need an interim summary of results. What is the historical cash value of the claim that a period when the liberal arts were pursued for their own sake and enjoyed autonomy was succeeded by a period in which the arts diminished in importance and were made subservient to other disciplines, this second period being identified with Scholasticism? While it is easy to concede that something significant happened as the twelfth century gave way to the thirteenth, the claim we are examining does not seem to be the best way of expressing that

29. "In his quippe generibus tribus philosophiae etiam eloquia divina consistunt.— C. Quomodo?—A. Nam aut de natura disputare solent, in Genese et in Ecclesiaste; aut de moribus, ut in Proverbiis et in omnibus sparsim libris; aut de logica, pro qua nostri theologiam sibi vindicant, ut in Cant. Cant. et in sancto Evangelio." *De dialectica, PL* 101:952. Alcuin's interlocutor in this dialogue is none other than Charlemagne.

30. Cf. *Didascalicon*, ed. Buttimer.

change. First, the standard way of regarding the liberal arts entailed from the beginning that they were viewed as propaedeutic, instrumental, *viae* to something else. Second, this something else in the early Middle Ages tended to be identified with the wisdom contained in Scripture. One wanted to study the liberal arts in order to be a better, more adroit reader of Holy Writ. Third, prior to the great change, when commentators confronted such a text as that of Boethius's *De trinitate*, where the Aristotelian division of speculative philosophy was reported, they did not immediately ask how such a division related to the liberal arts tradition. Gilbert of la Porée did not; Thierry of Chartres did not.[31] On the other hand, Thomas Aquinas in the thirteenth century was concerned to show how the liberal arts fitted into the Aristotelian scheme. So was Kilwardby in the *De ortu scientiarum*.[32] Fourth, in the earlier period, efforts to secularize the study of the arts, that is, to divorce them from their orientation to Scripture, were regarded as dangerous by such men as Hugh of St. Victor. Fifth, there was little uniformity in the earlier period and "arts schools" differed considerably from one another in the arts they emphasized and the authors read. Of course, there would be general agreement as to the number and identity of the liberal arts.

What then is the cash value of the claim? This: prior to the thirteenth century, it was possible to employ the schema of the seven liberal arts as an adequate summary of secular learning, even if this required stretching a point or two; after the introduction of the complete works of Aristotle, the Arabic commentaries, et cetera, et cetera,

31. In fairness, it should be pointed out that Thierry of Chartres did write an *Eptateuchon*, on the liberal arts. The prologue to this work has been edited by E. Jeauneau in *Mediaeval Studies* 16 (1954), pp. 174ff., and the work itself is discussed by A. Clerval in *Les écoles de Chartres* (Paris: 1895). Another twelfth-century figure, William of Conches, suggested the following division of knowledge that finds room for the liberal arts:

Knowledge
- Eloquence
  - Grammar Rhetoric Dialectic
- Wisdom
  - Theoretical
    - Theology Math. Physics
      - Arithmetic Music Geometry Astronomy
  - Practical
    - Ethics
    - Economics
    - Politics

See McInerny, pp. 167–69.

32. Cf. Robert Kilwardby, *De ortu scientiarum*, ed. Albert G. Judy, O.P. (London: 1976).

the inadequacy of the liberal arts scheme as a net in which to catch the entirety of secular learning could scarcely be ignored. In the words of Van Steenberghen:

La grande entrée d'Aristote au XIIIe siècle vint modifier de fond en comble la situation: pour la première fois, un système compact de disciplines scientifico-philosophiques forçait l'entrée du monde chrétien; l'aristotélisme, chef d'oeuvre de l'intelligence grecque, enrichi par les rapports du néoplatonisme grec, juif et arabe, se dressait soudain en face de la théologie; une sagesse païenne se trouvait tout à coup en présence de la sagesse chrétienne; le savoir profane n'était plus représenté par le cortège modeste et inoffensif des arts libéraux, mais par la puissante synthèse scientifique du péripatétisme.[33]

[Aristotle's grand entry into the thirteenth century radically altered the situation: for the first time, a compact system of scientific-philosophical disciplines entered the Christian world; Aristotelianism, the masterpiece of the Greek mentality, enriched by its contact with Greek, Jewish, and Arabic Neoplatonism, suddenly confronted theology; a pagan wisdom found itself face to face with Christian wisdom; profane knowledge would no longer be represented by the modest and inoffensive parade of liberal arts but by the powerful scientific synthesis of Peripateticism.]

Now the classical divisions of philosophy that had been handed down through the early Middle Ages, labels without their corresponding packages, could be matched with a hitherto unsuspected library of works. Thus, it is the adequacy or inadequacy of the liberal arts to gather all secular learning that is the issue. The liberal arts are not rejected; they are placed in a wider scheme by a Thomas Aquinas or a Kilwardby (radically different from the wider schemes of a William of Conches or a Hugh of St. Victor). Indeed, one might say that the liberal arts were *returned* to what had been their native habitat prior to the Dark Ages. These arts had been subservient parts of *paideia* for Plato and Aristotle.[34] In Islam, we are told, the liberal arts never enjoyed the separate existence they led during the early Middle Ages in the West.[35] That separate existence was a function of the *partial* inheritance of the classical patrimony. When this was remedied at the end of the twelfth century and later, the status of the liberal arts was bound to change, to revert to what it had been in the classical setting.

It must also be stressed that we cannot differentiate our two periods by dubbing the second Scholasticism or the Scholastic Age. It is, of

33. Fernand Van Steenberghen, *La philosophie au XIIIe siècle*, p. 287.
34. See the magnificent introduction by Ludwig Bauer to his edition of Gundissalinus's *De divisione philosophiae*, in Bauemker's *Beitrage*, vol. 4, II/III (1903).
35. See Majid Fakhry, "The Liberal Arts in the Mediaeval Arabic Tradition from the Seventh to the Twelfth Centuries," in ALPAMA, pp. 91–97.

course, no easy matter to define Scholasticism.[36] As a term of abuse, it is doubtless well that it should be as commodious as possible, the better to encompass all one's enemies. The tired example of the angels and the pinhead has been used again and again to suggest the fatuity and vacuousness of medieval school discussions. And yet, in a recent introduction to philosophy, Stephan Körner, no negligible figure on the contemporary scene, absolves that very discussion from blame. After all, it is a good illustration of a category mistake and we may take it that that was the point of the medieval discussion. That non-spatial entities are not circumscribed in place as are spatial ones is precisely the point. It is customary to refer to the exiguous and imper-sonal style of Scholastic writers as if this were the essence of Scholasti-cism. Well, one could equally well praise the care with which the medi-evals wrote and applaud the literalness of their style, seeing in it an apt instrument for a well-defined intellectual task. Philosophical styles change and it is a noteworthy fact that the philosophical style now dominant in English-speaking countries shares many characteristics with the philosophical (and theological) writings of the Middle Ages, early and late. Surely it is no accident that contemporary philosophers move easily into the analysis of medieval texts, feeling almost imme-diately at home with them. Doubtless this constitutes a subtle danger and one not always avoided. The very familiarity of the medieval style may deceive as to its burden, and knowledge of the historical setting, the origin of problems, of the evolution of the literary genre, is re-quired if anachronisms are to be avoided.

We find in Chenu a criticism of the Scholastic style that, since it con-tains a fairly accurate description of it, can easily be taken as the basis for an opposite appraisal.

Il est bien vrai que le style, extérieur et intérieur, du scholastique sacrifie tout à une technicité dont l'austérité le dépouille des ressources de l'art. Ou plutôt il se crée une rhétorique spéciale où les images, les comparaisons, les méta-phores, les symboles sont immédiatement conceptualisés, hors tout complai-sance sensible. Toutes les figures y sont ramenées à l'exemple, ou tournées à l'allégorie, procédés où la raison exploite crûment l'imagination, aux dépens de sa propre fécondité.[37]

36. Cf. Chenu, *Introduction à l'étude de Saint Thomas d'Aquin* (Montreal & Paris: 1954), pp. 51–60; Gilson, *History of Christian Philosophy in the Middle Ages*, pp. 246–50; M. De Wulf, *Histoire de la philosophie médiévale*, 6th ed. (1934), vol. 1, p. 15, note 2; M. Grab-mann, *Die Geschichte der scholastischen Methode*, 2 vols. (Freiburg: 1909–11); Astrik Gabriel, "The Cathedral Schools of Notre Dame and the Beginning of the University of Paris," in *Garlandia* (Frankfurt: 1969), pp. 39–64.

37. Chenu, p. 52.

[To be sure, both the inner and outward style of Scholasticism sacrifices everything to a technical standard whose austerity is not hospitable to artistic nuance. Or rather it fashions a special rhetoric in which images, comparisons, metaphors, and symbols are immediately conceptualized with little eye to sensible effect. All its figures are led back to the example or turned to allegory, procedures in which reason cruelly exploits imagination at the expense of its proper fecundity.]

It is really difficult to know what Chenu is demanding. Surely there is a rhetoric appropriate to philosophical and theological discourse, one element of which he hints at. That the style does not always come off, that even an impersonal style remains the man, is scarcely an objection to it as such. Brand Blanshard is one of the few, if he is not the only contemporary philosopher who has devoted serious thinking to the question of philosophical style.[38] The striking thing about Chenu's down-putting remarks about "Scholastic style" is that he ties it to the influence of the arts. Glossing his own *mot* that "Penser est un métier, dont les lois sont minutieusement fixées" (thinking is an occupation with minutely defined laws), he writes:

Lois de la grammaire, d'abord. Le premier des sept arts n'est pas relégué comme aujourd'hui dans la lointaine préparation de la culture; il en est le sol permanent, même en théologie, et il se trouvera au contraire quasi promu à la dignité de discipline philosophique, la grammaire spéculative. La scholastique médiévale demeure à base de grammairé, et son attention au langage est consciemment poussée à l'extrème, non pas seulement pour l'usage des *nominales* . . . mais en pleine substance philosophique et théologique.[39]

[First of all, the laws of grammar. The first of the seven arts is not relegated, as it is today, to the distant preparation of culture; it is its permanent soil, even in theology, and it will even be promoted to the dignity of a philosophical discipline, speculative grammar. Medieval Scholasticism reposes on a base of grammar and its attention to language is consciously pushed to the limit, not simply in the practice of nominalists . . . but in the very substance of philosophy and theology.]

Chenu sounds like a certain kind of critic of contemporary philosophical style with its emphasis on language. It is very difficult to know what his quip about grammar being as it were promoted to the dignity of a philosophical discipline means; indeed, throughout this section, Chenu adopts an arch, condescending manner, and his reader constantly feels the writer's elbow in his ribs, as it were. But the thing to notice is the linking of arts and Scholasticism. Scholasticism, as a style, arises naturally out of the liberal arts tradition and can scarcely be op-

38. Brand Blanshard, *On Philosophical Style* (Bloomington, Ind.: 1954).
39. Chenu, p. 52.

posed to it. Nonetheless, this apparent impasse brings us to the heart of the matter I have been asked to discuss.

I hope I have convinced you that we cannot regard the age of the universities, the age when an influx of classical and Arabic works changes the whole picture of the range and scope of human knowledge, as an age that pitched out the previous liberal arts tradition. After all, the base faculty of the university was the faculty of arts. From the age of fifteen to perhaps twenty-five, a man was engaged in pursuits that were the continuation of those previously studied in monastic and cathedral schools. Indeed, we are reminded by Delhaye of something important. There were perhaps twenty medieval universities all told, which is not a massive number when we think of the area over which they were scattered. Moreover, the monastic and cathedral schools continued to exist after the rise of universities and it appears that their curricula did not change radically.[40] Certainly there was pre-university schooling. Siger of Brabant, for example, likely studied at Liège before coming to Paris at about the age of seventeen.[41] In the faculty of arts, though only after many vicissitudes, condemnations, and heated exchanges, there came about the sort of integration of the liberal arts and Aristotelianism we have seen urged programmatically by Thomas Aquinas. The struggle in the first century of the university (I am thinking, of course, of Paris) was between the arts faculty and the masters of theology.

Thomas Aquinas occupied a chair of theology at the University of Paris and it was from that perspective that he attempted the reconciliation of the liberal arts and Aristotelianism that we examined earlier. In the arts faculty itself there grew up what Van Steenberghen calls "heterodox Aristotelianism," that is, an acceptance of Aristotle as interpreted by Averroes even if this led to conflict with Christian faith. This is a complicated and fascinating story in its own right. Bonaventure, who ascended to a chair of theology on the same day as Thomas Aquinas, is one of our sources for the initial reaction to what was going on in the arts faculty. In his *Conferences on the Ten Commandments* and in his *Conferences on the Gifts of the Holy Ghost*,[42] lenten ser-

40. Cf. Philippe Delhaye, "La Place des Arts Libéraux dans les Programmes Scolaires du XIIIe Siècle," ALPAMA, pp. 161–73.

41. Van Steenberghen, *Maître Siger de Brabant*, pp. 28–30.

42. *Collationes de Decem Preceptis*, collatio II, n. 25, in *Obras de San Buenaventura*, tom. 5 (Madrid: 1948). In the same volume, see *Collationes de Septem Donis Spiritus Sancti*, collatio VIII, and, on the historical setting of these sermons, see Van Steenberghen, *Maître Siger de Brabant*, pp. 40–46.

mons, he inveighs against those who accept the pagan philosophical tenets that are in clear conflict with the Christian faith. The controverted points are several but three must appear on any list: the eternity of the world, the denial of providence, the denial of personal immortality. These three claims, and others like them, were taken, following Averroes, to be the clear sense of Aristotle's philosophy. Thomas Aquinas enters the fray with his *De unitate intellectus contra Averroistas*,[43] and matters come to a head with the Condemnation of 1270 and, when that did not settle it, the further Condemnation of 1277.[44] The latter, three years after the death of Aquinas, also condemned several Thomistic teachings.

Why are these matters pertinent to our inquiry? They provide us with a parallel to the twelfth-century situation that exercised Hugh of St. Victor. Just as Hugh lamented the secularization of the liberal arts, so the great theologians of the thirteenth century objected to masters of arts who were teaching as philosophical truths claims clearly in contradiction with the faith. For a Bonaventure, such a conflict, when seen as such, was immediately resolved against the philosophical claim. Thomas, in his *De unitate intellectus*, quotes his adversary in the faculty of arts (who may have been Siger of Brabant) as saying:

But what he says later is still more serious: 'I necessarily conclude through reason that the intellect is one in number: but I firmly hold the opposite through faith.' Therefore he thinks that faith is concerned with some propositions whose contraries can be necessarily concluded. But since only a necessary truth can be concluded necessarily, and the opposite of this is something false and impossible, it follows, according to his remark, that faith would be concerned with something false and impossible, that not even God could effect. This the faithful cannot bear to hear.[45]

That is Thomas's concluding remark. The burden of his work has been to show that it is historically, that is, textually, inaccurate to interpret the text of Aristotle as did Averroes and Siger of Brabant. Thomas is concerned to protect Aristotle from his interpreters, not to protect the faith from Aristotle.

But let me return to what I suggested is truly the heart of our matter. If Scholasticism is taken to mean a style of thought and of

43. Saint Thomas, *De unitate intellectus*, ed. Leo Keeler, S.J. (Rome: 1946). English translation by Beatrice H. Zedler, *On the Unity of the Intellect against the Averroists* (Milwaukee: 1968).

44. Cf. Roland Hissette, *Enquête sur les 219 Articles Condamnés à Paris le 7 Mars 1277* (Louvain & Paris: 1977); John Wippel, "The Condemnations of 1270 and 1277," *Journal of Medieval and Renaissance Studies* 7 (1977), pp. 169–201.

45. Zedler translation of Keeler, n. 123.

writing, then we must recognize its continued existence across the Middle Ages; it cannot be seen as a new departure from a previously dominant medieval style. When Boethius turns into Latin the *Isagoge* of Porphyry and some logical writings of Aristotle, he accompanies them with commentaries whose style conveys to the West what we might call Greek Scholasticism. Boethius had been trained in a milieu where one commented on the works of Plato and Aristotle. One of the prominent literary genres was the commentary and it had become, as Boethius makes clear, a very stylized genre. For example, he lists the points that should be made by the commentator in his proemium.[46] To brood over a text, to explain its meaning, to paraphrase and unpack it, to reveal its order and arrangement—it is by doing these things that an adept can aid a novice. This is how one exhibits his mastery. So it was that Boethius's commentary on Porphyry generated commentary after commentary during the Middle Ages. Here is a major component of any description of Scholasticism, and it cannot be said that it shouldered out some previously dominant style. Heeding *auctores*, seeming always to be looking backward to a golden age, trying to retrieve it through the documents that have been handed down—even when a medieval wanted to say something original, he could be constrained by the tradition of commenting on *auctores*. Thus, Abelard's *Dialectica* pursues the same course as the canonical works in logic. It is not a commentary on those books—Abelard had written any number of those—but it is haunted by them.[47] As we move into the thirteenth century and the university milieu, the *expositio textus* continues.

Needless to say, though its style is continuous with preceding centuries, the Scholasticism of the university introduces variations on and additions to the Scholastic method. The *lectio*, the reading of the texts set for a given term, occurred in a dramatic setting, with the master aided by bachelors who were his apprentices, but the written result does not amount to a stylistic innovation. It is rather of the *Quaestio disputata* and the *Quaestio quodlibetalis* that we think when we seek

46. Cf. Boethius, *In Porphyrium Dialogi*, PL 64:9B–C: "Tunc ego: Sex omnino, inquam, magistri in omni expositione praelibant. Praedocent enim quae sit cujuscunque operis intention, quod apud illos *skopos* vocatur. Secundum quae utilitas, quod a Graecis *khrēsimon* appellatur. Tertium qui ordo, quod Graeci vocant *taxin*. Quartum si ejus cujus opus dicitur, germanus propriusque liber est, quod *gnēsion* interpretari solet. Quintum quae sit ejus operis inscriptio, quod *epigraphēn* Graeci nominant. . . . Sextum est id dicere, ad quam partem philosophie cujuscunque libri ducatur intentio . . ." Discussion in Pierre Courcelle, *Late Latin Writers and Their Greek Sources*, trans. Harry E. Wedeck (Cambridge, Mass.: 1969), pp. 286–95.

47. Peter Abelard, *Dialectica*, 2d rev. ed. L. M. De Rijk (Assen: 1970). See Maria Teresa Beonio-Brocchieri Fumagalli, *La Logica de Abelardo* (Firenze: 1969), infelicitously translated in the Synthese Historical Library, *The Logic of Abelard* (Dordrecht: 1970).

something peculiar to the Scholasticism of the university. These convey to us the dialectical setting of the university, the give and take prior to any magisterial resolution of the question. Of course these *quaestiones*, as they have come down to us, cannot be regarded as tapes or records of the debate itself, but as written they reflect their origin in a vital exchange before a "live audience." I suggested earlier that an article in the *Summa theologiae* has the same structure, simplified, as the disputed question. Thomas wrote the *Summa* in his cell, but it is as if he wished to engage in imaginary conversation, to write closet drama at least. Any strength is a potential weakness and it is easy to see how *amour propre*, the drive to win an argument rather than seize the truth, might take over and how subtlety might come to invite for its own sake or as a way to bedazzle an audience. Someone once wrote a piece on the vice of gambling and the virtue of insurance and I suppose one might alter this and speak of the vice of contention and the virtue of dialogue. It is the same activity that is done badly or well. There is no need nor justification for identifying Scholasticism with the bad employment of its methods.

Thus, while there are additions made to the method as we move into the thirteenth century, Scholasticism does not provide us with a way of distinguishing a later time from the earlier time when the liberal arts were dominant—where by 'dominant' we mean that they could be taken as adequately summarizing the range of secular knowledge.

The only sense we have so far been able to find for the claim that the liberal arts are replaced as we make the turn into the thirteenth century and into the fledgling university is that, with the introduction of the integral Aristotle, a new and wider conception of secular knowledge is gained such that the liberal arts must be seen as making up only a fraction of the *ancilla theologiae*. But surely, were we to content ourselves with this, we would be missing something terribly important, something that may not have been accurately expressed in the simple story with which we began but that, nonetheless, we *know* is there. Chenu's somewhat guardedly critical remarks about Scholastic style, which we cited earlier for their linking of the arts with the maligned style, hint at something else. In ticking off the supposed defects of Scholastic style, Chenu is obliquely expressing a preference for uses of language that, it could be argued, are not appropriate for the handling of philosophical and theological subjects. What is really at issue is a reappearance of that ancient quarrel between the philosopher and poet of which Socrates speaks in the *Republic*.

What is at issue, that is to say, and what I will have seemed disin-
genuous for ignoring so studiously, is what Van Steenberghen calls
l'exil des belles-lettres,[48] the leitmotif of Ernst Robert Curtius's *European
Literature and the Latin Middle Ages*.[49] Already in the twelfth century,
creativity and vitality in logic seem bought at the expense of grammar
in the sense of a prolonged immersion in the works of the great writers; so too, as the fortunes of philosophy rise, literature—belles-
lettres—and poetry feel neglected, feel themselves the object of hos-
tility, feel themselves engaged in battle. Gilson makes succinctly the
point Chenu was hinting at in a passage cited earlier: "On voit ap-
paraître une culture de type nouveau, fondée sur le minimum de
grammaire exigé pour l'usage courant d'un latin tout scolaire, consti-
tuée par l'étude de la logique et de la philosophie d'Aristote et cou-
ronnée par celle d'une théologie dont la technique s'inspire de cette
logique et de cette philosophie."[50] The fate of grammar may seem to
sum up the sort of evolution that is a result of the study of grammar
altering from a study of a Latin, as exemplified in the writings of its
best practitioners, to the study of rules and parts of speech and this
latter eventually becoming the phenomenon called speculative grammar. In this evolved form of grammar, one attempts to see beneath
the flesh of any living language the essential structure that any language must possess. Both Chenu and Gilson cite speculative grammar
as an *exemplum horribile*, and Van Steenberghen seems in agreement.
How swiftly fashions change. Few things are "hotter" at the moment
and one is no longer surprised to see analogies drawn between medieval speculative grammarians and Chomsky and his school.[51] But
however appraisals of its upshot differ, there can be agreement on the
evolution mentioned. A case can be made for the assertion that literary studies, to say nothing of the composing of literary works, do not
flourish where logic and philosophy thrive. Personally, I suspect that
this can be overstated. We need a careful presentation of precisely
what historical data sustain the case. It is doubtless overly dramatic to
speak of belles-lettres being exiled. Can John of Garland and Henry
Andeli be taken as sober historians of the matter? Moreover, pleasant
as it is to wallow in the Teutonic erudition of Curtius, I think he is a

---

48. Van Steenberghen, *La philosophie au XIIIe siècle*, pp. 527–29.
49. Translated by Willard R. Trask in the Bollingen Series (Princeton: 1953).
50. Gilson, *La Philosophie au Moyen Age des Origines Patristiques à la fin du XIVe Siècle*,
2d ed. (Paris: 1944), p. 401.
51. Cf. G. L. Bursill-Hall, *Speculative Grammars of the Middle Ages* (The Hague: 1971),
and J. Pinborg, *Die Entwicklung der Sprachtheorie in Mittelalter* (1967).

bad guide on the question. This is never more evident than when he discusses poetry and philosophy, notices that Jean de Meun speaks of writing poetry as "travailler en philosophie"[52]—doing philosophy, as we might say—and considers this a confusion. In summary of his discussion, Curtius writes:

> Scholasticism put an end to the confusion of philosophy with poetry, rhetoric, proverbial lore, and the various learning of the schools. The old connection between *artes* and philosophy is severed at a blow. The blow lay in Thomas's dictum: 'Septem artes liberales non sufficienter dividunt philosophiam theoreticam.' Yet Leopardi can still write: 'La scienza del bello scrivere e una filosofia, e profondissima e sottilissima, e tiene tutti i rami della sapienza.'[53]

This passage can be taken as a retrospective justification of my procedure in this paper. The remark of Aquinas, which Curtius quotes from Grabmann,[54] simply cannot bear the freight Curtius wants to put upon it. (The allusion to Leopardi baffles me; is he being cited as a backslider or as someone who failed to get the news of history as Curtius reads it?) Nevertheless, Curtius's reader begins to discern what he is really after. He wants to get literary studies, considered as bearing on the status of the poet and the act of writing poetry, recognized as wholly autonomous, as having won freedom from faith, philosophy, and other alien masters.[55] But that cannot be illuminatingly discussed as a severing of the liberal arts from philosophy, or vice versa.

To have written a paper on the fortunes of poetry in the Middle Ages would not have been, perhaps, to connect with what my predecessors at this podium have had to say, assuming of course that I am capable of writing on that topic. Ready or not, I am prompted to make, by way of conclusion, some animadversions on the relationship between poetry and philosophy.

The style, the language, the latinity of Scholasticism are frequent topics of discussion and, in introducing a remark of Chenu, I alluded to the familiarity many contemporary philosophers feel when they turn to medieval sources. The so-called analytic style of philosophizing finds resonance in the Scholastic. Indeed, one would not have to look far to find analogues of Thomas's description of poetry as *infima*

---

52. Curtius, p. 208.
53. Ibid., p. 213. The quote from Leopardi is from *Zibaldone*, n. 2728.
54. *Mittelalterliches Geistesleben*, vol. 1 (Munich: 1926), p. 190.
55. Curtius, p. 480.

doctrina[56] in contemporary discussions where the language of the poet is said to possess at best emotive meaning. It would be entertaining to lay side by side passages from medievals like Thomas, Ockham, or Abelard with passages from G. E. Moore, J. L. Austin, or Wilfrid Sellers. A family resemblance could be described, I think, though there is hardly a question of influence. I will not try to characterize this common style except to say that it is above all *literal* and that it strives with a moral passion for clarity of expression. Now it would be possible to think of a continuum of linguistic usage that would move from the literal at one extreme to the figurative and/or metaphorical at the other. Something like this is suggested by Aristotle when he sees philosophy as arising out of myth. Within the tradition of Aristotelian logic, we find a spectrum running from poetry through rhetoric through dialectic to the apodictic, the demonstrative, with works of Aristotle to represent the different styles of argument or discourse: the *Poetics*, the *Rhetoric*, the *Topics*, the *Analytics*.[57] Imagine that we developed a similar theory to the effect that there is a mode of language (call it literalness, for want of a better term) that is appropriate to the philosopher. A companion claim, I suspect, would be that there is also an appropriate literary genre in which to express philosophical thought. Don't we feel that we can immediately identify a piece of philosophical prose? Isn't there a sameness about the offerings in any given issue of a philosophical journal and indeed a sameness about journals? We may react to this as would John of Garland (or perhaps Roger Bacon), but the shock of recognition there would be.

Very well. Once one feels one has a manageable notion of philosophical style and the appropriate literary genre in which it expresses itself, one will be tempted to rank other styles and other genres as perhaps falling away from this austere ideal. Of course the assessment can be reversed. One isolates the essence of poetic language and ranks other uses of language as falling away from this golden ideal, with philosophical prose, *ça va sans dire*, ranking low, even lowest.[58]

Here is the source of the battle, a battle between poet and Scholastic, that is alluded to in the simple story with which I began. That it is not a fabrication, the passage from Curtius shows. I have myself felt the attraction of the view that there is a peculiar philosophical style,

---

56. *ST*, Ia, q. 1, a. 9, obj. 1; *In libros Post. Analytic.*, proemium, n. 6. For an interesting defense of Thomas's description of poetry, see Otto Bird, *Cultures in Conflict: An Essay in the Philosophy of the Humanities* (Notre Dame: 1976), p. 70.

57. What I am suggesting here is found in Thomas's proemium to his commentary on the *Posterior Analytics*.

58. Bird's book, cited above, is important for this whole discussion.

a use of language appropriate to the peculiar tasks the philosopher sets himself, easily distinguished from the uses to which poet and imaginative writer, historian and moralist, put language. I have been tempted by the notion that these differences exhibit themselves in a corresponding variety of literary genres. Well, whatever may be said for this as theory, it has little to do with the history of philosophy. For one thing, if we consider the genres in which recognized philosophers have expressed themselves, we are confronted with a bewildering variety: verse, aphorisms, meditations, dialogues, prayers, commentaries, *summae*, disputed questions, treatises, essays, et cetera.[59] Nor can it be maintained that these genres can be sorted out chronologically, as if the history of its literary genres matches the supposed history of its struggle toward the light, that is, our time. Consider the styles and works of Heidegger and Wittgenstein, perhaps the two most influential philosophers of this century. Consider Nietzsche and Kierkegaard in the last. Santayana wrote a little book called *Three Philosophical Poets* in which he discussed Lucretius, Dante, and Goethe.[60] It is a fascinating book though one may doubt that he succeeded in isolating the essence of the philosophical poet. I doubt that one could isolate the essence of the poetic philosopher, a genus that would include Parmenides and Plato as well as Nietzsche and Kierkegaard. We could draw a lesson from the synthesizing efforts of William of Conches, Hugh of St. Victor, Thomas Aquinas: we do not have to choose between poetry and philosophy, between the humanities and philosophy, between the arts and theology. What we want is a view that will embrace them all, not in an eclectic mishmash, but by seeing continuity and overlap as well as distinctions between the various uses of language, the various activities of mind.

I began with a quotation, "One ought not grow old in the study of the arts." The arts are part of a larger whole, a whole that, as Thomas Aquinas sees it, is capped by theology. It is in the study of ultimate causes, not in the pursuit of the arts, that man is meant to grow old. Not that wisdom entails a repudiation of the arts. Surely it is the mark of the wise man that he remains true to the dreams of his youth.

59. See Julian Marias, *Philosophy as Dramatic Theory* (University Park, Pa.: 1971).
60. George Santayana, *Three Philosophical Poets* (New York: 1953).

3

THE PRIME MOVER AND THE ORDER
OF LEARNING

The problem which I would like to discuss is the role which the proof for the Prime Mover plays in the natural approach to the science of metaphysics.[1] This proof, St. Thomas tells us,[2] gives us the most manifest and certain entree to a science above the philosophy of nature. In what follows, I will try to show the reason for the philosophy of nature's doctrinal priority to metaphysics. After the examination of this doctrine, a brief critique will be made of the position which maintains that there is a characteristically Thomistic metaphysics, an existential metaphysics, which is free from the exigencies of the order of learning. It is my feeling that an indirect support for the necessity of the order of learning can be found in the writings of one who opposes this order in the name of the authentic doctrine of our common master, St. Thomas.

1. REFLECTION ON THE ORDER OF LEARNING

The first thing that the intellect knows is being, for nothing is more knowable than being.[3] Since First Philosophy is the study of being, it

1. The following texts present the order to be observed in teaching all the philosophical sciences: *In librum de causis* (ed. Saffrey), proemium; *In VI Ethicorum*, lect. 7 (ed. Spiazzi), n. 1211; *In Boethii de trin.* (ed. Wyser), q. 5, a. 1, ad 9; ibid., (ed Calcaterra), lect. 1, q. 1, ad 1.
2. "Huius autem positionis [that of Plato] radix invenitur efficaciam non habere. Non enim necesse est ut ea quae intellectus separatim intelligit, separatim esse habeant in rerum natura: unde nec universalia oportet separata ponere et subsistentia praeter singularia, neque etiam mathematica praeter sensibilia: quia universalia sunt essentiae ipsarum particularium, et mathematica terminationes quaedam sensibilium corporum. Et ideo Aristoteles manifestiori et certiori via processit ad investigandum substantias a materia separatas, scilicet per viam motus."—*De substantiis separatis* (ed. Spiazzi), cap. 2, n. 50.
3. Cf. *Q. D. de ver.*, q. 1, a. 1; *ST*, Ia, q. 5, a. 2.

might seem that we are in formal possession of the subject of its inquiry at the very outset of the intellectual life. Nothing, of course, would please the opponents of metaphysics more than to think that it is being grasped in this obscure way which is the concern of the metaphysician. However, being as it is first known is not, we would say, the formal subject of metaphysics: the *ens primum cognitum* is the alpha and not the omega of the intellectual life. Being is first known confusedly; it is a whole which actually contains parts, but the intellect does not yet know them. It is in terms of being as it is first known that we make our first judgment, that of contradiction, and in terms of it also that we grasp certain transcendental properties. Moreover, the principles known at the outset and which are most knowable to us are in some way the concern of the metaphysician.[4] But, if this is the case, why do we insist that we are not immediately in metaphysics? Cajetan, in the proemium to his masterly commentary on the *De ente et essentia*, spells out the answer.

Being as it is grasped in the first abstractive act of the intellect is *ens concretum quidditati sensibili*, and its concept is the most confused and least evident of concepts.[5] The *primum cognitum* is often said to be the understanding of sensible being under its most universal predicate. This is not to say that being as it is first known is grasped as a universal which contains potentially its inferiors. Rather it is grasped as concretized in a sensible whatness; that is, it is discovered in some sensible nature not as in a state of abstraction whereby it relates to inferiors potentially contained within it—this would imply that being was already distinctly known as an actual whole—but rather as entering into the composition of the thing. To know being as a universal or potential whole follows on *ens primum cognitum*. However, in the words of John of St. Thomas, we say that the intellect begins with the most universal because it begins with that predicate which is apt to take on the greatest universality.[6] This universal knowledge implies imperfection, because the universality is on the part of what is known (the *quod*) and not on the part of the means of knowing (the *quo*). A knowledge *in*

---

4. "Universalissima principia sunt etiam quoad nos magis nota, sicut ea quae pertinet ad ens inquantum ens: quorum cognitio pertinet ad sapientiam sic dictam, ut patet in quarto Metaphysicae."—*In VI Ethic.*, lect. 5, n. 1181.

5. "Ille conceptus est omnium evidentissimus, sub quo intellectus positus magis remotus est a cognitione aliorum omnium, quam sub quocumque alio conceptu; conceptus actualis confusus entis est huiusmodi, scilicet quod intellectus habens ipsum, magis distat ab aliorum cognitione, quam habens quemcunque alium conceptum: ergo conceptus actualis confusus entis est inevidentissimus omnium."—Cajetan, *In de ente et essentia* (ed. Laurent), p. 9.

6. *Cursus philosophicus* (ed. Reiser), tom. 2, p. 25a40–43.

universali of the latter type would be perfect knowledge.[7] What is first known by the intellect is sensible being under what comes to be seen as its most universal predicate. "Being" can be said of whatever quiddity is abstracted from the things of sense experience. What is first known most confusedly is the quiddity of sensible things, grasped as being, that is, as actual and not merely as a possibility.[8] But in our investigation of the properties and causes of natural things, we arrive first at less common knowledge; that is, the causes that we come to know are of one genus or species; only after a great deal of consideration do we come to knowledge of universal causes. The universality which the *ens primum cognitum* can take on is a universality of predication; in our search for the causes of sensible being, we must move from particular to universal causes. We will return to the difference between these two types of community or universality.

The movement described here is, of course, that of the philosophy of nature. What we first know intellectually are the quiddities abstracted from the data of sense experience. But *sensibilia* come and go and, while they are, they seem constantly in movement. Thus *ens mobile* emerges as the formal subject of the philosophy of nature. In the first book of the *Physics*, the principles of this subject are discovered: matter, form and privation. In the second book, the principles of the science are discussed, the causes in virtue of which certain knowledge of this subject will be had. In the third book, the proper passion of the subject is demonstrated and the science proper is under way. When, in the eighth book, we arrive at a first efficient cause of the subject, something most important happens, for what had hitherto passed as synonymous with being, *ens mobile*, requires for its explanation a Prime Mover who is *ens* but not *mobile*.

This is our first demonstrative knowledge that "being" has a wider extension than material being. For the first time, the intellect sees that there is a possibility of a science of being as being which is distinct from the philosophy of nature. Prior to such a proof, "Being as being" is merely a more general way of designating material being which, ap-

---

7. ". . . cognitio enim qua cognoscitur aliquid solum in universali, est cognitio imperfecta, cognitio vero qua cognoscitur aliquid in propria specie, est cognitio perfecta; cognitio enim speciei includit cognitionem generis, sed non e converso; sequeretur igitur quod, quanto intellectus esset superior tanto esset eius cognitio imperfectior. Est ergo haec differentia universalitatis et particularitatis attendenda solum secundum id quo intellectus intelligit. Quanto enim aliquis intellectus est superior, tanto id quo intelligit est universalius, ita tamen quod illo universali eius cognitio extendatur etiam ad propria cognoscenda multo magis quam cognitio inferioris intellectus qui per aliquid magis particulare cognoscit."—*In librum de causis*, prop. 10a. Cf. *In II Sent.*, d. 3, q. 3, a. 2; *SCG*, II, cap. 98; *Q. D. de ver.*, q. 8, a. 19, ad 1; *ST*, Ia, q. 55, a. 3, ad 2; q. 89, a. 1.

8. *ST*, Ia, q. 5, a. 1, ad 1.

parently, is all the being there is. The consideration of being as being would be a more universal consideration, certainly, but would not the universality be simply of predication? The universality of metaphysics, however, is not simply a more general way of addressing ourselves to material being. And, prior to a proof that being is not synonymous with material being, this could only be a desirable concern if one preferred confusion to exactness in knowledge.[9]

It is the difficulty involved in arriving at knowledge of universal causes that makes metaphysics difficult, because, as we have seen, universality on the part of predication is had in some way at the very outset.[10] However, the community of predication of the terms is extended at the same time that we arrive at knowledge of beings which exist separately from matter and motion, which is what metaphysics presupposes.[11] The scope of such terms as "being," "act," "potency," "substance" and the like is going to be extended by the metaphysician in virtue of his knowledge that they are not confined to sensible things. We name as we know, and the less we know, the less our terms can signify. In metaphysics, we use the same terms, but their signification is extended in an analogous way. What seems to follow is that it is only in metaphysics that we realize the scope of our universal terms, how common the *communia entis* are. The common principles of metaphysics, then, are common in two ways, that of predication and that of causation.[12]

The argument for first learning the philosophy of nature if one is to see metaphysics as a possibility is presented most cogently by St. Thomas. An avoidance of this order of learning so as to begin with the consideration of being as being is foredoomed to be a vague and confused discussion which would have no excuse for itself. Why should one settle for indeterminate knowledge? Such a "metaphysics" would be an analysis of being which has not been shown to be more than material being, and it would merely be a discussion of material being in terms of universals in predication. Potential, universal, confused knowledge is all that one could legitimately expect from it.

The *via inventionis*[13] which proceeds from material being to immaterial being, from temporal to eternal things, is characterized as resolutive for it arrives at the causes of things.[14] The application of this notion to the relation of the various speculative sciences is expressed

9. Cf. *In I Metaphysic.*, lect. 2, n. 46.
10. *In VI Ethic.*, lect. 5, n. 1181.   11. Cf. *In Boethii de trin.*, q. 5, a. 3.
12. Ibid., q. 5, a. 4.   13. Cf. *ST*, Ia, q. 79, a. 9.
14. Cf. S. Edmund Dolan, "Resolution and Composition in Speculative and Practical Discourse," *Laval théologique et philosophique*, 6/1 (1950), p. 47.

in the statement that the other sciences resolve into metaphysics. That is, the rational is always resolved into the intellectual.[15] Metaphysics, which is intellectual in mode, is the term of the other speculative sciences whose mode is a rational one. The rational process is, however, of two kinds.

The first moves from one *thing* to another, as when a demonstration is had by extrinsic causes or effects. A compositive rational mode is had in this way when we reason from causes to effects; the resolutive rational mode is in the opposite direction, from effects to causes. The term of resolution in this order is had when we arrive at the supreme and most simple causes which are separated substances.

The second way in which we proceed rationally is according to intrinsic causes. This is compositive when we go from the most universal forms to the most particular; it is resolutive when the movement is the reverse, for we resolve into the most universal and simple forms. The highest universals are those which are common to all beings; therefore, the term of resolution in this order is the consideration of being and of those things which follow on being as such.

Once we arrive at the term of resolution, a *via iudicii* is possible.[16] Metaphysics provides principles to each of the particular sciences, because the intellectual consideration is the principle of the rational.

Nihilominus ipsa addiscitur post physicam et ceteras scientias, in quantum consideratio intellectualis est terminus rationalis, propter quod dicitur metaphysica, quasi trans physicam resolvendo occurrit.[17]

It should be remembered that the order of discovery is also the order of teaching, for efficacious doctrine traverses the same route that the student would have to if he were on his own.[18] It is presupposed that the teacher has acquired the various sciences and he may make use, at an early stage, of doctrine that can only be considered adequately later on; hence the maxim: *oportet addiscentem credere*.[19] The *proemia* to the commentaries on Aristotle are clear examples of the sapiential function of the teacher.

The order of learning, as the foregoing should serve to indicate, cannot be dismissed as a textual or historical oddity bearing no relation to St. Thomas's "personal" thought. The priority, for us, of the

---

15. *In Boethii de trin.*, q. 6, a. 1, ad tertiam quaestionem.
16. *ST*, Ia, q. 79, a. 9.
17. *In Boethii de trin.*, q. 6, a. 1, ad tertiam quaestionem. Cf. *In libros Metaphysic.*, proemium: "Haec enim transphysica inveniuntur in via resolutionis, sicut magis communia post minus communia."
18. *Q. D. de ver.*, q. 11, a. 1.
19. *In Boethii de trin.*, lect. 1, q. 1, a. 1. Cf. *Q. D. de ver.*, q. 14, a. 10.

philosophy of nature is dictated by the very nature of our mind. What else is St. Thomas saying when he points out that the other sciences are naturally prior to metaphysics as far as we are concerned?[20] To say that St. Thomas is not arguing his own case or that this doctrine on the order of learning is not applicable to another kind of metaphysics, would seem to rely on an equivocal use of terminology. Nonetheless, in the name of authentic doctrine, it has been maintained that there is a metaphysics which presupposes no other science; that it has a starting-point which does not require the laborious movement through the particular sciences, not even the philosophy of nature. It is helpful to see that one fairly full attempt to outline the trajectory of such a metaphysics exhibits it as far less independent than it claims to be.

2. REJECTION OF THE ORDER OF LEARNING

In his article "A Note on the Approach to Thomistic Metaphysics,"[21] Father Joseph Owens essays a sketch of a purely Thomistic metaphysics which uses the *De ente et essentia* as its base. As Father Owens traces the argument of the opusculum of St. Thomas, we have first some logical considerations arising from the study of predication, and secondly the establishment of the notion of abstracting without prescinding as exemplified in genera and species with regard to their inferiors. Thirdly, there is the application of this notion to the nature of things with respect to their being. However, although the genera include their species implicitly, the nature does not contain being in itself; being is an *adveniens extra* that cannot proceed from the principles of the nature, but has to be caused efficiently by something else and ultimately by subsisting being.[22]

This procedure suggests to Father Owens a distinctively Thomistic metaphysics.

The logical introduction of the *De ente et essentia*, apparently, may be necessary to obtain the correct Thomistic notion of essence, but as regards being it seems to function as an elaborate setting for *the crucial metaphysical starting-point*, that the being of a sensible thing is neither contained within the thing's nature nor caused by the principles of that nature. From this starting-point the act of being can be traced to its source in God, and can then be shown to be participated in all other things by a subject different from that act and so in potency to that act.[23]

20. *In Boethii de trin.*, q. 5, a. 1, ad 9; ibid., prologus, n. 3.
21. *The New Scholasticism* 28/4 (1954), pp. 454–76.
22. Ibid., p. 466.   23. Ibid., pp. 467–68.

Father Owens says that it appears difficult to find any other type of treatment in the text of St. Thomas which could be characterized as his typical metaphysical procedure, thus indicating that he feels it is likely that St. Thomas had a typical or personal metaphysical procedure.

The "crucial metaphysical starting-point" would seem to be the real distinction between essence and existence. Apparently, this distinction must be grasped at the outset, and then, with it in hand as a self-evident first principle, one can demonstrate the existence of God. Seemingly this is the first demonstration of Thomistic metaphysics, as well as of all philosophy since this metaphysics presupposes nothing. But how is the real distinction shown to be self-evident?

Being is seen evidently as an act or perfection by a simple comparison with non-being, for example in the case of a man existing or not existing in reality. To be is evidently different from not to be, and that difference is evidently the difference of a perfection from the lack of such perfection. The Aristotelian notions of act or perfection (energeia, entelecheia) were at hand. They could readily be used to describe the being of things. No difficulty whatsoever is felt by St. Thomas on this score.[24]

But it is just here that the reader of Father Owens begins to have difficulties. This Aristotelian terminology is rather advanced, and the terms adduced in fact signify with that type of equivocation which came to be called analogy. Is St. Thomas, in using these terms, relying on their previous impositions so that they are rather profound and complex instruments of communication? Is he presupposing the signification which they have in the science of their origin, the philosophy of nature? Father Owens guards against this interpretation. "Worthy of note is that this metaphysical procedure does not call upon natural philosophy to furnish its notions of potency and act."[25] But could not one agree with this and still maintain that their prior signification must be presupposed if their extended metaphysical use is to be meaningful? Not that this is the real point at issue. That the real distinction is simply not had in this evident way at the outset of the philosophical life is quite obvious in what follows.

What is not evident, however, and what is extremely difficult to establish, is that the nature of a thing is a potency to that being. This involves the long process just sketched. A consideration of sensible nature shows that being is accidental to such nature and yet prior to it.[26]

24. Ibid., p. 468.   25. Ibid.
26. Ibid., pp. 468–69.

Is the consideration of sensible nature properly a metaphysical consideration? Certainly St. Thomas's treatment of the essence of sensible substance is not independent of the treatment of the principles of mobile being in natural doctrine. As a matter of fact, in chapter two, after noting that the discussion of essence must begin with sensible substance,[27] St. Thomas clearly assumes a knowledge of matter and form. His treatment is a typically metaphysical one because it presupposes the philosophy of nature as already acquired. That such a presupposition provides the cognitive bridge into the discussion of non-material substances is the contention of the partisans of the order of learning. Any knowledge of matter and form presupposes an analysis of generation and corruption.[28] Nor does it seem to be an evasion of the demands of the order of learning to say that Aristotelian terms were at hand and could be put readily to use. Terms bring along with them the signification that has been imposed on them, and this is just why Aristotle uses the same terms from the beginning of the *Physics* to the end of the *Metaphysics*. The extension of the terms relies on the previous impositions, for metaphysical terminology reflects the dependence we have on the material if we are to arise to knowledge of the immaterial. Is it not just the analogous character of the terms the metaphysician uses, their reference back to their first imposition in virtue of which they signify the sensible things more knowable to us, that saves the metaphysics of Aristotle and St. Thomas from the charge of meaninglessness? This dependence, for us, on sciences prior to metaphysics, does not, of course, deny that metaphysics is a real contribution to our knowledge; rather it guarantees that our metaphysical knowledge has an anchor in common experience.

The *De ente et essentia* would seem to manifest quite clearly the necessity for us of the order of learning, so much so, that Father Owens's attempt to read it otherwise ends by being an indirect endorsement of the priority for us of the philosophy of nature.

A word on the "crucial metaphysical starting-point." If the *De ente et essentia* is a study in metaphysics, as most certainly it is, we may find it profitable to note that the real distinction is not presented until well along in the discussion,[29] which seems to suggest that one can be most emphatically in metaphysics before having made this distinction, that the proof of it is something within the science of metaphysics. Some-

27. "Sed quia illarum substantiarum essentiae sint nobis magis occultae, ideo ab essentiis substantiarum compositarum incipiendum est, ut a facilioribus convenientior fit disciplina."—*De ente et essentia*, cap. 2.

28. Cf. e.g., *In VIII Metaphysic.*, lect. 1, n. 1689.

29. *De ente et essentia* (ed. Spiazzi), cap. 4, n. 26.

times the *separatio* peculiar to metaphysics is thought to refer to a recognition of the real distinction between essence and existence, but in
the context of the most complete discussion of *separatio* that we find in
St. Thomas, what is being separated is being, substance, potency and
act, and the like, and what they are being separated from is matter
and motion.[30] Far from being self-evident, the real distinction between
essence and existence is one of the more difficult of metaphysical
truths to establish and one is well into metaphysics before one is
equipped to do it.[31]

One hesitates to put a final note to one's observations on a problem
which has called forth so many provocative and articulate contribu-
tions from both sides, for out of the dialectic of the discussion we all
must certainly benefit. The only conclusion which I offer is that the
order of learning which makes metaphysics consequent upon the philosophy of nature, not only for its terminology, which must be extended and purified, but even for the suggestion of its formal subject
as something not restricted to material conditions, follows on the very
nature of our mind and seemingly is not contradicted, either explicitly or implicitly, by an independent Thomistic text like the *De ente et
essentia.*

30. *In Boethii de trin.*, q. 5, aa. 1–3. Cf. Chapter 12 of this book.
31. Cf. W. Baumgaertner, "Metaphysics and the Second Analytics," *The New Scholasticism* 29/4 (1955), p. 415.

4

ONTOLOGY AND THEOLOGY IN THE *METAPHYSICS* OF ARISTOTLE

In his two major studies on Aristotle's *Metaphysics*,[1] Werner Jaeger set a style and approach for Aristotelian studies which, having reached a peak, seems at present to be going into a graceful decline.[2] By having recourse to the seemingly common sense view that there must have been a development in the thought of Aristotle over his long career, Jaeger was able to put an interpretation on choppy, enigmatic and apparently contradictory passages of the *Metaphysics* which seemed, and continues to seem, revolutionary. For there is something depressing and melancholy in the upshot of Jaeger's interpretation. Finally, I think one must say, he attempted to remove the *Metaphysics* of Aristotle from that class of books which contain a genuine and systematic achievement of thought and thereby provide the philosopher with an apt and precious instrument for repeating the performance and duplicating the achievement.

One who would seek a development of Aristotle's thought has ready to hand the historical commonplace that Aristotle was a member of

1. Werner Jaeger, *Studien zur Enstehungsgeschichte der Metaphysik des Aristotles* (Berlin: 1912); *Aristotle: Fundamentals of the History of His Development*, trans. R. Robinson (New York: 1934).

2. Jaeger has never been without his critics, of course, but most of the early ones either accepted his principles and doubted details of his application of them or, accepting the principles, offered radically alternative views of Aristotle's evolution. There were early critics who rejected the whole approach such as, for example, G. R. G. Mure, *Aristotle* (London: 1932), and Ernest Barker, *The Politics of Aristotle* (London: 1946). Joseph Owens, C. Ss. R., in *The Doctrine of Being in the Aristotelian Metaphysics* (Toronto: 1951), discusses genetic views, is influenced by them, but goes on to seek a unified philosophical doctrine. See too S. G. Nogales, *Horizonte de la Metafísica Aristotelica* (Madrid: 1955). A recent extremely original interpretation is that of Pierre Aubenque, *Le problème de l'être chez Aristote* (Paris: 1962). D. J. Allan, *Aristotle* (London: 1952), and Marjorie Grene, *A Portrait of Aristotle* (Chicago: 1963), indicate the current disenchantment with the genetic approach. Giovanni Reale, in *Il Concetto di Filosofia Prima* (Milan: 1961), gives an extensive interpretation of the *Metaphysics* designed to show the untenability of the evolutionary approach.

the Platonic Academy for nearly twenty years. Prior to Jaeger, this lengthy Platonic experience was not thought to have anything important to do with the Aristotelian *corpus* as we know it; *that* contained Aristotelianism, the revolt against and alternative to Plato. There were, to be sure, the dialogues attributed to Aristotle, but even the nineteenth-century editor of the fragments of those dialogues considered them to be spurious and non-Aristotelian. Why? Because they seemed so thoroughly Platonic in problem and development. But, if Aristotle was in effect a Platonist for some twenty years, it is at least plausible that the dialogues are genuine. There are few today who doubt that they are authentically Aristotelian. Jaeger's peculiar inspiration was to find in the Aristotelian treatises vestiges of that same Platonism and it is his purported discoveries of such traces in the *Metaphysics* which interest us here.

Jaeger was struck by a locution which occurs a significant number of times in the *Metaphysics* and which is certainly curious in a work presumably written by a post-Platonic Aristotle. Often, in discussing an issue, Aristotle will speak in a fashion that can be translated, "We Platonists say," or, "As we (Platonists) hold."[3] Furthermore, Jaeger found that passages in the first book of the *Metaphysics* and in the dialogue *Protrepticus* were remarkably similar.[4] If the latter had been written while Aristotle accepted the fundamental tenets and goals of Platonism, Jaeger conjectured that portions of the *Metaphysics* that has come down to us date from Aristotle's earliest period, his Platonic period. Other portions date from a later period when he had put away his Platonism and become an Aristotelian.

What makes Jaeger's interpretation of particular interest is his contention that Aristotle had two quite different and incompatible conceptions of the subject of First Philosophy, or metaphysics, and that nowhere in the *Metaphysics* as we have it was he able to fuse his two conceptions. The result is that metaphysics is not a science that Aristotle achieved; rather his treatises which bear that name testify to a noble attempt which nevertheless failed. Instead of a solution, the work presents us with a problem and Jaeger's way of solving that problem is by dissolving it into the biography of Aristotle.

It will be appreciated that Jaeger's interpretation, if valid, would put such efforts as that of St. Thomas in his commentary on Aristotle's *Metaphysics* in an absurd light. Aquinas seems to encounter little or no

3. Jaeger, *Aristotle*, p. 171.
4. Ibid., p. 69. Cf. Ingemar Düring, *Aristotle's Protrepticus: An Attempt at Reconstruction* (1961); A.-H. Chroust, *Aristotle: Protrepticus* (Notre Dame: 1964).

difficulty in rethinking the first twelve books of the *Metaphysics*, at least no difficulty that would lead him to doubt the fundamental unity of the work. And since what unifies a work which would develop a science is the subject of the science, it must be said that Aquinas finds no lasting ambiguity in Aristotle's conception of the subject of metaphysics. We could of course say that St. Thomas ignored the difficulties Jaeger underscores and in an irenic, independent and creative way uses the text of Aristotle to develop a conception of metaphysics that is not unequivocally in the text. This would not be consonant with the latter-day view that Aquinas "merely" explicates Aristotle in the commentary and gives us nothing of his own thought. Nevertheless, it would be a way out of an embarrassment.[5]

In a paper of the brief compass of the present one there can be no question of redeeming Aquinas's commentary in its entirety—should it stand in need of such redemption—or of examining Jaeger's view in all its particulars. Nevertheless I shall attempt to show that Jaeger's view when considered in the light of passages he regards as crucial does not have even a prima facie plausibility. On the other hand, prima facie, there is everything to commend the approach Aquinas took. Both points, which are but two sides of the same coin, will be made by reading Aristotle *ex Aristotele*.

Book Beta of the *Metaphysics* contains fourteen or fifteen problems which the science we are seeking, described as wisdom in Book Alpha, should resolve.[6] There is fairly general agreement that the first four problems are more methodological than substantive in the sense that their solution will involve statements on the subject and scope of the science sought.[7] About Beta in general Jaeger has two kinds of statements to make. First, he finds a sufficient number of instances of the "we" style to date the book early. Second, what it says reveals its Platonic bias. "Ever since Plato created the Ideas it had been absolutely *the* problem of philosophy. In formulating the task of metaphysics as he does, therefore, Aristotle starts directly from Plato's fundamental question. He expresses it, in fact, precisely as a Platonist would: the

---

5. See James C. Doig, "Science première et science universelle dans le 'Commentaire de la métaphysique' de saint Thomas d'Aquin," *Revue philosophique de Louvain*, février 1965, pp. 41–96. Doig argues that the commentary represents St. Thomas's understanding of Aristotle, a point he makes by considering the subject of the present article. His treatment represents a different approach from our own.

6. Cf. W. D. Ross, *Aristotle's Metaphysics* (Oxford: 1958), vol. 1, pp. 221ff.; S. Mansion, "Les apories de la métaphysique aristotélicienne," in *Autour d'Aristote* (Louvain: 1955); V. Décarie, *L'objet de la Métaphysique selon Aristote* (Paris: 1961), pp. 95–99; G. Reale, op. cit., pp. 54–98.

7. Father Owens disagrees. For his summary statement, see op. cit., pp. 140–46.

transcendental realities that we believe to exist in separation from sensible phenomena, such as the Ideas and the objects of mathematics—do they truly exist? And if not, can we posit, over and above sensible things, any other kind of supersensible reality? About the sensible world (*aisthete ousia*) he says nothing whatever."[8] Later, in his discussion of E.1,[9] Jaeger makes abundantly clear what his Platonic Aristotle's conception of metaphysics would be. Every science is concerned with a genus of being; there is a genus of beings which exist separately from matter and motion; and that is the genus with which metaphysics is concerned. A later Aristotle, having grown disinterested in such supersensible entities, having turned his attention toward sensible substance, would make metaphysics the general science of being without thereby arguing that there is another genus of beings apart from those studied by the particular sciences. E.1 contains Aristotle's unsuccessful attempt to put these two conceptions together.

Jaeger's interpretation and the contradiction between two possible conceptions of the subject of metaphysics which Aristotle was unable to reduce to unity involves the assumption that at some time in his career, a time presumably which does not antedate the writing of the *Analytics*, Aristotle held that supersensible substance, separated being, could be the subject (*genus subjectum*; *to genos to hypokeimenon*) of a science. If that assumption lacks plausibility, if it is explicitly excluded by Aristotle, then we can fairly conclude that there is a strong case against taking Jaeger's interpretation seriously.

First, with respect to Book Beta, which in Jaeger's view is early and Platonic, there can be no doubt that the structure of science as we are familiar with it from the *Posterior Analytics* is very much in Aristotle's mind. In speaking of whether or not this science should study the axioms, for example, he points out that any science studies a subject matter whose properties it attempts to demonstrate by having recourse to axioms.[10] Earlier, in speaking of metaphysics, Aristotle calls it the "science of the causes."[11] There has been a good deal of curious commentary written on that phrase; many have spoken as if the first causes could be the concern of this science, or any human science, in the sense of its *genus subjectum*. Could Aristotle himself have seriously entertained such a possibility?

It has already been pointed out that Jaeger sees in E.1 the clearest indication of Aristotle's failure to establish any unity in the various concerns of the First Philosophy; that is, Aristotle has no one view as

8. Cf. Jaeger, *Aristotle*, p. 195.   9. Ibid., pp. 215–18.
10. *Metaphysics*, 996b26–997a15. 11. Cf. Owens, op. cit., p. 125.

to the subject of the science. "For Physics deals with things which exist separately but are not immovable, and some parts of mathematics deal with things which are immovable but presumably do not exist separately, but as embodied in matter; while the first science deals with things which both exist separately and are immovable." [12] Aristotle here seems to be assigning as the subject of metaphysics those substances which exist separately from matter and motion. Such entities are divine if anything is and the science of them is called theology. Aristotle then poses Jaeger's question. "For one might raise the question whether first philosophy is universal, or deals with one genus, i.e. some one kind of being. . ." Not only does Aristotle pose the question, he goes on to answer it. "We answer that if there is no substance other than those which are formed by nature, natural science will be the first science; but if there is an immovable substance, the science of this must be prior and must be first philosophy, and universal in this way, because it is first. And it will belong to this to consider being qua being—both what it is and the attributes which belong to it qua being." [13]

What does Jaeger make of this passage? Aristotle has been talking of a special kind of being (*on ti kai genos ti*), namely, unmoved and transcendent being. He wants to make the study of this kind of being the task of a science other than mathematics or physics. But this is to make metaphysics but another special science. "But now this determination of the nature of metaphysics purely by means of its subject-matter, namely unmoved and transcendent being, makes it one special science among others." [14] If metaphysics has for its subject matter a special kind of being, how can it be the science of being as being, a general science distinguished from the particular sciences because the latter study only one type of being? The question and answer we quoted in our previous paragraph is described by Jaeger as a later note, added when Aristotle saw the contradiction he was in. "In a note that obviously breaks the train of thought, and must therefore be a later addition, he makes the following remarks." [15] Jaeger takes Aristotle's answer to mean that the first science is universal because it deals with the first object and he continues to suggest that it makes sense to speak of the divine as if it could be the subject of an Aristotelian science. One can only marvel at the self-assured clairvoyance which enables Jaeger to identify the passage as a later note. The final sentence of Aristotle's resolution of the problem does not detain

---

12. *Metaphysics*, E.1.1026a12–15.   13. Ibid., 1026a27–33.
14. Jaeger, *Aristotle*, p. 217.   15. Ibid.

Jaeger and of course in that sentence Aristotle speaks in a recognizable way of the subject of the science, namely being as being, whose per se attributes will be sought in the science of metaphysics.

What obvious checks to the hypothesis advanced by Jaeger are to be found in Aristotle? Can we find, for example, a clear statement that separate substance, God, could not be the subject of science in the strict sense called for? A first and very general impediment to the hypothesis is found in the fact that scientific knowledge is knowledge of something in its causes; if then there are first causes, they cannot enter into any science as its subject since this would suggest that there are causes of first causes. We do not have to rely on such a generality, however; Aristotle tells us quite explicitly that any explanation is of something complex and that without complexity no scientific question can be asked. "It is evident therefore that there is no investigation or instruction concerning simple entities; but there must be some other way of dealing with them." [16]

Simple substances cannot be the subject of a science in Aristotle's strict sense of science. Nevertheless it belongs to first philosophy or metaphysics to treat of divine being and thereby to be a theology. It must do so with reference to its subject matter which is being as being. The model of *propter quid* demonstration is saved in metaphysics insofar as the metaphysician asks after the commensurately universal properties of being as being; insofar as he asks what belongs to substance as such, i.e. not as material substance but insofar as it is substance; insofar as he asks what pertains to accident as such and not insofar as it is material, etc., etc. Knowledge of God can be had in metaphysics only through His commensurately universal effect, namely being as being.[17] Thus, metaphysics can be theology precisely insofar as its subject is common being, being qua being. The options Jaeger sees Aristotle vacillating between simply do not exist for Aristotle.

In the light of the foregoing it cannot be said that with respect to the problem Jaeger professed to find in the *Metaphysics* Aristotle would have been mute without Thomas (in the phrase of Pico della Mirandola); nevertheless, it is certainly true that the teaching of Aristotle has been made yet more explicit and clear by the presentations given of it by St. Thomas. Recall that Jaeger presents his prob-

16. *Metaphysics*, Z.17.1041b9–11. Cf. St. Thomas, *In VII Metaphysic.*, lect. 17, nn. 1669–71.

17. Cf. W. Baumgaertner, "Metaphysics and the Second Analytics," *The New Scholasticism* 29/4 (1955), pp. 403–26.

lem against the background of the Aristotelian doctrine on the division of theoretical philosophy into three kinds, a doctrine sketched in E.1. This doctrine leads inexorably, according to Jaeger, to the conclusion that first philosophy is concerned with separate or divine substance *as with its subject genus.* That is, it is concerned with a particular kind of being and cannot be at the same time a universal science of being as being. The latter would have a different subject genus distinct from the former's; that is, Aristotle is faced with a choice between theology and ontology. Let us sketch briefly how the presentations of St. Thomas preclude this interpretation even more explicitly than the text of Aristotle has already been shown to do.

In his exposition of the *De trinitate* of Boethius, Aquinas shows why removal from matter and motion is an essential requisite of science: the mental faculty is immaterial and science is of the necessary or unchanging.[18] Consequently, insofar as there are formally different ways in which objects of science are distinguished or separated from matter and motion there are formally distinct theoretical sciences. There are three such kinds of separation or abstraction. In natural philosophy, the mind abstracts from singular sensible matter although the definitions of this science include common sensible matter. The objects of mathematics are defined without including sensible matter but there is no commitment to the view that they exist in the fashion in which they are considered. Metaphysics excludes all matter from its definitions and is founded on the certainty that some immaterial and immobile things exist. If not every being is material, then materiality cannot pertain to being as such.

Of the things that exist, then, some are material and some are immaterial. Of course this is not known by intuition but is the result of proof.[19] A general science of being, the study of what belongs per se to being, cannot therefore be the study of sensible being as such or of immaterial being as such. Rather, it will be concerned with the *communia entis.* That is why St. Thomas distinguishes between the things which sometimes exist in matter and sometimes do not, on the one hand, and, on the other, things which never exist in matter.[20] Examples of the former are being, substance, act, potency, one, etc.; examples of the latter are God and the angels. The subject of metaphysics is said to be *ens commune* and what pertains to it per se and yet

18. St. Thomas, *In Boethii de trin.* (ed. Decker), q. 5, a. 1. Cf. Charles De Koninck, "Abstraction from Matter," *Laval théologique et philosophique* 13/2; 16/1; 16/2; 17/2.
19. Cf. *In IV Metaphysic.*, lect. 5, n. 593.
20. *In Boethii de trin.*, q. 5, a. 4.

the science is fittingly called theology because the chief thing it seeks to know is God. It is only to be expected that we should find all this summarized in St. Thomas's commentary on E.1.[21]

Since philosophy is the study of wisdom and wisdom is the knowledge of all things in their ultimate causes, philosophy is aimed from the beginning at whatever knowledge can be attained of God. However, given the debility of our knowing faculty, the ultimate object of human knowledge can never be the subject of a human science. In the study of natural things we are compelled to appeal to causes which are not themselves natural and we come thereby to see that not everything which is is material. This serves as the basis for seeking yet another science which will have as its subject, not being of a particular kind, but being as such. Proceeding horizontally, so to speak, this science will seek knowledge of what belongs per se to being after the fashion of properties of its subject. In what may be described as a vertical procedure, it will seek the cause of its subject, the efficient and, preeminently, the final cause of whatever is, of being as being.[22] The success of that effort puts one in possession of sapiential knowledge par excellence. Thus, in order to be a theology, metaphysics must have as its subject being as being. Once more, in the proemium to his commentary on the *Metaphysics*, it is St. Thomas who summarizes in magisterial fashion the doctrine concerning the unity of metaphysics and that summary makes it abundantly clear that, for one who understands Aristotle, Jaeger's "contradiction" could never be seriously entertained.

Ex quo apparet, quod quamvis ista scientia praedicta tria consideret [i.e. first causes, the most universal, God and the angels], non tamen considerat quodlibet eorum ut subiectum, sed ipsum solum ens commune. Hoc enim est subiectum in scientia, cuius causas et passiones quaerimus, non autem ipsae causae alicuius generis quaesiti. Nam cognitio causarum alicuius generis, est finis ad quem consideratio scientiae pertingit. Quamvis autem subiectum huius scientiae sit ens commune, dicitur tamen tota de his quae sunt separata a materia secundum esse et rationem. Quia secundum esse et rationem separari dicuntur, non solum illa quae nunquam in materia esse possunt, sicut Deus et intellectuales substantiae, sed etiam illa quae possunt sine materia esse, sicut ens commune. Hoc tamen non contingeret si a materia secundum esse dependeret.

21. Cf. *In VI Metaphysic.*, lect. 1, n. 1170.
22. Cf. *In VII Metaphysic.*, lect. 17, n. 1660.

5

THOMAS ON BOOK DELTA OF THE *METAPHYSICS*

There are two general problems associated with Thomas's commentaries on Aristotelian works, perhaps particularly his commentary on the *Metaphysics*. The first affects the whole tradition of commentaries from Hellenistic times and stems from the bombshell Werner Jaeger threw into Aristotelian studies during the first quarter of the century.[1] All the great commentaries on the *Metaphysics*, Greek, Arabic, Latin, presuppose that the work is a literary whole; indeed, a significant aspect of the commentator's task consists of showing the interrelation of the parts of the work, in short its order. If Jaeger is right about the literary disunity of the *Metaphysics*, the commentary tradition is called severely into question. The second great problem has to do with the value of Thomas's commentaries on Aristotle for determining what he, Thomas, thinks about this or that.

Discussions of the second point are many and various. From Chenu and Gilson to the 1974 essay by Father Joseph Owens, there has been a significant development of assessment.[2] It seems fairly clear that there

1. Werner Jaeger, *Aristotle: Fundamentals of the History of His Development* (Oxford: 1948).

2. M. D. Chenu, *Introduction à l'étude de saint Thomas d'Aquin* (Montreal: 1954), pp. 173–98; E. Gilson, *A History of Christian Philosophy in the Middle Ages* (New York: 1955), p. 367: "There is no philosophical writing of Thomas Aquinas to which we could apply for an exposition of the truths concerning God and man which he considered knowable in the natural light of reason. His commentaries on Aristotle are so many expositions of the doctrine of Aristotle, not of what might be called his own philosophy. As a commentator, Thomas could add to the text something of his own, but this was not his principal intention. We may find fragmentary expositions of his own philosophical conceptions in some particular treatises, for instance in the *De ente et essentia*. Generally speaking, however, we must resort to the theological writings in order to find them fully developed, but following a theological order. This is the only mode of historical existence they have, and whatever order of exposition he might have chosen to follow in philosophy, the theology of Thomas Aquinas remains for us the only place where his own rational view of the world is to be found." On this, see James Collins, "Toward a Philosophically Ordered Thomism," *The New Scholasticism* 32 (1958), pp. 301–26;

are no a priori literary and/or historical considerations which can settle the status of the commentaries. Finally, one must simply read them carefully and develop a theory of their nature against the background of that reading.

As for the first question, much post-Jaegerian study of the *Metaphysics* has devoted itself to finding larger or smaller ordered units within the fourteen books, clustering series of books in various ways, while conceding the main point that the fourteen books simply do not make up an ordered whole. Elsewhere, I have expressed my own views on the status of Jaeger's major claim about the *Metaphysics* as this is grounded on a reading of E.1.[3] In the present paper, I propose to consider the fate of Book Delta of the *Metaphysics* and then draw attention to Thomas's remarkable commentary on it.

I

Jaeger's remarks about Delta in his second work on the composition of Aristotle's work are succinct. In the course of providing an overview of the *Metaphysics*, he writes, "The postscript to the introductory book, the so-called little Alpha, comes after big A simply because they did not know where else to put it. It is a remnant of notes taken at a lecture by Pasicles, a nephew of Aristotle's disciple Eudemus of Rhodes; Alpha, Beta and Gamma belong together. Delta, on the other hand, was still known as an independent work in Alexandrian times, as a sound bibliographical tradition informs us. Epsilon is a short transitional passage leading to Zeta, Eta, Theta. These three form a whole, but their connection with the previous books seems to be problematical. . . ."[4] That isolation and dismissal of Delta from consideration sets the tone for the approach of later scholars.

Delta is evidently out of place where it is, and as evidently it is a genuinely Aristotelian work. It is referred to in Epsilon, Zeta, Theta and Iota, as well as in the *Physics* and the *De Generatione et Corruptione*—either by the vague phrase ἐν ἄλλοις or as τὰ περὶ τοῦ ποσαχῶς or by some variant of this title; and under this title it occurs in Diogenes Laertius' list, in which the *Metaphysics* does not occur. It is a useful preliminary to the *Metaphysics*, but it is not a preliminary to it in particular. Some of the notions discussed in it (κολοβόν,

Joseph Owens, "Aquinas as Aristotelian Commentator," *St. Thomas Aquinas 1274–1974: Commemorative Studies* (Toronto: 1974), vol. 1, pp. 213–38.

3. See Chapter 4 above. See too Pierre Aubenque, "La pensée du simple dans la *Métaphysique* Zeta 17 and Theta 10," *Etudes sur la Métaphysique d'Aristote*, Actes du VIe Symposium Aristotelicum (Paris: 1979), pp. 69–80, with discussion pp. 81–88.

4. *Aristotle*, pp. 169–70.

ψεῦδος) are not appropriate to the *Metaphysics*, and it is apparently earlier than the physical works while the rest of the *Metaphysics*, in its present form, is later.[5]

Ross takes it that Delta was inserted in its present place because Gamma 1004a28 was taken to promise an examination of varieties in the meanings of terms, perhaps because E.1026a34 is the first backward reference to Delta.[6]

Joseph Owens, in his magisterial *The Doctrine of Being in the Aristotelian Metaphysics*,[7] having reviewed the chronologies of others (who find no integral place for Book Delta) goes on to his own lengthy and illuminating effort to read *Aristoteles ex Aristotele* but, despite the crucial role he assigns *pros hen* equivocals, clearly accepts the view that Delta is an independent treatise which casts no light on whatever unified development there is in the fourteen books. This is not, of course, to say that Owens does not make extended use of Delta in his study.

Not all Aristotelian commentators have been willing to take the genetic and/or chronological approach as obligatory. Indeed, recent introductory works, after mentioning the incredible diversity of scholarly opinions on the structure and order of the *Metaphysics*, simply set the controversy aside and say, in effect, let's read Aristotle.[8] While this might seem slightly obscurantist, the same cannot be said of the remarks of Stephen Barker, who may be called a repentant evolutionist.[9] The judicious remarks of W. K. C. Guthrie in volume 6 of his *History of Greek Philosophy*[10] serve to introduce a needed sympathetic distance from the excesses of Jaeger and his more enthusiastic imitators.

But it should not be thought that doubts about the function of Book Delta within the *Metaphysics*, or indeed of its claim to a place among the other books, is a consequence of a genetic approach to Aristotle. The Everyman edition of the *Metaphysics* shifts Delta to the beginning of the work, thereby taking its cue, one might suppose, from the faintly dismissive title the Oxford translation gave the book: A Philosophical Lexicon—a vocabulary list, as it were, useful for finding one's way around the Aristotelian terrain.

5. W. D. Ross, *Aristotle's Metaphysics: A Revised Text with Introduction and Commentary* (Oxford: 1958), vol. 1, p. xxv.

6. Ibid., p. xxxi.

7. 3d ed. (Toronto: 1978).

8. D. J. Allan, *The Philosophy of Aristotle* (London: 1952); Marjorie Grene, *A Portrait of Aristotle* (Chicago: 1963); G. E. R. Lloyd, *Aristotle: The Growth and Structure of His Thought* (Cambridge: 1968).

9. Stephen Barker, *Aristotle's Politics* (Oxford: 1946).

10. W. K. C. Guthrie, *A History of Greek Philosophy*, vol. 6 (Cambridge: 1981).

If it is the case that in recent years, for whatever reason or reasons, Book Delta has been considered more or less out of place among the fourteen books of the *Metaphysics*, a notable exception to the trend is found in Giovanni Reale's *The Concept of First Philosophy and the Unity of the Metaphysics of Aristotle*.[11] Chapter 8 of his study is devoted entirely to Book Delta and Reale is quite aware that he is bucking a trend. But then Reale's general argument is that there is nothing to prevent a unitary reading of the *Metaphysics* as it has come down to us. For all that, his treatment of Delta comes at the end of his study, after his treatment of all the other books, and he concedes at the outset that Delta seems less amenable to the kind of reading he has been recommending.

The majority of modern interpreters consider Book Delta as a treatment originally conceived as a work standing by itself, only later inserted into the *Metaphysics* and not by Aristotle. It seems to us—and we will shortly prove it— that we possess good reasons for reading it precisely in the place and position in which the tradition has transmitted it.[12]

There are thirty chapters in Book Delta which is devoted to the analysis of that many terms. Contrary to scholars like Bonitz who could find no criterion or criteria for inclusion in the list, and no order among the terms on it, Reale holds that criteria are indeed discernible. Not only is there a repeated technique observed in the laying out of many meanings of a term and a subsequent attempt to reduce the plurality of meanings to unity, there is a plan, Reale feels, in the section of the terms for consideration.

First of all, negatively, terms which fall to the practical or productive sciences are not included. Second, most positively, Reale maintains that the book limits itself to theoretical concepts which specifically pertain to the object of first philosophy or which are in some way related to that object. We would be surprised, he remarks, to find such a discussion in the *Physics*, for example. It seems inescapable then that the terms "have been selected with the purpose of clarifying the metaphysical inquiry and thus not by chance."[13]

Reale then locates the view of Carlini midway between "the excessively schematic distinctions of Saint Thomas" and the overly empirical one of Ross.[14] In developing his view that there is a logical connection among the discussions of Delta, he argues for its fitting

---

11. Giovanni Reale, *The Conception of First Philosophy and the Unity of the Metaphysics of Aristotle*, trans. John R. Catan (Albany: 1980).

12. Ibid., p. 338.   13. Ibid., p. 340.

14. Ibid., p. 341.

placement where traditionally it has been placed and confronts some consequences of the genetic interpretation of Delta.

Reale's study of the *Metaphysics* is ample indication that the turning away from the host of problems raised by Jaeger need not be due to obscurantism or indifference to the historical vagaries involved in the transmission of texts. Without endorsing every aspect of Reale's argument, we can cite his book as counterevidence to the claim or suggestion that there is something amusingly naive in the way in which Hellenistic, Arabic, and Latin commentators, Thomas Aquinas among them, approached the works of Aristotle. There is thus no a priori scholarly impediment to taking Thomas's commentary as a guide in seeking to understand the *Metaphysics* of Aristotle.

For purposes of this article, we need not concern ourselves thematically with the second major issue mentioned at the outset, namely, the value of the commentaries for revealing Thomas's own thoughts on the matters under discussion in the book being commented on. Rather, I shall say some things about the way in which Thomas understands Book Delta. Reale summarized Thomas's view in the following way:

> Saint Thomas discovered an order even in the internal divisions of the material of Book Delta. For him, the book would be divided into three parts: the first part concerns the clarification of terms concerning the first cause (chapters 1–5); the second is dedicated to the terms indicating the object of first philosophy and the parts thereof (chapters 6–15); the third is concerned, finally, with terms indicating the various determinations of being (chapters 16–30).[15]

This is the interpretation that Reale regards as "excessively schematic" but he does not enlighten his reader as to the precise nature of the excess. His own understanding of the plan of the book[16] bears a strong family resemblance to that of Saint Thomas. But let us turn now to Thomas's commentary on Book Delta of the *Metaphysics*.

II

Whatever else can be said of Book Delta, it must be stressed that the terms it discusses are all instances of what Aristotle calls *pros hen* equivocals and Thomas calls—though he does not emphasize this in his commentary on Book V—analogous terms. Thus it is that Thomas

15. Ibid., p. 340.
16. Ibid., pp. 339–40.

says that Aristotle, having determined what this science considers, now in Book V begins his examination of those objects. "And because the things considered in this science are common to all things, and are not said univocally of them, but rather of some primarily and others secondarily, he first distinguishes the meanings of the words which fall to the consideration of this science." [17] The backward reference is to the preceding book and it is there Thomas makes clear that, in his usage, the adverb *analogice* and the adverbial phrase *secundum analogiam*, translate such Aristotelian phrases as *pollakhōs legetai*. [18] The Greek counterparts of *analogia* and *analogice* do not occur here in the Aristotelian text, despite the fact that the Latin words are loan words from the Greek. It seems to be the case that Aristotle nowhere uses *analogia* or *kat' analogian* in the way Thomas uses *analogice* and *secundum analogiam*, namely to speak of the relations among many meanings of the same term. [19] In any case, Thomas accepts Aristotle's argument that the way to get sufficient unity for a science of being as being is to see that "being" is an analogous term and that one sense of it takes priority over the others. The same will be true of other terms used in metaphysics and Book V is devoted to spelling this out.

Given this role of the book in the development of the science of being as being, we are prepared for the structure of the book. "Any science is concerned with a subject, properties and causes; that is why Book V is divided into three parts. First, it clarifies the meanings of terms which signify causes; second, the meanings of terms which signify the subject of the science, or parts of that subject. . . . Third, of those which signify the properties of being as being." [20]

Perhaps it would be well to recall the way in which the Aristotelian conception of science guides discussions in books prior to Delta. The great protreptic opening of the *Metaphysics* moves gracefully into the conception of science, the role of causes, and anchors the notion of wisdom to it. ". . . all men suppose what is called Wisdom to deal with

17. *In V Metaphysic.*, lect. 1, n. 749: "Et quia ea quae in hac scientia considerantur, sunt omnibus communia, nec dicuntur univoce, sed secundum prius et posterius de diversis, ut in quarto libro est habitum, ideo prius distinguit intentiones nominum, quae in huius scientiae consideratione cadunt."

18. Cf. *In IV Metaphysic.*, lect. 1, n. 534.

19. *Pace* G. L. Muskens, *De vocis ANALOGIAS significatione ac usu apud Aristotelem* (Groningen: 1943).

20. *In V Metaphysic.*, lect. 1, n. 749: "Cuiuslibet autem scientiae est considerare subjectum, et passiones, et causas; et ideo hic quintus liber dividitur in tres partes. Primo determinat distinctiones nominum quae significant causas; secundo illorum nominum quae significant subjectum huius scientiae vel partes eius. . . . Tertio nominum quae significant passiones entis inquantum est ens."

the first causes and the principles of things; so that, as has been said before, the man of experience is thought to be wiser than the possessors of any sense-experience whatever, the artist wiser than the man of experience, the master-worker than the mechanic, and the theoretical kinds of knowledge to be more of the nature of Wisdom than the productive. Clearly then Wisdom is knowledge about certain principles and causes" (981b28–982a1). The first three aporiae in Book Beta are unintelligible without reference to Aristotelian scientific methodology: whether the investigation of the causes belongs to one or to more sciences; whether such a science should survey only the first principles of substance, whether one science deals with all substances. Consider the following passages.

If there is a demonstrative science which deals with them, there will have to be an underlying kind, and some of them must be demonstrable attributes and others must be axioms (for it is impossible that there should be demonstration of all of them); for the demonstrations must start from certain premises and be about a certain subject and prove certain attributes. (B.2.997a5–10)

For every demonstrative science investigates with regard to some subject its essential attributes, starting from the common beliefs. (997a20)

Passages like these could be multiplied. In Book Beta, the demands of Aristotle's concept of science generate difficulties for the proposed inquiry, and it is quite clear that unless these difficulties can be resolved, the great project laid out at the outset of Alpha, as well as the Platonic version of that aspiration toward Wisdom, will be incoherent. That Aristotle holds that they can be resolved is clear from the crisp opening of Gamma: "There is a science which investigates being as being and the attributes which belong to it in virtue of its own nature." How can this be if the *genus subjectum* is also a predicable genus, univocally common to the more specific expressions of that subject matter? The theory of words said in many ways is, again, the answer to that difficulty. Being is not a genus, but the principal meaning of "being," *ousia*, provides the subject matter of the science we are seeking.

An attentive reader of the preceding books will look to Delta to continue this appeal to the structure of Aristotelian science. St. Thomas finds that that is precisely what Aristotle does in Delta. Some words of multiple meaning discussed in the book bear on causes, others on the subject, yet others on attributes of the subject of the science. Let us have before us the outline Thomas makes of Delta:

Words of interest to metaphysics having several meanings

I. Those which signify causes
    a. generally
        "principle" (lesson 1)
        "cause" (lessons 2–3)
        "element" (lesson 4)
    b. specially
        "nature" (lesson 5)
    c. modally
        "necessity" (lesson 6)

II. Those which signify the subject of the science
    a. as such
        i. "one" and "many" (lessons 7 & 8)
        ii. "being" (lesson 9)
        iii. "substance" (lesson 10)
    b. parts of the subject
        i. and first of "one"
            aa. first parts of "one" and "many"
                "same"
                "diverse"
                "different"
                "similar and dissimilar" (lesson 11)
            bb. secondary parts of plurality
                "opposites"
                "contraries"
                "diverse in kind" (lesson 12)
            cc. "prior and posterior" (lesson 13)
        ii. of "being"
            aa. as divided by act and potency
                "potency" (lesson 14)
                "impotency"
                a metaphorical sense of "potency"
            bb. as divided into categories
                "quantity" (lesson 15)
                "quality" (lesson 16)
                "relation" (lesson 17)

III. Words signifying properties of the subject
    a. those signifying perfection of being
        i. pertaining to perfection itself
            "perfect" (lesson 18)

      aa. signifying modes of the perfect
         "term" (lesson 19)
         "per se"
         "dispositive" (lesson 20)
         "habitus"
   ii. those pertaining to totality
      "part"
      "whole" (lesson 21)
      "genus"
 b. those signifying imperfection
   "false"
   "accident" (lesson 22)

This is the schema that can be gleaned from the taxonomic remarks Thomas makes at the beginning of the various lessons of the commentary and which is laid out for the reader in the Marietti edition of Cathala (1925). Reale found this structure excessively schematic despite the kinship, already noted, between his views and those of Thomas. One might say that Reale endorses the general schema while finding some difficulties with it, and that seems a reasonable reaction.

At the very outset it is clear that Thomas sees far more than the general order of the schema just given. For example, he suggests the reason why "principle" is discussed before "cause" and "cause" before "element." "Procedit autem hoc ordine, quia hoc nomen Principium communius est quam causa: aliquid enim est principium quod non est causa; sicut principium motus dicitur terminus a quo. Et iterum causa est in plus quam elementum."[21] This leads the reader to want to test the details of the ordering and to wish that Thomas had given a reason, as he does not, for the treatment of "one" preceding that of "being." What we are given at the outset of Thomas's discussion of the second main part of Delta, is this:

Postquam Philosophus distinxit nomina quae significant causas, hic distinguit nomina quae significant id quod est subjectum aliquo modo in ista scientia. Et dividitur in duas partes. Primo ponit sive distinguit nomina quae significant subjectum huius scientiae. Secundo ea quae significant partes subjecti. . . . Subjectum autem hujus scientiae considerandum, cujusmodi est ens et unum: vel sicut id de quo est principalius intentio, ut substantia. Et ideo primo distinguit hoc nomen unum . . . secundo hoc nomen ens . . . tertio hoc nomen substantiae. . . .[22]

We are given the reason for regarding "being" and "one" and "substance" as standing for the subject rather than for a part of the subject

21. Ibid., n. 750.   22. Ibid., lect. 7, n. 842.

of metaphysics, but none for the priority of the treatment of "one." Elsewhere[23] Thomas says things which suggest that any discussion of the meaning of "one" is going to presuppose the meaning of "being." "Unum enim addit indivisionem supra ens. Dicitur enim unum ens indivisibile vel indivisum." Indeed, this point is made at the outset of the book of the *Metaphysics* devoted to the discussion of unity.[24]

When Thomas goes on to the second part of the second part, that is, to the words which signify parts of the subject of metaphysics, he subdivides it into two: the words which signify parts of one and those which signify parts of being. Why is there no third division, words signifying parts of substance? "Substantia enim quae etiam posita est subjectum huius scientiae, est unum solum praedicamentum non divisum in multa praedicamenta."[25] This reason might seem to militate against "substance" being listed along with "one" and "being" as signifying the subject of the science. Thomas has said that "substance" is not as common as "being" and "one" but it is what the science chiefly aims to discuss. In order to understand that, we must understand the way Thomas explains the opening of Gamma.

"There is a science which considers being as being and that which belongs to it *per se*."[26] None of the particular sciences considers being as being as its subject. How can something so general provide sufficient focus for a science? The whole point of the introduction of the discussion of analogous names at that point is to show that the primary analogate of such a word gives us the focus we need for a science. But substance is the primary analogate of "being." Ergo, etc. Here is Thomas's statement of the argument.

Hic ponit quod haec scientia principaliter considerat de substantiis, etsi de omnibus entibus consideret, tali ratione. Omnis scientia quae est de pluribus quae dicuntur ad unum primum, est proprie et principaliter illius primi, ex quo alia dependent secundum esse, et propter quod dicuntur secundum nomen; et hoc ubique est verum. Sed substantia est hoc primum inter omnia entia. Ergo philosophus qui considerat omnia entia, primo et principaliter debet habere in sua consideratione principia et causas substantiarum; ergo per consequens ejus consideratio primo et principaliter de substantiis est.[27]

Thus, in Delta, words which signify parts of the subject of the science as designated by "being" are based on the division of being by act and potency and by the categories, but substance is not listed among the latter. Indeed, the terms which are listed are "quantity," "quality" and "relation." Why don't the names of the other categories occur here?

23. Cf. *In X Metaphysic.*, lect. 3, n. 1974.   24. Ibid., lect. 1, n. 1920.
25. *In V Metaphysic.*, lect. 11, n. 906.   26. *Metaphysics*, Γ1.1003a17.
27. *In IV Metaphysic.*, lect. 1, n. 546.

"Alia vero praedicamenta praetermittit, quia sunt determinata ad aliquod genus rerum naturalium; ut patet praecipue de agere et pati, et
de ubi et quando."[28] If we think Thomas has forgotten the last remark
when "passio" comes up in the discussion of "habitus," he makes it
clear that he has not.[29]

These few soundings indicate why one tends to agree with Reale to
the degree that his position is that, while in the main the schema
Thomas finds in Delta expresses what is in the book, there are occa-
sional puzzles that Thomas does not dispel. A further example of the
latter would be the bewildering way in which "accident" keeps showing up in Delta. In discussing "one," Thomas distinguishes what is one
per se and one per accidens.[30] The same distinction is made when the
modes of "being" are discussed. In lesson 22, we find "accidens" coming up for discussion again. Given Thomas's search for order in the
book, we are likely to think he should have said something about that.

It is important to stress that such expectations are aroused by
Thomas's illuminating remarks about the detailed interrelations of
the parts of Delta. The fact that he does not explicitly spell everything
out does not, of course, mean that he would be unable to reply to such
requests. However that may be, Thomas's commentary enables us to
see the link of Delta with Gamma.

Gamma has brought to the fore, and not for the first time, the role
that Aristotle's conception of science, developed in the *Posterior Analytics*, plays in his efforts to find a science beyond physics and mathematics. It is as if the formal conception of science is already had and
one is asking how it is instantiated in the case of a putative science of
being. Aristotle's recognition that "being" is not common to the things
that are, or to the kinds of thing there are, as a univocal term is common to its subjects, enabled him to find sufficient focus for a science of
being. Such common terms as "being" and "one" range over kinds,
again not univocally but, as Thomas will put it, analogically. This
means that one meaning of such terms takes precedence over the
others. The privileged position of the discussion of substance in metaphysics is thereby established.

Now, in Delta, as Thomas reads it, we are confronted with something a good deal more organized than a random list of words. This is
not a philosophical lexicon, *sans phrase*. The words under discussion
are chosen because of their significance for the science we are seeking.
If "being" and "one" are analogous, it will be necessary to distinguish

---

28. *In V Metaphysic.*, lect. 15, n. 977.
29. Ibid., lect. 20, n. 1069.   30. Ibid., lect. 7, nn. 843–47.

their several meanings and to look for an order among them. The same turns out to be true of words signifying parts of the subject, properties of the subject and causes of the subject. No one can fail to see that Delta is a collection of words "said in many ways," of analogous terms. Gamma has prepared us to expect such a discussion of analogous terms and has given us an inkling of the criteria for inclusion in or exclusion from a list which would be useful to a metaphysician. There are all kinds of analogous terms which are of little interest to the metaphysician.

III

The student of Thomas's commentary on Aristotle's *Metaphysics* cannot fail to be impressed by its relentless search for, and discovery of, the order of the twelve books which made up Thomas's version. This is something which must be judged as such, by comparing the text and Thomas's remarks upon it, not by appeals to "the nature of commentaries" or allegedly established characteristics of them. Many students of Thomas are in the grips of the idea that he somehow, genially, read into texts his own agenda, making them say things they do not mean, for purposes of his own. It may be that some version of that claim can be established in the case of one or another Thomistic commentary. That would enable us to conclude nothing about the commentary on the *Metaphysics*.

Thomas's reader will, at the very least, dismiss as unserious the view that Delta is simply a list of words, a lexicon which functions as an introduction to Aristotelian vocabulary. The pattern that Thomas sees among the words discussed, appealing to the Aristotelian concept of science, of subject, cause and attribute, is securely grounded in the text itself, thus linking it to the preceding books in terms of something formal and fundamental to what is going on. It would be a task of Quixotic dimensions to argue that Thomas is *reading into* the text what is not there. Clearly what he is doing is *reading out* of the text what is plainly before the reader.

One who agrees that Delta, in its main lines, is structured as Thomas sees it, can nonetheless, as the foregoing indicated, question some of the more detailed claims for order. He may also notice difficulties for the claim to order that Thomas does not deal with. But the appeal to the structure of Aristotelian science in reading Delta, far from being the importation of thirteenth-century predilections into a mid fourth-century B.C. text, is indeed the key to the book.

6

ULTIMATE END IN ARISTOTLE

In what follows I am concerned with three interrelated and over-lapping questions: What does Aristotle mean by *end* and *ultimate end*? Where and how does he show that man has an ultimate end? In what sense is man's ultimate end one? I shall confine myself almost exclusively to the first book of the *Nicomachean Ethics*.

"Every art and every inquiry, and similarly every action and pursuit, is thought to aim at some good; and for this reason the good has rightly been declared to be that at which all things aim." Thus begins the *Nicomachean Ethics*. The sentence attempts, I should say, a swift inventory of human acts or deeds. They are all and as such teleological, undertaken for some purpose, done with an end in view. Furthermore, a first determination of the meaning of "good" is given. The good is the aim, purpose or end of an action, where of course "good" means the good for man since we are speaking of human deeds. This is a startling way to begin a treatise on ethics. If every human act aims at an end, and if the end and good are one, then each and every human action is, as human action, good. In order to escape this leveling consequence, Aristotle is going to need some criterion whereby he can distinguish between the real and the apparent good. How will he find one?

His procedure seems roughly this. If any action is undertaken with an end in view, with an eye to some good, what is sought as good is taken to be perfective of the agent. That is, the not-doing is less perfect than the having or doing. One seeks what one does not have and seeks it because having it is preferable, is the completion of a capacity, the fulfilment of a need. Whatever a man does or seeks is done or sought under this broad assumption. But not everything so sought is really perfective of the agent. Thus Aristotle will proceed on the assumption that knowledge of the kind of agent we are will provide a criterion for distinguishing in the things we seek those which are truly perfective of us from those which are not. Hence the traditional talk of real and apparent goods.

In a manner familiar to his faithful reader, Aristotle clarifies the issues involved by appeal to artistic or technical activities. Just as the human artifact is the basic metaphor through which he speaks of natural objects, so here, and even more fittingly, before turning explicitly to human doing, the meaning of terms will be anchored in human making. No one can doubt the pedagogical utility of this, but here as elsewhere we must be extremely careful lest the aid become an impediment. "But a certain difference is found among ends; some are activities, others are products (*erga*) apart from the activities that produce them. Where there are ends apart from the actions, it is the nature of the products to be better than the activities." Though it is not quite as neat as this, I take the distinction between action-as-end and product-beyond-action-as-end to be an adumbration of the distinction between *technē* and *phronēsis*. If the former casts light on the latter, it can also mislead, not least when we are speaking of ends and means. In the case of art, activity is a means relative to the product-as-end, so that in art the aim is the good or perfection of the artifact. In the case of man as doer, action is not a means but the end. This remains true even if we should say that action of a certain kind is that whereby the agent becomes good: his goodness here is his disposition to perform acts of the kind in question.

"Now, as there are many actions, arts, and sciences, their ends also are many . . ." This remark reminds us, should we need reminding, that the opening sentence of *Nicomachean Ethics*, I, if true, tells us something of each and every human deed, whether art, science or choice, but the unity of the remark is that of generality. That is, some one thing is true of everything we do. If every action aims at some end, this does not mean that there is some one end at which all actions aim. Never loath to be explicit, Aristotle gives a list: the end of the medical art is health, that of shipbuilding a vessel, that of strategy victory, that of economics wealth. And so on and on. If any game is a recreational activity, this truth does not inform us on the immense variety of kinds of game. If any action has an end, this truth cannot substitute for the immense variety of endlike objects. The picture that thus emerges is this: while we can soar above the arena of human activity and say that whatever man does aims at an end, when we descend we seem faced with the prospect of piecemeal analysis of now this end, then that, then the next, and so on ad infinitum.

But there may be another way of gathering goods or ends, of unifying actions into clusters, a way which is not that of predicable universality but rather that of subordination and superordination. (Of course The Porphyrian tree might be spoken of, is spoken of, in terms of subordination and superordination so that the task might be distinguishing modalities of those terms.) How can actions or goods be clustered? "But where such arts fall under a single capacity [*dunamis*] . . . in all these the ends of the master arts are to be preferred to all the subordinate ends; for it is for the sake of the former that the latter are pursued." The end of bridle-making is bridles, of stirrup-making stirrups, of saddle-making saddles. These ends or goods are for the sake of riding, of horsemanship. But horsemanship may be subordinated to military strategy, the art of war, whose end is victory. Activities and their ends can be so clustered around one particular end which is superordinate and all the others subordinate. Once more, these prefixes should not be read in terms of greater or less predicable scope: the picture is not that of species subordinated to a genus.

Having indicated (a) how we can say something which while generally true of every action leaves open the need of examining the ends of particular actions, or kinds of action, one at a time, and (b) that the sheer diversity of human teleological activity can be mastered somewhat by clustering actions when the ends of several are subordinate to the end of another activity, Aristotle now, in chapter 2, suggests that the second mode (b), if pursued, can lead to the grand sweep of the first mode (a). "If, then, there is some end of the things we do, which we desire for its own sake (everything else being desired for the sake of this), and if we do not choose everything for the sake of something else (at that rate, the process would go on to infinity, so that our desire would be empty and vain), clearly this must be the good and the chief good." What is the force of this passage? If we were to ignore the second parenthetical remark, it would seem to be a mere hypothesis, a subjunctive, perhaps optative, remark. However, if we do take into account that second parenthetical remark, we seem to have an argument to the effect that there must be such an ultimate superordinating end of all we do.

Even if one were to take the quoted passage as an hypothesis, one would have to say that it is soon rendered categorical by appeal to two quite different sorts of fact. In the immediate sequel of chapter 2, we find Aristotle proceeding thus. If there were such an ultimate end, knowledge of it would be of the greatest usefulness; like archers and their target we would then be in a position to aim in the right direction. Furthermore, if there should be such an ultimate superordinating end, concern with it would fall to politics, the master art of human affairs. It is this observation that leads Aristotle forth from his hypothetical reverie. When we consider the political order, we find that such an ultimate end is presupposed. Aristotle has in mind the statesman in his guise of legislator. Laws are passed concerning every conceivable human activity; no overt human behavior seems to escape the purview of the law, if only because a law might be passed saying that such and such an activity is not to be interfered with. If law is proscriptive, regulative, permissive or protective, it would seem that in principle any and every human activity can be covered by it. For this to be the case, however, the lawmaker must have some vantage point, some end in view, some good in mind, when he thus takes into account the whole of human activity. And would this not be some ultimate superordinating end to which the ends of all activities are subordinated? Thus, whether or not the passage with which chapter 2 begins is understood as an argument to the effect that there must be an ultimate end of human activity, it is clear that later on, by appeal to the law, Aristotle asserts that men do recognize such an ultimate end.

There is another so to speak factual appeal whereby Aristotle turns his hypothetical into a categorical. In chapter 4 he says that there is at least verbal agreement among men that there is an ultimate end, verbal because they have a name for it, *eudaimonia*, happiness. This then is one way of reacting to the passage quoted above. If there were an ultimate superordinating end of human action, it would be our chief good. But both legislation and the way men speak of happiness suggest a recognition of an ultimate end. Ergo, etc.

Nonetheless, friend and foe alike have taken the opening passage of chapter 2 to be an argument, not an hypothesis, and the second parenthetical remark supports this interpretation. If there is no ultimate end, our desire would be vain and empty. That is, if human action is not to be nonsensical, there must be an ultimate end. Presuming that this is an argument, how good an argument is it? There are some standard objections to it.

(a) Aristotle is here misled by the linear analogy of subordinate and superordinate ends. Real life revolves in lazy circles. I want A in order that B and B in order that C and C in order that A. That is, I exercise in order to be healthy in order to work in order to earn a vacation and go to Florida where I will loll in the sun and exercise my eyes in order to be healthy in order to acquit my obligations to Notre Dame, etc., etc. such that what was for-something-else may later become the aim of its erstwhile aim.

(b) No doubt there are people who sacrifice everything to some one dominant passion of their lives, but why put so high a premium on a particular psychological type? Henry James and Disraeli were driven

men, everything in their lives subordinated to a single-minded purpose and deriving its importance therefrom, but not everyone is like
that. There are more pleasant people—you and I—who seek to or-
chestrate their aims in such a way that no one of them achieves domi-
nance over the others. What we want is harmony of ends rather than
one overriding purpose.

(c) Aristotle is guilty of a foolish fallacy. He passes from "All chains
must end somewhere" to "There is somewhere that all chains end." Or
from "Every road comes to a stop someplace" to "There is some place
where all roads stop." All roads lead to Rome.

One's first reaction to these objections is that Aristotle ought not be
open to them—call this the pious reaction. If the notion of ultimate
end makes sense it ought not do so at the expense of what the objec-
tors remind us. As for the third objection, if it has force, it amounts to
an Aristotelian criticism of Aristotle. The point it makes is precisely
the point Aristotle makes in chapter 1. The common truth that every
action has an end is not an argument for a common end of all actions.
Has the introduction of what we have called clustering, of subordination and superordination, clouded Aristotle's mind on this point and
in so short a space? As to the second parenthetical remark in the passage which now concerns us, it could be said that it too goes against
the grain of chapter 1. Why should we think that in the absence of an
ultimate end our desire would be vain and empty? An end is an end.
If this action has an end, that saves our desire from being vain and
empty. So too with the next one and the next and so on. It is not its
subordination to a further end which makes an end an end in the first
place. Without that subordination it remains an end. The parenthetical remark seems to treat any particular end as if it were "for the
sake of something" in the sense that it is not sought for its own sake.
But that would make every end less than the putative ultimate one
merely instrumental, not desirable in itself: they would all be like
bitter medicine taken for the sake of health. What in the world is
Aristotle trying to say? (I shall abstain from the scholarly dodge of
suggesting that the parenthetical remark is an interpolation by a later
hand.)

The way out of the woods here, I think, is to see that the examples
Aristotle brought forward to illustrate what he means by subordination and superordination, helpful as they are, can be productive of a
bad picture. The examples show how several particular activities can
be subordinated to the end of another particular activity. But surely
Aristotle is not suggesting that among the myriad of particular acts we
perform there is one particular act to which all others are subordi-

nable. What then can he mean by ultimate end? Perhaps this. We know what bricklaying is and what its end is; so too with plumbing, fiddling, teaching French irregular verbs, ice-fishing, playing scrabble, and on and on. But all of these are human acts. If there are criteria for fiddling and fishing, are there none for human action as such? Of course this is a surprising direction for Aristotle to take. We know how to go about ascribing actions and/or products to a man qua fiddler or qua fisher or qua geometer, but what would it mean to ascribe an activity to man qua man? Must we not simply say that human acts are the things men do on the model of that familiar phrase "Philosophy is what philosophers do"? To be sure, the latter is a go-away definition and vulnerable to some such sorites as this: Philosophy is what philosophers do; Socrates is a philosopher; Socrates can shimmy like my sister Kate; philosophers can shimmy like my sister Kate. The go-away definition has a come-back here, even if my sister Kate is herself a philosopher. But how can we move from "Human acts are what humans do" to "do qua human"? What conceivable contrast could we have in mind? Another surprising feature of this apparent turn in Aristotle's argument is that it seems to take him right back to the opening sentence of the *Nicomachean Ethics*. I think it does. But in returning to his opening remark Aristotle now treats it *intensive, ut ita dicam*, rather than *extensive*. Lest you think that I regard lapsing into Latin as in and of itself a clarification, I propose to turn now to chapter 7 where my archaic adverbs can be replaced by substantive doctrine.

Chapter 7 begins with a brief summary of chapters 1 and 2. The good is related to actions as their end. There are as many goods as there are actions. The actions in question are human actions. Are there criteria for an action being human as there are criteria for a particular action being the kind of action it is (e.g. fiddling, plumbing, etc.)? If we could find a criterion for human action as such, we would be able to speak of the human good, i.e., the goal of human action as human. Let us put all this schematically.

Let x and y be human actions;
   (a) then both x and y aim at ends or goods;
   (b) the end of x differs from the end of y;
   (c) doing x well or badly is read from the end at which it aims; so too with y;
   (d) doing x well differs from doing y well;
   (e) if doing x well and doing y well are both instances of good human activity, can we give an account of "acting humanly well" which is not just as such an account of "doing x well"?

(f) such an account of "acting humanly well" is what is meant by an ultimate superordinating end.

We must now make a terminological point. The human good, man's chief good, is expressed by the following synonyms: *eudaimonia*; *eu prattein* (acting well); *eu zēn* (living well); *hou kharin* (that for the sake of which); *ariston teleion* (ultimate end). What these terms mean is not some particular good among others (1097b17–19). Thus, the human good cannot be the end of a particular action, of one human action distinct from all other human actions. The ultimate good, then, must be that which makes the infinity of goods at which human actions may aim human goods. We know how to describe the end of man qua flautist, qua fiddler, qua fisher. How can we describe the end or good of the human agent qua human?

"This might perhaps be given, if we could first ascertain the function of man. For just as for the flute-player, a sculptor, or any artist, and, in general, for all things that have a function or activity, the good and the 'well' is thought to reside in the function, so would it seem to be for man, if he has a function." "Function" here translates *ergon*; I say "here" advisedly; in chapter 1 *ergon* is used to designate the product-beyond-the-activity. It is clear that function explicates the qua-locution. If you know what an activity aims at you are thereby able to assess whether it is done well or badly. This is what I was trying to express in step (c) of the above schematism. Man's function would enable us to interpret the *eu* (well) in the list of synonymous expressions given in the preceding paragraph. As it happens, Aristotle illustrates what he means by function in two quite different ways.

(1) "Have the carpenter, then, and the tanner certain functions or activities, and has man none? Is he born without a function?"

(2) "Or as eye, hand, foot, and in general each of the parts evidently has a function, may one lay it down that man similarly has a function apart from all these? What can this be?"

Ad 1. This passage establishes the notion of function as we have been suggesting: man qua carpenter, qua tanner, qua harpist, qua sculptor, etc. Such qua-locutions designate man from a particular activity which has its own end, good or purpose and the activity can be assessed as well or badly done by reference to its end. If the human agent could be designated qua human we would then be able to explicate the *eu* in *eu prattein* and *eu zēn*.

Ad 2. This passage suggests the way to isolate human action as such, human life as such. Here we are given activities of parts of man (eye, foot, etc.) as opposed to particular human activities. The first passage can speak of *ergon kai praxis*, the second only of *ergon*. Further, the second passage mentions vital processes, manifestations of life, which can be truly predicated of man. The first passage treats human activities *extensive*; the second shows how we can get at human activity or human life *intensive*, that is, unpack it in such a way that we discover its formal note.

In search of an account of "living humanly well," Aristotle will now suggest that there are types of vital activity which can be truly predicated of man, but not qua man. Think of the difference between "Socrates' beard is growing" and "Socrates is growing a beard." Aristotle puts it this way: (a) "Life seems to be common even to plants, but we are seeking what is peculiar to man. Let us exclude, therefore, the life of nutrition and growth." The important word here is "common." Some vital activities which are found in man are also found in nonhuman things; therefore they are not peculiar to man and cannot be the kind of activity or function we are seeking whose *eu* will be the human good. (b) "Next there would be a life of perception, but it also seems to be common even to the horse, the ox and every animal." This is reminiscent of the second illustration of what he means by *ergon*. (c) "There remains, then, an active life of the element that has a rational principle; of this, one part has such a principle in the sense of being obedient to one, the other in the sense of possessing and exercising thought."

Those vital activities of man which exhibit a rational principle pertain to man qua man. It is now clear that this account of activities of man qua man discriminates among activities which can be truly predicated of man; not all such activities belong to man as man because not all of them are peculiar to him. Just as "shimmying like my sister Kate" is not what philosophers do as philosophers, so growing, seeing, hearing, etc. do not pertain to man as man. These are no more confined to man than shimmying like my sister Kate is confined to philosophers. We see too that, in his first illustration of what he means by *ergon*, Aristotle is not distinguishing human action from fiddling, fishing and flauting; rather he is after what each embodies in its way, namely, rational, conscious activity.

It will have been noticed that Aristotle no sooner introduces a criterion from human action as such, namely, that it exhibits a rational principle, than he hastens to point out the ambiguity of this criterion. Activity can be called rational (or human) either because it is the activity of reason itself or because it is an activity obedient to reason, in some way under the sway of reason. This suggests that, if reason is what will enable all human acts, as strategy or architecture enable us to cluster subgroups of human acts, "rational" is a floating criterion. The way in which Aristotle first suggests that his criterion may be taken in several ways (activity which is essentially rational and activity which partakes of or is obedient to reason) adumbrates the distinction between intellectual and moral virtues; the former are the *eu* of rational activity in the first sense, the latter the *eu* of rational activity in the second sense. To do an act well is excellence or virtue for that activity. But the picture becomes swiftly more complicated. The rational faculty itself is subdivided into theoretical and practical. Thus, while human action and rational activity are identified, we are faced with at least three great groupings: theoretical rational activity; practical rational activity; activities of faculties other than reason which come under the sway of reason and are thus rational by participation.

Thus we arrive somewhat prepared at our third and final question: In what sense is the ultimate end one? At the beginning of chapter 7, Aristotle says this: "Therefore, if there is an end for all that we do, this will be the good achievable by action, and if there are more than one, these will be the goods achievable by action." At the end of the chapter, he writes: "human good turns out to be an activity of soul in accordance with virtue, and if there are more than one virtue, in accordance with the best and most complete." Does this not suggest that the ultimate end or happiness, since it is not one particular good among others, is constituted by the whole set of human actions done well? When from this vantage point we look back at the objections already listed, we see that it is mistaken to assume that Aristotle is suggesting that there is some particular action to whose end the ends of all other particular actions must be subordinated. He is not saying that some particular kind of action must become our dominant passion as writing was for Henry James and politics was for Disraeli. Nor could he have committed the simple fallacy of the third objection; he is not saying that there is some one end, the same one, of all particular actions. "Virtuous activity" or "living humanly well" do not name one thing because there are different kinds of rational activity and thus different kinds of virtue and our happiness or perfection or ultimate end is constituted not by some one virtue but, to the degree this is possible, by them all. If there are difficulties with the notion of ultimate end they are not captured by the usual objections to it.

But have we given a completely faithful picture of Aristotle's thought? If *eudaimonia* turns out to be a name for a set of virtuous activities, is it not nonetheless the case that for Aristotle this is an ordered set? Rational activity is various, no doubt, but the phrase would appear to be not equivocal but an instance of something said in many ways but with reference to one (*pollakhōs legomenon pros hen*). Theoretical reasoning, whose end or good is the perfection of the faculty of reason itself, namely, truth, seems to claim priority; furthermore, *theōria* or contemplation seems spoken of as the preeminent good for man. But then it would seem that contemplation, like writing novels for Henry James, is the indicated dominant passion for man. Well, much depends on how this is understood. It cannot mean that contemplation would be the exclusive concern of any man; for Aristotle, this activity seems necessarily episodic. Nor, since life for anyone must include far more than contemplation, could the ends of other rational activities be "for" contemplation in the sense that they are not first ends of and for themselves. It is difficult to know what could be meant by sacrificing moral virtues to the dominant passion of contemplation. Living well for any man is going to involve a plurality of virtues. The set of virtuous activities is ordered in several ways. From the point of view of necessity, of temporal priority (and this is an abiding not an evanescent priority), the moral virtues and the virtues of practical intellect take precedence. Of the task of metaphysics Aristotle says that all other human activities are prior to and more necessary than it, but none is better. Which is a way of saying that contemplation could never be an exclusive or dominant concern of anyone. So we are left with the view that man's ultimate end is not some particular good among others but is constituted by the set of virtuous activities. That set may be seen as ordered in several ways, in terms of necessity, on the one hand, and, on the other, in terms of the graded senses of rational activity according to which theoretical reason the *eu* of which is contemplation is highest and best. But there is always a set of virtuous activities constitutive of *eudaimonia*. "Let this serve as an outline of the good."

7

BOETHIUS AND ST. THOMAS AQUINAS

The influence of Boethius on the thought of St. Thomas may seem so pervasive as to make it impossible to speak of it with any brevity. As the "first Scholastic," Boethius helped shape the methodology Thomas was to make his own.[1] Chenu has called the twelfth century the *Aetas Boetiana* and, if the same cannot be said of the thirteenth, Boethius continued to influence, directly and indirectly, medieval thought.[2] Read prior to the influx of the complete *corpus Aristotelicum*, the works of Boethius could be expected to appear in a more Platonic light even though, as translator and commentator, Boethius was a major conduit through which the Stagirite entered the Latin West. How does Thomas Aquinas, the Aristotelian, react to the platonizing Boethius? Thanks to the works of Fabro, Geiger, Little, Henle and Courcelle, our understanding of the Aristotelianism of Thomas and of the Platonism of Boethius has been considerably altered.[3] Indeed, if students of St. Thomas were once in need of the warning that reading St. Thomas as largely a footnote to Aristotle is too narrow a viewpoint, they may soon need to be warned away from too heavy an emphasis on the role that Platonism and Neoplatonism played in the Thomistic synthesis.

Thomists will be forever in the debt of Father Cornelio Fabro for his magisterial studies on participation in the thought of St. Thomas. It is noteworthy that his studies began where St. Thomas is explicating the context of the following: "Diversum est esse et id quod est."[4] The

1. Cf. M. Grabmann, *Die Geschichte der scholastischen Methode*, vol. 1 (Freiburg: 1909).
2. M. D. Chenu, *La théologie au XIIe siècle*, Etudes de Philosophie médiévale, 45 (Paris: 1957).
3. Cf. C. Fabro, *La Nozione Metafisica di Partecipazione*, 3d ed. (1963); *Partecipazione e Causalità* (1960); L. B. Geiger, *La participation dans la philosophie de saint Thomas d'Aquin* (1942); P. Courcelle, *Late Latin Writers and Their Greek Sources* (1969; trans. of the 2d French ed. of 1948), pp. 273–330 on Boethius. Courcelle establishes to his own satisfaction that Boethius studied with Ammonius in Alexandria.
4. Cf. Fabro, *La Nozione Metafisica*, pp. 24ff.

words are taken, of course, from the Boethian tractate that the medievals called the *De hebdomadibus*. In this essay, I hope to make some small and tentative contribution to our understanding of what the phrase meant for Boethius and what it came to mean for St. Thomas when he commented on the tractate of Boethius.[5] I shall, however, preface my discussion of "Diversum est esse et id quod est" with a discussion of an equally enigmatic and not unrelated remark that is found in Boethius's *De trinitate*: "Reliqua enim non sunt id quod sunt." I am not the first to suggest that an understanding of the latter can throw some light on the former.

I. RELIQUA ENIM NON SUNT ID QUOD SUNT

In *De trinitate*, cap. 2, Boethius sets down the familiar Aristotelian division of speculative science into natural, mathematical and theological science. If we ask ourselves why he begins his discussion of the dogma of the Trinity in this way, the answer must surely be that he means to place his discussion in its proper niche. This raises a problem, of course. Is theology as envisaged by the philosophers the proper locus for a discussion of the Trinity? It is not surprising that St. Thomas, in his *expositio*, gives the necessary division of types of theology.[6] Our own interest lies in the seemingly Aristotelian character of the text.

"Nam cum tres sint speculativae partes, *naturalis*, in motu inabstracta *anupexairetos* (considerat enim corporum formas cum materia, quae a corporibus actu separari non possunt, quae corpora in motu sunt ut cum terra deorsus ignis sursum fertur, habetque motum forma materiae coniuncta), *mathematica*, sine motu inabstracta (haec enim formas corporum speculatur sine materia ac per hoc sine motu, quae formae cum in materia sint, ab his separari non possunt), *theologica*, sine motu abstracta atque separabilis (nam dei substantia et materia et motu caret)."[7] This text immediately recalls those pithy remarks of Aristotle's in *Metaphysics*, E.1.1026a13–16. Philip Merlan professes to find in the text of Boethius a hopeless tangle of "epistemonic and ontic points of view."[8] On the contrary, one finds a classic clarity in the passage. As

5. My conclusions in this chapter are admittedly tentative. Firmer and more mature positions are taken in my *Boethius and Aquinas*, to be published by the Catholic University of America Press.

6. *In Boethii de trin.*, ed. Decker, q. 2, aa. 2–3.

7. *De trinitate*, chap. 2, ll. 5–16 in the Stewart and Rand ed., Loeb Classical Library (London: 1918).

8. *From Platonism to Neoplatonism*, 2d ed., pp. 77–78.

the immediate sequel makes clear, what is formal in the thing is the object of knowledge. Natural science considers the forms of bodies with their matter since such forms cannot be actually separated from their bodies. Given the relation of matter and motion, such forms are *in motu inabstracta*. Mathematics *considers* the forms of bodies without matter and thus without motion, forms which, since they are in matter, cannot *be* separate from matter and motion. Theology considers forms which lack matter and motion. Such form(s) is (are) *sine motu abstracta atque separabilis*. Merlan is misled because he takes abstract to refer here to the "epistemonic" rather than to the "ontic" side. Of course he is wrong. *In motu* and *sine motu* modify *considerat* and *speculatur* and are, in Merlan's terminology, epistemonic. *Inabstracta* and *abstracta atque separabilis* refer to the way forms exist and are thus, as Merlan would say, ontic. Indeed the parallelism with the Aristotelian text is all but perfect.[9]

> (*a*) in motu inabstracta = περὶ ἀχώριστα ἀλλ' οὐκ ἀκίνητα
> (*b*) sine motu inabstracta = περὶ ἀκίνητα οὐ χωριστὰ
> (*c*) sine motu abstracta = περὶ χωριστὰ καὶ ἀκίνητα

The key phrases thus contrast our mode of consideration, on the one hand, and the mode of existence of forms, on the other hand. This contrast is of the utmost importance for deciding on the Platonism or Aristotelianism of Boethius. We recall that St. Thomas, like Aristotle before him, found fault with Plato's penchant for identifying our way of knowing with the way things are. "Et quia Plato non consideravit quod dictum est de duplici modo abstractionis, omnia quae diximus abstrahi per intellectum, posuit abstracta esse secundum rem."[10] One way of testing the Platonism of Boethius would be to ask if he himself ever makes this confusion.

As is well known, there is a passage in Boethius's *In Porphyrium Dialogus* which parallels that of *De trinitate*, cap. 2. In order to fulfill his task as expositor, Boethius must inform the reader of the intention of the work, its usefulness, its order, its authorship, its title, and its place in philosophy.[11] The discussion of the utility of Porphyry's *Isagoge* involves Boethius in a discussion of what philosophy is and of what its parts or divisions are. As "amor et studium et amicitia quodammodo sapientiae" (10D), philosophy is "studium divinitatis et purae mentis illius amicitia" (11A).

9. *Metaphysics*, E.1.1026a13–16.
10. *ST*, Ia, q. 85, a. 1, ad 2.
11. Migne, *PL* 64:9B.

Est enim philosophia genus, species vero ejus duae, una quae *theōrētikē* dicitur, altera quae *praktikē*, id est speculativa et activa. Erunt autem tot speculativae species, quot sunt res in quibus justae speculatio considerationis habetur. Quotque actuum diversitates, tot species varietatesque virtutum. Est igitur *theōrētikēs*, id est contemplativae vel speculativae triplex diversitas, atque ipsa pars philosophiae in tres species dividitur. Est enim *theōrētikēs* pars una de intellectibilibus, alia de intelligibilibus, alia de naturalibus . . .

(*a*) Est enim intellectibile quod unum atque idem per se in propria semper divinitate consistens, nullis unquam sensibus, sed sola tantum mente intellectuque capitur. Quae res ad speculationem Dei atque ad animi incorporalitatem considerationemque verae philosophiae, indagatione componitur. Quam partem Graeci *theologian* nominant.

(*b*) Secunda vero pars est intelligibilis, quae primam intellectibilem cognitatione atque intelligentia suscipiens, ea comprehendit quae sunt omnium coelestium supernae divinitati operum causae, et quidquid sub lunari globo beatiore animo atque puriore substantia valet; postremo humanarum animarum conditionem atque statum, quae omnia cum prioribus intellectibiles substantiae fuissent, sed corporum tactu, ab intellectibilibus ad intelligibilia degenerarunt, ut non magis ipsa intelligantur quam intelligant, et intelligentiae puritate tunc beatiora sunt, quoties sese intellectibilibus applicarint.

(*c*) Tertia *theōrētikēs* species est, quae circa corpora atque eorum scientiam cognitionemque versatur, idest physiologia, quae naturas corporum passionesque declarat.[12]

There is scarcely any need to point how different an intellectual ambience we sense in this division of theoretical or speculative philosophy. It is not simply that the order of treatment is reversed, with theology coming first; the very principle of division is straightforwardly "ontic." There are as many parts of speculative philosophy as there are distinct levels of being. How then could we be surprised to see that the soul takes the place of mathematics? As Boethius goes on to say, it is only fitting that *intelligibilium substantia* should occupy the middle rank since it has a dual function, first, to animate and vivify bodies and, second, to contemplate *intellectibiles*.[13] Furthermore, the mention of degeneration from the status of intellectible to that of intelligible arrests the reader. The Neoplatonic flavor of the text is inescapable. How can we explain its difference from the division given in *De trinitate*, cap. 2? One is reminded of Boethius's addendum to the resolution of the problem of universals in his second commentary on Porphyry. "Altioris enim est philosophiae [to resolve the difference between Plato and Aristotle], idcirco vero studiosius Aristotelis sententiam exsecuti sumus, non quod eam maxime probaremus, sed quod hic liber ad praedicamenta conscriptus est, quorum Aristoteles

12. Ibid., 11A–C.   13. Ibid., 11D.

auctor est." [14] Boethius was under no such constraint in the *De trinitate* and we must return to that work to find if Boethius there means to *maxime probare* Aristotle or Plato.

We have shown above that the very language Boethius uses in setting forth the division of speculative philosophy in the *De trinitate* echoes that of Aristotle. Nonetheless, as we continue our reading of chapter 2, keeping in mind the surprisingly different presentation in the first commentary on Porphyry, we encounter locutions reminiscent of Plato. Thus, having said that we should treat natural things *rationabiliter*, mathematicals *disciplinaliter* and divine things *intellectualiter*, Boethius goes on: "neque deduci ad imaginationes, sed potius ipsam inspicere formam quam vere forma neque imago est et quae esse ipsum est et ex qua esse est. Omne namque esse ex forma est" (Rand, 18–21). The distinction between *forma* and *imago* is important but more important still is what is said of form which is truly form: "esse ipsum est et ex qua esse est." The last claim is tied to a general law: "omne esse ex forma est." One thinks: to be is to be something or other and form is the measure of the being a thing has. The illustrations Boethius gives are familiar and Aristotelian. The statue is a statue, not because of the bronze which is its matter, but because of its form, the likeness of a living thing impressed upon it. As for bronze, it is not bronze because of its element, earth; that is its matter. Earth, in its turn, is what it is, not because of unqualified matter, but because of its form. The general law is thus arrived at by induction: "nihil igitur secundum materiam esse dicitur sed secundum propriam formam" (28–29). Returning now to divine substance, which is form without matter, Boethius says: because it is form without matter, it is one and it is what it is. "Reliqua enim non sunt id quod sunt" (31). Only by understanding this claim can we make sense of what has been said of divine substance.

Substances other than the divine are not what they are. Surely it is odd to say of a thing that it is not what it is. This sounds too much like saying, "A is not A." Boethius cannot be asserting that. What then is his point? Well, divine substance is form alone; other substances are complex, composed of form and matter. He uses man as an example. Man is composed of body and soul. He is this + that. Now, whatever is a "this + that" is neither this alone nor that alone. It is easy to agree. What is not clear is that Boethius's maxim is thereby illumined. Man may not be body alone nor soul alone, but if man is body-and-soul,

14. *PL* 64:86A.

that is, if what he is is a compound, then of course to say that a compound is not one of its components alone is not tantamount to saying that a compound is not what it is, namely, a compound. Boethius's point is clearly a subtle one.

We have seen that form is the key to the distinction of the theoretical sciences as this is stated in the *De trinitate*. Furthermore, "omne namque esse ex forma est": form is the key to being and intelligibility. Compounds of form and matter are the sorts of thing they are, not because of their matter, but because of their form. What-a-compound-is is read from the side of form, not of matter. That is why a simple thing, something which is form alone, is identical to what it is, to what makes it be the kind of thing it is. "Reliqua enim non sunt id quod sunt. Unumquodque enim habet esse suum ex quibus est, id est ex partibus suis, et est hoc atque hoc, idest partes suae coniunctae, sed non hoc vel hoc singulariter, ut cum homo terrenus constet ex anima corporeque, corpus et anima est, non vel corpus vel anima in partem; igitur non est id quod est" (31–37).[15] Compound substances, the suggestion is, since they are not simply form, although it is thanks to form that they are the kind of thing they are, are not what they are, are not solely what they are. Is this Platonism or Aristotelianism?

In the passage we have just quoted, Boethius illustrates what he means by appeal to *homo terrenus*. Is the phrase pleonasm or Platonism? Earthly man suggests a contrast with some other sort of man, perhaps an ideal man. Does the context encourage this line of thought? Well, consider lines 51–53: "Ex his enim formis quae praeter materiam sunt, istae formae venerunt quae sunt in materia, et corpus efficiunt": the forms which are in matter and which effect bodies come from forms which exist apart from matter. The plural is suggestive. We seem justified in thinking that *humanitas*, or perhaps *anima humana*, is one of the separate forms (*praeter materiam*) envisaged. True form is apart from matter; indeed, to call forms in matter forms is an abuse of language. Better to call them images. These images imitate (*adsimulantur*) the forms which are not in matter (51–56).

But let us return to the earlier discussion. Having explained what he meant by saying that substances other than the divine are not what they are, Boethius repeats that the substance which is form alone "vere est id quod est; et est pulcherrimum fortissimumque quia nullo nititur" (39–40). Its unity is such as to exclude number. In chapter 1, Boethius explained that numerical difference is caused by variety

---

15. Edition of Stewart and Rand already cited, ll. 30–37. Migne has ". . . in parte igitur non est id quod est."

of accidents: "sed numero differentiam accidentium varietas facit" (24–25). If true form cannot be the subject of accidents, it cannot be the abode of numerical diversity. "Neque enim subiectum fieri potest; forma enim est, formae vero subiectae esse non possunt" (42–43). If a form like humanity is subject to accidents this is not because of what it is ("non eo quod ipsa est") but because matter is subjected to it and, when the matter subjected to humanity receives an accident, it can seem that humanity itself does. Clearly a form which does not subject matter to itself will not even seemingly be the subject of accidents. Being more truly form, it more truly exhibits the truth that form is not a subject. Those forms which appear to be subjects, though not even they really are, are best called images.

The beginning of *De trinitate*, cap. 2, so clearly Aristotelian, thus seems to conflict with its ending, which is so obviously amenable to a Platonic interpretation. *Homo terrenus*, a soul + body, is a form in matter. But such a form is more accurately called an image. Image-forms, which are in matter and which actuate bodies, come from true forms which are outside matter. Furthermore, image-forms imitate true forms. The final sentence of the chapter, it is true, puts a brake to this interpretation. Quite suddenly, Boethius switches from the plural to the singular. "Nulla igitur in eo diversitas, nulla ex diversitate pluralitas, nulla ex accidentibus multitudo atque idcirco numerus" (56–58). It seems only right that the English translation should begin, "In Him, then, there is no difference. . . ."

What would the Aristotelian reading of "reliqua enim non sunt id quod sunt" be? It might seem that there can be none. After all, one of the major concerns of *Metaphysics*, Z, is to deny that a thing and what it is differ. "Each thing itself, then, and its essence are one and the same in no merely accidental way. . . ."[16] "But indeed not only are a thing and its essence one, but the formula of them is also the same, as is clear even from what has been said; for it is not by accident that the essence of One, and the One, are one."[17] Despite such passages, it is possible to see affinities between *De trinitate*, cap. 2, and *Metaphysics*, Z.

In asserting the unity of forms which exist apart from matter, Boethius observes that such forms cannot be the subject of accidents. That which is subject of accidents is less perfectly one than that which is not so subject; a substance of which predicates can be truly affirmed which do not express *what* the substance is, what belongs to it *per se*, is a less perfect substance. Such a substance is not only or simply what belongs to it per se; it is not only what it is.

16. 1031b18–20.   17. 1031b31–a2.

Aristotle begins his discussion of substance by pointing out that *ousia* can mean the individual thing, the universal, the genus or the essence.[18] In the *Categories*, he distinguished between first and second substance; the latter is the species or genus, the former the individual thing, *tode ti*. It is sometimes said that, in the *Metaphysics*, this priority is reversed and second substance becomes primary. This is absurd, since then we would have to understand Aristotle as saying that the universal or genus is primarily substance and his whole anti-Platonic polemic would be worse than confused. The text of Boethius is not a bad guide here. Consider the primary substance of the *Categories*, the *tode ti*, the individual thing. It is composed of matter and form and is neither the one nor the other alone. In *Metaphysics*, Z, the question is asked: to which of its components does the compound substance chiefly owe its status as substance? The answer, of course, is form.[19] When we ask of the *tode ti, ti esti?* (What is it?), our answer will emphasize form rather than matter. That answer, the τὸ τί ἦν εἶναι[20] or essence, is sometimes equated with form, but clearly Aristotle is not saying that a compound is one of its components to the exclusion of the other.

What Aristotle does do is to distinguish what is predicated of substance per se from what is predicated of it per accidens. This distinction is one of the most sustained themes of *Metaphysics*, Z. Let us attempt a short and simplistic statement of it. (a) That which can be truly predicated of an individual throughout its career in time belongs to it *per se*; (b) that which is sometimes true of an individual and sometimes not, belongs to it *per accidens*. Predicates of the first sort belong to the individual because of what it is, because of its essence; predicates of the second sort do not. Among per se predicates, a distinction is made between those which enter into the definition of the thing and those into whose definitions the substance enters *ex additione*.[21] An example of the first kind of *per se* predicate is rational, of the second, risible. Now it is just at this point that Aristotle seems to go back on his claim, against Plato, that a thing and its essence are one. Although some predicates are true of the individual per se and others per accidens, a set of the first set, the essence or τὸ τί ἦν εἶναι, is not identical with the individual. The reason is to be found in the fact that some predicates are true of the individual per accidens. That

18. *Metaphysics*, Z.3.1028b33ff.   19. Ibid., Z.2.
20. Ibid., Z.4.
21. Cf. *In VII Metaphysic.*, lect. 4, n. 1344.

is, the individual is *more than*, not simply, what is true of it per se or essentially.[22]

We have then the hint of an Aristotelian way of understanding the Boethian maxim: "reliqua enim non sunt id quod sunt." Both Aristotle and Plato, in their different ways, deny that the individual and its essence are identical. For Aristotle, the distinction between individual and essence is not a distinction between two things; the essence does not exist apart from the individual, separately. Plato, on the other hand, thinks of the essence of compound things as itself an οὐσία χωριστή. We have returned, it can be seen, to the problem of universals and to the two classical and perennial solutions of it. The Platonic solution, Aristotle maintains, confuses our way of knowing and the way things are, our way of conceiving essence and its mode of existence. That confusion is always a test of Platonism. The enigma of Boethius resides precisely in the difficulty we encounter in putting him to this test. Chapter 2 of the *De trinitate* contains features of Aristotelianism and features of Platonism. Troubling as that is, it cannot be forgotten when we turn to the *De hebdomadibus*.

II. DIVERSUM EST ESSE ET ID QUOD EST

Most scholars have seen the advantage to be gained from approaching the *De hebdomadibus* from the *De trinitate* and if many have noticed the vacillation of Boethius between Aristotle and Plato, the preponderance of scholarly opinion is that Boethius maintains an Aristotelian view of the "structure of the concrete." This Aristotelianism is then thought to carry over to the *De hebdomadibus*. Obviously if it is also assumed that there are profound differences between Aristotle and St. Thomas on the matter of *esse* and *quod est*, the commentary of St. Thomas on the *De hebdomadibus* will be expected to go far beyond the scope of the Boethian text. Much depends, of course, on what one takes the doctrine of St. Thomas himself to be. My procedure will be as follows. First, I will set down the axioms with which the *De hebdomadibus* begins; second, I will sketch as briefly as possible the way in which St. Thomas clarifies these axioms; thirdly I will look at some representative claims to the effect that what St. Thomas makes of the text is not what the text says.

22. Ibid., lect. 5, nn. 1378–80.

The Boethian Axioms

(1) Diversum est esse et id quod est:

(*a*) ipsum enim esse nondum est, at vero quod est, accepta essendi forma, est atque consistit.

(*b*) Quod est participare aliquo potest, sed ipsum esse nullo modo aliquo participat (Fit enim participatio cum aliquid iam est; est autem aliquid cum esse susceperit).

(*c*) Id quod est habere aliquid praeterquam quod ipsum est potest; ipsum vero esse nihil aliquid praeter se habet admixtum.

(2) Diversum est tantum esse aliquid et esse aliquid in eo quod est:

(*a*) illic enim accidens hic substantia significatur.

(*b*) Omne quod est participat eo quod est esse ut sit; alio vero participat ut aliquid sit.

(*c*) Ac per hoc id quod est participat eo quod est esse ut sit; est vero ut participet alio quolibet.

(3) Omni composito aliud est esse, aliud ipsum est.

(4) Omne simplex esse suum et id quod est unum habet.

Expositio Divi Thomae

I have deviated from the usual way of presenting the axioms, taking my cue from the exposition of St. Thomas, in order to show how seriously he takes Boethius's claim to be proceeding in a highly orderly, even mathematical, way. St. Thomas clearly does not see these axioms as a random list of presuppositions. What in the text of Boethius is listed as the first axiom, is actually a meta-axiom which makes the familiar distinction between conceptions self-evident to all and conceptions self-evident only to the learned. Propositions will be evident to all when they are composed of terms no one can fail to understand. "Ea autem quae in omni intellectu cadunt, sunt maxime communia quae sunt: ens, unum et bonum. Et ideo ponit hic Boethius *primo* quasdam conceptiones pertinentes ad ens. *Secundo* quasdam pertinentes ad unum, ex quo sumitur ratio simplicis et compositi. . . ."[23] (1) and (2) in our list pertain to being, while (3) and (4) pertain to unity in the way St. Thomas has just suggested.

With respect to being, *ens*, St. Thomas continues, notice that *ipsum esse* is something common and indeterminate which is determined in two ways, on the side of the subject which has *esse*, and on the side of the predicates affirmed of the already constituted subject. (1) in our

---

23. *In de hebdomadibus*, ed. Calcaterra, lect. 2, n. 23.

list deals with the determinations of *ipsum esse* by its subject, while (2) in our list deals with the comparison of *esse simpliciter* and *esse aliquid*. St. Thomas's procedure here suggests a logical image. One imagines *ipsum esse* as the copula freed from the proposition and thereby made indeterminate, indefinite, an infinitive. Then both subject and predicate appear as ways of determining or tying down the scope of *ipsum esse*, making it finite. The image has its limitations, of course, since not all predicates are accidental predicates, but St. Thomas expresses himself with considerable care.[24]

The suspicion that St. Thomas is proceeding *logice* is borne out by n. 22 of lect. 2. Here we read that the axiom stating that "diversum est esse et id quod est" is not an affirmation about things, but rather about the meaning of terms. That is, *esse* and *quod est* have different meanings, *rationes* or *intentiones*, but this diversity does not necessitate a diversity in the things to which they may refer. (3) and (4) in our listing of the axioms will speak of the diversity, or lack of it, between *esse* and *quod est secundum rem*. For now, the diversity is one of meanings.

This division of the axioms into those expressing diversity *secundum intentiones* and those which ask whether a diversity *secundum rem* answers to the diversity of meanings, is important in itself and for applying what we have called the test for Platonism. To take the first axiom in our list to be establishing a metaphysical truth would be to confuse, if St. Thomas is right, the intentional and real orders and thereby to embrace Platonism. But what precisely is the diversity *secundum rationes seu intentiones*? To say that it is a difference in the meanings of terms is clearly not sufficient. *Man* and *horse* have different meanings; we would normally give different accounts of what the two terms mean. Furthermore, we would normally use them to refer to quite different things. What St. Thomas has in mind is more subtle, namely, a difference in *modi significandi*. St. Thomas uses *significare* in much the same way as speakers of English use *mean*. Sometimes a term is said to mean or to signify individuals, at other times meaning or signification of a term is identified with the account (*logos*) or *ratio* we should give to explain it. *Man* signifies$_1$ or means$_1$ rational animal and it signifies$_2$ or means$_2$ Socrates, Plato, etc. Signify$_2$ can be replaced by *supponit pro* in the first and clearest sense of that phrase.[25] That is, a

---

24. "Circa ens autem consideratur ipsum esse quasi quiddam commune et indeterminatum: quod quidem dupliciter determinatur: uno modo, ex parte subiecti, quod esse habet; alio modo, ex parte praedicati, utpote cum dicimus de homine, vel de quacumque alia re, non quidem quod sit simpliciter, sed quod sit aliquid, puta album vel nigrum."—ibid., lect. 2, n. 21.

25. See Boethius, *De duabus naturis*, ed. cit., chap. 2, l. 66.

common term supposes for (or means$_2$) those individuals of which it is predicated.[26]

In the text before us, St. Thomas is using *significare* in the first sense, as signify$_1$ or mean$_1$. Thus our attention is drawn to the accounts or *rationes* of the terms in question. Now every *ratio* is complex, which is why a synonym cannot be a *ratio*.[27] The *ratio* of a term is composed of a *res significata* and a *modus significandi* and the most obvious examples of *modi significandi* are the abstract and concrete ways of signifying the same form or act. As St. Thomas makes clear, what he is saying is this: *quod est* and *esse* have different *rationes*; moreover, this difference is not to be sought in their meaning$_1$ different forms or acts, but in the *way* they signify$_1$ the same act or form. In the light of this, we grasp without difficulty the examples St. Thomas gives.[28]

Significatur in concreto	*Significatur in abstracto*
album	albedo
currens	currere
ens	esse

This diversity of modes of signifying is, St. Thomas tells us, manifested in three ways by Boethius, namely by (1a), (1b) and (1c) in our list.

(1*a*) "Ipsum enim esse nondum est, at vero quod est, accepta essendi forma, est atque consisit."

Because of its mode of signifying, *ipsum esse* cannot function as a subject of which are predicated finite modes of signifying the same act. No more does the mode of signifying of *currere* permit it to be a subject of which a finite form of that verb could be predicated. We can no more say "Ipsum esse est" than we can say "Currere currit." That is, we cannot do it and obtain well-formed sentences. Syntax dictates that *est* and *currit* be attached to expressions like *ens* and *currens*. Notice that we are now dealing with triplets of *modi significandi* and not merely couplets: *currens/currere/currit*; *ens/esse/est*. The variety is of modes of signifying the same act or form: the act signified indeterminately, abstractly, as infinitive; the act signified as concretized in a

---

26. See *Q. D. de pot.*, q. 9, a. 4.
27. *In VII Metaphysic.*, lect. 3, nn. 1329–30.
28. "Dicit ergo primo, quod diversum est esse, et id quod est. Quae quidem diversitas non est hic referenda ad res, de quibus adhuc non loquitur, sed ad ipsas rationes seu intentiones. Aliud autem significamus cum dicimus currere, et aliud per hoc quod dicitur currens. Nam currere et esse significantur in abstracto, sicut et albedo, sed quod est, idest ens et currens, significantur sicut in concreto, velut album."—ibid., lect. 2, n. 22.

subject which has or exercises it; the act exercised, *in actu, in exercitio*. How can the couplet *album/albedo* become a triplet? What is the *ratio albi? Id quod habet albedinem*. What is the *ratio currentis? Subjectum currendi*. It is interesting that the *ratio entis* is sometimes formed on the adjectival model, viz. *quod habet esse*, and sometimes on the participial model, viz. *subjectum essendi*.[29] In order to form a triplet of the adjective, we would have to engage in linguistic artifice: *album/albedo/albedit*. But cannot "album est" do service for *albedit*?

It is especially important in the case of *ens* to see the triple mode of signifying: participial (*ens*), abstract or infinitive (*esse*) and finite verb form (e.g. *est*). The rationes of *ens* and *esse* are mutually dependent. *Ens* = "quod habet esse, habens esse." *Esse* = "id quo aliquid est ens." *Album* = "quod habet albedinem." *Albedo* = "id quo aliquid est album." *Currens* = "subjectum cursus vel currendi." *Currere* = "id quo aliquid currit." But how explicate *est* and *currit? Currit* = "actus ut exercitus ab currente." *Est* = "actus essendi." Of course *currit* is the exercise of *esse accidentale*. A more determinate *esse substantiale* is *vivere*: "vivere est esse viventibus."

ens/esse/est
vivens/vivere/vivit

These verbal niceties which may, alas, seem tiresome, are of importance if we are to avoid some widespread misunderstandings of the doctrine of St. Thomas. In order to parse his use of *esse* accurately, we must pay careful attention to the hints he gives us in such passages as the one before us.

Ipsum enim esse nondum est, quia non attribuitur sibi esse sicut subiecto essendi; sed *id quod est, accepta essendi forma*, scilicet suscipiendo ipsum actum essendi, *est atque consistit*. Non enim ens dicitur proprie et per se, nisi de substantia, cuius est subsistere. Accidentia enim non dicuntur entia quasi ipsa sint, sed inquantum eis subest aliquid, ut postea dicetur.[30]

This passage enables us to see the importance of the introduction of the abstract and concrete modes of signifying. What *ens* signifies con-

---

29. "Deinde cum dicit, Ipsum enim esse, manifestat praedictam diversitatem tribus modis: quorum primus est, quia ipsum esse non significatur sicut ipsum subiectum essendi, sicut nec currere significatur sicut subiectum cursus: unde, sicut non possumus dicere quod ipsum currere currat, ita non possumus dicere quod ipsum esse sit: sed sicut id ipsum quod est, significatur sicut subiectum essendi, sic id quod currit significatur sicut subiectum currendi: et ideo sicut possumus dicere de eo quod currit, sive de currente, quod currat, inquantum subiicitur cursui et participat ipsum; ita possumus dicere quod ens, sive id quod est, sit inquantum participat actum essendi."—ibid., n. 23.

30. Ibid.

cretely, *esse* signifies abstractly. "Ipsum esse nondum est": *esse* is time-less, not yet, indefinite, an infinitive. The verb *est* consignifies time and can be affirmed only of what *iam est*.[31] *Ens* signifies *quod habet esse* and of course *ens* is a common term, universal, indeed *communissimum*. Furthermore, it is a *commune analogicum*.

We remember that the analogous term involves a plurality of *rationes* related in such a way that each signifies the same *res significata* but in different ways. That is, the *rationes* of the analogously common term differ in their *modi significandi*.[32] The many *rationes* of *sanum*, for instance, have the same *res significata*, expressed by *sanitas*, but they signify it in different ways: *subjectum sanitatis*, *causa sanitatis*, *signum sanitatis*, etc. The *ratio propria* of the analogous term is that way of sig-nifying the form or act which is required to explain the other ways of signifying that form or act. Thus, the *ratio propria sani* is *subjectum sani-tatis* because, when I call urine healthy, I explain what I mean by say-ing that urine is a *signum sanitatis*, understanding *sotto voce*, "in eo quod est subjectum sanitatis." "Ratio propria non invenitur nisi in uno."[33] As is well known, St. Thomas considers *sanum* to illumine the claim that "ens dicitur multipliciter seu analogice," that is, "ens non dicitur proprie et per se nisi de substantia, cuius est subsistere. Accidentia enim non dicuntur entia quasi ipsa sint, sed inquantum eis subest aliquid . . ." (n. 23).

We are now in a position to see why it was so difficult to find a per-fect fit between *esse* and either *currere* or *vivere*. "Currens est subjec-tum currendi; album est quod habet albedinem; vivens est quod vivit, quod habet vitam, subjectum vivendi." *Currere*, *albedo*, *vivere* all ex-press some determinate actuality, however abstract their mode of ex-pressing it. But *esse* is the "actus omnium actuum, etiam formarum."[34] It is *quiddam maxime commune* and thus *maxime indeterminatum*. What will tie it down and make it determinate? "Omne namque esse ex forma est; aliquid dicitur esse secundum propriam formam." How suggestive these remarks from the *De trinitate* now seem. They il-lumine "id quod est, accepta essendi forma, est atque consistit." *Forma essendi* or, as St. Thomas glosses it, *actus essendi*. "Ens habet esse per aliquam formam, vel substantialem vel accidentalem." Through sub-stantial form, the concrete thing, *quod est*, enjoys *esse substantiale*; that is, for *est* we can substitute *subsistit*. And, in the case of some sub-stances, for *subsistit* we can substitute *vivit*, for yet others, *intelligit*, be-cause "vivere est esse viventibus" and "intelligere est esse intelligen-

---

31. *In I Periherm.*, lect. 5.   32. See my *The Logic of Analogy* (1961).
33. *ST*, Ia, q. 16, a. 6, c.   34. *Q. D. de pot.*, q. 7, a. 2, ad 9.

tibus." But this, as St. Thomas remarks, is to anticipate the text of Boethius.

(1*b*) "Quod est participare aliquo potest, sed ipsum esse nullo modo participat (Fit enim participatio cum aliquid iam est; est autem aliquid cum esse susceperit)."

This passage occasions St. Thomas's justly famous statement of the modes of participation. "Est autem participare quasi partem capere; et ideo quando aliquid particulariter recipit id quod ad alterum pertinet universaliter, dicitur participare illud" (n. 24). Universal and particular: Man is animal; Socrates is man. The subjects of these propositions "non habet rationem praedicati secundum totam communitatem." There is a second mode of participation when ". . . subiectum participat accidens, et materia formam, quia forma substantialis vel accidentalis, quae de sui ratione communis est, determinatur ad hoc vel ad illud subiectum." Third, the effect may be said to participate in its cause, particularly a non-univocal cause. Given these three modes of participation, we can ask what kind is affirmed of *quod est* and denied of *ipsum esse.*

If we ignore the third mode of participation, St. Thomas says, we see that *ipsum esse* cannot participate in either of the other two modes. "Non enim potest participare aliquid per modum quo materia vel subiectum participat formam vel accidens, quia ipsum esse significatur ut quiddam abstractum." That would seem to be reason enough to reject the first mode of participation too, but St. Thomas denies this. Being abstractly signified does not as such disqualify something from being a subject of predication. We say, "Albedo est color." Of course we knew that all along.[35] Later, in n. 25, St. Thomas will contrast predications of abstract and concrete terms. Thus, the fact that *ipsum esse* signifies abstractly does not suffice to exclude the first mode of participation from it. "Similiter autem nec potest aliquid participare per modum quo particulare participat universale: sic enim etiam ea quae in abstracto dicuntur participare aliquid possunt, sicut albedo colorem; sed ipsum esse est communissimum: unde ipsum quidem participatur in aliis, non autem participat aliquid aliud" (n. 24). No abstract term or infinitive form of a verb is more indeterminate, vague and thus more common than *ipsum esse.* Any other verb, noun or adjective expresses a mode of being and thus determines the indeterminateness of *ipsum esse.* And what of the concrete term, *ens?* "Sed id

---

35. Of course much depends on the kind of supposition the term is taken to be exhibiting.

quod est, sive ens, quamvis sit communissimum, tamen concretive dicitur; et ideo participat ipsum esse, non per modum quo magis commune participatur a minus communi, sed participat ipsum esse per modum quo concretum participat abstractum" (n. 24).

We are entitled to be surprised here. St. Thomas wants us to understand a passage in which Boethius says *quod est* can and *ipsum esse* cannot participate. He gives us the etymology of *participare*, of *partake*: it is to take a part of something. He then exhibits three modes of participation, one of which he sets aside; it is then made clear that *ipsum esse* cannot participate in either of the remaining modes. Is any of the three modes helpful in understanding the positive claim, namely, that *ens* or *quod est* can participate? Is the participation of the concrete in the abstract, of *ens* in *esse*, an instance of the first mode of participation? St. Thomas denies it. The second mode would seem to relate to it but not to be identical with it. In any case, we seem to be offered a fourth mode of participation, that of the concrete in the abstract. But of course this mode of participation has been in play from the beginning of the discussion of "diversum est esse et id quod est." Any concrete term can be said to participate in its corresponding abstract term. That which is white participates in whiteness, that which is human participates in humanity and, generally though not generically, *quod est* participates in *esse*. Participation pertains to that which *iam est*, and *ipsum esse nondum est*. "Fit enim participatio cum aliquid iam est; est autem aliquid cum esse susceperit." By taking *susceperit* to be a synonym of *participat*, St. Thomas can speak of *quod est* as participating in *esse*.

(1c) "Id quod est habere aliquid praeterquam quod ipsum est potest; ipsum vero esse nihil aliud praeter se habet admixtum."

This is the third clarification of "diversum est esse et id quod est." The first pointed out that while "est atque consistit" can be predicated of *ens*, they cannot be predicated of *ipsum esse*. The second pointed out that while *ens* can participate, *ipsum esse* cannot.

Ens est atque consistit.   Ipsum esse non est neque consistit.
Ens participat aliquid.   Ipsum esse nullo modo aliquid participat.

To these St. Thomas now adds a third contrast of *ens* and *esse*. Boethius tells us that *ens* can have something beyond what it is, *ipsum esse* cannot.

Circa quod considerandum est, quod circa quodcumque abstracte consideratum, hoc habet veritatem quod non habet in se aliquid extraneum, quod scilicet sit praeter essentiam suam, sicut humanitas, et albedo, et quaecumque hoc modo dicuntur. Cuius ratio est, quia humanitas significatur ut quo aliquid est homo, et albedo quo aliquid est album. Non est autem aliquid homo, formaliter loquendo, nisi per id quod ad rationem hominis pertinet; et similiter non est aliquid album formaliter, nisi per id quod pertinet ad rationem albi; et ideo huiusmodi abstracta nihil alienum in se habere potest.[36]

We have here the first mention in lectio 2 of the *quo/quod* couplet as exemplified by *esse/ens*. The concrete is denominated from the same form or act which is abstractly expressed: man is denominated from humanity, white from whiteness, etc. Something is true of man *qua* man or of the white *qua* white just insofar as it enters into what is meant by humanity and whiteness, or vice versa. Man *qua* man is rational, but man is not white *qua* man. The white is colored *qua* white, but it is not large or heavy *qua* white. These qua-locutions enable us to see that, just as things are true of the concrete thing, *formaliter loquendo*, only when they pertain to it because of the form from which it has been denominated such-and-such, so too and a fortiori, nothing can be truly said of the abstractly signified which is not part of what it is. But if the concrete, understood formally, shares in this restriction on the abstract, thanks to its concrete way of signifying it can be the subject of true predications which are not founded on what it formally is.

Aliter autem se habet in his quae significantur in concreto. Nam homo significatur ut qui habet humanitatem, et album ut quod habet albedinem. Ex hoc autem quod homo habet humanitatem vel albedinem, non prohibetur habere aliquid aliud, quod non pertinet ad rationem horum, nisi solum quod est oppositum his: et ideo homo et album possunt aliquid aliud habere quam humanitatem vel albedinem. Et haec est ratio quare albedo vel humanitas significantur per modum partis, et non praedicantur de concretis, sicut nec sua pars de suo toto.[37]

That which is and subsists because of its participation in humanity can participate in other forms and acts just so long as they are not incompatible with one another. That which has humanity can also have whiteness. Thus, man is white, though not of course *qua* man since whiteness is not part of humanity. The concrete thing can thus have what is outside what it is.

Up to this point, St. Thomas has taken Boethius to be exhibiting the diversity of *ens* and *esse* in terms of *ens commune* and *esse commune*. As has been obvious throughout, since *ens* is not a genus, the relation of *ens* to *esse* can only be discussed with reference to *esse substantiale* or *esse*

36. Loc. cit., lect. 2, n. 25.   37. Ibid.

accidentale. The emphasis has appropriately been on substance, on that which "est atque consistit, cuius est subsistere" because "ens non dicitur proprie et per se nisi de substantia" (n. 23). It is this which is now made explicit.

(2) "Diversum est tantum esse aliquid et esse aliquid in eo quod est."

If, as (1c) maintains, what is signified concretely can have something which does not belong to it because of what it is, we must distinguish a twofold *esse*: "ex quo id quod est, potest aliquid habere praeter suam essentiam, necesse est quod in eo consideretur duplex esse."

Quia enim forma est principium essendi, necesse est quod secundum quamlibet formam habitam, habens aliqualiter esse dicatur. Si ergo forma illa non sit praeter essentiam habentis, sed constituit eius essentiam, ex eo quo habet talem formam, dicetur habens esse simpliciter, sicut homo ex hoc quod habet animam rationalem.

The phrase "accepta essendi forma" has already provided St. Thomas with an occasion to show how the concrete being participates in or receives *esse*, namely, through a form. "Ipsum enim esse nondum est": it is indeterminate and common and it is a *commune analogicum.* A proper, more determined, designation of *esse* is *subsistere.* "Quod est, idest subsistit, est ens proprie et per se." *Esse* is participated in only via form, first and properly via essence or substantial form, secondarily and less properly via accidental form. That is why the categories are called *modi essendi.* The being or *esse* which a thing has because of a form not its essence is called *esse aliquid.* In short, the individual substance has *esse simpliciter seu substantiale* through its essence; it has *esse aliquid* through accidents. According to St. Thomas, Boethius gives three differences between *esse simpliciter* and *esse aliquid.*

(2a) "Illic enim accidens hic substantia significatur."
When a thing is said to be such-and-such and not to be without qualification, accident is signified; the form which explains this kind of *esse* is *praeter essentiam rei.* When a thing is said to be without qualification, substance is signified, "quia scilicet forma faciens esse constituit essentiam rei."

(2b) "Omne quod est participat eo quod est esse ut sit; alio vero participat ut aliquid sit."

Participation is invoked to explain both having *esse substantiale*, via essence, and having *esse aliquid*, via an accidental form: "sicut homo ad hoc quod sit albus, participat non solum esse substantiale, sed etiam albedinem." Obviously the phrase *participat ipsum esse* cannot be understood as participating *esse* tout court as an act over and beyond *esse substantiale* and *esse accidentale*. There is no such *esse commune*; for there to be such an *esse*, *ens* would have to be a genus.

(2*c*) "Ac per hoc id quod est participat eo quod est esse ut sit; est vero ut participet alio quolibet."[38]

That participation whereby a thing is a substance is presupposed by its participation in accidental forms whereby it has *esse aliquid*. "Nam aliquid est simpliciter per hoc quod participat ipsum esse; sed quando iam est, scilicet per participationem ipsius esse, restat ut participet quocumque alio, ad hoc scilicet quod sit aliquid."[39] It would of course be absurd to suppose that there are three participations being distinguished here: participation in *ipsum esse*, participation in *esse substantiale*, participation in *esse aliquid*. "Omne namque esse ex forma est." *Esse commune* is immediately divided into *esse substantiale* and *esse accidentale*, *per prius et posterius*; these are not species of a generic *esse*. Rather the one is *esse simpliciter*, the other *esse secundum quid*. To overlook this simple and obvious truth gives rise to fanciful and ungrounded accounts of the difference between Aquinas and Boethius, Aquinas and Aristotle. But more of that in a moment.

We have reached the end of the axioms which turn on the different meanings of *esse* and *ens*. Now the question arises as to whether this difference in meaning answers to a difference *secundum rem, realiter*. What is the point of this distinction? One would have to be a Platonist in the sense already defined simply to equate our mode of knowing, which is expressed in our language and meanings, with the way things are. Whether what we are speaking of is in itself simple or composite, our mode of knowing, and therefore our mode of talking too, suggests complexity. Sometimes the things of which we speak are *res compositae*, sometimes we attempt to speak of *res simplices*. What has been said so far does not, therefore, establish any diversity *ex parte rerum, realiter*, between *ens* and *esse*.[40]

(3) "Omni composito aliud est esse, aliud ipsum est."

---

38. Ibid., n. 27.   39. Ibid., n. 30.
40. Ibid., n. 31.

St. Thomas suggests that we can deduce from what has already been said that, in composite things, *esse* and *quod est* differ *realiter* and not simply *secundum intentiones*.

> (i) "Ipsum esse neque participat aliquid, ut eius ratio constituatur ex multis, neque habet aliquid extraneum admixtum, ut sit in eo compositio accidentis";
> (ii) "et ideo ipsum esse non est compositum";
> (iii) "res ergo compositum non est suum esse."[41]

(i) Recalls (1*b*) and (1*c*) and there is no need to repeat our explanations of those illustrations of "diversum est esse et id quod est." The *ratio ipsius esse* is simple because there is nothing, abstract or concrete, more universal and more undetermined than *esse* itself. *Esse*, unlike *ens*, does not signify in such a way that it could be the subject of accidental predication; it signifies as a *quo*, not a *quod*. Two modes of complexity are thereby denied of *esse*; its *ratio* is not composed, since there is nothing more universal than it which could function as its quasi-genus, and it is not signified in such a way that it could be a whole consisting of what it is and accidents. On the basis of these denials, we can conclude (ii): "ipsum esse non est compositum." Does (iii) thereby follow? Does "res ergo composita non est suum esse" follow from "ipsum esse non est compositum"? Simple conversion of (ii) would yield (iia): "compositum non est ipsum esse." But how can we move from (iia) to (iii): "res composita non est suum esse"?

> (iv) "ens sumitur ab esse rei";
> (v) "ens componitur ex essentia et esse";
> (vi) "ens non est idem quod suum esse";
> (vii) "esse suum simplex est";
> (viii) "ens compositum non est suum esse."

(viii) is, of course, identical to (iii).

> (4) "Omne simplex esse suum et id quod est unum habet."

If there were a composition of *esse* and *quod est* in the simple thing, it would not be simple. The complexity of the *res composita* at issue in (3) is multiple: there is composition of *essentia* and *esse*; within essence there is the complexity of matter and form and, because of that, there is a composition of individual and nature or essence. Obviously a thing which is such that, although there is in it a composition of *essen-*

---

41. Ibid., n. 32.

tia and *esse*, nonetheless its essence is not composed, is relatively less complex, more simple, than what was spoken of in (3).

Si ergo inveniantur aliquae formae non in materia, unaquaeque earum est quidem simplex quantum ad hoc quod caret materia, et per consequens quantitate, quae est dispositio materiae; quia tamen quaelibet forma est determinativa ipsius esse, nulla earum est ipsum esse, sed est habens esse.[42]

To be is to be something or other, even when it is a question of separate forms; each is what it is and not another thing. They would not differ from one another *inquantum sunt* unless *esse ipsorum* were determined, and determined differently. "Omne namque esse ex forma est."

Manifestum erit quod ipsa forma immaterialis subsistens, cum sit quiddam determinatum ad speciem, non est ipsum esse commune, sed participat illud . . . unaquaeque illarum, inquantum distinguitur ab alia, quaedam specialis forma est participans ipsum esse; et sic nulla earum erit vere simplex.[43]

We can see now what would be required for something to be truly simple. The truly simple would not participate in *ipsum esse* and thus possess an *esse inhaerens* measured by its form; it would be *ipsum esse subsistens*.

Hoc autem non potest esse nisi unum; quia si ipsum esse nihil aliud habet admixtum praeter id quod est esse, ut dictum est, impossibile est id quod est ipsum esse multiplicari per aliquid diversificans: et quia nihil aliud praeter se habet admixtum, consequens est quod nullius accidentis sit susceptivum. Hoc autem simplex unum et sublime est ipse Deus.[44]

The *applicatio ad res* of the diversity of meanings, of modes of signifying, presupposes that there are things composed of matter and form. Furthermore, the application to separate forms is not intended to demonstrate that there are such separate forms. Indeed, St. Thomas is willing to take his examples indiscriminately from Plato or Aristotle.[45] By the same token, we are not here given a proof of God's existence. Rather, presupposing God, St. Thomas is analyzing the import of talk about Him. However complex our terms, in meaning, mode of meaning, connotation, what we are talking about when we talk of God is utterly simple.

Perhaps the single most important thing to notice about this explication of the Boethian axioms is the way in which *ipsum esse*, from meaning something indeterminate and common, comes to mean something unlimited and unique. That is, we witness the formulation

42. Ibid., n. 33. 43. Ibid., n. 34.
44. Ibid., n. 35. 45. See n. 34.

of the least inadequate divine name from the most general and common term in our language.[46] Earlier we spoke of the logical image St. Thomas suggests with his statement that *ipsum esse*, "quiddam indeterminatum et commune," is tied down and restricted by subject and predicate which give it a determinate content. That progression is from the vague to the distinct, from the empty to the full, from the more to the less universal. When the *vere simplex* is discussed, on the other hand, *ipsum esse* is treated, not as vague, empty, undetermined, but as fullness, as unrestricted, unique reality. Almost as surprising is the discussion of the *esse rei compositae* in n. 32 in a way identical with the *esse subsistens* of n. 35. But of course the *esse* of the composed thing is not unrestricted or undetermined actuality; it is measured and limited by form. *Esse participatum* (or *participati*) will be specified through the form of the participator.

III. A GLANCE AT SOME OTHER INTERPRETATIONS

For Roland-Gosselin, the interpretation of Boethius in both the *De trinitate* and the *De hebdomadibus* is remarkably easy. "En bon et strict aristotélicien, Boèce n'avait parlé que de substance première, *quod est*, et de forme, *quo est*."[47] Aristotle recognized a logical distinction between essence and existence, but not their real distinction.[48] Boethius was a good Aristotelian; ergo, etc. While this approach can seem to work fairly well with "reliqua enim non sunt id quod sunt," it runs into difficulties with the axioms of the *De hebdomadibus*. Roland-Gosselin has trouble with the remark in the *De trinitate* "omne namque esse ex forma est." But he makes short work of it. Boethius does not quite mean "omne esse forma est"; rather, form is the controlling element in stating what a being is. But what of the axioms? "Il nous paraît donc certain que Boèce ne parle jamais de l'existence distincte de l'essence. L'identité qu'il pose en Dieu est l'identité de la substance et de la forme divine, la distinction qu'il établit dans la créature, une distinction entre la substance première et la forme. Boèce est resté en cette doctrine entièrement fidèle au point de vue d'Aristote."[49]

The reading Roland-Gosselin suggests of the axioms would begin as follows, presumably: Essence and individual are diverse. But that is about as far as he could go. The next phrase in Boethius is, "Ipsum

46. *ST*, Ia, q. 13, a. 11.
47. M.-D. Roland-Gosselin, *Le "De ente et essentia" de saint Thomas d'Aquin*, p. xix.
48. Ibid., pp. 138ff.   49. Ibid., p. 145.

enim esse nondum est, at vero quod est, accepta essendi forma, est atque consistit." How would Roland-Gosselin render this? "The essence is not an individual; the individual, having acquired an essence, is an individual"? What Boethius is explaining here is *est atque consistit*. That is the actuality of the individual substance which *results* thanks to the form it receives. We saw earlier how important it is to see here a triplet, not just a couplet; not just *quo/quod*, but *esse/ens/est*. Boethius wishes to explain such claims as that Socrates is human. If *human* here can be expressed by τὸ ἀνθρώπῳ εἶναι, the *is*, ἔστι, *est*, of such propositions as "Socrates is human" can scarcely be reduced to a sign of identity introduced between components of the essence. And if Socrates *has* the τὸ ἀνθρώπῳ εἶναι, his *having* it is what is expressed by *est atque consistit*. Actually having is not the same as the actuality had. What can Roland-Gosselin make of Boethius's remark that "omne quod est participat eo quod est esse ut sit"? "Ens habet esse ut sit." Roland-Gosselin sees that *habens esse* entails *accipiens essendi formam* and somehow thinks that is not meant to explicate the *est* or *sit*. The distinction between individual and essence is not identical to "diversum est esse et id quod est." The latter follows from the former.

Father Cornelio Fabro has given us three major interpretations of the *De hebdomadibus*.[50] Those familiar with the work of Fabro need not be told that he possesses at once a Teutonic thoroughness and scope as well as a more Mediterranean subtlety and sympathy. *Da buon tomista*, Fabro is as concerned as anyone to exhibit the originality of the Angelic Doctor, particularly in his analysis of the structure of concrete being; nevertheless, he sees the thought of Thomas growing more or less naturally out of its sources and antecedents. One is not surprised to read "che l'interpretazione più corretta dei testi boeziani non suggerisce, *almeno direttamente*, una distinzione reale fra essenze ed esistenza, poiché essa n'è completamente assente."[51] In examining St. Thomas's exposition of the *De hebdomadibus*, Fabro distinguishes "la partecipazione come composizione nozionale" from "la partecipazione come composizione reale." Somewhat misleadingly, he identifies the first with what St. Thomas had called the diversity *secundum ipsas intentiones*. The notional and real compositions are also linked with predicamental (formal) and transcendental act (*actus essendi*). This leads him to suggest that what had earlier been seen as a twofold participation becomes threefold. Here are the texts. "L'*id quod est* ha una

50. See note 3 above. For a survey of the literature, see G. Schrimpf, *Die Axiomenschrift des Boethius De hebdomadibus als philosophisches Lehrbuch des Mittelalters*, 1966.
51. C. Fabro, *La Nozione Metafisica*, p. 102.

doppia partecipazione, una sostanziale all'*ipsum esse*, per essere *simpliciter*, ed un'altra agli accidenti che sono dei modi di essere secondari; e queste due partecipazioni sono ordinate in modo che non si può avere la seconda partecipazione 'esse aliquid', se prima non si è avuta la prima, quella dello 'ipsum esse'."[52] But later we read this: "'Diversum tamen est esse aliquid in eo quod est, et esse aliquid, illic enim accidens, hic substantia significatur', pone S. Tommaso nell'imbarazzante ma logica per lui situazione di distinguere nel concreto partecipante un duplice *esse*: uno che non è 'praeter essentiam' ed uno invece che resta 'praeter essentiam': il primo fa essere *simpliciter*, il secondo *secundum quid*. Nella sottile spiegazione che segue si ribatte l'osservazione che prima si dà la partecipazione all'*esse* come tale, onde il soggetto si costituisce in sè ed è capace di partecipare alle altre formalità (accidentali). Evidentemente Boezio qui non può parlare che dell'*esse* formale (*sostanziale*) e non dell'*actus essendi*, tanto che il Commentatore per un istante lo riconosce, ma senza rinunciare al suo significato di *esse* come *actus essendi*, e facendo dell'unica differenza (molto facile a comprendersi) tre, passa gradualmente dalla prima alla terza per concludere il suo intento."[53] The reader has the unsettling suspicion that Fabro wishes to distinguish the *actus essendi* from the *esse substantiale* and the *esse accidentale*. But of course the *esse substantiale* is the *actus essendi* he is speaking of and what, for Aquinas, it is distinct from is *essentia* and *forma substantialis*. Fabro's use of the phrase "praeter essentiam" bears little relation to the text of St. Thomas. Surely he does not mean to deny that the *esse substantiale* is *praeter essentiam*?[54]

In *Partecipazione e causalità*, Fabro is less irenic in his treatment of the relationship between Boethius and Aquinas.[55] Here there is more emphasis on the way in which, in his commentary, St. Thomas uses the text of Boethius to soar to altitudes undreamt of by the author of *De hebdomadibus*. Completely different intellectual orientations are suggested. Thus, unlike Boethius and Aristotle, for whom *ipsum esse nondum est*, St. Thomas, like Parmenides, Proclus, Spinoza and Heidegger, in their different ways, holds that *ipsum esse* alone properly is. We are now, of course, in the land of Fabro's *esse ut actus intensivus*. "L'originalità della metafisica tomistica ha il suo fulcro in questo 'passaggio al limite dell'essere funzionale' aristotelico all'*esse subsistens* supremo, ovvero in questa *promozione metafisica* dell'*esse formale* aristotelico, che non è ancora, all'*esse reale subsistens* (Dio) che sempre e

52. Ibid., p. 25.
53. Ibid., p. 30.   54. Ibid., p. 28.
55. C. Fabro, *Partecipazione e Causalità*, pp. 204–13.

anzitutto è e dà agli altri esseri tutti di essere e di esistere."[56] Finally, in an illuminating section of his *Intorno al fondamento della Metafisica tomistica*, reprinted in *Tomismo e pensiero moderno*,[57] Fabro summarizes his views on the axioms of the *De hebdomadibus*, based on a careful study of the *De trinitate*. "Continuando il discorso, in conformità ai significati riscontrati nel *De Trinitate*, dobbiamo dire che anche queste proposizioni non trattano tanto dei rapporti tra astratto e concreto, fra il possibile e il reale, ma del reale stesso in quanto esso è considerato o come l'atto della forma (*esse*) o come il tutto esistente (*quod est*) che risulta dei vari atti (sostanze e accidenti)."[58] In sum, he concludes, for Boethius, "Esse è quindi qui la realtà della forma."[59]

IV. CONCLUDING SUMMARY

Comparisons of Boethius and St. Thomas will inevitably be made on the basis of the *De trinitate* and *De hebdomadibus*, and the latter must occupy pride of place because of the occurrence in it of that enigmatic phrase: "Diversum est esse et id quod est." By and large, it is Thomists who make the comparison and they share two presuppositions: (*a*) the doctrine of St. Thomas is pellucidly clear, if only to the individual scholar writing, and (*b*) Boethius cannot have taught the same thing St. Thomas did on the diversity of *esse* and *quod est*. An effort must therefore be exerted to make some pre-Thomistic and properly Boethian sense of the axioms. A general fault, from which not even Fabro is exempt, is that almost exclusive attention is paid to the axioms and almost none to the use Boethius makes of them in the treatise itself. The importance of the *De trinitate* for an understanding of the *De hebdomadibus* is seen but, again, that importance is not traced beyond apparent parallels to the axioms. Given the fact that, in such comparisons, the doctrine of St. Thomas is marshalled from throughout his writings and juxtaposed to the axioms taken almost in abstraction from the Boethian corpus, the results seem predetermined. It is unfortunate that other works of Boethius, if only the other theological tractates, are not taken into account. One need only glance at that tractate known to the Medievals as the *De duabus naturis* to see that it is replete with texts which bear on the structure of concrete being. For example, chapter 2, where "person" is defined, and chapter 3, where

56. Ibid., pp. 212–13.
57. C. Fabro, *Intorno al Fondamento della Metafisica Tomistica*, repr. in *Tomismo e Pensiero Moderno* (Roma: 1969), pp. 173–90.
58. Ibid., p. 188.   59. Ibid., p. 189.

Boethius adjusts his Latin vocabulary to the Greek, provide precious and enlightening distinctions between *persona, substantia, essentia, subsistentia*, etc. Only when Boethius is more fully studied for his own sake will comparisons of his doctrine with that of St. Thomas move beyond the currently received opinions. In reading Fabro's identification of form and *esse* in Boethius, one is bound to notice that *est* is not predicated of the form of the composite, but of the concrete whole. Like Roland-Gosselin, Fabro seems sometimes to equate the having of an actuality with the actuality had. Yet are not the axioms aimed at precisely that distinction? I have seen no serious treatment by anyone of that significant phrase, in the body of the treatise, "et quoniam actu non potuere exsistere, nisi illud ea quod vere bonum est produxisset."[60]

If our understanding of Boethius is at best thin and partial, the interpretations of St. Thomas opposed to the teaching of Boethius are often difficult to reduce to the texts. To speak of *esse ut actus intensivus* is helpful when it is a question of *ipsum esse subsistens*. Fabro's "passaggio al limite dell'essere funzionale" enables us to press against the limits of thought and language to envisage God as one in whom the many and diverse perfections seen in creatures are found in a unified and infinitely rich way. But of course we have no concept answering to this use of *ipsum esse*: it stands for a dialectical process. We can handle far more easily the *esse commune* which must be declined according to the categories as *esse substantiale* and *esse accidentale*. Surely it is misleading to think of this *esse commune* as containing intensively within itself all formal perfections. It is, rather, *quiddam indeterminatum et commune*. Perhaps the best use for seeing *esse creatum* as *actus intensivus* is the Aristotelian phrase, which St. Thomas made his own: "vivere est esse viventibus."[61] For the living thing, its *esse substantiale* is *vivere*, and *vivere* as *actus intensivus* is the act of a soul which is a unitary substantial form and the source of all the substantial perfections of the thing, both living and non-living. As a general rule, however, I prefer St. Thomas's own attitude toward Platonic and Neoplatonic sources. "Haec igitur Platonicorum ratio fidei non consonat nec veritati, quantum ad hoc quod continet de speciebus naturalibus separatis, sed quantum ad id quod dicebant de primo rerum Principio, verissima est eorum opinio et fidei christianae consona."[62] Any confusion of *esse commune*, analogically common to creatures, and *ipsum esse subsistens*, would be Platonism indeed.

60. Stewart and Rand ed., ll. 143–44.
61. *In I de anima*, lect. 19, n. 209.
62. Proemium to Thomas's exposition of the *De divinis nominibus* of Pseudo-Dionysius.

8

ALBERTUS MAGNUS ON UNIVERSALS

Hoc enim per rationes logicas ad plenum sciri non poterit, sed metaphysico determinanda relinquuntur.[1]

To ask after Albert the Great's teaching on the problem of universals, seemingly a pedestrian question, leads one swiftly into a bewildering thicket, but one in which to thrash about is both historically interesting and philosophically worthwhile. Of course we want to know how Albert handled the three Porphyrian questions which constitute the traditional problem of universals, and we expect that his treatment of them will profit from his unparalleled knowledge of the Aristotelian corpus as well as of the Arabs. We are also provided with materials that must influence our judgment of the Platonism of Albert. At the same time, his conception of what logic is and of how it differs from other disciplines is everywhere at work in the passages that must be considered. Once we know Albert's views on the status of the concerns of the logician and the fact that he considers the discussion of universals to be the first task of the logician, we are likely to think that his resolution of the problem of universals is fated and predictable. As we shall see, this is far from being unequivocally or unambiguously so. On this matter, Albert is profound, prolix and unfailingly surprising.

My procedure in this paper is quite straightforward. I shall first set forth Albert's discussion of why universals must interest the logician, in the course of which his view on the nature of logic and the status of its concerns will be sketched. With this in hand, I shall turn to three places in his writings where Albert considers the problem of universals, taking the texts in descending order of importance. The passages in question are (1) the second tractate of the work Albert devoted to

1. *Liber de Praedicabilibus*, tractatus 2, cap. 2, p. 20a. I cite this work from the Borgnet ed. of the *Opera Omnia*, vol. 1 (Paris: 1890).

the *Isagoge* of Porphyry, the *Liber de Praedicabilibus*, (2) the second tractate of the *De Intellectu et Intelligibili*, and (3) an important passage
from Albert's paraphrase of the *Metaphysics*. Although there is intrinsic evidence that Albert wrote the Porphyrian paraphrase after he
wrote on the *Physics*,[2] I will not be concerned with questions of chro-
nology, nor, given the constraints of space, will anything be said of the
more and less immediate historical sources of Albert's views. All in all,
what I have to say will be of a preliminary and largely expository
nature, but, given the relative ignorance of Albert's thought, this is as
it should be.

I. THE LOGIC OF UNIVERSALS

After dutifully repeating Porphyry's demur about discussing in an
introductory work the questions that make up the problem of universals, Albert, like so many others before him, launches with gusto into a
prolonged discussion of them. Porphyry thought these questions too
difficult; Albert, as the motto of this paper indicates, felt that the
problem of universals raises questions that are best left to the metaphysician. Nonetheless, he argues that the logician must study universals. Indeed, they are his chronologically first concern. This follows
from the nature and scope of logic.

Logic has for its subject argument: "Logicae subjectum est argumentatio."[3] Argumentation involves a plurality of propositions and
thus the analysis and understanding of the proposition is a logical task
presupposed by the study of argumentation as such. But, if the proposition is an element of argument, the proposition itself can be broken
into terms, and thus the logic of the definition of terms comes before
the logic of propositions. To cast this point in the framework of the
works of the Organon, we see that such books as the *Topics* and *Analytics* presuppose *On Interpretation*, which in turn presupposes the
Categories.[4] Since Porphyry's little work is an introduction to the *Categories*, Albert, in discussing the five predicables, takes himself to be on
the very threshold of logic.

Logic is also—and most frequently—described by Albert as the science or art of coming to knowledge of the unknown through what is

2. Ibid., cap. 4, p. 28b.
3. Ibid., tractatus 1, cap. 4, p. 7b.
4. See Albert's discussion in the first chapter of the first tractate of his exposition of
On Interpretation: Perihermeneias, Liber I, ed. cit., pp. 373–76.

already known.[5] It is the mode of all knowledge and/or science[6] and concerns itself, not with things, but rather with the way in which things are ordered as we know them.[7] Since our knowledge is expressed in language, the logician must be concerned with language though it does not constitute his essential object.[8] In short, Albert denies that logic is a *scientia sermocinalis*. The logician is essentially concerned with things insofar as they are in the mind of one seeking to come to knowledge of what he does not know through knowledge already had. One can say, accordingly, that logic is not a *scientia sermocinalis* but rather is concerned with second intentions; that is, it bears not on language as such but on the ordering of known things in the mind of a human knower.[9]

Tractatus 2 of the *De Praedicabilibus* begins by asking why universals, of which the five predicables (genus, species, difference, property, and accident) are instances, should be considered by the logician. The answer derives from the nature of predicability. Only that can be truly and properly predicated of another which is in that of which it is predicated. Now, nothing is in itself, either as the essence or accident of itself, and from this it follows that nothing can be truly or properly predicated of itself. From the fact that what is truly and properly predicated is in another, it necessarily follows that it is communicable to all those things it is signified as being in. To be communicable is to have an aptitude to be in and of many. Whatever is thus in another is for that very reason predicable. The nature itself (*ratio et causa*) of the predicable is that it is universal. Whatever is predicable, in the sense of predicable meant here, is universal. If the first act of one seeking to discover the unknown from the known involves the ordering of the predicables, clearly this presupposes that one knows why the predicable is predicable. Since something is predicable because it is universal, logic begins with the study of universals.

The universal is that which, though it is in one, is capable of being

5. See, for example, *De Praedicamentis*, tractatus 2, cap. 1, p. 149.

6. *De Praedicabilibus*, p. 2a.

7. Ibid., p. 9.

8. "Propter quod logicus et ad se et ad alterum utitur sermone per accidens, et non per se: quia sine sermone designativo procedere non potest ad notitiam ejus quod ignotum est." P. 7a.

9. Ibid., p. 9a: "Quia autem logica omnia considerat prout sunt in anima sive in intellectu ejus, qui quaerit per notum sibi venire in notitiam ignoti." Richard F. Washell, in "Logic, Language and Albert the Great," *Journal of the History of Ideas* 34/3, pp. 445–50, criticizes Norman Kretzmann for saying that Albert both challenged the claim that logic is a *scientia sermocinalis* and maintained that it is a science of mental entities (*intentiones*). I think Kretzmann right. However infrequently Albert uses the phrase *secundae intentiones*, that phrase best captures his conception of logic.

in many: "Universale autem est, quod cum sit in uno, aptum natum est esse in pluribus." [10] Thus it pertains to the logician to study the universal insofar as it is the basis of predicability. The study of what is universal, insofar as it is a certain nature, a kind of being, falls to the metaphysician. [11] To predicate or to be predicated derives from the mental activity of one ordering and combining predicables according to the proper notion of predicables.

How precisely are we to understand this division of labor between the logician and metaphysician? The logician considers the universal as such, as universal, that is, as predicable, as likely to be in and of many. The metaphysician, on the other hand, considers the universal insofar as it is a certain nature or type of being. Now clearly the nature meant cannot be the nature of the universal properly speaking, since this involves predicability and that is the concern of the logician. It must therefore be the nature known to which predicability attaches, not as such, but *per accidens*: insofar as it is known. The logician considers the nature, not as such, in its ontological constituents, so to say, but just insofar as it is predicable. Speaking of the five predicables, Albert writes, "Per hoc enim accidentia diversum modum accipiunt praedicandi in quid vel in quale." [12] Predicability, universality, is not a constituent of the natures studied by the metaphysician; it is not a feature of real natures as they exist independently of our knowing and talking about them. The logician is thus concerned with the way in which we order and arrange things as we know them in our quest of the unknown through what we already know, an order and arrangement distinct from the order among existent things, the real order. This is Albert's abiding conception of the nature of logical entities, and doubtless that is what Kretzmann had in mind in making the remark to which Washell seems to take exception.

Logic may not be as such a *scientia sermocinalis*, but its concerns cannot be understood apart from language, inner or outer. [13] Albert distinguishes logic's dependence on or concern with language from that of grammar, poetry, and rhetoric. Logic's involvement with language is one with its being the mode of moving from the known to the unknown. Then comes this precision:

10. *De Praedicabilibus*, tractatus 2, p. 17b.
11. "Et hoc modo prout ratio est praedicabilitatis, ad logicum pertinet de universali tractare, quamvis secundum quod est natura quadam et differentia entis, tractare de ipso pertineat ad metaphysicum. Praedicare enim et praedicari rationis est ordinantis et componentis praedicabilia secundum praedicabilium propriam rationem." Ibid.
12. Ibid., p. 18a.
13. Ibid., p. 7a.

The proof of this is that the known (through which knowledge of the unknown is gained) can be considered in two ways, namely as a thing outside the mind of the knower and as a certain notion in the mind of the knower. It is not causative of knowledge of the unknown insofar as it exists outside the mind of the knower, but rather insofar as it is a notion of the thing existing in the knower's mind, for in the latter sense it is significant and grounds for inference, by a perfect comprehension of which the intellect in some way perceives the unknown. It is in this way that the logician considers words significant of things and not otherwise.[14]

The logician is concerned with argumentative or syllogistic discourse and with whatever linguistic constituents of such discourse there may be. That is, he is concerned with simple as well as complex discourse, but with the former as it is presupposed by the latter.[15]

Just as the thing known may be a real thing but the fact that it is known by me (or anyone) is not a constitutive property of it, so for things to be talked about in simple or complex discourse is not a constitutive feature of things:

Complexity and incomplexity do not belong [*accidunt*] to a thing insofar as it is a thing, nor even to the vocal sound insofar as it is a vocal sound, but they belong to the vocal sound insofar as it is referred to simple or composed understanding.[16]

The basis of this remark is the definition of the *vox significativa* found in *On Interpretation*, and it enables Albert to distinguish the common or universal from the proper name:

Further the vocal sound insofar as it is referred to the understanding of one seeking to discover the unknown through the known is such that it is divided into the common or universal and the proper or singular, neither of which belongs [*accidit*] to it insofar as it is referred to the designated thing. All the things that are sensed and insofar as they are constituted by nature are singular: the note of the common that they take on derives from mind.[17]

14. "Huius autem probatio est, quod notum (per quod ignoti scientia accipitur) dupliciter consideratur, scilicet prout est res extra animam noscentis accepta, et prout est notio quaedam in anima noscentis. Non autem facit notitiam ignoti prout est res extra animam noscentis accepta, sed potius prout est notio rei in anima noscentis existentis: sic enim significativa est et illativa ejus quod ignotum est: quod ignotum ipsi aliquo modo percipit intellectus perfecta comprehensione. Hoc ergo modo voces significativas rerum considerat logicus et non aliter." Ibid., p. 8a.

15. In the *De Praedicabilibus* (p. 8b) Albert says that there are two parts of logic based on the division of simple and complex linguistic expressions.

16. "Complexio autem et incomplexio non accidunt rei secundum quod res est, nec etiam voci secundum quod vox: sed accidunt voci secundum quod refertur ad intellectum simplicem vel compositum." Ibid., p. 9b.

17. "Adhuc autem vox secundum quod refertur ad intellectum ejus qui quaerit invenire ignotum per notum, habet quod dividitur in commune, seu universale: et proprium, sive singulare: talium enim nihil accidit ei secundum quod ad rem designatum

Any term that is imposed from a form communicable to many, whether substantial or accidental, whether or not actually shared, is a common or universal term. Singular terms, whether proper names or definite descriptions, signify what can only belong to one.[18]

Given the definition of the universal as that which is predicated of many things, in which it is either substantially or accidentally, Albert provides the following scheme of the five predicables discussed in Porphyry's *Isagoge*:

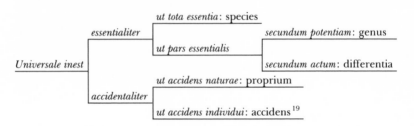

He adds the by now familiar point that he is not here concerned with the things themselves (*res ipsas*) which take on this ordering according to predicability. For things to be genera or species and the like is an accident and not a constituent of them.[20] He seems to contrast the predicables with the categories or predicaments, however, as if the former were a concern with the accidents that things take on as known and named by us and the latter a concern with the things themselves. But, if logic is concerned with things as they are known and the *Categories* is concerned with the things themselves, it should follow that the *Categories* is not a logical work. Either that or logic has been badly defined. Albert's thoughts on the matter are easily discovered:

Because the predicables must be considered insofar as they are signified by vocal sounds, Boethius says that this science, namely that contained in the *Categories*, deals with the ten first words signifying the first genera of things, for this order is not in the things themselves, but it is necessary that reason impose the order, just as it makes composite collections.[21]

---

refertur. Res enim omnes sunt singulares quae cadunt sub sensu et secundum quod constituuntur a natura: et commune quod est in eis accipitur ab intellectu." Ibid., p. 10a.

18. Ibid., p. 10b.   19. Ibid., pp. 17b–18a.
20. Ibid., p. 18a.

21. "Propter quod praedicabilia oportet considerare secundum quod vocibus significantur: propter quod dicit Boethius quod haec scientia, scilicet liber Praedicamentorum, est de decem primis vocibus prima genera rerum significantibus: ordo enim non est in rebus ipsis, sed oportet quod ratio ponat ordinem, sicut et facit complexionem et collectionem oppositorum." *De Praedicamentis*, p. 150a.

Albert seems to go out of his way to stress the point, summarizing the task before him thus: "Cum ergo tam utile sit hoc negotium istarum rerum *prout universalia quaedam sunt*, istarum quinque rerum *prout in ratione sunt*, speculatione sive consideratione tentabo traditionem compendiosam faciens doctrinam monstrare."[22]

Albert's view on the status of the entities with which the logician is concerned seems clear enough. The logician is concerned with that ordering of things known that the mind introduces into its own activity as it moves from the known to the unknown. But, if it is concerned with mental entities, logic is equally and perforce concerned with the linguistic expression of them. And that is Washell's point against Kretzmann. The logician cannot ignore language. To say that the logician "is concerned with discourse only incidentally, if at all" may be taken to set logic off from such *scientiae sermocinales* as grammar, poetry, and rhetoric. Nonetheless, the order among the predicables, for example, "cannot be determined unless the predicable is taken as designated by some vocal sound."[23] "From all this, it is plain what the subject of this book is: it is that which can be ordered according to the notion of the predicable or its subject insofar as this order is signified by some vocal sound."[24] In denying that logic is *sermocinalis*, Albert appeals to Avicenna, and, not insignificantly, he points out that, insofar as language is the concern of the logician, namely as *significativus concepti*, it is something a man may engage in with himself as well as with others. That is, as John Damascene suggests, there is an inner as well as an outer language.[25]

It is true that the phrase "second intention" does not often occur in Albert; indeed, so far as I know, it never occurs in the logical writings. But surely the doctrine is there. Universality, predicability of many, is an accident of the nature as abstracted by mind.[26] If the intellectual grasp of a thing by way of abstraction is called an *intentio*, as it is,[27] and if we also find talk of the *intentio generis* and *intentio speciei*, as we do,[28] and if universality attaches to, is accidental to, intentions in the first sense,[29] we have a warrant for calling the universal and its types,

---

22. Ibid., p. 19a.

23. ". . . ordo praedicabilium non potest determinari, nisi secundum quod sub voce habet praedicabile designari." Loc. cit., p. 150a.

24. "Et ex his planum est quid sit hujus libri subjectum: est enim sujectum ordinabile in ratione praedicabilis et subjicibilis, secundum quod stat sub voce talem ordinem signante." Ibid. See as well pp. 377b–78a and p. 459: ". . . cum omnis et total logica sit scientia disserendi."

25. P. 7a–b.

26. P. 29a; see too p. 34a.

27. E.g., p. 10a and p. 22b.

28. See p. 18b.

29. See p. 24b.

genus, species, etc., second intentions. But surely what is important is whether or not Albert holds what is meant by "second intention" and not whether he uses this terminology profusely or at all. Thomas Aquinas is not prodigal with the terminology himself.

By way of summary, we can say that, for Albert, the universal is a concern of the logician because the logician is concerned with argumentation in all its amplitude. This concern embraces all the constituents and presuppositions of argument, propositions, their terms, and the ordering of terms according to predicability and subjectability. A very first concern of the logician, by way of preparation for undertaking the inquiry into the categories, is universality. Universality, predicability of many, is something that attaches to a nature as abstracted by our mind from the individuating and particularizing conditions due to matter. As known, the nature is something one related to the many in which it can be found. Just as "to be known by men" is not a constitutive feature of natural things, so "to be talked of by men" is not a constitutive feature of natural things. The relations, properties, and accidents that things take on as known by men are the concern of the logician. Thus logical entities are mental, mind-dependent, and do not enjoy extra-mental existence.

If all this is roughly true, it will seem that Albert is unlikely to have any problem with the ontological status of universals and that he will make short shrift of the three questions of Porphyry that make up the problem of universals. That this is far from being the case, we shall now see.

II. THE PROBLEM OF UNIVERSALS

Of the three discussions of universals mentioned earlier, that found in Albert's discussion of Porphyry's *Isagoge*, his *Liber de Praedicabilibus*, is by far the most extensive. It is also the most surprising. The whole second tractate of this work deals with the three Porphyrian questions that constitute the problem of universals. In the Borgnet edition, the discussion covers twenty-four pages and comprises nine chapters. The first chapter argues that the logician must handle the question of universals, establishes the number of the predicables as five, and points out the usefulness of the discussion for logic. The second chapter sets forth the three Porphyrian questions and gives several preliminary interpretations of the first question, but not of the second and third. Albert then devotes separate chapters to the discussion of the three questions and adds four more chapters dealing with allied matters. The treatment is anything but perfunctory, therefore, and the reader rightly expects an illuminating and nuanced handling of the issues.

Now it is well known that Porphyry's questions are set forth in such a way that the second presupposes that a certain answer has been given to the first and the third presupposes that the second has been answered in a particular way. That is, the first question asks if genera and species subsist in reality or exist only in concepts, and the second question, presupposing that we have answered the first by saying that genera and species subsist, asks whether they are corporeal or incorporeal. The third question, on the assumption that they are incorporeal, asks if genera and species are found in sensible particulars or exist separately from them. Given Albert's views on the status of logical entities and given that genera and species are logical entities, we might expect that he would handle the first question with a distinction or two and wrap up the whole problem of universals rapidly. *Au contraire.*

Albert devotes a great deal of space to the first question. First, he sets forth seven of the strongest arguments on behalf of the view that genera and species pertain to the conceptual order and are not subsistent entities, arguments that can be roughly characterized as Aristotelian. He follows these with seven arguments on behalf of the view that universals are subsistent entities, and these arguments can be characterized as Platonic. Then, having given his own view, he states that the seven Platonic arguments are valid and necessary and proceeds to refute one by one the seven Aristotelian arguments.

What I propose to do is this: First, I shall set forth Albert's own solution; second, the solution in the *De Praedicabilibus* will be compared with that in *De Intellectu et Intelligibili* and in the paraphrase of the *Metaphysics*; third, I shall comment on Albert's refutation of the seven arguments that deny genera and species subsist; finally, I shall ask how coherent Albert's several treatments of universals are.

1. Albert's Solution in *De Praedicabilibus*

Albert begins by distinguishing three ways in which the universal can be considered, "namely, in itself as a simple invariable nature; as referred to understanding; and as it is in this thing or that."[30] Taken in the first way, it is the simple nature that gives being and definition

---

30. ". . . dicimus quod universale triplicem habet considerationem, scilicet secundum quod est in seipso natura simplex et invariabilis: et secundum quod refertur ad intelligentiam: et secundum quod est in isto vel in illo." P. 24a.

and a name; it is among the things that are most truly a being, having no alien nature mixed with it, nor is it subject to variation by some other nature. Insofar as it is in this thing or that, many things pertain to it, the first of which is that the nature is particularized and individuated, the second that it is multiplied, and the third that it is incorporated and thereby subject to an infinity of diverse characteristics, since an infinity of things can inhere in matter. Considered in the second way, that is, as in the intellect, one must further distinguish between its reference to the First Intelligence knowing and causing it and its reference to the intellect knowing it by way of abstraction. The First Intelligence causes it to be a ray and light (*radium et lumen*) of itself, to be simple, pure, immobile, incorporeal, both perfectible and moving with regard to the possible intellect. The intellect that does not cause the nature but knows it abstractly confers universality on it by separating it from matter and individuating notes. At this point Albert invokes the Aristotelian dictum: "universale est dum intelligitur, particulare vero dum sentitur."[31] Having said that universality pertains to a nature insofar as it is known by such an abstractive intellect as ours, Albert enigmatically adds, "quam de natura sua ante habuit" (which of its own nature it had before).[32] Obviously, universality cannot be both what the nature has of itself and what is conferred on it when it is known by an abstractive intellect. Albert seems to be suggesting that the human intellect, by abstracting the nature from individuating notes, restores it, as it were, to its condition prior to being received in matter.

This interpretation is bolstered by the next distinction Albert draws,[33] that among forms *ante rem*, that is, taken in themselves as being the principles of things, *in re*, that is, taken with the thing in which form exists as individuated and particularized, and *post rem*, as abstracted and separated from individuating conditions and having universality conferred upon them by the mind. The first are the substantial principles of things, the second the substances of things, the third accidents and qualities which are called the notes of things received in the soul.

With these distinctions in hand, Albert can say that

universals, that is, the natures which are called universals, taken in themselves, most truly are and are ingenerable, incorruptible and invariable. They are outside, beyond, bare and pure concepts, as the second group of argu-

31. P. 24b.   32. Ibid.
33. Ibid.

ments incontrovertibly show; in some sense, however, they are in things and individuated. . . . Furthermore, they enjoy existence in the mind and this in a twofold way, namely, in the intellect which causes and effects them, and in the intellect knowing them by way of abstraction and effecting and educing them through universality.[34]

What then is Albert's answer to the first Porphyrian question? Genera and species, universals, may be considered in three ways and will be said to exist differently according to these different considerations. If we consider the natures or forms that are dubbed universals, they are, in themselves, changeless, neither coming to be nor passing away. Moreover, they are not mere concepts. This is decisively settled, according to Albert, by the second set of seven arguments. The natures or forms which are called universals are not mere features or creatures of our mind. These forms or natures can be considered as they exist in matter, and there they are particularized and individuated. Thus, insofar as they exist in particulars, natures are particular and not universal. Finally, natures can be considered with reference to intellect, and it is with respect to a mind knowing them in an abstract way, as something one over and above the many particulars, that universality is effected. The short answer would thus seem to be that to be a universal, to be a genus or species, happens to natures as they are abstractly known by such a mind as ours. But Albert exhibits singular reluctance to state and settle for this short answer. And, to the reader's vast surprise, he embraces without question seven Platonizing arguments and undertakes to refute Aristotelian arguments.

2. Other Albertine Solutions

When we turn to the second tractate of Albert's *De Intellectu et Intelligibili*,[35] we seem to be moving in a somewhat different ambience. The opening chapter asks whether only the universal is the object of understanding and Albert provides two sets of arguments, but this time he prefers the set that is compatible with Peripatetic philosophy. The sec-

---

34. ". . . universalia, hoc est, naturae quae universalia vocantur, secundum se accepta, sunt et verissime sint ingenerabilia et incorruptibilia et invariabilia. Sunt etiam extra, vel praeter intellectum solum, nudum, et purum, sicut incontradicibiliter probant secundum esse individuatum. . . . Ad huc autem secundum quoddam esse sunt in intellectu: et hoc dupliciter, scilicet in intellectu per cognitionem causante et agente, et in intellectu cognoscente per abstractionem ea per universalitatem agente et educente." Pp. 24b–25a.

35. The text is found in Borgnet, vol. 9, pp. 477–502, with the second tractate on pp. 490–97.

ond chapter poses, in effect, the first Porphyrian question. Albert sets down four arguments on behalf of the view that the universal exists in the soul and only three on behalf of the view that universals must enjoy an extra-mental existence. This time Albert does not choose sides, but characterizes his own view as midway between those represented by the two sets of arguments: ". . . we say that the essence of anything can be considered to exist in two ways."[36] In the first way, the nature is taken to be different from matter or any subject in which it is found; in the second way, it is considered as in matter, as individuated. Each of these ways is further subdivided:

And the first way can be further subdivided into two. First, insofar as it is a certain essence absolute in itself, and thus it is called *essence*, and it is one something existing in itself, nor does it have any other being than that of essence, and thus it is one alone. Second, as communicability according to aptitude belongs to it: and this pertains [*accidit*] to it from the fact that it is an essence apt to give being to many, even if it never does so, and thus it is properly called a *universal*.[37]

The particularized nature may be said to have the aptitude of being in many, but only in the mind is the reference to many actuated: "That is why the Peripatetics say that the universal is only in the mind, meaning by universal that which is in and of many actually and not merely by way of aptitude."[38]

There is certainly a family resemblance between this treatment and that in *De Praedicabilibus*, but the differences are remarkable. One is struck by the phrase *essentia quaedam absoluta in seipsa*, a harbinger of Aquinas's *natura absolute considerata*. Furthermore, the distinction given above seems to avoid the ambiguity between the nature dubbed a universal because of what happens to it as known by us and the nature spoken of with respect to its intrinsic constituents. Just as a physical object can be referred to by way of an accidental property, e.g., "the red one," or substantively, e.g., "the checker," so a nature

36. "Nos autem in ista difficultate mediam viam ambulantes, dicimus essentiam uniuscujusque rei dupliciter esse considerandum."—p. 493a.

37. "Et primo quidem modo adhuc dupliciter consideratur. Uno quidem modo prout est essentia quaedam absoluta in seipsa, et sic vocatur *essentia*, et est unum quid in se existens, nec habet esse nisi talis essentiae, et sic est una sola. Alio modo ut ei convenit communicabilitas secundum aptitudinem: et hoc accidit ei ex hoc quod est essentia apta dare multis esse, etiamsi numquam det illud, et sic proprie vocatur universale."—p. 493a.

38. ". . . et ideo dixerunt Peripatetici quod universale non est nisi in intellectu, referentes hoc ad universale quod est in multis et de multis secundum actum existendi, et non secundum aptitudinem solam."—p. 493b.

can be referred to as a universal or as a kind of being, e.g., human. It is one thing to ask whether the nature which takes on, when known, the property of universality can exist outside the mind and quite another to ask whether the nature considered as having the property of universality can exist outside the mind. In this second text, Albert observes this distinction far more faithfully than he does in the *De Praedicabilibus*.

In his presentation of the seventh book of the *Metaphysics*, Albert provides a crisp account.[39] Identifying the substance of man as that which is expressed in the definition, he notes that this substance can be considered in two ways, in itself and with respect to the accidents it takes on. In the second sense, one is concerned with the existence the substance takes on by comparison with something other than itself. Thus to consider the nature or substance as it exists in the mind or as it exists in matter is to see it taking on properties or accidents which are not essential constituents of it. To speak of the universal as being in one way or the other is not to assert that it is something *per se existens*. Of course, these remarks on the *Metaphysics* cannot be disengaged from the problematic of that work, but it could be argued that they state a clearer position than that found in the *De Praedicabilibus*.

3. Albert's Refutations

When we look at Albert's refutation of the seven arguments he had set down on behalf of the claim that universals do not enjoy separate existence, outside the mind, we find him not at his best. The first argument had maintained that whatever exists is numerically one thing. In reply, Albert says that universals do not exist as do the products of natural processes. Furthermore, he suggests that the nature is itself one, even numerically one.[40] Of course, humanity is one nature and equinity is another, but it seems odd to equate this with numerical unity, particularly when the claim is supported by saying that many men are one in nature. Surely they are numerically many and specifically one.

A similar oddity is found in his refutation of the second argument. That argument had held that whatever exists separately must be a subsistent thing (*hoc aliquid*) whereas the nature is a kind (*quale quid*). Albert suggests that we distinguish two senses of "having separate existence." If it means undivided in itself and divided from all others,

39. *In VII Metaphysic.* (ed. B. Geyer, Cologne: 1960), tractatus 5, cap. 1.
40. *De Praedicabilibus*, p. 25a.

the objection holds, but if it means having independent existence, the objection fails, "because the universal, separate in this way, enjoys existence in reality although it is not a subsistent thing."[41] This could mean something as tame as: the nature which takes on universality as known enjoys existence in particular things. Nothing in the first set of seven arguments suggests that so tame an interpretation is being contested and one wonders what Albert means to say.

In refuting both the fifth and sixth arguments, Albert seems guilty of the fallacy of the *per accidens*. The sixth argument had likened the universal to the form in the mind of the artisan which relates to many exemplars, but as exemplified it is always singular and particular. In refuting this, Albert makes the point that what is true of the nature as it exists in individuals is only *per accidens* true of the nature, that is, is not true of it as such. He then goes on to say that to be universal and common belongs to the nature as such (*secundum se*). To this it must be said that to be universal is equally accidental to the nature as such, something Albert himself elsewhere insists on. The same fallacy of the *per accidens* is committed in Albert's refutation of the seventh argument where he asserts that to be common belongs to the nature *secundum se*.[42]

It is difficult to avoid the thought that, in writing the *De Praedicabilibus*, Albert was insufficiently in command of the necessary clarity to deal effectively with the Porphyrian questions. The whole drift of his presentation of the nature of logic and of the status of the concerns of the logician suggests a quite different treatment of the problem of universals from what we in fact find. That drift suggests that Albert should have embraced the first set of seven arguments, those we have characterized as roughly Aristotelian. One can only wonder how he would have gone about showing that the second or Platonic set incontrovertibly establishes the separate existence of universals. In seeking to refute the first set, Albert seems to argue against the grain of his own views and is led into patently fallacious reasoning. We learn from Albert the necessity of distinguishing between what belongs to the nature as such and what happens to it as it is known by an abstractive intellect like ours. And then we see him smudging this distinction and attributing to the nature as such what is only true of it as known abstractly. Later, in the *De Intellectu et Intelligibili*, he proceeds with sureness and clarity and explicitly rejects the Platonic position.

41. Ibid.: ". . . quia universale sic separatum, habet esse in natura, et tamen non est hoc aliquid."
42. Ibid., p. 26a.

III. CONCLUSION

It is unavoidable to conclude that Albert only gradually won through to a clear position on the problem of universals. In the *De Praedicabilibus* we find a complicated and often incoherent outlook that is notably different from that of the *De Intellectu et Intelligibili*. It is noteworthy that, in the former work, the threefold distinction of forms as *ante rem*, *in re*, and *post rem* is presented by Albert in his own name whereas in the latter he identifies it as a Platonic distinction and is critical of it.[43] One finds adumbrations of the far clearer outlook of Aquinas in reading Albert—we have mentioned the seeming harbinger of the Thomistic *natura absolute considerata*[44]—but any comparison of the two giants of the thirteenth century leads inexorably to the conclusion that Albert, great though he undeniably was, is a precursor of his famous disciple. Doubtless he is someone without whom Thomas would have been far less than he was, and it would be churlish not to grant him the admiration he richly deserves. But, as this brief glance at his treatments of the problem of universals suggests, there is a groping, prolix, and unsure aspect of Albert's thought that cannot be denied.

43. Chap. 5, p. 496.
44. See M.-D. Roland-Gosselin, *Le "De ente et essentia" de saint Thomas d'Aquin* (Paris: 1948), pp. 24–29.

9

ALBERT AND THOMAS ON THEOLOGY

Albertus Magnus and Thomas Aquinas are usually seen as linked with one another by the quite new conception of the science of theology which they share and which sets them off against the Augustinian tradition.[1] Needless to say, there are many other ways in which one might speak of the affinity between Albert and Thomas, not least their receptive attitude toward Aristotle. In this paper, I shall be making a somewhat pedestrian examination of passages where the two saints explicitly discuss the nature of theology. In doing this, I do not mean to beg any questions concerning their actual theologizing—that is, there may be differences in theological practice which do not manifest themselves on the level of methodological and preliminary considerations. In the passages to be examined, similarities and differences between the two men will be noticed, similarities and differences which may recall their respective attitudes toward Aristotle.

Both Albert and Thomas commented on the *Sentences* of Peter Lombard, both men wrote a *Summa theologica*. Albert in his treatment of distinctio 1 and Thomas in his prologue discuss the nature of theology; Albert in the Prima Pars of his *Summa*, tractatus 1, considers the nature of theology, and Thomas Aquinas does the same in the first question of the First Part of the *Summa theologiae*. What I intend to do is, first, examine Albert's views, comparing passages from the *Sentences* commentary and the *Summa*, second, do the same thing with Thomas Aquinas, and, finally, say something about Albertine and Thomistic variations within the new conception of the science of theology.[2]

1. See for example Alfonso Pompei, *La Dottrina Trinitaria di S. Alberto Magno, O.P.* (Roma: 1953), p. 11.
2. For purposes of this examination all that is required is that Albert's commentary on the *Sentences* is considerably earlier than his *Summa*. For the vexed question of the dating of Albert's writings, see, for example, O. Lottin, *Commentaire des Sentences et Somme théologique d'Albert le Grand* in *Recherches de Théologie Ancienne et Médiévale* 8 (1936), pp. 117–53.

ALBERT THE GREAT

"Veteris ac novae legis continentiam, diligenti indagine, etiam atque etiam considerantibus nobis, praevia Dei Gratia, innotuit sacrae paginae tractatu circa res vel signa praecipue versari." This famous opening sentence of Book 1, distinction 1, is Albert's guide for his discussion of the nature of theology in his commentary on Lombard. At the end of his *divisio textus*, Albert enters a caveat about the view of the subject matter of theology which, of course, Peter Lombard took from St. Augustine.

Et hoc ideo inducitur, quia tam res quam signa communioris significationis sunt quam in hac scientia intendantur: et ideo non omnes proprietates rerum, nec omnes proprietates signorum inquiruntur hic: et ideo oportet determinare secundum quas proprietates de rebus et signis inquiratur. (*In I Sent.*, d. 1, Borgnet, p. 15a)

Within the ambit of Lombard's designation of the subject, seen to require a great deal of restriction in its scope, lest theology embrace the totality of knowledge, Albert sets forth the following topics of investigation: (1) "Quomodo investigat subjectum Theologiae?" (2) "Quid sit subjectum Theologiae?" (3) "An Theologia sit una scientia vel plures?" (4) "An Theologia sit scientia speculativa vel practica?" (5) "De modis exponendi sacram Scripturam." (6) "An divisio bona sit in res et signa?" (7) "An Sacramenta veteris legis conferebant gratiam?"

When we turn to the *Summa theologica*, we find a somewhat different list of preliminary questions. The tractatus begins "Cupientas igitur petitionibus fratrum . . . ," and this must have been a conscious echoing of Lombard's beginning, "Cupientes aliquid de penuria ac tenuitate nostra . . ." Just as the *Sentences* commentary begins with an allusion to Aristotle's scientific methodology, so the *Summa* invokes an Aristotelian maxim: "Et quia dicit Philosophus, quod solvere non potest qui nescit nodum, de quolibet nodum questionis praemittemus, et singulis solutiones congruas, prout Deus dederit, annotabimus." Albert accordingly asks six things about this science: (1) "An est?" (2) "Quid est?" (3) "De quo sit ut de subjecto?" (4) "Qualiter ab aliis scientiis separata est?" (5) "Quis proprius modus ejus est?" (6) "Ad quid est sicut ad finem?"

For our purposes, we will select three points of comparison between these two texts: (a) how does theology differ from philosophy? (b) how does theology differ from Scripture? (c) the character of theology.

1. How Theology Differs from Philosophy

One could cite numerous passages in which Albert acknowledges the difference between a philosophical and theological discussion. For example, in replying to the forty-three problems on which he had been consulted by the Master General, Albert writes, "Hanc autem secundum philosophiam vultis nobis determinari, quia secundum fidem catholicam dubitare non licet quin Deus Filius corpus quod assumpsit et immediate et corporaliter et distincte impleat et moveat."[3] In what precisely does the difference consist? In commenting on the *Sentences*, Albert proceeds in such a way that his reader must hunt around for the distinction; it does not become thematic. Thus, in article 2, in the course of discussing the proposal that the subject of theology could be the "credible," he writes:

quidam antiqui dixerunt, quod credibile generaliter acceptum est subjectum Theologiae. Voco autem *credibile generaliter acceptum*, praeambulum articulo, sicut Deum esse veracem, Deum esse, sacram Scripturam a Spiritu Sancto esse factam, Scripturam non posse excidere . . . (p. 16b)

Clearly, what Albert here refers to as preambles to articles of faith cannot be identified as philosophical considerations. The same must be said of the "antecedens ad articuli fidem" in the *Summa* (p. 25b). It is with reference to an objection to the Augustinian-Lombardian designation of the subject of theology as "res et signa" that Albert gives an indication of the formal difference between theology and philosophical sciences. If one took the designation seriously, theology, being concerned with "res et signa," would be concerned with everything, including what philosophers take up in a plurality of different sciences. Augustine's remark seems clearly false if meant to cover each and every doctrine. In the commentary on the *Sentences*, there is only one passage which gives anything like a formal statement of the difference between theology and other sciences, and that occurs in the discussion of theology as wisdom.

ista scientia principalissime dicitur sapientia, eo quod ipsa est de altissimis, et altissimo modo: quia de Deo per principia fidei; aliae autem scientiae quae a Philosophis sunt inventae, etsi sapientiae dicantur, quia sunt de altis, non tamen sunt altimissimo modo, sed potius per principia quae sub ratione sunt. (*In I Sent.*, ed. cit., p. 19a)

No doubt, when we encounter a passage like this, we instinctively think of the more nuanced discussions elsewhere in Albert, but it

3. James Weisheipl, "The *Problemata Determinata XLIII* Ascribed to Albertus Magnus (1271)," *Mediaeval Studies* (1960), p. 19.

must be said that the commentary on the *Sentences*, despite the fine list of preliminary questions, is very thin on what precisely the formal distinction between theology and other sciences is. Reference is made to First Philosophy and how its subject is unified, and a contrast between it and Theology emerges, but only in that First Philosophy considers things "proportione ad unum quod subjectum sit aliorum" whereas Theology considers many things "proportione ad unum quod est finis beatificans" (p. 17b), but no further contrast is made. So too Theology is contrasted with Moral Philosophy, with Albert rejecting the notion that his view of Theology would subalternate it to Moral Philosophy (p. 19a).

From this point of view, the *Summa theologica* represents a considerable advance. By means of a distinction between different senses of "lumen," of "revelatio," of "fides" and of "principia," Albert is able to set theology off from the philosophical sciences. Thus, by means of "principia quae intellectus apud se habet" (p. 8a) man can know the divine but "ex lumine quidem connaturali non elevatur ad scientiam Trinitatis et incarnationis et resurrectionis" (p. 10a). What can philosophers know of God?

Sed non intellexit Boetius, quin posset esse subjectum de quo multa probantur, quae per modum relationis et attributionis conveniunt ei: talia enim multa etiam Philosophi probaverunt de Deo, sicut quod sit simplex, et aeternus, et principium, et hujusmodi alia quae de ipso ut de subjecto probata sunt. (p. 16a)

So too, although Theology is concerned with all things, this is not "sub ratione diversa quae differunt singula, sed sub una ratione, quae est utile esse significando vel disponendo ad id quo fruendum est" (p. 15a). Its difference from Metaphysics is put thus:

Theologia autem non est de ente ut ens est, nec de partibus entis ut entis partes sunt: sed est de ente determinato per formam analogiae ad id quo fruendum est, et de partibus ejus secundum quod specialem habet analogiam ad illud. (p. 19b)

As noted above, the suite of methodological discussions taken up in the *Summa* includes an explicit discussion of the way Theology is distinguished from other sciences. It is here that Albert confronts what for Thomas is the first question: what need is there for theology? Is it not superfluous when one considers the range of philosophy? Albert introduces a distinction between knowledge which is "*acquisita*" and that which is "*per revelationem*": the former is based on sense experience, the latter on faith. Earlier (p. 10a), he had distinguished this sense of "faith" from a philosophical sense of an opinion supported by argument. Now he distinguishes two senses of "revelation" to accommodate such Scriptural texts as Romans 1 : 19 and this involves the distinction between a "lumen generale" and a "lumen supermundana" (p. 20b and p. 21b). So we get this crisp distinction:

prima philosophia de Deo est secundum quod substat proprietatibus entis primi secundum quod ens primum est. Ista autem de Deo est secundum quod substat attributis quae per fidem attribuuntur. (p. 20b)

Obviously, when we discuss Albert's characterization of Theology this distinction will be further clarified.

2. Theology and Scripture

The most surprising thing about the two Albertine texts is their lack of a clear-cut, consistently observed distinction between Theology and Sacred Scripture. In both of them we constantly encounter questions raised about Theology which are answered as if they bore on Scripture as such. Thus, in the *Summa*, when it is asked whether Theology is speculative or practical, the solutio begins: "Ad hoc dicendum quod in veritate Sacra Scriptura practica est . . ." This is not a momentary lapse; it is a constant feature of both the *Commentary on the Sentences* and the *Summa theologica*. Still citing the latter text, when the question of the subject of theology is discussed, we find such remarks as these: "Et ita videtur quod res et signa materia non possunt esse sacrae Scripturae" and "Statim in principio Genesis theologia est de operibus conditionis" (p. 14a).

It is easy to see how the continuity between Scripture and Theology would lead to such locutions. Clearly, if the principles of theology are gained through faith and revelation, Scripture contains the principles of Theology. But we want to know the difference between the canonical books and such works as Peter Lombard's *Sentences*, not to mention Albert's commentary on it. We find such a distinction, in the latter text, when Albert discusses the senses of Scripture. St. Paul has promised both sound doctrine and the refutation of those contradicting it. The former is accomplished by the historical, allegorical, moral and anagogical senses of Scripture.

In quantum autem finis est, scilicet contradicentes revincere, habet alium modum. Contradicens enim non revincitur nisi duobus, scilicet probatione veritatis, et manifestatione erroris. Hoc autem non fit nisi per argumentationem congruam a ratione auctoritatis, vel naturalis rationis, vel similitudinis congrue sumptam: et sic hoc modo argumentatio talis erit instrumentum ejus, et (ut patet in proemio) *iste modus est scientiae istius libri, alii autem modi sunt observati in Biblia.* (p. 20a)

In question 5 of the first tractate of *Summa theologica*, Albert offers this contrast between Scripture and Theology: Scripture deals with particulars, the Fathers proceed otherwise.

Tamen quia in particularibus latent theoriae universales, multae a patribus pulcherrime extractae sunt et scientialiter traditae et artificiose in originalibus eorum, sicut patet in libris Dionysii et Augustini, Gregorii et aliorum. (p. 22a)

This scientific and artful method is sometimes foreshadowed in Scripture itself, as when Paul argues for the general resurrection from Christ's resurrection (p. 25b). Albert distinguishes the "dictum" of Sacred Scripture from the "ratio dicti": it is the latter that Theology supplies, but only for one who accepts Scripture.

Ita in theologia ad eum qui negat sacram Scripturam verum dicere, non est disputatio de fidei articulis, sed ad eum qui concedit hoc, multae rationes possunt induci. (p. 26b)

One might say that, on the subject of the relation between Theology and Scripture, Albert is more satisfying early and late than he is on the distinction between Theology and the philosophical sciences, where the distinction is far clearer in the *Summa* than in the commentary on the *Sentences*, though the clarity wanted is oddly submerged so that the distinctions emerge almost as obiter dicta rather than as matters of supreme importance.

3. The Characterization of Theology

If there is a single Scriptural passage which broods over the Albertine conception of theology in both texts under examination it is from Paul's Epistle to Titus 1 : 1, "Secundum fidem electorum Dei, et agnitionem veritatis quae secundum pietatem est." From the time of the commentary on the *Sentences*, this governs what Albert says.

Thus, in discussing the subject of Theology and accepting as good money the Augustinian designation offered by Peter Lombard, Albert makes clear that Theology is not concerned with "res absolute," but "prout ordinantur ad perfectionem beatitudinis et fruitionis" nor with signs except as they provide a "dispositio ad beatitudinem" (p. 16a–b). So too in arguing that the unity of the subject of Theology is a proportional one, he makes it clear that all theological discussions refer "ad unum quod est finis beatificans" (p. 17b). Before asking whether Theology is a speculative or practical science, Albert has put it among those sciences whose aim is "ut boni fiamus" (p. 18a). The discussion of the practical or speculative nature of Theology is in effect a gloss on the verse from the Epistle to Titus.

Veritatis autem quae secundum pietatem est sunt duo: unum scilicet secundum pietatem cultus Dei in se et in membris . . . Alterum autem est finis intentionis, et hic est conjungi intellectu et affectu et substantia cum eo quod colitur prout est finis beatificans: et ideo ista scientia proprie est affectiva, id est veritatis quae non sequestratur a ratione boni, et ideo perficit et intellectum et affectum. Talis autem finis in rebus creatis non invenitur: et ideo Philosophi non tractaverunt hujusmodi scientiam: sed diviserunt unam ad verum quod est in rebus, aliam autem ad bonum quod est in ipsis. (p. 18b)

Theology makes us good ("ut boni fiamus") precisely because its chief concern is "veritas quae est affectiva beatificans" (p. 19a).

Here we have Albert's characterization of Theology, one to which he remained loyal throughout his long career. Certainly there is no change of attitude in the *Summa*. "Theologia scientia est secundum pietatem, hoc est, quod non est de scibili simpliciter ut scibile est, nec de omni scibili, sed secundum quod est inclinans ad pietatem" (p. 11b). Piety comes from the "cultus Dei" which is perfected by faith, hope, charity, prayer and sacrifice. And when in the *Summa* the question arises as to whether Theology is speculative or practical, the answer, as previously noted, is expressed in terms of Scripture: "dicendum quod in veritate Sacra Sciptura practica est." What follows is in warm continuity with the view of the commentary on the *Sentences*.

verum quod inquirit, de Deo et operibus ejus inquirit, non ut verum simpliciter, sed ut summe beatificans, in quod referat totam pietatis intentionem in affectu et opere. Sicut etiam Aristotelis in X *Ethicorum* felicitatem contemplativam determinat, ut ad finem ad quem referantur actus virtutum intellectualium et moralium et heroicarum: propter quod et ipsa quae tractat de felicitate contemplativa, moralis sive practica est sicut et caeterae partes moralis scientiae. (p. 18b)

In the final discussion of tractatus 1 in the First Part of his *Summa*, Albert distinguishes two senses of "end," an intrinsic end and an end without or beyond. "Finis intra in ipsa scientia est, et finis extra in sciente" (p. 31b). This science of Theology could not have some other science as its end; rather it is the end of all the other sciences.

Finis autem in sciente, potius finis est studii, quam scientiae. Et ille triplex est, proximus scilicet operi, ut habeatur notitia theologicorum. Secundus proximus perfectioni, ut ex hoc quis perfectus sit ad actus felicitatis contemplativae. Ultimus ut ex hoc per habitum beatitudinis creatae beatitudinem increatam in prima veritate consequatur.

The composite Albertine position can thus be stated as follows: Theology differs from the philosophical sciences because it proceeds from revealed principles and these are contained in Scripture; theology differs from Scripture in its mode, which is scientific or artful although there are some adumbrations of theological argumentation in Scripture itself. God as the ultimate beatifying end is the subject of Theology and everything else is taken up under that formality: God as the source and then the end of all other things. Is Theology a science undertaken for knowledge ("sciendi gratia") or in order that we might become good ("ut boni fiamus")? If we consider the end of the science, it is doubtless truth about God as ultimate beatifying end that is the end, but what the knower wants is not only knowledge but that he may be enabled to engage in contemplation and ultimately enjoy union with God.

THOMAS AQUINAS

The prologue of Thomas's commentary on the *Sentences* considers the following matters:

ad evidentiam hujus sacrae doctrinae, quae in hoc libro traditur, quaeruntur quinque: 1. de necessitate ipsius; 2. supposito quod sit necessaria, an sit una vel plures; 3. si sit una, an practica vel speculativa; et si sit speculativa, utrum sapientia vel intellectus; 4. de subjecto ipsius; 5. de modo.

One can see a more orderly and logical arrangement of questions here and, in their phrasing, the promise of differences with Albert. In the First Part of the *Summa theologiae*, question 1, Thomas is concerned "De sacra doctrina, qualis sit et ad quae se extendat," a discussion involving ten articles. (1) Whether there is any necessity for any science beyond the philosophical disciplines? (2) Is Sacred Doctrine a science? (3) Whether it is one science? (4) Whether it is a practical science? (5) Whether it is more worthy than other sciences? (6) Whether it is wisdom? (7) Whether God is the subject of this science? (8) Is this doctrine argumentative? (9) Whether Sacred Scripture should use metaphors? (10) Whether Sacred Scripture involves many senses in one letter?

We shall put the same three questions to Thomas as we did to Albert.[4]

---

4. See Ralph McInerny, *Saint Thomas Aquinas* (Boston: 1978; repr. Notre Dame: 1982).

1. How Theology Differs from Philosophy

It is noteworthy that in both texts, the first question that Thomas proposes is why should there be any science beyond the philosophical sciences. More precisely, he wants to know why there should be any inquiry into and doctrine about God beyond that attainable in philosophy. All right-thinking persons recognize that the goal of human life is the contemplation of God. But God can be contemplated in two ways, in one way, through creatures, which is imperfect but which is the contemplation envisaged by philosophers. This is a contemplation "ex rationibus creaturarum" and it must be distinguished from that which is possible to man on the supposition of faith: "non a creaturis sumptam sed immediate ex divino lumine inspiratam; et haec est doctrina theologiae" (*In I Sent.*, prolog., a. 2, c.).

It is a feature of Thomas's discussion of theology and philosophy in both our principal texts that he dwells on their respective knowledge of God. The philosopher can come to knowledge of God from principles known by the natural light of reason; by faith we have knowledge of God by a divine illumination and theology can develop by way of argumentation what is given by faith.

Unde ista doctrina magis etiam divina dicenda est quam metaphysica: quia est divine quantum ad subjectum et quantum ad modum accipiendi; metaphysica autem quantum ad subjectum tantum. (ibid., a. 2, sol. 1)

There is a limit to what can be known of God through the principles of natural reason; faith puts us in possession of truths about God which exceed the range of reason.

In the *Summa theologiae*, as he had in his exposition of the *De trinitate* of Boethius, Thomas makes a most important point. Faith and revelation are required not only for knowledge of God which exceeds the reach of the natural principles of reason, but even, practically speaking, for naturally knowable truths about God. Thomas notices that naturally knowable truths about God, e.g. that God exists, that He is one, etc., are included in Scripture. Thus, though they be de facto believed, they need not be, and in this they differ from those truths about God which can only be held on the authority of Deus "*revelans.*" Thomas uses the phrase "praeambula fidei," to designate truths about God which have been revealed but which are in principle naturally knowable. This differs from Albert's use of the same term.

Ad ea etiam quae de Deo ratione humana investigari possunt, necessarium fuit hominem instrui revelatione divina; quia veritas de Deo per rationem

investigata, a paucis hominibus et per longum tempus et cum admixtione
multorum errorum proveniret: a cujus tamen veritatis cognitione dependet
tota hominis salus, quae in Deo est. (*ST*, Ia, q. 1, a. 1, c.)

Faith and revelation are thus seen to be a practical necessity even for
naturally knowable truths about God; they are a fortiori necessary for
truths which exceed the capacity of human reason.

Philosophy terminates in knowledge of the divine and represents a
laborious ascension from the realm of sense to the adumbration of the
divine that is to be found in that realm. The principles of theology are
not, any more than the principles of natural reason, acquired: faith is
not an attainment, it is a gift. The basic difference then is the principles in the light of which truths are established.

2. How Theology Differs from Scripture

Theology is in continuity with Scripture because its principles have
been revealed and are accepted by faith. If faith is a gift and not an
acquisition, it is otherwise with theology.

in hac doctrina non acquiritur habitus fidei, qui est quasi habitus principiorum; sed acquiritur habitus eorum quae ex eis deducuntur et quae ad eorum
defensionem valent. (*In I Sent.*, prolog., q. 1, a. 3, sol. 3)

Theology does not prove its principles, but accepts them; having accepted them it proceeds by way of argumentation in their articulation
and defense. Thus, the theologian might argue against one who denies one article of faith by showing him his denial is incompatible with
his acceptance of others.

Si vero adversarius nihil credat eorum quae divinitus revelantur, non remanet
amplius via ad probandos articulos fidei per rationes; sed ad solvendum rationes si quas inducit contra fidem. (*ST*, Ia, q. 1, a. 8, c.)

Theology's method thus entails that it make use of natural reason as
well as what has been received by faith. Sacred doctrine makes use of
human reason, not to prove the faith (which if it were possible would
remove the merit of faith) but to make manifest what has been handed
down (*ST*, Ia, q. 1, a. 8, ad 2). "Et ex istis principiis, *non respuens communia principia*, procedit ista scientia; nec habet viam ad ea probanda,
sed solum ad defendum a contradicentibus . . ." (*In I Sent.*, prolog.,
a. 3, sol. 2, ad 3).

3. The Characterization of Theology

"Theologia est scientia de rebus quae ad salutem hominis pertinent." This remark is found in the *contra* of quaestiuncula 2 in *In I
Sent.*, prolog., q. 3, but for all that expresses Thomas's own thought. It
occurs where he is asking whether theology is speculative or practical.
He has already argued that theology is a single science, seeing everything under one formality. Is it speculative or practical? Given its origin, because of the efficacity of the divine light, it suffices for complete
human perfection.

Unde perficit hominem et in operatione recta et quantum ad contempla-
tionem veritatis: unde quantum ad quid practica est et etiam speculativa. Sed
quia scientia omnis principaliter pensanda est ex fine, finis autem ultimus
istius doctrinae est contemplatio primae veritatis in patria, ideo principaliter
speculativa est. (*In I Sent.*, prolog., a. 3, sol. 1)

Theology is primarily speculative because man's end, the contemplation of God, is speculative. It is not meritorious actions which are the
end of theology, but rather what they make possible. "Blessed are the
pure of heart, for they shall see God." Thomas speaks of theology as a
science which is as it were subalternated to God's knowledge of Himself and as aimed at a beatifying knowledge of Him hereafter.

The distinction Thomas makes between two types of judgment, that
"per modum inclinationis" and that "per modum cognitionis," illus-
trating them respectively in terms of the chaste man's judgment as to
what he should do and the moral theologian's judgment, is of importance for understanding Thomas's characterization of theology. The
chaste man judges out of his affinity with the good of chastity; the
moral theologian's judgment is not measured by his own virtue but by
the principles of his science. "Secundus autem modus judicandi pertinet ad hanc doctrinam, secundum quod per studium habetur; licet
ejus principia ex revelatione habeantur" (*ST*, Ia, q. 1, a. 6, ad 3).

CONCLUSION

A perusal of what Albert and Thomas have to say at the outset of
their respective commentaries on the *Sentences* as well as at the beginning of their *Summae*, makes it abundantly clear why the two men
should be linked in their conception of theology. One senses in each
man's repertoire a vast knowledge and acceptance of Aristotle's conception of what a science is, how sciences are distinguished from one

another, the division of sciences into speculative and practical. To see the contents of the *Sentences* through the lens of Aristotelian methodology certainly transports that enormously important work from a twelfth- into a thirteen-century setting. The scholastic method does not wait the thirteenth century for its commencement, but it undergoes a remarkable transformation then. If the *Sic et Non* suggests the Aristotle of the *Topics*, the works of Albert and Thomas examined here call into play the *Analytics*. Moreover, they invoke those writings of Aristotle unknown to either Abelard or Peter Lombard, most notably the *Metaphysics*, to say nothing of Arabic commentators. What would Peter Lombard have made of the preliminary discussions of Albert and Thomas in their commentaries on his most famous work?

Yet, looking backward, both Albert and Thomas are at pains to adjust their view of theology with that incorporated in the *Sentences* and with the Augustinian tradition which is present in the designation of the subject of theology by the phrase "res et signa." But, whatever their piety in regard to the tradition, it is undeniable that Peter Lombard's understanding of the subject of theology, while never flatly rejected by Albert or Thomas, becomes peripheral to their own elaboration of theology's subject.

But if Albert and Thomas are moving in a changed intellectual universe, there are differences of emphasis in the two men. Nowhere is this more evident than in their treatments of the question: is theology practical or speculative? They both want theology to be speculative and practical, but Albert's tendency is to stress its practical side. We engage in theology in order to become good and Albert takes this goal to put theology closer to the moral than to the theoretical sciences. Thomas, while maintaining that Sacred Doctrine is sufficient for complete human perfection, stresses that contemplation of God is man's end and that moral virtue is instrumental to the attainment of that end. "Blessed are the pure of heart for they shall see God." Purity of heart is a good and it is a prerequisite for an activity which is not practical but contemplative.

Do these different emphases argue for a greater or lesser distance from traditional Augustinianism? Perhaps. If so, that is not unimportant. But, however important, it scarcely destroys the fundamental community of vision of these two great thirteenth-century Dominicans, Albert the Great and Thomas Aquinas.

10

ST. BONAVENTURE AND ST. THOMAS

They were both born in Italy; each joined a new mendicant order; they were elected to professorial chairs at the University of Paris on the same day; both died in 1274. Bonaventure and Thomas Aquinas, Franciscan and Dominican, respectively; both canonized by the Church—saints. One could go on enumerating the similarities between these two men; indeed, one is inclined to do so when one thinks of them across that gap of seven hundred years. Whatever their differences, they can seem all but indistinguishable to the twentieth-century eye. Whether read in translation or in the original Latin (and to the classically trained, medieval Latin itself will seem an odd patois), their works may seem only historical curiosities, contents of a time capsule, alien. The assumption of this paper is that Bonaventure and Aquinas can be read as Plato and Aristotle and Kant are read, namely, as contributors to ongoing philosophizing, as voices to be taken into account. I shall concentrate on what my two medievals had to say about knowing and believing.

The topic is chosen not simply because it provides a good sample of their thought but also because it bears directly on what has seemed to many the basic impediment to learning anything philosophical from the medievals. Plato and Aristotle are distant from us in time, but their works are recognizably philosophical (as if our criteria for applying the adjective did not derive in large part from these two); Descartes and Kant may have been Christians, but that fact does not seem to animate their philosophy. The medievals, on the other hand, got things all mixed up. After all, were not Bonaventure and Aquinas Masters of Theology? Would we go to Barth for philosophy? Histories of philosophy have been written which ignore the Middle Ages, the historian assuring us that no genuine philosophy was being done during those centuries: was not being done because it could not be done, and the impossibility is one of principle. Medieval thought is permeated by faith and fervor; one who shares the religious beliefs of such authors may be interested in them, but the benefits he gains are not philosophical ones. Proscribing, censorship, ecclesiastical authority, the preeminence of theology—these features of the times indicate that prejudices against medieval thought are not unfounded. What is perhaps not sufficiently known is that the oppositions and distinctions which medievals are said not to have grasped or honored are among the most discussed topics in their writings. Any run-of-the-mill medieval author will provide you with a complex and subtle discussion of the differences between knowing and believing, philosophy and theology. Indeed, speaking historically, our way of making such distinctions is part of an unacknowledged medieval inheritance.

So much for protreptic and mild polemic. My main hope is to remove impediments to following a discussion of some medieval ways of distinguishing knowing and believing as well as such corollaries of the distinction as the differentiation of philosophy from theology. My emphasis is on Thomas Aquinas, but Bonaventure makes an important and essential contribution to what I have to say.

On several occasions St. Thomas makes use of the phrase *praeambula fidei*, preambles to faith, in speaking of those truths about God which are accessible to unaided human reason. It is well known that Thomas thought that pagan philosophers, notably Aristotle, had succeeded in proving that God exists and had come to knowledge of some of His attributes. These are the matters that "preambles of faith" is meant to cover, and it can be seen that a discussion of it can hope to cast some light on the notion of Natural or Philosophical Theology, the culminating concern of metaphysics in its traditional form.[1]

An attempt to make sense of Thomas on preambles of faith is as good a way as any to exhibit the complex and profound infrastructure which sustains a clear surface meaning. I am suggesting, again, that we have here a good sample of how Thomas works. The further significance, for our purposes, is clear. Thomas Aquinas, Christian and priest, had believed from his mother's knee in the truth of the proposition "There is a God." The proposition is an object of faith. Yet he is saying that, for philosophers, it was an object of knowledge. More, he himself fashioned what he considered to be valid and cogent proofs of

---

1. The central difficulty addressed in this paper is expressed in the first objection in a. 2 of q. 1 of the *Summa theologiae*, Ia. In being asked whether it is demonstrable that God exists, the objector points out that it is of faith that God exists, what is believed cannot be known or demonstrated, ergo, etc. In his reply, Thomas distinguishes articles of faith from matters which are preambles to those articles and counts among the latter that God exists. The phrase *praeambula fidei* is already present in such an early work as Thomas's exposition of the *De trinitate* of Boethius (q. 2, a. 3, resp.; ed. Decker, p. 94).

God's existence. That must mean that the proposition "There is a God" is at once an object of knowing and believing. Nonetheless, Thomas insists that one cannot simultaneously know and believe the same truth. Bonaventure seems to be of another mind on the matter. The view of Aquinas suggests some strange overlap of knowledge and religious belief and of philosophy and theology. Is he caught in an inconsistency? He thinks not. The preambles of faith are the locus of clarification.

In order to go on, indeed, in order to grasp the incompatibility mentioned above, we must be clear on the difference between knowing and believing, a difference Thomas establishes with reference to yet other mental acts and/or states.[2] One knows or believes that something or other is true, so we can express the object of these mental acts by the usual variable for a proposition, p. Thus, what we want to know from Aquinas is the difference between "knowing that p" and "believing that p." In discussing it, as I have suggested, Aquinas will add to the mix such mental acts as "thinking (opining) that p" and "doubting that p."

   (1) When I know that p, p is true and $-p$ is false.

Values for p are such that they are either true or false. Knowledge is had when there is a determination of the truth of p. St. Thomas's way of discussing the matter derives from the following elementary consideration. If p is either true or false, then if p is true, $-p$ is false, and if $-p$ is true, p is false. Thus, Thomas will say that, in knowing, the mind assents determinately to one side of a contradiction. To know that p is to know that p is true and that $-p$ is false.

St. Thomas finds it useful to make a subdistinction between knowing as *intelligere* (*intellectus*) and knowing as *scire* (*scientia*). In a narrow and proper sense of knowing, our determination of the truth of p is inferred from the truth of other propositions; to know something in this strong sense is mediated cognition. For Thomas, *scire* and *scientia* are tied to syllogism, so much so that the object of science or knowledge is the conclusion of a demonstrative syllogism which is known to be true because it follows validly from true premises. Not every proposition to which the mind gives determinate assent is mediate, however.

---

2. I develop the distinctions between knowing, opining, doubting, and believing with particular reference to *Quaestio disputata de veritate*, q. 14, aa. 1 and 2. This seems to me the most concise and in several ways most precise expression given of matters which are put forth again and again in various works of Thomas. Of course, the treatise on faith in the *Summa theologiae*, IIaIIae, is an obvious parallel text, but there Thomas permits himself a more spacious although no less orderly discussion.

St. Thomas also allows for immediate or self-evident truths, that is, propositions such that the connection between predicate and subject is not grasped through a middle term but is grasped as soon as one knows the meaning of the constitutive terms. Needless to say, for Thomas, knowing what the terms mean is not simply a matter of knowing how we use words. When I know that the whole is greater than its part, this is not as such to know a truth about "whole" and "part," but about wholes and parts. But that is a long story.

(2) When I think (opine) that p, $-p$ may be true.

Opinion embraces a proposition whose contradictory might turn out to be true. Needless to say, there are certain values of p, such that p and $-p$ are simultaneously true. Some men have beards and some men do not have beards. In such a case, p and $-p$ are not contradictories. We have contradictory propositions only when, if p is true $-p$ is false and if $-p$ is true p is false. When we think or opine that p, we do not with confidence reject $-p$ as false. In the case of knowledge, whether it bears on self-evident truths or, in the proper sense of the term, on mediated or inferred truths, the contradictory is determinately excluded. The object of opinion may also be arrived at as a conclusion from premises but the premises do not express evidence which is conclusive for the truth of p. No doubt there are degrees of opinion. Perhaps that is why doubt can be associated with opinion.

(3) When I doubt that p, I think that $-p$.

To think that $-p$ is not to be completely sure of $-p$ and thus to fear that p may be true. But this is not to say that in thinking that $-p$, I equally think that p. If the evidence indicates the truth of $-p$, I will doubt that p. To hold that p v $-p$ is not to have an opinion. A jury that reports that the accused is either innocent or guilty as charged has not delivered a verdict.

Perhaps this can suffice as a first sketch of "knowing that p," "thinking that p," and "doubting that p." For our purposes, knowing and opining are the important mental acts or states, since it is with reference to them that Aquinas will express what he means by "believing that p." It may be well to say here once and for all that Aquinas, like ourselves, often uses "thinking" or "opining" to express what is here defined as "knowing." So, too, he will often use "knowing" and "believing" interchangeably, and the same can be said of "believing" and "thinking." What we have just witnessed is his assigning definite meanings to these terms for a specific purpose. In doing this, he appeals to the way we talk, and he is guided by ordinary Latin as we should be by ordinary English, but he is not engaged in an effort to say what these terms ordinarily or always mean for all purposes. The fact that "think" and "know" and "believe" can be interchangeable in some contexts is, while true, not helpful when our purpose is to assign meanings to the terms which will distinguish *different* mental acts. It is the mental acts which differ even though we may sometimes speak of them in one way and sometimes in another. Once the difference between the mental acts is clarified, "know," "think," and "believe" can be given more or less technical meanings which will cause the remarks in which they occur to diverge slightly from ordinary talk.

Given his quasi-technical accounts of "knowing that p" and "thinking that p," St. Thomas adds his account of "believing that p."

(4) We believe that p is true and that -p is false on the basis of authority.

Given his definitions, Aquinas will argue for the following theses:

(5) It is impossible for a person simultaneously to know that p and to believe that p.
(6) It is impossible for a person simultaneously to think that p and to believe that p.

If "believing that p" differs from both "knowing that p" and "thinking that p," belief nonetheless bears similarities to both knowledge and opinion. In common with "knowing that p," "believing that p" totally excludes the possibility that -p might be true. To believe that p is true is to have no doubt that -p is false. In common with "thinking that p," "believing that p" is not grounded on conclusive evidence of the truth of p. For purposes of completeness, we can add that "believing that p" is unlike the "knowing that p" which occurs when the value of p is a self-evident truth.

If like "knowing that p," "believing that p" entails the falsity of -p, this is not because the believed p follows validly from true premises, nor is it because, as with "thinking that p," the preponderance of the evidence indicates the truth of p. I may think that Notre Dame will defeat Alabama; I may think that bald-headed males are more amorous than their hirsute confreres and in both cases marshal evidence to support my claim, even as I agree that one who maintains the contradictory is not willfully opaque, ignorant, obtuse, and so on. In the case of belief in the Trinity or Incarnation, it makes little sense to say that the evidence seems to indicate their truth. One's assent to the truth of p and rejection of -p as false is explained, in the case of belief, not by conclusive evidence, but by reliance on authority.

It will be seen that, in this discussion, St. Thomas is concerned to clarify the nature of religious belief. Nonetheless, we can get some help toward understanding the contrasts he is drawing by appealing to instances of belief which involve one man's trusting another. Let us say that, in conversation with you, I assert that p and you ask me why I say that. I answer that my Uncle Seymour told me that p. My assertion that p resides on the fact that I trust my Uncle Seymour. I did not mention him when I asserted that p, in the scenario I have in mind, but, if pressed, I would admit to the avuncular source of my confidence. Let us assign a value to p. Let us imagine that what I said was, "People who lay their ungloved hands on hot stoves get burned." When you ask why I say this, I bring in Uncle Seymour. Now I could be the empirical type and arrange for a hot stove and lay my ungloved hand on it. More cautiously, I could secrete myself in a broom closet and observe the reactions of others when they lay their ungloved hands on the hot stove. Then, when you ask me why I say that p, I need no longer bring in Uncle Seymour as explanation of my assertion. This situation can be generalized. The student of science, the specialist in a given area of science, may assert that p where the value of p is some scientific result and yet reply, when pressed, that he asserts that p because Professor Seymour said so or because he has just read an article in the *Alaskan Journal of Tropical Studies*. In such cases, believing that p is in principle replaceable by knowing that p. Trust or faith here, acceptance of p as true on the basis of authority, need not be a terminal mental act but only a stage on the way to knowledge. *Oportet addiscentem credere*, Aristotle said; the student must trust or believe, but not because that is his goal. His goal is knowledge.[3]

In the case of religious belief, believing that p is the acceptance of the truth of p (and the falsity of -p) on the authority of another and is, moreover, a mental state or attitude toward p that cannot, at least in this life, be replaced by knowing that p. When the believer asserts that there is a Trinity of Persons in the Godhead or that Christ is both God and man, the basis of his conviction is the authority of God. As St. Thomas put it, the formality under which assent is given to one side of a contradiction in the act of faith is *Deus revelans*: God revealing.[4]

The distinction between knowledge and opinion on the one hand,

---

3. The Aristotelian maxim is found in *On Sophistical Refutations* (161b3) and is often quoted by St. Thomas. For a citation of it in connection with our concerns here, see *ST*, IIaIIae, q. 2, a. 3, c.

4. Cf. *ST*, Ia, q. 1, a. 3, c.

and faith on the other, seems to come down to a distinction between evidence and motive. When I assert a self-evident truth, the evidence is intrinsic to the judgment made. When I assert a mediated truth, as I do in both knowledge and opinion, the grounds or evidence for what I assert is found elsewhere than in the proposition I assert. The elsewhere, of course, is the premises from which the proposition is derived as a conclusion. If the evidence, whether conclusive or probable, of the conclusion is said to be extrinsic to it, it is not extrinsic in the same way or to the same degree as is the motive for assent to a believed truth. My knowledge that the internal angles of a scalene triangle add up to 180° may be necessarily derived from other truths, and my opinion that life exists only on earth may be grounded on a great deal of information, but in both cases there is a connection between the proposition known or opined and the propositions which express the evidence from which it is concluded. One need only think of the relation between the terms of a syllogism. In the case of belief, the motivation for assent, namely the trustworthiness of the authority, is quite extrinsic to the content of the proposition believed.

As has already been seen, we can distinguish two sorts of belief, the ordinary kind in which we take another's word that something is the case and the extraordinary kind where our authority is God revealing. Let us use subscripts to distinguish them.

(4a)   When I believe$_1$ that p, I accept p as true on someone's say-so, but I can in principle establish the truth or probability of p and thus dispense with the appeal to someone's say-so.

(4b)   When I believe$_2$ that p, I accept p as true on God's authority, and I cannot, in this life, replace my dependence on his authority with knowing that p.

Values of p as the object of believing$_2$ would be such truths as "There are three persons in one divine nature," and "Christ has both a human and a divine nature." In believing$_1$, so long as my mental state is one of belief, I have a motive for assenting to or accepting a proposition as true, but I have no evidence for it. The same is true of believing$_2$ with the addendum that my condition is not even in principle corrigible or alterable in this life.

In the case of believing$_1$, when attention is shifted from the content of the proposition believed to be true to our motive for thinking so, we can of course inquire into our justification for thinking that so-and-so is trustworthy. It might be said that in trusting Uncle Seymour on the truth of p, we are believing both p and Uncle Seymour. St. Thomas will say that we believe someone and something. This does not preclude our having reasons for trusting our source. In the case of believing$_1$, that justification may be found in the fact that on many occasions in the past Uncle Seymour has told me things which I took on his say-so and subsequently found to be true on the basis of evidence. Thus, the scientist might give as justification for his taking as true what he reads in a learned journal the fact that often in the past he has established to his own satisfaction the truth of its reports. In believing$_1$, taking another's word can thus be seen to be an expedient, a *pis aller*, a corrigible condition, since in any given instance of it *p* can in principle be known. Of course, it would be practically impossible to prove out every claim accepted on the word of others in the scientific community, say, but this is a practical and not a theoretical constraint.[5]

The veracity or trustworthiness of the authority on whom we rely for our conviction of the truth of *p* when we believe$_2$ that *p* is a different matter. It would not do to suggest that, since divine revelation has proved its veracity in the case of the Trinity, I am justified in relying on it in the case of the Incarnation, or vice versa. All instances of believing$_2$ are on the same footing. We may wish to circumvent the problem in one fell swoop by saying that God is truth or God is veracious, and that therefore it makes no sense to doubt what God says. While any human witness is fallible and may mislead, God, being what and who He is, cannot deceive. The assertion that God can neither deceive nor be deceived enters into the Catechism's Act of Faith, and this suggests that the veracity of God is an object of faith, is itself within the circle of faith, and thus could not be external to it as a truth which might prop up or support the truths constitutive of faith. We cannot show that faith is reasonable by invoking what is itself an object of faith.[6]

These distinctions and clarifications of what St. Thomas means by

5. It is a simplification for present purposes to regard believing$_1$ as bearing on claims like scientific ones which are amenable to a proving procedure. Of course, it is anything but clear that all or most or indeed many of the humanly most significant examples of taking another's word fall under this rubric. See Chapter 16 below.

6. Signs, wonders, and miracles will occur to us as possible antecedents to the assent of faith; one who produces signs and wonders, who works miracles, gains our attention to what he says and his miracles may serve as motives for accepting as true the claims that he makes about himself. I am proceeding on the assumption that while a miracle or sign is observable by both the believer$_2$ and the unbeliever, the two interpret differently what they see. The believer interprets them as works of God, the unbeliever does not. My reasons are complex but can be suggested by the following: crowds saw and heard and witnessed Christ, yet not everyone believed. Of those who saw and heard and did not believe, we cannot say that witnessing works they recognized as divine they did not recognize them as divine. The reader is reminded of what Johannes Climacus says in *Philosophical Fragments*. For Thomas on this, see *ST*, IIaIIae, q. 6, a. 1.

knowing, opining, doubting, believing$_1$ and believing$_2$ are a necessary preliminary to understanding his conception of *praeambula fidei*. That phrase, we have seen, is taken to cover those truths about God which can be known by men independently of revelation. In other words, the truths covered by the phrase "preambles of faith" are possible objects of knowledge. The truths of faith are not, of course, possible objects of knowledge in this life.

Let us recall the thesis set down earlier that is taken to follow from the clarifications we have been examining.

(5) It is impossible for a person simultaneously to know that p and to believe that p.

Given the distinction that we have made between kinds or sorts of believing, this thesis can be construed in a number of ways. While the thesis as expressed in (5) is true of both believing$_1$ and believing$_2$, it can be restated with the types of believing in mind.

(5a) It is impossible for the same person simultaneously to know that p and to believe$_1$ that p.

The point of this restatement is to bring out the fact that objects of believing$_1$ can also be objects of knowledge. The teacher may know an astronomical truth and the pupil believe$_1$ the same truth on the teacher's say-so, the two mental acts bearing on the same truth at the same time. And, of course, the same person can believe$_1$ that p at t_1 and know that p at t_2. The thesis expressed in (5) can be restated for believing$_2$ as follows:

(5b) It is impossible for any man in this life to know that p if p is an object of believing$_2$.

This is the strongest form of the thesis. With it before us, let us select the following as examples of preambles of faith: there is a God, there is only one God. It is not our concern to give, if it could be given, a complete inventory of the preambles of faith. The ones we have mentioned are more than enough for our purposes.

We have already suggested the way to distinguish preambles of faith from truths of faith. The former are those truths about God which men can *know* in reliance on their natural powers alone; the latter are those truths God has revealed about himself, which could not otherwise be assented to, and which are accepted as true because He has revealed them, never because we know them to be true.[7] Relying on

---

7. Of course, we can know what is to be or is believed in the sense of being able to

Romans 1 : 19–20, St. Thomas, like many others before and after him, held that men can, from the visible things of this world, come to knowledge of the invisible things of God. At the very least, this means that the world provides evidence of the existence of God. Indeed, St. Thomas took Aristotle's proof from motion to be valid and conclusive. Thus, "God exists" can be a value for p in the schema: I know that p. But is not "God exists" an obvious value for p in the schema: I believe$_2$ that p? There would be no difficulty here if we were faced only with the thesis as expressed in (5), since that could be construed as in (5a). But is it not (5b) that comes into play, thus rendering St. Thomas's position incoherent?

To see how St. Thomas avoids contradicting himself, we must allow that the faith of the religious believer comprises both believing$_1$ and believing$_2$. That is, it seems to be a common state of affairs for the religious believer to accept on the authority of divine revelation both truths about God which are in principle knowable and truths about God which are not knowable in this life. One brought up in the faith would believe that there is a God, that there is only one God, that He is intelligent, etc., where the *et cetera* is meant to embrace any or all preambles of faith. But preambles of faith are by definition knowable in principle. Nor would the believer normally distinguish these from such other believe truths as the Trinity and Incarnation. But, if God's existence can be known, and if a believer comes to know it, he can no longer be said to believe this truth. If he knows that there is only one God, he can no longer believe it. The doctrine of preambles of faith comes down to this: among the things which the religious person believes there are some truths which are really objects of believing$_1$, although the bulk of the objects of his faith are objects of believing$_2$. Only the latter are *de fide*, of faith in the strict sense; the former are preambles of faith since they need not be believed, being in principle knowable. When this is recognized, there is no inconsistency in saying that one who first believed that there is a God comes to know that there is a God. (5a) applies to this situation; (5b) applies only to what is *de fide*.[8]

There are, of course, other ways of handling the difficulty. It might be said that the proposition "God exists" does not have the same va-

---

identify the claims, propositions, and so on. Not to know what one believes in this weak sense of 'know' is a possible human condition, and it is easy to imagine situations describable in that way. Nonetheless, this recognition-knowledge is not what is being denied when it is said that the believer does not know (understand) the proposition to which he gives his assent.

8. See note 1 above.

lence when it is the conclusion of a demonstration, and thus a philosophical achievement, that it has when it is an object of faith. Pascal distinguished the God of the philosophers from the God of Abraham and Isaac, suggesting that the God who is known is not the God who is believed.[9] The position may perhaps be developed in this way. It is clear from St. Thomas's presentation of the Five Ways that he does not think that "God exists" would ever as such appear as the conclusion of a proof. After each proof, he observes that what has been shown to exist is what we mean by God.[10] What functions as the subject of the conclusions of the proofs is a given description of God, e.g., first unmoved mover, first efficient cause, and so on. It is this variety of descriptions which makes a plurality of proofs of God's existence possible. We can now put the Pascalian point in this way: God is known to exist or is proved to exist under descriptions which differ from those self-descriptions God provides in revelation. Of particular interest for our purposes, one is reminded of Bonaventure's contention that one can simultaneously know and believe the same truth, for example, that God is one, a contention which seems to conflict with (5), (5a), and (5b). His subsequent exposition nonetheless makes clear that the object of simultaneous knowledge and belief is not really the identical object. If one can know and believe at the same time that God is one, Bonaventure interprets this to mean that one knows that there is not a plurality of gods and believes that the one God is a Trinity of Persons. Since "one" is taken in several senses, "there is one God" is not the same proposition as known and as believed.

We have interpreted Pascal's point about the God of the philosophers and the God of Abraham to mean that God is known under some descriptions and believed under quite different descriptions. We then suggest that Bonaventure's point about the simultaneity of knowledge and belief is a version of this, since the divine unity turns out to be two different descriptions insofar as it is an object of knowledge and an object of faith. While there is nothing wrong with this position as stated, it is questionable whether some of its assumptions are true. If we should say, for example, that the philosopher can come to know God as first cause (and Thomists who think Thomas granted Aristotle too much in interpreting the Stagirite as proving this, themselves go on to say that Thomas himself fashioned such a philosophical proof), it is difficult to see how knowing God in this way differs from what believers have believed of Him since their mother's knee.

9. See Romano Guardini, *Pascal for Our Time* (New York: 1966), pp. 113ff., and J. H. Broome, *Pascal* (New York: 1966), pp. 75ff.
10. See *ST*, Ia, q. 2, a. 3, c.

True, there are those who suggest that creation is a theological concept, apparently meaning by that, that apart from faith one could not grasp the total dependence of other things on God suggested by the phrase *creatio ex nihilo*.[11] While this contention, if true, would preserve the radical difference between knowledge and faith, the difference seems bought at too high a price. Indeed, it seems headed in the direction of saying that whatever philosophers claim to know about God is false.

Bonaventure's position is actually compatible with our own earlier suggestion to the effect that religious faith incorporates both believing$_1$ and believing$_2$ and that it is therefore possible that some believers who believed$_1$ that God is one, later came to know that God is one and it is the same truth which was once believed and later known.[12] That God is one in the sense that there cannot be a plurality of gods is a truth which could first be believed$_1$ and later known. There is, as it happens, an analogous situation in the moral order. Many truths of practice have been revealed which in principle need not have been because they are naturally knowable by men. One need only utter the phrase "Natural Law" to make the point, adding St. Thomas's view that precepts of the decalogue are natural law precepts.[13] God told men that murder is wrong, although this is something men can see apart from revelation. Moreover, it must be the same truth which is believed$_1$, accepted on the authority of God, and later known and thus no longer believed. While it is often misunderstood, the Catholic position on Natural Law is quite clear. Precepts which have been revealed and thus can be accepted on the authority of God revealing are, so far as their content goes, such that the divine authority is not necessary to grasp their truth. God told men that murder is wrong but it is not wrong because He said so and thus in insisting on the precept one is not demanding religious faith of everyone. Now, the same sort of thing would seem to be true of descriptions of God. We would make a shambles of the concept of precepts of faith if we should say that the objects of believing$_1$ differ from what men can in principle know. For

11. Thomas himself seems to hold, as in *De aeternitate mundi*, that it is creation in time and not creation *ex nihilo* which distinguishes the believer's understanding of the way in which divine causality is exercised from the mere philosopher's.

12. I have attempted a discussion of Bonaventure on this point, along with the major texts, which are found in his exposition of the *Sentences* of Peter Lombard, in *Philosophy from Augustine to Ockham*, which is vol. 2 of *A History of Western Philosophy* (Notre Dame: 1970), pp. 259–67. I coauthored this five-volume history of philosophy with my late colleague A. Robert Caponigri.

13. The point I am making here relies on putting together a number of texts from the *Summa theologiae*, IaIIae, namely, q. 90, q. 94, and q. 100, aa. 1–3.

this reason, the Pascalian point, unless it is restricted to believing$_2$, is unacceptable. With respect to some descriptions of God, the God of the philosophers and the God of believers (as believing$_1$) is the same. Of course none of this in any way contests the truth that the vast majority of the objects of religious faith are objects of believing$_2$.

The animus against the concept of preambles of faith, particularly as it is associated with the traditional natural theology, arises from the apparent connotations of the term "preamble." St. Thomas chose this term because he felt it expressed well the general maxim that grace presupposes nature, builds on it, and does not destroy it. He does not, of course, mean to suggest that the community of believers consists by and large of people who, having first acquired knowledge of God, that He is, is one, and so on, come to believe$_2$ truths that He has revealed of Himself. The fact is that revelation includes things knowable in principle as well as things that can never be known in this life and that ordinary religious believers do not as a rule distinguish the one kind of truth from the other. But if the concept of preambles of faith does not entail that natural theology is chronologically prior to faith in the strong sense, it does mean that some of the truths to which we have given our religious assent are knowable *in via* and thus can be seen to be objects of believing$_1$. Our condition relative to them is not unlike the belief of the scientist that certain claims he himself has not verified are nonetheless true. As for St. Thomas, it is abundantly clear that his contention that the objects of believing$_1$ can be replaced by knowledge in no way commits him to the thesis that, in this life, the objects of believing$_2$ can be known to be true.

Now we approach the most delicate matter of all. If some of the truths to which we have given the assent of faith can be known, what is the importance of this knowledge, when had, for those truths which are and remain *de fide*? It will be appreciated how easily the claim that men can come to know truths about God which they previously believed can be misunderstood if we have not distinguished believing$_1$ from believing$_2$. And yet, do we not want to say that believing$_2$ is affected in some way by the success of the program suggested by the phrase *praeambula fidei*? No doubt, but let us be clear as to how it is not affected. The fact that we can come to know a truth that we previously believed$_1$, for example, that there is a God, that He is one, in no way diminishes the necessity that the believer, be he wise or simple, accept as true, solely on the authority of God, the Trinity, the Incarnation, the Resurrection, the Forgiveness of Sins, and so forth. The most accomplished metaphysician is in exactly the same condition as the most unsophisticated sacristan with respect to what is *de fide*. What is more, and this is of crucial importance, knowing that there is a God, knowing that He is one, knowing any of the preambles of faith, does not entail any of the *de fide* truths. That accomplished metaphysician we mentioned may very well be a nonbeliever; his knowledge that there is a God does not compel him to believe₂ what God has revealed of Himself. It was Kierkegaard's unfounded fear that natural theology commits one to this absurdity. The mental state of believing₂ remains anomalous; in it the intellect is rendered captive in that its assent is gained, not because of the clarity and intelligibility, for us, of what is proposed, but by the promise of an eternal happiness if we will but restrain that hubris which demands that whatever is intelligible be seen to be so by us.[14] By definition, the believer does not know, does not understand, the truths to which he gives his assent. Is religious faith thereby irrational?

A negative answer to the question reposes on such considerations as the following. First, the believer believes that the truths to which he gives his assent are intelligible and make sense even though he does not see that they do. It is a false description of religious faith to say that it is the teleological acceptance of manifest nonsense. Second, the notion of preambles of faith gives indirect support to this conviction. If some of the things God has revealed can be known to be true, this suggests that the rest is intelligible, although it is not the case that what is and remains *de fide* can in any way be deduced or known from what is understood. And, of course, it is basic to faith that the believer hold that eventually, *in patria*, faith will give way to seeing. Again, no proponent of the absurdity or irrationality of faith has, to my knowledge, maintained that one truth of faith contradicts another truth of faith. Thus, internally to the body of believed truths, the basic demand of rationality, the principle of contradiction, is honored. St. Thomas held further that nothing we know to be true can be in conflict with what we believe₂ to be true. If this is itself a truth of faith, it is also a program for the theological task, or at least a part of it. Indeed, we can find here one of the motives for the interest the community of believers has always taken in the task of natural theology. It is not that a proof of God's existence is direct support for truths of faith in the strong sense. But if God is known to exist, one impediment to accepting that He has revealed truths about Himself is removed. Nor could

14. In Chapter 16, I have argued for the compatibility of the views of Thomas and the Kierkegaard of *Philosophical Fragments*. Knowing the truth of the proposition that there is a God in no way commits one to the acceptance of truths about God which cannot be known, but if we knew the falsity of the proposition that there is a God, this would have devastating effects on all truths of faith.

the community of believers ignore claims that it is nonsense to assert that there is a God. Believed$_2$ truths cannot be derived from truths known about God but, negatively, if it were known that there is not a God, believed$_2$ truths would *eo ipso* be destroyed. A God known not to exist cannot reveal truths about Himself.

As for attacks on faith proper, St. Thomas maintained that the theologian could either refute the attack or, if that be impossible in the strong sense of refutation, he can at least show that the attack is not compelling, necessary, cogent. This seems to allow for cases where evidence would tell against a truth of faith, although the evidence would not be conclusive.[15] I think it is clear that none of these activities would make any sense if religious faith were indifferent to rationality, if it were indeed a leap into the manifestly absurd entailing a general devaluation of reason and logic. Nevertheless, there is much truth in the Kierkegaardian description of faith as a crucifixion of the understanding. Faith is humbling for one who honors the demands of reason as themselves deriving from God and yet assents to truths which he does not understand but holds to be in themselves understandable.

Our discussion has suggested the all but identical views of Aquinas and Bonaventure and, so far as the matters discussed go, in the way we have discussed them, this is accurate enough. Nonetheless, it would be misleading in the extreme to leave the impression that Thomas and Bonaventure were of one mind on the relation between faith and philosophy. It has been said that the Bonaventure of the commentary on the *Sentences* of Peter Lombard, an early work which reflects the saint's brief university career, must not be identified with the man who, shortly after receiving his chair of theology at Paris, was elected Master General of the Franciscans and eventually became a cardinal.[16] The writings of Bonaventure which reflect his pastoral concerns see Aristotle not as the apotheosis of natural reason but as an antagonist, an enemy of the faith. Were we to take three positions which were either held by Aristotle or thought to be held by him, namely, the eternity of the world, the unicity of the agent intellect with its consequences for personal immortality and, finally, the description of the

15. On these various tasks of the theologian, see, for example, Thomas's exposition of Boethius's *De trinitate*, q. 2, a. 3.

16. For the many and diverse differences between Thomas and Bonaventure, see Fernand Van Steenberghen, *La philosophie au XIIIe siècle* (Louvain: 1966); Joseph Ratzinger, *The Theology of History in St. Bonaventure* (Chicago: 1971), pp. 119ff. Here, as in so many other instances, the work of Etienne Gilson has been seminal. A late expression of his interpretation can be found in *A History of Christian Philosophy in the Middle Ages* (New York: 1955). My own modest contribution can be found in the book cited in note 12.

divine knowledge as thought thinking itself with the implication that God knows only Himself with obvious consequences for the notion of Providence, we could exhibit the differences between Thomas and Bonaventure in a striking way. Thomas, confronted with such difficulties, is first of all concerned to see what exactly, behind the filigree of the Islamic commentaries, Aristotle meant and, given that, whether it is indeed inimical to the faith. On all three points, he ends with an interpretation of Aristotle which makes the great pagan philosopher compatible with Christian belief. I myself reject the view that he was either consciously or actually reading Aristotle wrong when he did this. Others, alas, hold that Aristotle did not say what Thomas takes him to say on these matters and that Thomas either knew this but interpreted him "genially" or did not know it and was simply wrong. A surprising number of Thomas's defenders portray him as wrenching texts to his own fleeting advantage. My reading of the *De unitate intellectus* and the *De aeternitate mundi* prevents me from finding this devious explicator.

Bonaventure, confronted with the three difficulties mentioned, is quite willing to assume that Aristotle said what he is said to have said and that what he said is incompatible with the faith. From this enormous difference in antecedent attitude toward the most impressive representative of philosophy known to the two men flow a great many other differences. But that is another and lengthy discussion.

11

SCOTUS AND UNIVOCITY

This paper actually has more to do with Aquinas than with Scotus and more to do with analogy than with univocity. I am not particularly embarrassed by this in the present gathering since, as we all know, the Scotistic doctrine of the univocity of being has been discussed, more often than not, with reference to the apparently opposed Thomistic tenet that being is analogous and cannot be univocal. There is nothing particularly novel in the suggestion that Scotus and Aquinas are only apparently at odds here; indeed, we are no longer surprised to find that it is the Thomist who suggests this. The reconciliation is accomplished in a number of ways. We are told that Scotus was opposing himself to Henry of Ghent rather than to Thomas and that once this is recognized, the difference between Scotus and Aquinas is diminished if it does not disappear. Or, we are told that the opposition between Scotistic univocity and Thomistic analogy is developed in terms of a notion of analogy which is Cardinal Cajetan's rather than that of Aquinas himself. This sort of thing is familiar enough and there is no need to repeat it here. I am not wholly convinced by the attempts at reconciliation I have seen, but I do not propose to develop my own thoughts with close reference to those attempts. Rather I want to recall briefly Scotus's reasons for asserting that being is univocal with respect to God and creature, with respect to the various modes of being and, having done this, I want to ask whether St. Thomas's doctrine of analogy, as I understand it, can handle the difficulties Scotus sees. Finally, I will offer a few tentative remarks about a reconciliation of Scotus and Aquinas on the community of being.

Speaking as simple disciples of the Subtle Doctor, we can bring the force of Scotus's several arguments in favor of a univocal concept of God and creature [1] to a focus in the following statement. Granted that

---

1. *Ordinatio*, I, d. 3, nn. 26–38.

God is infinite being and the creature a finite being, there must be a first and preliminary way in which we know God as a being and the creature as a being in which *being* prescinds from these different modes and expresses only what God and creature have in common. If there were no minimal common meaning of the term *being*, we could not argue to the existence of God without committing the fallacy of equivocation. The term *being* expresses either a perfection common to God and creature, or a perfection proper to creatures, or a perfection proper to God. If either of the last two possibilities is entertained, we seem to be prevented from speaking of God at all. To choose the first possibility, that is, to maintain that God and creature share a perfection meant by the term *being*, is to accept the Scotistic doctrine of univocity:

Et ne fiat contentio de nomine univocationis, univocum conceptum dico, qui ita est unus quod eius unitas sufficit ad contradictionem, affirmando et negando ipsum de eodem; sufficit etiam pro medio syllogistico, ut extrema unita in medio sic uno sine fallacia aequivocationis concludantur inter se uniri.[2]

Scotus gives a succinct statement of his position by sketching the normal route of any metaphysical inquiry:

Omnis inquisitio metaphysica de Deo sic procedit, considerando formalem rationem alicuius et auferendo ab illa ratione formali imperfectionem quam habet in creaturis, et reservando illam rationem formalem et attribuendo sibi omnino summam perfectionem, et sic attribuendo illud Deo. Exemplum de formali ratione sapientiae (vel intellectus) vel voluntatis: consideratur enim in se et secundum se; et ex hoc quod ista ratio non concludit formaliter imperfectionem aliquam nec limitationem, removentur ab ipsa imperfectiones quae concomitantur eam in creaturis, et reservata eadem ratione sapientiae et voluntatis attribuuntur ista Deo perfectissime. Ergo omnis inquisitio de Deo supponit intellectum habere conceptum eundem, univocum, quem accepit ex creaturis.[3]

There are certain perfections which are first encountered in creatures and therefore in a finite mode; the name signifying such perfections can be taken as signifying that perfection in abstraction from the creaturely or any other mode and, so taken, it is predicable univocally of creatures and God, both of whom possess the perfection in question. Preeminent among such words would be that of *being* and Scotus may be taken to hold that the term *being* signifies a perfection distinct from the creaturely or divine modes of possessing it and that, thanks

2. Ibid., n. 26.
3. Ibid., n. 39.

to this, there is a way of understanding the term *being* which makes it predicable univocally of God and creature.

Aquinas follows a not dissimilar procedure in speaking of the meaning of certain divine attributes as well as in speaking of the meaning of *being* as attributed to or predicated of God. However, where Scotus speaks of univocity, Aquinas speaks of analogy and, if we were to hold ourselves simply to the two descriptions of univocity given by Scotus and quoted above, we could effectively identify Scotist univocity and Thomistic analogy. The analogous term, for Aquinas, is sufficiently determinate in meaning to give rise to contradictory propositions and it is sufficiently one to function as the middle term in a syllogism. But since the univocal term also possesses these characteristics, Aquinas would regard them as necessary and not sufficient characteristics of the analogous term. Therefore, one swift and cheap way of reconciling Scotus and Aquinas must be foregone, since it would do credit to neither man. Rather, we must ask if analogy, as Aquinas understands it, involves the common core of which Scotus speaks and, if it does, why Aquinas did not say, as Scotus will, that a term involving such a common core is univocal.

I do not propose to bore you by recalling the well-known features of Aquinas's doctrine of analogous terms. Suffice it to say that we are faced here with a subdivision within a doctrine of naming which arose, against an Aristotelian background, from the assumption that when we speak we are expressing what we know and that one element of speech is the name or noun. The Thomistic doctrine of naming is triadic, involving as it does the *vox*, the *ratio* and the *res*, or verbal expression, mental concept and extra-mental entity to which reference is made by the word through the mental conception. There are, of course, all kinds of difficulties with this doctrine and there would be no hope of handling even a modest number of them here. Analogous names fall within a broader context of a view on the community or predicability of names. Some names are predicable of several things in such a way that they preserve the same meaning in each use; that is Aquinas's understanding of the univocal term. Some names are used of several things but in each use their meanings are quite different; that, of course, is Aquinas's understanding of equivocal or ambiguous terms. The analogous term, in the well-worn phrase, lies midway between the univocal and equivocal term. It does so because there is a common core of meaning but in order to understand this, we must see something of Aquinas's conception of the *ratio nominis*.

What the name principally signifies or means is the mental concept or *ratio* and this, Aquinas holds, is always complex. A frequent way in which he expresses this complexity proceeds in terms of *res significata*, *modus significandi*. The *res significata* of the name is the perfection from which the name is imposed to signify, the formality or actuality or distinguishing characteristic we have in mind when we use this name as opposed to that. In univocal predication, not only does the name have the same *res significata*, it also signifies that perfection in the same way, i.e., it has the same *modus significandi*. The equivocal term is one which, when used, is understood to mean a plurality of *res significatae*. Now, it goes without saying that, when we speak of the "same name" in talking of univocity and equivocity, we are thinking of *several uses* of the same name, just as Scotus, in his two descriptions of univocity, refers in effect to several occurrences of the same term as, e.g., in more than one proposition of the syllogism. The same is true of the analogous term. We may consider the discussion to arise against the background of two sentences: God is wise, Man is wise; or, God is, Socrates is. Of such statements, we say that they have the same predicate and in trying to determine whether the term is univocal, equivocal or analogous, we are in effect asking whether the same term means exactly the same thing, utterly different things or the same thing in a modified way in these various occurrences.

Now, in order to see the force of the Scotist contention of univocity of being, we can look first of all at the most frequent example of an analogous term in Aquinas, namely *healthy*. The discussion proceeds against the background of multiple use. It occurs to us that we say, or hear said, that dogs are healthy, food is healthy, urine is healthy, etc., and we want to know what *healthy* means in those various occurrences. Scotus can be imagined as saying that in all these occurrences, whatever differences we may later want to point out, *healthy* has the core meaning of health. Understood as signifying only that *res significata* and prescinding from the various ways in which that perfection is signified, why can't we say that *healthy* is a univocal term in the instances cited or, more exactly in Scotus's words, that healthy is a univocal concept thanks to the core perfection of health?

What we are brought to by these considerations is the Thomistic view that there is a *ratio communis* of the analogous name. Aquinas, like Scotus, felt that there is a familiar and obvious meaning of terms according to which they embody a creaturely mode—at least when we are speaking of some terms that are common to God and creature. Sometimes Aquinas speaks of that familiar meaning of the common term as the *ratio propria*; it is the "per prius secundum impositionem

nominis." Sometimes, the *ratio propria* of the analogous term is constituted by the ontologically most perfect way of possessing the *res significata* of the common name. This shift is what underlies Aquinas's
apparent vacillation between saying, on the one hand, that created perfection is the *per prius* of a name common to God and creature and, on
the other, that the divine perfection is the *per prius* of such names.
Now this seems to lead to something that Scotus resisted mightily,
namely that an analogous term as signifying several similar concepts
suffices for passing from creature to God. He wants terms common to
God and creature to possess a core of meaning thanks to which there
is one concept, a univocal concept. Isn't he opposed to Aquinas on this
score?

In one sense, there is certainly opposition. Aquinas will speak of an
analogously common name as signifying a range of *rationes*, as having
different meanings, which meanings are related *per prius et posterius*.
Thus the analogously common term *being* signifies either the substantial or accidental mode of being, but the first principally, the second
secondarily and with reference to the first. We seem to have, accordingly, many concepts analogous or similar to one another. Let us look
somewhat more closely at this business of a common term signifying
many *rationes* related *per prius et posterius*.

In the case of *healthy*, again, the *res significata* of the term is health
which is, let us say, a proportion of the humors. Some things called
healthy possess health as a quality; other things called healthy cause
that quality in entities susceptible of it; yet other things are signs of
that quality in things susceptible of it. In all uses of *healthy*, therefore,
we have meanings which include as their *res significata* the quality,
health. However, and this is Aquinas's main point and, I fear, his ir-
reconcilable difference from Scotus, the various things called healthy
do not relate to the quality or *res significata* equally or in the same way.
It would be impossible to explain the way in which urine is said to be
healthy without making reference to the way in which animals are
called healthy, *but the reverse is not true*. In short, there is a privileged
meaning of *healthy* and this privileged meaning is what Aquinas means
by the *ratio propria* of the term.

There is, nonetheless, provision made by Aquinas for a *ratio communis* of the analogous term. The *ratio communis entis* is variously expressed by Aquinas as *quod est, quod habet esse* or *habens esse*. I have elsewhere suggested that it is possible to regard such a *ratio communis*
along the lines of a propositional function, that is, as '. . . *esse*', where
the blank can be filled in with the modes of being, one of which is primary and privileged, namely, that of substance: "id quod debet esse in

se et non in alio." So too, despite Cajetan, it is possible to formulate a *ratio communis* of healthy: what relates in any way to health. This kind of talk requires that we see that the "blank" in the *ratio communis* may be filled in a variety of ways or modes and that, when this is done, we have a plurality of *rationes* related *per prius et posterius*.

Against the background of this hurried and unsatisfactory sketch, what can we say of the possibility of reconciling Scotus and Aquinas on the community of being? They are certainly in agreement on this, that in the statements "God is wise" and "Socrates is wise," *wise* possesses a common core, what Aquinas calls the *res significata*. Where perhaps they differ, and irreconcilably, is in this, that Scotus speaks as if such a term as *wise* could be taken to mean only the *res significata* and that it must be so taken in the examples given. Aquinas, on the other hand, would maintain that a name always involves in its meaning both a *res significata* and a *modus significandi*. It is that conviction which underlies his melancholy reminder that, in any effort of ours to speak of God, "omne nomen cum defectu est."

12

A NOTE ON THOMISTIC EXISTENTIALISM

According to the traditional order of learning, First Philosophy or metaphysics is said to be last for us. However, although St. Thomas sets down this order in several places,[1] many contemporary Thomists[2] feel that the order of learning does not apply to the doctrine of St. Thomas himself and that in learning that doctrine we can begin with metaphysics. The texts in which St. Thomas gives us this order of learning are dispensed with as either observations about Aristotelianism, or as commentaries on a passing historical situation. There are two ways in which one can deal with this position. First, one might defend the order of learning as something consequent upon the nature of our intellect and the objects of the various sciences. Secondly— and this is the purpose of the present paper—one can examine the underlying tenet which prompts the rejection of the traditional order of learning. The presupposition of that rejection is that the philosophy of St. Thomas, as distinguished from that of Aristotle, is an existentialism.

It is being said with increasing frequency that the metaphysics of St. Thomas began after long reflection on the remark in Exodus where God refers to Himself as "He Who is." The saint was then led to see the primacy of the act of existence and accordingly his metaphysics is existential, whereas that of Aristotle, who never had an opportunity to read Exodus, is a sterile essentialism. Now first of all, it is obvious that revealed statements do not, as revealed, yield conclusions in a naturally acquired science. Secondly, although revealed truth can serve as an extrinsic guide for the philosopher, it would never dictate an order

---

1. *In VI Ethic.* (ed. Spiazzi), lect. 7, n. 1211; *In librum de causis* (ed. Saffrey), proemium; *In Boethii de trin.* (ed. Calcaterra), n. 3; q. 5, a. 1, ad 9.
2. Cf. G. P. Klubertanz, "The Teaching of Thomistic Metaphysics," *Gregorianum* 35 (1954), pp. 3–17 and 187–205.

other than the natural one. Thirdly, no subalternation of the known types, according to principles, subject or end, is possible.

1. A CONTROVERSIAL TEXT

The text most frequently invoked in support of the alleged existentialism of St. Thomas is *In Boethii de trinitate*, q. 5, a. 3,[3] where we find discussed the various degrees of removal from matter proper to each of the speculative sciences. This being the third article of a question which proposes to show the division of the speculative sciences, it seems only fitting that it be read in the context of the preceding articles.

Having made the preliminary distinction between speculative and practical science by a consideration of their respective ends and objects, St. Thomas observes that the object of the speculative faculty, the *speculabile*, possesses two properties, immateriality and necessity, the first of which is due to the knowing power, the second to the exigencies of the habit of science. Since this is so, *speculabilia* will be distinguished according as they are removed by varying degrees from motion (opposed to the necessity required by science) and from matter (opposed to the immateriality required for intellection).

There follows the familiar doctrine on the three degrees of removal from matter.[4] Certain things require matter both in order to exist and in order to be understood, but are understood as having common sensible matter and not individuating matter. Other *speculabilia* require matter in order to exist, but can be understood without sensible matter for reasons to be given in article three. Finally, there are *speculabilia* which are separated from matter in existence as well as in being understood, but these are two kinds. Either they never exist in matter, as God and the angels, or they do not necessarily exist in matter, sometimes doing so and sometimes not, such as substance, quality, potency and act, the one and many, and the like. It is to be noted that St. Thomas speaks of these three levels as kinds of separation from matter:[5] *separatio* receives a proper signification in article 3, but even there remains an analogical name.

From these fairly universal and common considerations St. Thomas turns in the following articles to a more particular determination of

---

3. I follow the edition of Paul Wyser (Fribourg, 1948).

4. *In de sensu et sensato*, lect. 1, n. 1; *ST*, Ia, q. 85, a. 1, ad 2.

5. "Sic ergo speculabili . . . per se competit *separatio* a materia et motu, vel applicatio ad ea."—op. cit., a. 1, c.

each of the speculative sciences. Thus, in article 2 it is a question of the philosophy of nature and of precisely how its object is removed from matter and motion. We are rendered attentive by an allusion to the difficulty of the question and to the errors to which the inability to resolve it has led. We are shown the differences here, in a determinate fashion, between matter as it enters into the definitions of the philosopher of nature, and matter as it individuates existing mobile things. In the body of the article and in the answer to the fourth objection, St. Thomas introduces the necessary distinction between the object of science as the universal ratio (*res scita*) and the universal as the means of knowing (*ut medio sciendi*) the particular mobile things by a reflexive act of thought, a return to the phantasm.

In article 3 St. Thomas sets about explaining the abstraction or separation or distinction peculiar to mathematics whereby the *speculabile* is understood without matter although, when it exists, it exists in matter.[6] It is of paramount importance to show that such an abstraction is not mendacious.[7] St. Thomas begins by noting that our intellect can abstract in various ways following on its two-fold operation. According to the first operation, simple apprehension, it can distinguish by removing from matter: it can separate things which are conjoined in reality, and this precisely because it is the first operation and does not claim that what it is knowing actually exists in this abstract mode. Formal truth is had only in the second operation, composing and dividing. By the first operation we can distinguish or separate in two ways: (a) by abstracting the whole from its parts, the universal from particulars, or (b) the form—not, be it noted, substantial form—from its matter. The philosophy of nature, and indeed every science, proceeds in the first way; mathematics proceeds in the second way, abstracting the accidental form of quantity from sensible matter. Accidents inhere in substance following a definite order, first quantity, then the qualities, etc. Therefore, we can consider substance as quantified while ignoring sensible matter.

The two kinds of abstraction which follow on the first operation of the mind are said to consider the nature or quiddity; the separation which follows on the second operation of the mind is said to look to the very existence of the thing. It is precisely here that some rather novel interpretations of the genesis of metaphysics have arisen.[8]

6. Thus "mathematica non sint bona." Cf. *Q. D. de ver.*, q. 21, a. 2, ad 4.
7. *In Boethii de trin.*, q. 5, a. 3, ad 1; *In II Physic.*, lect. 3 (ed. Pirotta), nn. 330–33; *ST*, Ia, q. 85, a. 1, ad 1.
8. Cf. Marie-Vincent Leroy, Annexe to "Le savoir speculatif," *Revue thomiste*, Maritain volume, p. 335.

2. THE EXISTENTIAL INTERPRETATION

What St. Thomas is saying, we are told, is that the mind is separating by a negative judgment the act of existence from the nature or essence of material things, i.e. arriving at knowledge of the real distinction, and with this metaphysics begins. Armed with this interpretation, it has seemed possible to some to reject the order of learning the philosophical sciences. That order, it seems, is true perhaps of Aristotelian or Avicennian philosophy, but not applicable to the existential philosophy of the Angelic Doctor himself. Such a reading of this passage, aside from the difficulties involved in maintaining that philosophy begins with metaphysics and metaphysics with a recognition of the real distinction, most certainly does violence to the context. Article 3, far from repudiating the doctrine on the acquisition of the sciences, presupposes it and has no meaning aside from it.

We are reading an article which, in the context of the question, is concerned with the way in which the various *speculabilia* are separated from matter. The judgment of separation is the distinction from matter that constitutes the *speculabile* which is the object of metaphysics; it is a judgment that the *speculabilia* of metaphysics are removed from all matter, common sensible, and intelligible, and this not only in the order of understanding, but also in the order of existence.[9] This can only mean that when one is equipped to make a judgment that there are certain things which not only are understood without matter and motion, but can actually exist apart, metaphysics can begin. It is because of certain conclusions reached in the philosophy of nature that one is justified in making the judgment of separation.[10]

This interpretation, which is the obvious one, is the cause of unrest among existential Thomists; they find in this text a deeper, less Aristotelian meaning. For them, the judgment of separation is a distinction between essence and existence. The recognition of the real distinction, accordingly, is the beginning of metaphysics, and it can be had independently of the philosophy of nature. Moreover, it would seem that the real distinction is grasped is some intuitive manner and is not the fruit of any demonstration; hence, the first demonstration of all philosophy would, in this existential view, conclude to the exis-

---

9. "Substantia autem, quae est materia intelligibilis quantitatis, potest *esse* sine quantitate. Unde considerare substantiam sine quantitate magis pertinet ad genus separationis quam abstractionis."—*In Boethii de trin.*, q. 5, a. 3; cf. *Q. D. de spiritualibus creaturis*, a. 1, ad 10 and ad 23.

10. Cf. *In IV Metaphysic.*, lect. 5, n. 593; ibid., lect. 13, n. 690; lect. 17, n. 748; *In XII Metaphysic.*, lect. 6, n. 2517.

tence of God. Surely this exhibits a Cartesian penchant which would tailor reality to the measure of man; the priority of metaphysics becomes a priority for us, and there would seem to be no reason other than subjective indisposition or preoccupation to prevent any man's becoming a metaphysician at one fell blow. And not only is the traditional order of learning being rejected; metaphysics itself is altered beyond recognition. Far from being a science which moves laboriously toward knowledge of separated substance, it begins with the proof of the *Actus Purus*, of the *Esse Subsistens*. What is of present interest is the fact that appeal is made to *In Boethii de trinitate*, q. 5, a. 3, for support of the contention that metaphysics begins with the recognition of the real distinction between essence and existence. What are the implications of this interpretation?

The judgment of separation is a judgment that what is separated can *exist* apart from all matter and motion. If this judgment were that of the real distinction between essence and existence, it could only mean that either the essence of this material thing, or its existence, can exist apart from all matter and motion. Certainly, St. Thomas is not telling us that the existence of material things can exist apart; the very redundancy of "exist" is a material warning against this interpretation. And, with regard to essence, if one should say that the human soul is subsistent and thus can exist apart from the body, we need only point out that this is a truth which is proved in the philosophy of nature, and that therefore the judgment of separation presupposes certain proofs from prior sciences. Q.E.D. But, should it be said that reflection on the notion of existence must convince us that it can be separated from essence, or at least that it need not only be found as the act of a material essence, even granting that such a sophisticated consideration could be indulged in at the beginning of the philosophical life, we note that the implication of this objection is that *ens inquantum ens* is synonymous with existence qua existence. For what we are separating is the subject of metaphysics. If this separation is said to be the separation of existence from essence, existence alone would be the subject of metaphysics. Being is defined, however, as *id quod habet esse*: a whole—essence and existence.

3. THE REAL DISTINCTION—LOGICAL OR METAPHYSICAL?

With regard to the initial assumption that the real distinction between essence and existence is *per se nota*, we observe that any distinction presupposes knowledge of the terms to be distinguished. But what possible meaning can essence have for one who is embarking on the philosophical way? Certainly we could assume nothing more than a merely nominal grasp of what is designated. In other words, no account is being taken of the difference between essence as "whatness," object of definition, and essence as substance, the prime subject of metaphysics and the subject of existence. The two are by no means synonymous, unless we want to identify our mode of understanding with the mode of being *in rerum natura*. It is true that it is precisely by way of an analysis of essence as expressed by the definition that we arrive, in metaphysics, at the notion of essence as substance. In any other science, such a mode of procedure would be dialectical, but for metaphysics it is a proper mode.[11] It is of course the kind of discussion to be found in the seventh book of the *Metaphysics*; however, a careful distinction is always retained between the logical intention and the existing substance.

That there can only be a nominal understanding of essence at the beginning of philosophy can be shown from a consideration drawn from logic concerning the questions which are asked with regard to the incomplex term. We first ask *an sit*, and then *quid sit*. This is the scientific approach, for we do not seek the essence of something which is not known to exist; only existing things, indeed, properly speaking, only existing substances have essences.[12] Our quidditative definitions, it follows, are of real existent things. But what of the notions we have of non-being, of chimeras, etc.? Is not some kind of definition presupposed by the question *an sit*, since we are not inquiring into existence *tout court*, but whether some thing exists? Precisely, and what precedes the question is knowledge of the *quid est quod dicitur*, a nominal definition which does not necessarily designate anything in reality.[13] What then would be the initial knowledge of the real distinction between essence and existence? Surely the real distinction is between what responds to the question *an sit* and what responds to the question *quid sit*, but the reply to this second question is rather hard to come by, and determinate knowledge of existence as an act must await that reply. Would, then, the alleged initial knowledge of the real distinction be a distinction, not between essence and existence, but between two questions, *an sit* and *quid sit*? If this is the case, as it must be, any immediate leap to the conclusion that God exists is clearly precluded. Either this is what is meant by the initial recognition of the real distinction or,

---

11. Cf. *In Boethii de trin.*, q. 6, a. 1; *In I Post. Analytic.*, lect. 20, n. 5.

12. *In II Post. Analytic.*, lect. 6; *In VII Metaphysic.*, lect. 3.

13. *In Boethii de trin.*, q. 6, a. 3; *In II Post. Analytic.*, lect. 1, nn. 5−6; lect. 6, n. 4.

even more crudely, it would be a distinction between the *quid est quod dicitur* and the *an sit*. In neither case do we have knowledge of essence as substance, essence in the real order, which is the basis for the real distinction. The above two possibilities are the only "real distinctions" had at the beginning of metaphysics which have an intelligible meaning in the light of the doctrine of St. Thomas.

Is it not only after the lengthy discussion in Book VII of the *Metaphysics* which leans so heavily on the logic of definition, and after Book VIII where these notions are applied to the real order, and after the treatment of act and potency in Book IX, that the metaphysician finds himself equipped to treat of the real distinction between essence and existence? Only at that point does essence have the meaning it must have if the real distinction is to be intelligible; only at that point are we armed with the doctrine which enables us to speak of the act of existence.

4. THE AMBIGUITY OF EXISTENTIALISM

There is another danger latent in the *soi-disant* existential approach, a danger which has its source in the recognition that God is He Who is, and that *esse* is the first of all created perfections.[14] For although whatever we know about a thing is grounded in the fact that it exists or has some relation, positive or negative, to existence, and although the most proper name we can have of God is *Qui est*, we must beware of erecting that which is most perfect *secundum quid* into the most perfect *simpliciter*. Surely the very least we can know of a material thing is that it is: once this is gained we are but on the threshold of scientific knowledge. There is a dangerous ambiguity in the notion of "existential knowledge," for it may seem to mean only an affirmative answer to the question *an est*. It is not because we "take existence frivolously for granted" that we plunge immediately ahead to the question that asks what a thing is; rather it is because we want to know what it means for this thing to exist. This is by no means to identify essence and existence; rather it is to affirm that simply to know that a thing is, is to know next to nothing about it.

Moreover, there is much to learn from reading St. Thomas's statements as to why "He Who is" is the most perfect name of God. Does he not say that it is precisely because our knowledge of God is inadequate and imperfect that this name, which signifies indeterminately,

14. *Q. D. de pot.*, q. 7, a. 2, ad 9; *In librum de causis*, prop. 4a.

responds to the knowledge we have? [15] Thus the very perfection of the name can be seen as a commentary on the imperfection of our knowledge. Since this is so, the ambiguity of "existential knowledge" is set into relief and we become aware that it could quite easily mean putting a premium on imperfect knowledge. Is this why metaphysics is so easy for existential Thomists? They are content with what would appear to be nominal or dialectical knowledge. And again, the parallel does not seem forced when we recall that Descartes assumed that he knew *what* the soul and motion were simply because he was certain *that* they were. We are all reasonably certain that things exist: this is the beginning and not the end of inquiry.

5. CONCLUSION

There is no basis in *In Boethii de trinitate*, q. 5, a. 3 for a rejection of the traditional order of learning, nor for the contention that St. Thomas teaches that metaphysics begins with a recognition of the real distinction. There is, then, no shortcut to wisdom; the judgment of separation, and thus metaphysics itself, becomes possible only after certain demonstrations had in the philosophy of nature.

What we have been saying is not a denial of the importance of the real distinction between essence and existence for Thomistic thought. Rather, it is meant to be a safeguard of the meaningfulness of that distinction, for it makes it a piece of knowledge which must be earned. It should be realized that the real distinction is not the answer to every question raised in philosophy, a crude procrustean bed on which to measure every thought. There are other questions and other answers, and unless they are first dealt with, metaphysics will become either an aesthetic experience or a science more charismatic than acquired.

15. *ST*, Ia, q. 13, a. 11; *In I Sent.*, d. 8, q. 1, a. 1; *Q. D. de pot.*, q. 7, a. 5; q. 10, a. 1, ad 9.

13

BEING AND PREDICATION

A.

Recently the nature of the so-called existential proposition has been the object of renewed discussion among logicians as well as metaphysicians. I say "renewed" because, as is recognized by at least some contemporary disputants, the problems involved have long been recognized. It is not surprising, then, that Thomists should feel moved to bring to the attention of others the thought of St. Thomas on existential propositions. Indeed those who profess to see in the metaphysics of St. Thomas a kind of existentialism have been especially drawn to his views on this matter and purport to find in his remarks a basis for some rather startling statements about the concept of being. In this paper I propose to consider some of the relevant passages in St. Thomas as well as an influential existential interpretation of them. I take it that this consideration will lay bare a number of historical inaccuracies and doctrinal flaws in "Thomistic Existentialism."

1. The Existential Proposition

It is not surprising that it is in his commentary on Aristotle's *De interpretatione* that St. Thomas speaks of what is called the existential proposition. In the course of a comparison of enunciations which include an "infinite noun," Aristotle distinguishes those in which *is* is predicated as *tertium adiacens* from others in which it is not.[1] *Is* is a *tertium* when it attaches to a noun or verb, e.g., "Socrates is just." Opposed to such enunciations are others, e.g., "Socrates is." In the latter kind, *is* is the principal predicate. In "Socrates is just," *is* is not the principal predicate but, together with *just*, forms one predicate.

---

1. *De interpretatione*, 10.19b19–22: "When the verb 'is' is used as a third element (*tertium adiacens*) in the sentence, there can be positive and negative propositions of two sorts. Thus in the sentence 'man is just' the verb is used as a third element, call it verb or noun, which you will" (Oxford translation).

With regard to the first [i.e., that when the verb "is" is used as a third element in the sentence, there can be positive and negative propositions of two sorts], two things must be understood.

The first of these is the meaning of his [Aristotle's] statement, '*Is* is predicated as a third element [*tertium adiacens*].' To understand this one must consider that the verb *is* is sometimes predicated in an enunciation according to itself, as when it is stated, *Socrates is*—by which we intend to signify no more than that Socrates exists in reality [*in rerum natura*].

But sometimes *is* is not predicated *per se* as though the principal predicate, but as though conjoined to the principal predicate in order to connect it to the subject, as when it is stated, *Socrates is white*, it is not the intention of the one speaking to assert Socrates to be in reality, but to attribute whiteness to him through the intermediary of this verb *is*. And therefore in such cases *is* is predicated as adjacent to the principal predicate.[2]

From this passage it is clear that in "Socrates is," *is* is the predicate; the existential proposition, like any other simple enunciation, is composed of a noun and a verb, a subject and a predicate. In propositions in which *is* is a *tertium adiacens* there are not two predicates but one, e.g. is-white. "And it is called *third*, not because it is a third predicate, but because it is a third expression [*dictio*] placed in the enunciation, which, along with the word predicated, constitutes one predicate, in such a way that the enunciation is divided into two parts and not into three."[3] St. Thomas also notes the obvious signification of *is* in "Socrates is": when we make such an assertion, we mean that Socrates is *in rerum natura*. It is important to stress that St. Thomas asserts (1) that existence is a predicate, and (2) that existence, *is*, signifies something. Both of these assertions have been denied in the interests of an existential interpretation of St. Thomas's doctrine.

M. Gilson tells us, in *Being and Some Philosophers*, that logic, apparently Aristotelian logic, cannot handle the existential proposition. "Propositions are usually defined as enunciations which affirm or deny one concept of another."[4] M. Gilson divides the proposition into

2. *In II Periherm.*, lect. 8, n. 2: "Circa primum duo oportet intelligere: primo quidem, quid est hoc quod dicit, 'est tertium adiacens praedicatur.' Ad cuius evidentiam considerandum est quod hoc verbum *est* quandoque in enunciatione praedicatur secundum se; ut cum dicitur, 'Socrates est,' per quod nihil aliud intendimus significare, quam quod Socrates sit in rerum natura. Quandoque vero non praedicatur per se, quasi principale praedicatum, sed quasi conjunctum principali praedicato ad connectendum ipsum subiecto; sicut cum dicitur, 'Socrates est albus,' non est intentio loquentis ut asserat Socratem esse in rerum natura, sed ut attribuat ei albedinem mediante hoc verbo *est* praedicatur ut adiacens principali praedicato."

3. Ibid.: "Et dicitur esse tertium, non quia sit tertium praedicatum, sed quia est tertia posita in enunciatione, quae simul cum nomine praedicato facit unum praedicatum, ut sic enunciatio dividatur in duas partes et non in tres."

4. E. Gilson, *Being and Some Philosophers* (Toronto: 1949; 2d ed., 1952), p. 190.

"one-term" and "two-term" propositions. "Man is rational" is said to be a two-term proposition. *Man* and *rational* are the terms; *is* is not a term "because it designates, not a concept, but the determinate relation which obtains between two terms."[5] "John is," is an example of a Gilsonian one-term proposition: *John* is the only term. This leaves *is* unexplained and M. Gilson pronounces the breakdown of logic. "In short, if all propositions entail either a composition or division of concepts, how can there be a proposition in which there is only one concept?"[6] One could point out, of course, that the integral parts of the enunciation, according to Aristotle, are the noun and the verb, that "John is" clearly qualifies as an enunciation in Aristotelian logic. However, there are reasons for following further M. Gilson's analysis, for it leads us to the heart of his Existentialism.

M. Gilson observes that logicians have a way of turning "one-term" propositions into "two-term." Thus, "Peter runs" can be rendered "Peter is running."

Now, in such cases, as *I am* or *God is* the transformation is not even possible, because in *I am being* or *God is being*, the predicate is but a blind window which is put there for mere verbal symmetry. There is no predicate even in the thus-developed proposition, because, while *running* did not mean the same thing as *is*, *being* does. In other words, *is-running* does not mean *is*, and this is why, in the first case, the verb is a copula, which it is not in the second case. The metaphysical truth that existence is not a predicate is here finding its logical verifications.[7]

In "John is," according to M. Gilson, *is* is neither predicate nor copula. Since *is* clearly is a predicate in "John is," one may well wonder what M. Gilson is getting at. The following remark, summarizing his denial that *is* is a predicate in such propositions as "John is" gives us the clue. "All the rest is mere verbiage calculated to make us believe that existence falls under the scope of conceptual predication."[8] M. Gilson's denial that *is* is a predicate is closely linked to his view on the manner in which the intellect grasps existence.

2. Existence and Conception

If existence is not predicated in existential propositions this is because predicates are concepts and, M. Gilson contends, there is no concept of existence. What then is being asserted in existential judgments?

Noting that there is no *a priori* reason to doubt that human thought

5. Ibid.
7. Ibid., p. 193.

6. Ibid., p. 191.
8. Ibid.

at the very outset goes straight to what is the core of being,[9] M. Gilson says that existence is attained in the judgment. And the judgment must be distinguished from abstract representation.[10] What can be grasped and represented abstractly is essence; if then we assume that existence is not essence, it seems to follow that existence cannot be abstractly represented. Intellect attains existence only by means of the judgment.

The concept which expresses an essence cannot be used as a complete expression of the corresponding being, because there is in the object of every concept something that escapes and transcends its essence. In other words, the actual object of a concept always contains more than its abstract definition. What it contains over and above its formal definition is its act of existing, and, because such acts transcend both essence and representation, they can be reached only by means of judgment. The proper function of the judgment is to say existence, and this is why judgment is a type of cognition distinct from and superior to pure and simple abstract conceptualization.[11]

Touching on the theme of his book, M. Gilson notes that "essentialistic" metaphysics identifies what can be understood, the essence of the thing, with the whole of reality and intelligibility. Judgment, which has existence and not essence as its object, corrects this penchant and guards against abstract speculation. Philosophy "must use judgment to restore essence to actual being."[12] In judgments of existence, my mental act answers the existential act of the known thing. "Let us rather say that such a judgment intellectually reiterates an actual act of existing. If I say that *x is*, the essence of x exercises through my judgment the same act of existing which it exercises in x."[13] That all of this is the doctrine of St. Thomas is clear, M. Gilson feels, from *In Boethii de trinitate*, q. 5, a. 3.

M. Gilson's analysis of existential propositions, then, involves the view that existence cannot be conceived, that it functions neither as copula nor predicate in such propositions as "John is." However, existence, the core of being reached at the very outset of the intellectual life, can be attained in the judgment when we return the abstracted essence to its existence: we say that it is and our act of judging reflects in its structure the structure of reality where essence is composed with existence. It will be appreciated that all this has a decided effect on the question of the concept, not of existence, but of being.

---

9. Ibid., p. 201.
11. Ibid.
13. Ibid.

10. Ibid., p. 202.
12. Ibid., p. 203.

3. The Concept of Being

Being in the view of M. Gilson, cannot be the object of purely abstract cognition nor can essence be legitimately severed from its act of existence.[14] If, in existential judgments, we correct the essentializing tendency of our mind by restoring essence to existence, this will be *a fortiori* necessary when it is a question not of *this* being, but of Being. Describing the "abstract essence of being" as a "metaphysical monster," M. Gilson adds:

For, indeed, there is no such essence. What is conceivable is the essence of *a being*. If the correct definition of being is "that which is," it necessarily includes an *is*, that is existence. To repeat, every *ens*, is an *esse habens*, and unless its *esse* be included in our cognition of it, it is not known as an *ens*, that is, as a *be-ing*. If what we have in mind is not this and that being, but being in general, then its cognition necessarily involves that of existence in general, and such a general cognition still entails the most fundamental of all judgments, namely that being is.[15]

What is surprising here, of course, is the introduction of "existence in general" which surely involves knowing in general what existence is, that is, having a concept of it. And, in "Being is," a judgment spoken of as necessary for metaphysics, to what existence would we be returning the essence of being (the "metaphysical monster")? Surely not to some existence outside the mind, as seemed to be suggested when existential propositions having singular subjects were being discussed, for there is no existence in general outside the mind. And, if existence in general is general thanks to being in the mind, then abstraction, representation, indeed everything M. Gilson was concerned to rid metaphysics of lest it become "essentialistic," seem involved.

As a matter of fact, if *ens* signifies *id quod habet esse*, it would seem that in the concept of being we already have the *esse* to be introduced by the general existential judgment, "Being is." Is this to be taken to mean "Essence exists"? This would be a strange issue of M. Gilson's analysis, since being is then equated with essence. The real point, it emerges, is that *being* signifies "essence exists." Despite the fact that this makes of "Being is" a compound proposition, it is indeed what M. Gilson intends, something quite clear from the second edition of his book.

There, in an appendix, M. Gilson considers a number of objections posed by Fr. Regis, O.P. in his review of the first edition.[16] The appen-

14. Ibid., p. 204.   15. Ibid.
16. *The Modern Schoolman* 28/2 (January 1951), pp. 121–27.

dix is particularly important since in it M. Gilson seems to reject what he had maintained in the first edition. Fr. Regis had noted that, in the commentary on the *Perihermeneias*, St. Thomas speaks of existence as a predicate, and, since M. Gilson's intention was to present the viewpoint of St. Thomas, the texts referred to by Fr. Regis are matters of serious concern. Faced with these texts, M. Gilson seemingly must make some adjustments in his earlier position if it is to be identical with that of St. Thomas. What he does is to reduce the difference between his views and those of St. Thomas to the level of language; the appendix is introduced under the heading *Sapientis enim non est curare de nominibus*. It soon becomes clear, however, that something more than language is at stake.

The remarks of Fr. Regis are fully justified. No Thomist aiming to express the point of view of Thomas Aquinas as he himself would express it should write that existence (*esse*) is not known by a concept. Historically speaking, our own formulas are inaccurate, and had we foreseen the objections of Fr. Regis, we would have used another language, or made clear that we were not using the language of Saint Thomas. We should avoid as much as possible unnecessary misunderstandings. The question is: can these misunderstandings be completely avoided?[17]

M. Gilson is now willing to admit that existence is known by means of a concept. Indeed, he feels that his earlier distinction between *conceptus* and *conceptio*[18] indicates that in some sense of the word *concept* he had allowed that there is a concept of existence. He notes that Fr. Regis, O.P. does not seem to honor this distinction. M. Gilson had earlier used the term *conceptio* to cover the composite act whereby essence is grasped and judged to exist. But the point at issue is not whether we agree that *conceptio* can be used to signify a judgment, but whether there is a *conceptus* of existence analytically prior to any existential judgment. It is difficult to interpret M. Gilson as affirming this. He notes that the more restricted term, *conceptus*, has been taken over by unidentified essentialists as their own and confined to the apprehension of essence. Because of the difficulties of making himself understood in the alleged essentialistic atmosphere of the day, he has restricted his use of *concept* to the "simple apprehension of an essence." Existence can be the object of *conception*. "Otherwise how could it be known? But it cannot be known by the simple conceptual apprehension of an essence, which it is not."[19] This is ambiguous. It can mean either that the concept of the essence of any creature does not

---

17. Gilson, op. cit., pp. 221–22.   18. Ibid., p. 190, note 1.
19. Ibid., p. 223.

include its existence, or that there is no concept (*conceptus*) of existence. M. Gilson notes that anyone is free to reject his distinction of *conceptio* and *conceptus*, but the question is whether the use made of it here can be accepted as the thought of St. Thomas. "John is," can be the object of a *conceptio*; of John we can have a *conceptus*. But can there be a *conceptus* of existence? If not, it is clear that there will be no predication of existence and hence no *conceptio* of "John is." [20]

Admitting that St. Thomas speaks of existence as a predicate, M. Gilson feels that such talk is nowadays misleading. "For, if we tell them [non-Thomists] that existence is a predicate, they will understand that, according to Thomas Aquinas, actual existence, or *esse*, can be predicated of its essence as one more essential determination." [21] If the meaning of *predicate* has changed, one might feel that a clarification of the old and new meanings would be of help in avoiding misunderstanding. M. Gilson, however, seems intent on questioning the adequacy of Aristotle's logic.

In his commentaries on Aristotle does Saint Thomas always express his deepest personal thought on a given question? Unless we admit that logic is a strictly formal science wholly unrelated to metaphysics, it is hard to imagine that the true Thomistic interpretation of a logic applicable to *habens esse* can be identically the same as that of a logic applicable to a metaphysics of *ousia*.[22]

This is a most unfortunate turn in the discussion. M. Gilson's hint at the possibility of an "existential logic" can only be as valuable as his estimate of Aristotle's metaphysics, as his analysis of the logical intentions of proposition, predicate, etc., and as any indication he may be able to give that the difficulties he has raised are due to the logic of Aristotle. Of course, only the second and third points concern us here.[23]

M. Gilson recalls[24] that St. Thomas assigns three meanings to *esse*: it can mean essence, the actuality of essence, or the truth of a proposition (*In I Sent.*, d. 33, q. 1, ad 1). Only the first two are real being. When we use *est* in logic, it is not a *tertium praedicatum*, for in "John is white," *is-white* is the predicate. So too in "John is," *is* is the predicate

20. Cf. *In IV Metaphysic.*, lect. 10, n. 664: "Significatio autem orationis a significatione nominum dependet. Et sic oportet ad hoc principium redire, quod nomina aliquid significant. . . ."

21. Gilson, op. cit., p. 224.

22. Ibid. On all this, cf. E. Trepanier, "Premières Distinctions sur le mot 'être,'" *Laval théologique et philosophique* 11/1 (1955), pp. 25–66.

23. On the first point, cf. John D. Beach, "Aristotle's Notion of Being," *The Thomist* 21/1 (January 1958), pp. 29–43.

24. Gilson, op. cit., p. 224.

according to St. Thomas. Far from being the solution it is just this that remains M. Gilson's problem, a problem, according to M. Gilson, "whose solution is not to be found in the excellent texts so aptly quoted by Fr. Regis."[25] In "Socrates is," *Socrates* "refers to an essence, but does its predicate refer to an essence as in the case of *albus*? There is no problem as to its conceivability: I have the concept of 'existing Socrates' which is the intelligible import of this judgment. Our own question is: if *est* is a predicate, what kind of a predicate is it?"[26] It has to be noted that an unexplained shift takes place here. We are told that *Socrates* refers to an essence and asked if *is* does. But the original question was: is there a concept of *esse*?—not whether *esse* is an essence. To identify *essence* and *concept* is simply to beg the question. Moreover, it is noteworthy that the conceivability of existence is only through the conception of "existing Socrates." That this is all that is meant by the conceivability of existence is clear from the following passage.

Let us agree that in Thomas Aquinas the verb *est* is a predicate; what is the nature of the cognition we have of what it predicates? This is no longer a logical problem; it is a problem in noetics and in metaphysics, because it deals with the nature of being and of our knowledge of it. When we predicate *est*, we are not predicating the 'quidditas vel natura rei.' Nor for that matter do we predicate something which belongs to the essence of Socrates (such as 'homo'), or that inheres in it (such as 'albus'). Logically speaking, it could be said that *esse* inheres in the subject Socrates, but metaphysically, it does not, because where there is no *esse* there is no Socrates. Granting that *est* is a logical denomination of Socrates as existing, the metaphysical status of the denominated still remains an open question. Among those who refuse the composition of essence and *esse*, quite a few have been misled precisely by the fact that their metaphysical inquiries were conducted in terms of logic. For, indeed, as soon as we do so, *est* becomes a predicate like all other predicates, and we imagine ourselves in possession of a distinct concept of *esse* in itself, apart from the concept which we do have of Socrates-conceived-as-existing.[27]

Since the only way in which existence can be conceived is in such a conception as "existing Socrates," it is clear that existence is attained only in the judgment, that there is no concept (*conceptus*) of existence. Surely, then, there is no point in speaking of existence as a predicate. If existence can only be conceived in a conception of an existential judgment (which does not involve a *conceptus* of existence), any talk of the predication of existence would be concerned with the predication of a proposition.

25. Ibid., p. 225.
26. Ibid.   27. Ibid.

4. The Simple Apprehension of Being

The contention of "Existential Thomism" that the concept of being is a judgment or proposition contradicts explicit remarks of St. Thomas. In order to see this is so, it must be made clear that this view on the concept of being has to do with what the intellect first knows, *ens primum cognitum*. M. Gilson, in the context of his argument that *being* involves at once apprehension and judgment notes that there is no *a priori* reason to doubt that reason "at the outset" goes to what is the core of being, i.e. existence.[28] The composition of essence and existence in a judgment which is the conception of being seems to answer to the being which, as St. Thomas says, *primo cadit in intellectu*.[29] Now, although it is certainly the thought of St. Thomas which M. Gilson wishes to expose, it is with St. Thomas that he seems to disagree.

In many places, St. Thomas writes that being is what the intellect first grasps.[30] Moreover, being (*ens*) is said to be attained by simple apprehension, by the first operation of the mind, which is analytically prior to judgment.

But it should be stated that those things which are more universal according to simple apprehension are the first known, for that which falls first upon the intellect is being. . . .[31]

As evidence of this, it should be understood that since there is a two-fold operation of the intellect—one in which it knows "what something is" [*quod quid est*], which is called "the understanding of indivisibles"; the other, by which it composes and divides—in both there is some first thing. In the first operation, indeed, of the intellect there is some first thing which falls upon the conception of the intellect, namely, that which I name "being."—nor is anything able to be conceived by the mind in this operation unless "being" be understood.[32]

Both Cajetan and John of St. Thomas have discussed this doctrine at length. Being as first known by our intellect is, Cajetan maintains, *ens*

28. Ibid., p. 201.
29. Ibid., p. 205. Cf. J. F. Anderson, *Review of Metaphysics* 11/4 (June 1958), p. 557.
30. Cf. *De ente et essentia*, proemium; *Q. D. de ver.*, q. 1, a. 1.
31. *In I Metaphysic.*, lect. 2, n. 46: "Sed dicendum quod magis universalia secundum simplicem apprehensionem sunt prima nota, nam primo in intellectu cadit ens. . . ."
32. *In IV Metaphysic.*, lect. 6, n. 605: "Ad huius evidentiam sciendum est, quod cum duplex sit operatio intellectus: una, qua cognoscit quod quid est, quod vocatur indivisibilium intelligentia: alia, qua componit et dividit: in utroque est aliquod primum: in prima quidem operatione est aliquod primum, quod cadit in conceptione intellectus, scilicet hoc quod dico ens; nec aliquid hac operatione potest mente concipi, nisi intelligatur ens."

concretum quidditati sensibili.[33] The formula was carefully chosen. St. Thomas will often say that it is the quiddity of material things which is the connatural object of the human intellect, since our concepts are abstracted from the sense image, the phantasm. The intellect is said to be able to know *what* the things are whose sensible qualities are attained by the senses, and, of course, what sensible qualities are. Since the *whatness* or quiddity, though not a *per se* object of sense, is intellectually attainable by us thanks to the instrumentality of the senses, it is denominated 'sensible'. The sensible quiddity, however, is not something which can be sensed *per se*. The concepts or ideas formed by the mind are first of all means of knowing sensible things—and nothing more. Of course, as it happens, knowledge of what sensible things are can lead us to the certainty that there are things which are not sensible, either *per se* or in the *per accidens* way sensible quiddity is. Whatever we come to know of such things will be by an analogy with sensible things, via the connatural objects of our intellect. That is why our knowledge of "separate substance" is always radically imperfect. At the outset of the intellectual life, there will be no question of forming a concept which will be applied to anything other than what is attained by the senses. And, if the first concept is that of being, as St. Thomas teaches, it will be sensible quiddity which is known as being. *Concretum*, in Cajetan's formula, is opposed to *abstractum*. He wants to insist that *ens primum cognitum* is not grasped by what he calls formal abstraction. If it were, it would be *ens commune*, the subject of metaphysics. It is nonsense to say that being is known in this way at the outset of the intellectual life. By means of what Cajetan calls total abstraction, being is grasped as a universal whole predicable of its subjective parts.[34] It may seem odd that Cajetan will not allow that being is first known as a universal whole. Does not St. Thomas explain the priority of being in terms of *magis universalia*? And, after all, it would seem that *being* can be predicated of whatever the senses attain. Cajetan in a very subtle, exhaustive and illuminating discussion[35] has argued that a nature must first be known as a definable whole, an integral whole, before it can be known as a predicable or universal whole. And, since confused knowledge precedes distinct knowledge of the same thing, Cajetan has concluded that *ens primum cognitum* is *being* grasped confusedly as a definable whole. *Ens concretum quidditati sensibili*, then, is not known by total abstraction or by formal abstraction.

33. Cajetan, *In de ente et essentia*, proemium, n. 5.
34. *ST*, IaIIae, q. 120, a. 2.
35. Cajetan, loc. cit.

But, as John of St. Thomas notes: "The intellect is said, nevertheless, to begin from that which is more universal, since it begins from that predicate which is disposed to sustain the greater universality." [36]

We may object to this *concretum* on the grounds that intellectual knowledge is by definition abstract. If being is the first concept formed by the mind, isn't it, like any other concept, abstracted by the agent intellect from a phantasm? Cajetan, of course, has no intention of denying this. "In a third way, as having neither of these conditions, yet nevertheless abstracted from singulars." [37] The first concept is freed from materiality and singularity and in that sense is abstract. But Cajetan, aware that even total abstraction implies distinct knowledge of what it is that is predicable of many, and wanting to retain the truth insisted on by St. Thomas [38] that the first act of our intellect is attended by a maximum of confusion and potentiality, speaks of the *primum cognitum* as *concretum quidditati sensibili*.

John of St. Thomas, in discussing the same matter, raises the objection that the singular or singularity is what the intellect first grasps. In handling this, he introduces an explanation of the first confused knowledge of being that "Existential Thomists" should find sympathetic. John answers the objection by pointing out that intellectual knowledge of singularity presupposes distinct knowledge of the nature of which *this* is a singular instance. The objector continues: let us say that at the outset the intellect grasps singularity, not as to its *quid sit*, but as to its *an sit*. John's reply is interesting.

But let it be that the intellect begins to know the quiddity of its object not quidditatively, but as to "whether it is" [*an est*], in such a way that neither concerning the nature itself, nor concerning the singularity does it attain any other predicate than the "whether it is" [*an est*]—nevertheless by this fact it does not know the singular as it is singular, but in a confused way, and under a certain most common notion of its being, in such a way that of the singularity it knows nothing other than that it is being. Now this is to know something common to the singular and to the nature—for of both there is had knowledge as to the "whether it is" [*an est*], and thus being or "whether it is" as in concretion with, or applied to, some sensible singular, will be that which is first known [*primum cognitum*] by the intellect. For which reason—and this is very much to be noted—when the intellect knows something as to "whether it is," it does not prescind from the "what it is" [*quod quid est*] or quiddity, for this is impossible since it is its formal object and what is first and *per se* intelligible.

36. John of St. Thomas, *Cursus theologicus*, tom. 2, p. 25a40–43: "Dicitur tamen incipere intellectus ab universaliori, quia incipit ab eo praedicato quod maiori universalitati substerni aptum est."

37. Cajetan, loc. cit.: "Tertio modo ut neutram istarum conditionum habens, abstractum tamen a singularibus."

38. Cf. *ST*, Ia, q. 85, a. 3.

Rather, solely it does not know it quidditatively, i.e. by penetrating the proper constitution of its quiddity and the cause of its being, but in the quiddity itself it attains alone a certain predicate which is overwhelmingly common and confused, which is being; and this is what it knows at that time as "what it is" [*quod quid*].[39]

What John of St. Thomas seems to be saying is that the first concept formed by the intellect is a means of knowing sensible quiddities, not with respect to what they determinately are, but under the formality of having existence. Doubtless what existence means here is presence to sense. In other words, being is *id quod habet esse*. It is noteworthy, however, that although John speaks of this first concept as the most confused predicate, he does not speak of any actual predication. That could hardly take place without a predicate.

Being as first conceived or apprehended by our intellect is the most common predicate; it can be predicated of that from whose image the concept has been abstracted. What-is, being, like any concept, may enter into composition and division, i.e. become subject or predicate of an enunciation. Like any other concept, being, what-is, is not of itself a judgment or assertion susceptible of truth or falsity in itself. However, unlike most other concepts, it can appear to assert or affirm existence. For this reason, Aristotle and St. Thomas go to special pains to show that this is not the case.

The noun and the verb are parts of speech (*oratio*); alone neither one signifies what is true or false.[40] Indeed, only that *oratio* which is an enunciation does. What nouns and verbs have in common is that they both signify and that neither signifies what is true or false. With respect to the verb, the second point is best shown in the case of that verb which seems an exception to it, i.e. *to-be* or *esse*. "For although every finite verb implies existence [*esse*] since to run is to *be* running,

39. John of St. Thomas, loc. cit., pp. 23b38–24a27: "Sed esto ita sit, quod intellectus incipiat cognoscere quidditatem sui obiecti non quidditative, sed quoad an est, ita quod neque de ipsa natura neque de ipsa singularitate attingat aliud praedicatum quam ipsum an est, tamen hoc ipso non cognoscitur singulare ut singulare, sed sub confusione et ratione quadam communissima ipsius esse, ita quod de ipsa singularitate non cognoscit nisi quod sit ens. Hoc autem est cognoscere aliquid commune ipsi singulari et ipsi naturae; de utroque enim datur cognitio quoad an est, et sic ipsum esse seu an est ut concretum seu applicatum alicui singulari sensibili erit primum cognitum intellectus. Quare (quod valde advertendum est) quando intellectus cognoscit aliquid quoad an est, non praescindit a quod quid seu a quidditate, hoc enim est impossibile, cum sit formale eius obiectum et primo et per se intelligibile, sed solum non cognoscit quidditative, id est penetrando constitutionem propriam quidditatis et causas essendi, sed in ipsa quidditate solum attingat praedicatum quoddam valde commune et confusam, quod est ipsum esse; et hoc est quod tunc cognoscit ut quod quid."

40. *In I Periherm.*, lect. 5, n. 16.

and every infinite verb implies non-existence [*non esse*], since not to run is *not* to *be* running, nevertheless no verb signifies this whole which is for a *thing to be* or *not to be*." [41]

Here, in the Oxford translation, is Aristotle's text. "Verbs in and by themselves are substantival and have significance, for he who uses such expressions arrests the hearer's mind and fixes his attention; but they do not as they stand express any judgment, either positive or negative. For neither are 'to be' and 'not to be' and the participle 'being' significant of any fact, unless something is added; for they do not themselves indicate anything, but imply a copulation of which we cannot form a conception apart from the things coupled." [42] The Latin translation St. Thomas had did not translate τὸ ὄν as *being*, but as *is*. St. Thomas is aware of this [43] and comments on both readings, i.e. *ipsum est* and *ipsum ens*.

He begins with the latter. "For in order to prove that verbs do not signify a thing to be or not to be, he [Aristotle] takes that which is the fount and source of existence, namely, being itself—concerning which he says that it is nothing. . . ." [44] St. Thomas, before giving his own explanation of this, examines the readings of other commentators. Alexander takes the statement that "being is nothing" (*ens nihil est*) to refer to the equivocal signification of *being*. An equivocal noun, taken by itself, signifies nothing. St. Thomas disagrees. Not only does *being* not signify nothing, it signifies many (*multa*), but according to prior and posterior in meanings (*secundum prius et posterius*)—"whence it is understood absolutely speaking of that which is said in the prior way." [45] Moreover, Alexander's approach has little to do with Aristotle's point. Porphyry says that "*being* does not signify the nature of anything, as does the word 'man' or 'wise,' but solely designates a certain conjoining." If this were the case, St. Thomas observes, *being* would be neither noun nor verb, but would be like the conjunction and preposition.

What Aristotle does mean, as Ammonius pointed out, is that *ens* does not signify what is true or false. Nevertheless, even Ammonius didn't get to the heart of the matter.

41. Ibid., n. 16: "Quamvis enim omne verbum finitum implicet *esse*, quia currere est currentem esse, et omne verbum infinitum implicet *non esse*, quia non currere est non currentem esse; tamen nullum verbum significat hoc totum, scilicet *rem esse*, vel *non esse*."

42. *On Interpretation*, 16b19–25.

43. *In I Periherm.*, lect. 5, n. 19.

44. Ibid.: "Ad probandum enim quod verba non significant rem esse vel non esse, assumpsit id quod est fons et origo ipsius esse, scilicet ipsum ens, de quo dicit quod nihil est. . . ."

45. Ibid.: ". . . unde simpliciter dictum intelligitur de eo, quod per prius dicitur."

And therefore, to follow the words of Aristotle more closely, one should consider that he said that the verb does not signify a thing *to be* or *not to be*, even *being* [*ens*] does not signify a thing to be or not to be. And thus he says, "It is nothing" [*nihil est*]—i.e. does not signify anything to be.

For this was most clear with the expression *being*: since being is nothing other than *what is* [*quod est*]. And thus it appears both to signify a *thing*, by the expression QUOD, and *existence* by the expression EST. And indeed if this expression *being* should signify *existence* principally, as it signifies a *thing* which has *being*, without doubt it would signify that something exists.

But it does not principally signify that composition which is implied in the expression EST, but it "consignifies" it insofar as it signifies a *thing* having being.

Whence such a "consignification" [or implied signification] does not suffice for truth or falsehood—since the composition in which truth and falsehood consist cannot be understood except insofar as it connects the extremes of the composition.[46]

Being signifies what-is, not "something exists." *Being* names the thing from the formality of existence, but it does not signify that the thing exists. Only an enunciation can do this and therefore signify the kind of composition which is true or false. Thus, St. Thomas teaches that *being*, although it names a thing from existence, principally signifies *what* has existence; it is the *res* that is named and signifies by the word *being*, not the factual existence of it. It seems clear, then, that *id quod habet esse, quod est, habens esse*, etc. are not propositions but phrases; the present text clearly expresses the doctrine that *ens* does not involve a judgment in its signification. It is also clear that *est*, since it is a verb, i.e. a *vox significativa*, signifies something. This last point emerges once more when St. Thomas comments on the translation which gives *ipsum est* instead of *ipsum ens*.

"For that no verb signifies a thing *to be* or *not to be*, he [Aristotle] proves by the verb EST, which stated in itself does not signify *something* to be, although it does signify *being*."[47] The composition (or affirma-

46. Ibid., n. 20: "Et ideo ut magis sequamur verba Aristotelis considerandum est quod ipse dixerat quod verbum non significat rem *esse* vel *non esse*, sed nec ipsum ens significat rem esse vel non esse. Et hoc est quod dicit 'nihil est,' idest non significat aliquid esse. Etenim hoc maxime videbatur de hoc quod dico *ens*; quia *ens* nihil aliud est quam *quod est*. Et sic videtur et *rem* significare, per hoc quod dico QUOD, et *esse*, per hoc quod dico EST. Et si quidem haec dictio *ens* significaret *esse* principaliter, sicut significat *rem* quae habet *esse*, procul dubio significaret aliquid esse. Sed ipsam compositionem, quae importatur in hoc quod dico EST, non principaliter significat, sed consignificat eam inquantum significat *rem* habentem esse. Unde talis consignificatio compositionis non sufficit ad veritatem vel falsitatem: quia compositio, in qua consistit veritas et falsitas, non potest intelligi, nisi secundum quod innectit extreme compositionis."

47. Ibid.: "Quod enim nullum verbum significat rem *esse* vel *non esse*, probat per hoc verbum EST, quod secundum se dictum, non significat *aliquid* esse, licet significat *esse*."

tion) seemingly signified by this verb is had only when what it composes is stated. Then there can be truth or falsity. *Est* is said to consignify composition and not to signify it. It consignifies it because it is a verb: "For it signifies primarily that which falls upon the intellect in the manner of actuality in the absolute sense—since EST, absolutely speaking, signifies *to be in act*, and therefore it signifies after the manner of a verb."[48] The actuality principally signified by this verb *is* or *exists* is generally the act of any form, whether it be substantial or accidental act. Thus, when we want to signify any form or act actually to be in (*inesse*) some subject, we do so by means of the verb *is*. Such actuality is signified *simpliciter* by the present tense, *secundum quid* by the other tenses.[49]

5. Interim Summary

The foregoing analysis indicates why one cannot agree with M. Gilson when he writes: "There is a point on which Aristotle and Thomas fully agree: taken alone, *is* means nothing."[50] What each man says is that *is* alone, like *being* alone, does not assert anything; that therefore neither *is* nor *being* signifies a judgment which would be true or false.

We may take it as shown, I think, that for St. Thomas there is a concept (*conceptus*) of being; that *being* is a term signifying a simple apprehension and not a judgment. If the latter were the case, *being* would signify something susceptible of truth or falsity. But this is clearly not the case. *What-is* (*id quod habet esse*), affirms nothing; but this is not to say that they mean nothing. Moreover, *is* is a significant term, if it were not a *vox significativa*, it could hardly be a verb.

Given these seemingly clear doctrines of St. Thomas, the position we examined earlier may seem merely capricious. However, as has already been indicated, it claims foundation in the texts of St. Thomas, particularly in the saint's exposition of the *De trinitate* of Boethius. There St. Thomas writes:

The first operation, indeed, regards the nature itself of the thing, accordingly as the thing understood obtains a certain grade in beings, whether it be a complete thing, or some certain whole, or an incomplete thing, such as a part or an accident.

48. Ibid.: "Significat enim primo illud quod cadit in intellectu per modum actualitatis absolute: nam EST, simpliciter dictum, significat *in actu esse*; et ideo significat per modum verbi."
49. Ibid.
50. Gilson, op. cit., p. 229.

The second operation, however, regards the being itself of the thing, which indeed results from the collecting together of the principles of the thing in composite things, or accompanies the simple nature of the thing, as in the case of simple substances.[51]

This passage has been interpreted to mean that simple apprehension grasps essence alone, and that only in judgment is existence attained. In the light of our previous examination, it is clear that existence is not grasped by the first operation as it is by the second. In judgment, the mind asserts that a thing is or that it is such-and-such. We have already seen that the concept of being does not assert that anything is and that, although *being* means "that-which-has-existence," this *ratio* is the term of the operation called simple apprehension. So too the concept of substance (which is the *ratio propria entis*), i.e. that to which existence belongs *per se et non in alio*, does not assert the existence of any *res*. No more does the concept of existence (i.e. *esse in rerum natura, in actu esse*) assert that something exists. When it is said that the second operation of the mind, "qua componit et dividit, respicit ipsum esse rei," what is meant is that the mind can assert the composition only of what exists together *in rerum natura* and can assert the separation only of that which exists separately *in rerum natura*—if its judgments are to be true. By means of the first operation, it can consider one thing apart from another even when these could never exist apart. (That the mind does not have absolute freedom here, is shown at great length in the text in question.) In the case of the existential judgment, if existence were not first conceived, grasped as the term of the first operation of the mind as to what it is, no existential judgment would be possible. What is composed in the affirmative enunciation which signifies the existential judgment "Socrates is," is precisely Socrates and existence. The exposition of the *De trinitate*, then, is certainly not teaching a different doctrine from the texts examined above nor does it demand a logic other than that of Aristotle. The logic taught by St. Thomas, like his metaphysics, is most profitably sought in his commentaries on Aristotle. The hypothesis of a "personal" metaphysics of St. Thomas, an existential metaphysics, like the consequent hypothesis of an existential logic to fit the existential metaphysics, exhibits an unfortunate tendency to derogate Aristotle in

51. *In Boethii de trin.*, q. 5, a. 3 (ed. Wyser): "Prima quidem operatio respicit ipsam naturam rei, secundum quod res intellecta aliquem gradum in entibus obtinet, sive sit res completa ut totum aliquod, sive res incompleta, ut pars vel accidens. Secunda vero operatio respicit ipsum esse rei, quod quidem resultat ex congregatione principiorum rei in compositis, vel ipsam simplicem naturam rei concomitatur, ut in substantiis simplicibus."

such a way that the obvious sense of the texts of St. Thomas is rapidly obscured and lost.[52] It remains true that the best way to imitate St. Thomas is to become, with him, a faithful disciple of Aristotle.

B.

Thus far we have considered the nature of the existential proposition against the background of an interpretation of St. Thomas which claims that existence cannot be a predicate because it cannot be conceived. Existence, on this view, is attained intellectually only in the judgment. Thus, since *being* means "that which is," the concept of being comprises a simple apprehension of essence and the judgment that it exists. The *conceptio* whereby we grasp what has thereby been judgmentally united is taken to be the concept of being which, as St. Thomas says, *primo cadit in intellectu*. Against this we argued that existence can be conceived, that it can be a predicate and that the concept of being does not include a judgment.

When it is recognized that existence is the predicate in such propositions as "Socrates is," difficulties still remain for the student of the texts of St. Thomas. With Professor Gilson we must pose a number of questions.[53] When we affirm that Socrates exists, we predicate existence of him, but in so doing "we are not predicating the 'quidditas vel natura rei.' Nor, for that matter do we predicate something that belongs to the essence of Socrates (such as 'homo'), or that inheres in it (such as 'albus')."[54] When we predicate existence of Socrates, are we predicating something which is of his essence, or something which is an accident? If neither, what kind of a predicate is existence? Allied problems in the text of St. Thomas are these: only God has *being* predicated of Him *essentialiter*, yet being is said to be predicated *essentialiter* of whatever falls under the categories. But, if *being* is predi-

52. M. Gilson, in his essay "Cajetan et l'existence," makes this curious remark: "L'histoire de ce que l'on nomme commodément l'Ecole Thomiste n'a jamais été écrite. Nous ne prétendons donc pas la connaître, mais ce que nous en savons nous invite à penser que le principal obstacle à la diffusion du Thomisme de saint Thomas, même à l'interieur de l'Ordre Dominicain, fut l'influence d'Aristote. Cette assertion d'apparence paradoxale, étant donnée l'interpretation traditionelle de saint Thomas, est sans doute destinée à devenir une banalité dont on s'étonnera qu'il y ait jamais eu lieu de la dire." *Tidjschrift voor philosophie* (June 1953), p. 284. Doubtless St. Thomas himself would not be the least of those who would find this assertion paradoxical. General statements about the relationship between the doctrine of Aristotle and that of St. Thomas can be tested only by particular cases—like that of the existential proposition.
53. E. Gilson, *Being and Some Philosophers*, p. 225.
54. Ibid.

cated *essentialiter* of what falls under the categories, what are we to make of statements that *being* is an accidental predicate of any creature?[55] The present part hopes to contribute something towards an understanding of St. Thomas's meaning and thereby the truth of the matter.

1. Being *Per Se* and Being *Per Accidens*

In Book Delta of the *Metaphysics*, Aristotle is concerned with distinguishing the various meanings of words signifying things which fall to the consideration of metaphysics. "And because the things considered in this science are common to all, they are not said univocally but according to priority and posteriority of different things, as was pointed out in the fourth book; hence he [Aristotle] first distinguishes the intentions of the words which fall to the consideration of this science."[56] St. Thomas divides the words analyzed in this book into those which signify the subject, or parts of the subject, of the science; those which signify its causes; and those which signify its properties: a fitting division, since every science considers the properties and causes of its subject. It is clear that St. Thomas does not look on Book Delta as a neutral "philosophical lexicon," something which plays no integral role in the development of the science of metaphysics. It is not surprising, on this interpretation, that the various meanings of the term *being* should be discussed in this book, and in commenting on Aristotle, St. Thomas has a number of things to say which pertain to the problems mentioned above.

"Things," Aristotle says,[57] "are said to 'be' (1) in an accidental sense, (2) by their own nature." Despite this initial two-fold division, we find four modes of *being* distinguished in this chapter. It will be of interest to see if the two-fold division is retained despite this subsequent complexity and in what way *being* is divided not univocally but according to priority and posteriority into these modes.

St. Thomas divides chapter 7 of Book Delta in the following manner. "Here the Philosopher distinguishes how many ways being is

55. See the meditative and stimulating study of Father Joseph Owens, "The Accidental and Essential Character of Being in the Doctrine of St. Thomas Aquinas," *Mediaeval Studies* 20 (1958), pp. 1–40.

56. "Et quia ea quae in hac scientia considerantur sunt omnibus communia, nec dicuntur univoce sed secundum prius et posterius de diversis, ut in quarto libro est habitum; ideo prius *distinguit intentiones nominum, quae in huius scientiae consideratione cadunt.*"—*In V Metaphysic.*, lect. 1, n. 749.

57. *Metaphysics*, V.7 (Oxford translation).

said, and he does three things. First, he distinguishes being into being
per se and being *per accidens*."[58] Then Aristotle goes on to distinguish
the modes of being *per accidens* and the modes of being *per se*. All
but the first of the four modes fall under being *per se*. "He distinguishes the modes of being *per se*, and he does three things. First, he
distinguishes the being which is outside the mind into the ten categories, and this is perfected being. Secondly, he sets down another mode
of being according to which it is only in the mind . . . Thirdly, he divides being by potency and act, and being so divided is more common
than perfected being, for being in potency is being only imperfectly
and in a certain sense."[59]

What is the meaning of this initial division of being into being *per se*
and being *per accidens*? What causes difficulty is the fact that the being
per se which is distinguished from being *per accidens* is itself divided
into substance and the nine accidents. Noting this difficulty, St. Thomas
writes: "Being therefore is divided into substance and accident according to an absolute consideration of being, as whiteness itself, considered in itself, is said to be an accident and man a substance. But
being *per accidens* [i.e. as opposed to being *per se* which is divided by
substance and accident] has to be understood in terms of a comparison of accident to substance, a comparison signified by this verb *is*,
as when we say, 'Man is white.' Hence this whole 'Man is white' is being
per accidens. Thus, it is clear that the division of being in itself [*secundum se*] and accidentally [*secundum accidens*] is based on something's
being predicated of another either *per se* or *per accidens*. The division
of being into substance and accident is based on this that something in
its nature is either substance or accident."[60]

We may find this comment anything but a clarification. If *ens per accidens* here is had by a comparison of predicate to subject whereas *ens
secundum se* is based on an absolute consideration, how can being *per se*
be distinguished from being *per accidens* "secundum quod aliquid
praedicatur per se vel per accidens"? That is, isn't being *per se* itself had
by a comparison of predicate to subject? Isn't it simply a matter of distinguishing *per se* from accidental predication and, if that is the case,
how can accident fall under being *per se* if this is based on *per se* predi-

---

58. *In V Metaphysic.*, lect. 9, n. 885.
59. "Distinguit modum entis per se: et circa hoc tria facit. Primo distinguit ens, quod
est extra animam, per decem praedicamenta, quod est ens perfectum. Secundo ponit
alium modum entis, secundum quod est tantum in mente. . . . Tertio dividit ens per
potentiam et actum: et ens sic divisum est communius quam ens perfectum. Nam ens in
potentia est ens secundum quid tantum et imperfectum. . . ."—ibid., n. 889.
60. Ibid., n. 885.

cation? Certainly, something can be predicated *per se* of an accident (e.g. white is a color), but we are concerned here with modes of *being* and can being be predicated *per se* of accident? Moreover, if being *per se* is designated by an absolute consideration, how can it be divided into substance and accident "secundum diversum modum praedicandi"? In order to resolve these difficulties and arrive at a proper understanding of the text (all of this with a view to discussing the overriding problems of this part), we want to discuss *per se* and *per accidens* predication and their relation to predicable and predicamental accidents.

(a) "Per Se" and "Per Accidens" Predication

Predication is a logical relation; it does not pertain to things as they exist *in rerum natura* but follows on our mode of knowing. Having grasped separately what exists as one, our mind composes by attributing one thing to another, the predicate (that which is affirmed) of the subject (that of which it is affirmed). What is meant by predication *per se*? The preposition *per*, St. Thomas notes,[61] suggests a relation of causality. *This* is through, by, thanks to, *that*. (Sometimes too *per* refers to the fact that a thing is by itself, alone; a meaning important for the third mode of perseity distinguished in the *Posteriora*.) It is the causal import of the preposition which is at play when we speak of predication *per se*. In the statement "Man is an animal," the predicate is said to be predicated *per se* of man, because animal pertains to the form and consequently to the definition of man. This first mode of perseity is based on formal causality. The second is based on material causality. If I say, "Every number is odd or even," I am not predicating of number something which enters into its definition. Number is not oddness nor evenness nor a kind of oddness or evenness; rather these are accidents of number. That is, number enters into the definition of what is here predicated of it. Oddness and evenness are accidents of number (although any number must be odd or even, neither is what number is) and are said *per se* of their proper subject.

Restricting ourselves to these two modes of *per se* predication (and, as St. Thomas points out,[62] the third and fourth modes of perseity are reducible to these), we can say that *per se* predication is had whenever the predicate is the definition or part of the definition of the subject or, on the other hand, when the subject enters into the definition of the predicate. Predicates said of their subjects in neither of these ways

61. *In I Post. Analytic.*, lect. 10, n. 2.
62. Ibid., lect. 35, n. 4.

"sunt accidentia, idest per accidens praedicantur, sicut musicum et album praedicantur de animali per accidens."[63]

Whatever is not predicated *per se* is predicated *per accidens*. An example of the latter is "Man is white." The predicate does not enter into the definition of the subject nor is that of which the predicate is said its proper subject since many things other than man are white. If "Man is white" is true this is so only because a man, say Socrates, happens to be white. Numbers, on the other hand, do not just happen to be odd or even.

Despite this clear distinction of *per se* and *per accidens* predication, we must take note of a wider use of the adverb *accidentaliter* applied to predication. The predicate is what is said of another in a proposition. However, it is sometimes said, the predicate is said of the subject in either of two ways. Sometimes we predicate that which is of the very nature of the subject, sometimes we predicate that which is in the subject. This distinction, which recalls the terminology of the *Categories*, is used by Aristotle in the *Perihermeneias*. St. Thomas explains as follows. "For it seems that something is said to be *of* the subject when it is predicated essentially, e.g. 'Man is animal'; *in* the subject, however, as an accident is predicated of the subject, e.g. 'Man is white.'"[64] That which is *de subiecto* is said to be predicated *essentialiter*; that which is *in subiecto* is predicated *accidentaliter*. The subject truly is what is predicated of it *essentialiter* or *substantialiter*. The latter term occurs in the commentary on the *Metaphysics*.[65] There it is argued that the substantial predicate must be one: the subject is what is predicated of it substantially and whatever is is one. The subject is not truly that which is predicated of it accidentally. When we say that a man is white, white is not *what* the subject is, which is why white is said to be predicated accidentally. This is not to say, of course, that nothing can be truly predicated accidentally[66] nor that there is only one predicate *tout court* which can be predicated essentially or substantially of a subject. Many generic predicates are said *in quid* of the subject, but there is only one adequate substantial predicate, i.e. the definition.

It is clear that what can be predicated essentially or substantially is predicated *per se* in the first mode. Therefore, the second mode of *per se* predication involves that which is predicated *accidentaliter*. That is

63. Ibid., lect. 10, n. 5.

64. "Videtur enim aliquid dici ut *de* subiecto, quod essentialiter praedicatur; ut 'homo est animal'; *in* subiecto autem, sicut accidens de subiecto praedicatur, ut 'homo est albus.'"—*In I Periherm.*, lect. 5, n. 9.

65. *In IV Metaphysic.*, lect. 7, n. 628.

66. Cf. *In II Post. Analytic.*, lect. 4, n. 5: ". . . non omne quod vere praedicatur de aliquo, praedicatur in eo quod quid est, nec significat essentiam eius."

why we find the somewhat arresting phrase "*per se* accidents" used. These are not opposed to *per accidens* accidents but to what *contingit inesse*. That is, the distinction is between accidents which are in their subjects necessarily and those which are in their subjects contingently. An example of the necessary accident is that which is predicated *per se* in the second mode. This necessity must have its source in the subject and necessary accidents are distinguished according as some have the principles of the species for their cause whereas others have the principles of the individual of the species as their cause. "Man is risible" is an example of the first type. This accident is called a property; it is a result of the difference, rational, which enters into the species and consequently definition of man. Accidents following on the individual and not on the nature are called *inseparable* accidents.[67] Opposed to such accidents are contingent or *separable* accidents, e.g. "Man is white."[68] What is common to every accident is the fact that it is not of the essence of its subject. "Est autem commune omni accidenti," St. Thomas says elsewhere, after having made the same two-fold division just discussed, "quod non sit de essentia rei, et ita non cadit in definitione rei."[69]

(b) Predicable and Predicamental Accident

It may be well to relate this discussion to the distinction of predicable and predicamental accident, for that distinction seems relevant to *Metaphysics*, V.7. This distinction divides accidents into two kinds. The first is the accident which is other than substance and comprises the nine genera of accidents. When accident is understood in this way there is no midway point between substance and accident, for they divide being by affirmation and negation: substance is what is not in a subject, accident what is in a subject. Secondly, accident may be understood as it is numbered among the five universals or predicables by Porphyry (*Isagoge*, cap. 4). In this use, accident does not signify what is common to the nine genera, but "the accidental relation of predicate to subject, or of the common to what is contained under it."[70]

That the second use of *accidens* is different from the first is clear from this that if accident were understood in the second way, where it is distinguished from genus and species, nothing in the nine genera of

---

67. *Q. D. de anima*, a. 13, ad 7.
68. *In I Post. Analytic.*, lect. 14, n. 2.
69. *Q. D. de anima*, a. 12, ad 7.
70. ". . . sed habitudinem accidentalem praedicati ad subiectum, vel communis ad ea quae sub communi continentur."—*Q. D. de spiritualibus creaturis*, a. 11, c.

accidents could be called a species or, more strangely, a genus. But color is the genus of white, number the genus of two. Given the difference of these two uses of *accident*, then, we can note that, in the second sense, we can speak of a mean between substance and accident, between the substantial predicate and the accidental predicate, namely what is predicated as a property, i.e. in the second mode of perseity. The property has this similarity with the substantial predicate that it is caused by the substantial principles of the species; it agrees with the accidental predicate in this that it is not of the essence of the thing. "Differt autem ab accidentali praedicato, quia accidentale praedicatum non causatur ex principiis essentialibus speciei, sed accidit individuo sicut proprium speciei; quandoque tamen separabiliter, quandoque inseparabiliter."[71]

If we take the property as our point of reference, we see that it is included among things said *per se* as opposed to those said *per accidens*. It is distinguished from what is said *essentialiter* and included among those predicated *accidentaliter*, being more closely related to the inseparable accident of the individual. Sometimes, as in the last text examined, it is distinguished from both the substantial and accidental predicate.

The linking of separable and inseparable accidents to the individuals of the species and substantial predicates and property to the species is often done by St. Thomas. Consider the following unquantified propositions:

(1) Man is rational,
(2) Man is risible,
(3) Man is white.

(1) and (2) could be preceded by the universal quantifier, *every*, which means the predicate is said of everything of which the subject is said.[72] We would not want so to quantify (3): at best this indefinite proposition would be quantified as "Some man is white," appealing to the *individuum vagum*, or we would form the singular proposition, "Socrates is white."[73] Indeed, it is only because Socrates happens to be

---

71. Ibid.   72. *In I Periherm.*, lect. 10, n. 13.

73. In view of the criticisms of the *Categories* as 'ontological', it may be well to observe that the distinction of things into universal and singular is a logical one, at least in the sense 'logic' has for Aristotle and St. Thomas. (Not that Aristotle used *logikē* to designate the doctrine of the Organon, any more than he himself called the relevant books the Organon, though the designation is utterly Aristotelian. Cf. *Metaphysics*, 995a12–14.) "Quia igitur hanc divisionem dedit de rebus non absolute secundum quod sunt extra animam, sed secundum quod referuntur ad intellectum, non definivit universale et singulare secundum aliquid quod pertinet ad rem, puta si diceret quod universale

white, or happens to be walking, that we can say, man is white, or man walks. With any separable accident it is the case that it is predicated *per prius* of singulars, of the individual, and *per posterius* of the universal nature. With *per se* predicates just the reverse is true: they are predicated *per prius* of the universal and *per posterius* of the individual. Thus, man walks, is true if it is true that Socrates (or some other individual) walks. But "Socrates is rational and risible" is true because it is true that man is rational and man is risible.[74]

(c) Predication "Per Essentiam" and "Per Participationem"

In a text which will occupy us again later, St. Thomas speaks of predication in yet another way. "Dicendum quod dupliciter aliquid de aliquo praedicatur: uno modo essentialiter, alio modo per participationem. Lux enim praedicatur de corpore illuminato *participative*; sed si esset aliqua lux separata, praedicaretur de ea essentialiter."[75] In order to understand this text, we will examine some other uses of the same terminology. In some texts the distinction between what is predicated *per essentiam* and *per participationem* is the same as that between what is predicated *essentialiter* and *accidentaliter*. ". . . those things of which the genus is predicated according to participation cannot be defined by that genus unless it is the essence of that which is defined. As 'fired iron', of which fire is predicated by participation, is not defined by fire as by its genus, since iron is not fire in its very essence but participates something of it. The genus is not predicated of the species by participation, but by essence. Man is essentially animal, not only something participating animal, for man truly is what animal is."[76] To be said by way of participation is proper to that which is not of the essence of that of which it is predicated. In the same way, what is predicated by way of participation can be said to be predicated *denominative*, and both are distinguished from "univocal predication,"[77] which

extra animam, quod pertinet ad opinionem Platonis, sed per actum animae intellectivae, quod est praedicari de multis vel de uno solo."—*In I Periherm.*, lect. 10, n. 9.

74. Cf. *In V Metaphysic.*, lect. 7, nn. 845–47; ibid., lect. 11, n. 910; *In I Periherm.*, lect. 10, n. 9.

75. *Quodlib.* II, q. 2, a. 1.

76. ". . . ea de quibus genus praedicatur secundum participationem, non possunt definiri per illud genus, nisi sit de essentia illius definiti. Sicut ferrum ignitum, de quo ignis per participationem praedicatur, non definitur per ignem, sicut per genus; quia ferrum non est per essentiam suam ignis, sed participat aliquid eius. Genus autem non praedicatur de speciebus per participationem, sed per essentiam. Homo enim est animal essentialiter, non solum aliquid animalis participans."—*In VII Metaphysic.*, lect. 3, n. 1328.

77. Ibid., lect. 2, n. 1288.

is had when the predicate is of the very essence of the subject. In "Man is white," *white* can be said to be predicated by way of participation or denominatively [78] of man.

St. Thomas does not always use predication by way of participation as something opposed to predication *per essentiam*. Thus, he will often say that the species participates the genus. "Omne quod de pluribus praedicatur univoce, secundum participationem cuilibet eorum convenit de quo praedicatur: nam species participare dicitur genus, et individuum speciem. De Deo autem nihil dicitur per participationem: nam omne quod participatur determinatur ad modum participati, et sic partialiter habetur et non secundum omnem perfectionis modum." [79] If we recall the three-fold manner of participating distinguished by St. Thomas in his comments on the *De hebdomadibus* of Boethius, we see that the texts already alluded to are not contradictory. Prior to the division, we are given the common notion of participation. "Est autem participare quasi partem capere; et ideo quando aliquid particulariter recipit id quod ad alterum pertinet universaliter, dicitur participare illud." [80] Then participating is distinguished into the three modes:

(1) sicut homo dicitur participare animal, quia non habet rationem animalis secundum totam communitatem; et eadem ratione Socrates participat hominem;

(2) similiter etiam subiectum participat accidens, et materia formam, quia forma substantialis vel accidentalis, quae de sui ratione communis est, determinatur ad hoc vel ad illud subiectum;

(3) et similiter effectus dicitur participare suam causam, et praecipue quando non adaequat virtutem suae causae; puta, si dicamus quod aer participat lucem solis, quia non recipit eam in ea claritate qua est in sole. [81]

In the immediately preceding texts, predication *per participationem* or *denominative* is distinguished from that *per essentiam*; the former answers to the second mode given in the *De hebdomadibus* and the latter to the first mode of participating, explaining why elsewhere he can speak of the species participating its genus. What now are we to make of the text with which we began this section? What meaning of *essentialiter* is there opposed to *participative*?

The example given suggests the third mode of participating listed

78. Denominative predication in turn is taken either from something within or from something without the subject. Cf. *In III Physic.*, lect. 5, n. 15; and the commentary of Sylvester of Ferrara on *SCG*, II, cap. 13, n. 2.
79. *SCG*, I, cap. 32.
80. *In de hebdomadibus*, lect. 2 (ed. Calcaterra), n. 24.
81. Ibid.

in the *De hebdomadibus*: an effect is said to participate in its cause *particulariter* (i.e. *partem capere*) when it is not equal to, adequate to, its cause.[82] However, the distinction given in the *Quodlibet* need not be restricted to the third mode. Of present interest is its relevance to the first mode. In what way can that which is predicated *in quid*, e.g. genus of species, species of individual, be said to be predicated, not *essentialiter*, but only *per participationem*? An answer seems suggested by the *De hebdomadibus*. *Man* is not a "universal predicate" of Socrates, nor *animal* of *man*. We are thinking here of the universal predicate of the *Posterior Analytics*,[83] which adds to the *dici de omni* and *dici per se* the note of perfect adequacy with its subject and permits the universal affirmative proposition in which it occurs to be simply converted. The example of the *Posteriora* is this: having interior angles the sum of which is equal to the sum of two right angles is a universal predicate not of plane figures nor of isosceles triangle but precisely of triangle. The species, isosceles, participates in this property via its participation in the generic nature of triangle. If we should select an example from the genus of substance, an objection arises which is relevant to the doctrine of the *Quodlibet*. Thus, having noted that such-and-such is a universal predicate of animal, but not of man, we might object: but there exists no animal apart from these men and these brutes. So too the significant remark of the *Quodlibet*: ". . . sed si esset lux separata, praedicaretur de ea essentialiter." If the mode of existence of the subject were equivalent to the mode of signifying of the predicate, the predicate would be said of it *essentialiter*. If there were some subsistent individual who was what-it-is-to-be-a-man, man would be predicated of him *essentialiter*; since there is no such man, there is nothing of which man is predicated *essentialiter* in the sense of the *Quodlibet*. To be sure, man is predicated *per essentiam* of such individuals as Socrates, but as well *per participationem*. None of them is what-it-is-to-be-a-man, is the species, has *man* predicated of him *essentialiter* in just that sense. This would seem to be the problem raised in Book Zeta of the *Metaphysics*: is the essence other than the individuals? Aristotle, we remember, answers the question in two ways, first negatively and then affirmatively. The thing and its essence are one in this sense that the essence does not enjoy any existence in separation from the individuals, as Plato maintained. If there were a man separate from the particular men of our experience, that Man would be man *essentialiter*. As things are, the essence expresses only part of what the individuals are:

82. Cf. *In II Metaphysic.*, lect. 2, nn. 293–96.
83. Cf. *In I Post. Analytic.*, lect. 11.

thus as signified in precision from the individuals, i.e. as signified abstractly, it cannot be predicated of them. We cannot say, "Socrates is humanity," because Socrates is not man *essentialiter* in the sense of the *Quodlibet*.[84] In anticipation, we can note with St. Thomas: "Si autem est aliqua res, in qua non sit aliquod accidens, ibi necesse est, quod nihil differt abstractum a concreto. Quod maxime patet in Deo."[85] By way of conclusion here we could adapt the text of the *Quodlibet* in this fashion: "*Man* is predicated of the individual man *participative*; but if there were some separated man it would be predicated of him *essentialiter*."

(d) Being "Per Accidens"

With a view now to resolving the difficulties raised concerning *Metaphysics*, V.7, let us examine the text in a somewhat summary fashion. By considering what is discussed under being *per accidens* and being *per se*, we should be able to grasp the principle of their difference.

Since being *per accidens* is had by a comparison of the accident to its subject, we find a three-fold subdivision: (1) when an accident is predicated of an accident, e.g. The just is musical; (2) when an accident is predicated of a subject, e.g. Man is musical; (3) when the subject is predicated of the accident, e.g. The musical is man. "In omnibus enim his, Esse, nihil aliud significat quam accidere."[86] Now, to predicate accidentally, which is tantamount to asserting that two things are accidentally one, is to be understood as meaning that the predicate is not of the essence of the subject. This can be examined easily enough in (2), but (1) and (3) present certain difficulties. If being *per accidens* is had by a comparison of accident to subject, that comparison is ob-

---

84. Cf. *De ente et essentia*, cap. 3, in fine. When we say that the essence expresses only part of what individuals are, the emphasis is on *expresses*. 'Humanity' signifies *per modum partis*, 'man' *per modum totius* (cf. *Quodlib.* IX, q. 2, a. 1, ad 1). This is not to say that 'man' expresses more than 'humanity' does; both the abstract and the concrete terms signify only the essence. They differ in the way they signify it, and because 'man' in its mode of signifying does not prescind from accidents, it can be predicated of Socrates. But 'man' does not signify the accidents. Cf. *In VII Metaphysic.*, lect. 5, n. 1379.

85. Ibid., n. 1380. With respect to the text of *Quodlib.* II, q. 2, a. 1, consider the following remark from *SCG*, II, cap. 26: "Quod est commune multis non est aliquid praeter multa nisi sola ratione: sicut *animal* non est aliud praeter Socratem et Platonem et alia animalia nisi intellectu, qui apprehendit formam animalis exspoliatam ab omnibus individuantibus et specificantibus; homo enim est quod vere est animal; alias sequeretur quod in Socrate et Platone essent plura animalia, scilicet ipsum animal commune, et homo communis, et ipse Plato. Multo igitur minus est ipsum esse commune aliquid praeter omnes res existentes nisi in intellectu solum. Si igitur Deus sit esse commune, Deus non erit aliqua res nisi quae sit in intellectu tantum."

86. *In V Metaphysic.*, lect. 9, n. 887.

scured in (1) and (3). St. Thomas links the two of these together because both refer to the subject only indirectly.[87] "When we say, 'The
white is wood,' what is meant is that the universal predicate *wood* is
predicated of the subject which happens to be white, namely of this
particular wood in which whiteness is. It is the same thing to say, 'The
white is wood,' as to say, 'This wood which happens to be white is
wood.' It does not mean that white is the subject of wood."[88] So too
when we say, "The just is musical," *musical* is predicated of *just* because
it is predicated of the subject of just.[89] "There is this difference, therefore, in the three foregoing modes that when the accident is predicated of the subject, it is not predicated through some other subject;
however when the subject is predicated of the accident, or an accident
of an accident, the predication is made by reason of that which underlies what occupies the position of subject. Of *that* subject [i.e. the
merely grammatical subject] an accident is predicated accidentally; of
the species of the subject, however, it is predicated essentially."[90]
Being *per accidens*, then, always arises from the comparison of accident
to its subject and the accident is not of the essence of its subject. Being
per accidens is designated by the copula of such propositions where *is*
means happens-to-be; the proposition, in its composition, signifies
what is one only accidentally.

(e) Being "Per Se"

The term "being" is divided into two modes at the outset of *Metaphysics*, V.7: the *per accidens* and the *per se*. Having looked at the discussion of the first mode, we turn now to the second. As we have seen,
being *per se* is further subdivided into three modes: *ens perfectum*, *ens
ut verum* and being said according to act and potency. Perfected being
is divided by the ten categories. This division (no more than the initial
division of the chapter, as we shall argue below) is not that of a genus

87. Ibid.
88. ". . . cum dicitur 'album est lignum' hoc significatur, quod illud universale
praedicatum, quod est 'lignum', praedicatur de subiecto, cui accidit esse album, scilicet
de hoc particulari ligno, in quo est albedo. Idem enim est sensum cum dico, 'album est
lignum' ac si dicerem, 'hoc lignum, cui accidit esse album, est lignum'; non autem est
sensus quod album sit subiectum ligni."—*In I Post. Analytic.*, lect. 33, n. 4.
89. *In V Metaphysic.*, lect. 8, n. 887.
90. "Est ergo differentia in tribus modis praedictis: quia cum praedicatur accidens
de subiecto, non praedicatur per aliquod aliud subiectum; cum autem praedicatur subiectum de accidente, vel accidens de accidente, fit praedicatio ratione eius quod subiicitur termino posito in subiecto; de quo quidem praedicatur aliud accidens accidentaliter, ipsa vero species subiecti essentialiter."—*In I Post. Analytic.*, lect. 33, n. 4. *Essentialiter* means of itself as opposed to thanks to something else.

into its species; rather it is based on different modes of predicating.[91] Now since of those things which are predicated, some signify *what*, some *how*, some *how much* and so on, to be (*esse*) will have as many meanings as there are distinct modes of predicating. In "Man is animal" *is* signifies substance; in "Man is white," quality, and so forth.[92] The mention here of "Man is white" enables us to return to the problems raised earlier. This same proposition was used as an example of being *per accidens*; how now can it exhibit a kind of being *per se*? Or, more particularly, how can accident be a mode of being *per se* and thereby be distinguished from being *per accidens*? If we recall that being *per accidens* involves a comparison of accident to subject, we must also recall that the genera of accidents are distinguished on the basis of modes of predicating. What is meant by "secundum absolutam entis considerationem" as opposed to "per comparationem accidentis ad substantiam"?[93]

To begin, let us recall that the division of *ens perfectum* into categories on the basis of modes of predicating is a brief resume of something first taught in Aristotle's logical work, the *Categories*. And, since that work is concerned with logical intentions analytically prior to those which attach to composing and dividing, i.e. judging, its concern with predication must differ from that of the *Perihermeneias*. That difference is brought out by the terms *praedicabilitas/praedicatio*.[94] A genus is that which is predicable of many differing in species. The intention of genus attaches to a concept not as actually predicated but as able to be predicated. The categories or predicaments are divisions of predicates, not as actually parts of propositions, but considered in themselves. In the examples already given, "Man is animal," "Man is white," what interests us is the being attributed to the subject: *is-animal*, *is-white*, considered just in themselves. In being *per accidens*, on the other hand, we look to the accidental togetherness of man and white, i.e. *white-man*, and that *whole* is what we are saying *is* accidentally.

St. Thomas makes this point somewhat indirectly by disputing Avicenna's reading of the passage before us. The Arabian commentator maintained that the things in the genera of accident principally signify substance and only secondarily accident, as if *album* and *musicum* first and primarily signified substance and signified accident only *per posterius*. St. Thomas argues that this is false.[95] First, he gives his own

---

91. Cf. *In III Physic.*, lect. 5, n. 15.
93. Ibid., n. 885.
95. *In V Metaphysic.*, lect. 9, n. 894.

92. *In V Metaphysic.*, lect. 9, n. 890.
94. Cf. *De ente et essentia*, cap. 4, in fine.

interpretation and then he gives the reason for it, a reason which enables us to see that his is the correct and Avicenna's the incorrect reading. First, then, St. Thomas asserts that white (*album*) as it is placed in a category, signifies only quality (*solam qualitatem significat*). It does, of course, signify its subject *ex consequenti*, indirectly, insofar as it is a concrete term; by the same token, its subject is included *ex consequenti* in its *ratio* or definition. For an accident to be is for it to be in substance, but it is not its subject, is not substance, and thus the concrete name of an accident will not principally signify its subject. It is different for the abstract name of the accident, e.g. whiteness, which signifies *per modum substantiae* and not *per modum accidentis* as does its concrete name. *Whiteness* in no way consignifies substance, which is why we read elsewhere that when things other than substance are signified abstractly, we can doubt that they are beings at all.[96]

Secondly, St. Thomas gives a textual argument to show his understanding of Aristotle is correct. If, as Avicenna thought, accidents primarily signified their subject, Aristotle would have placed them under being *per accidens* and not under being *per se*. The whole, subject-accident, white-man, is being *per accidens*, but the accident considered in itself, *per se*, is not being *per accidens* in that sense.

With a view to addressing ourselves to the questions raised at the beginning of this article, we turned to an analysis of *Metaphysics*, V.7, where Aristotle distinguishes the various modes of the term "being." Our analysis thus far has led to a discussion of predication *per se* and *per accidens*, of predication *essentialiter* as opposed to that *accidentaliter*, of predication *per participationem* as opposed to that which is *essentialiter*. These distinctions helped us to understand the basic divisions of *Metaphysics*, V.7, and to resolve the difficulty following on the use of accidental being to signify the whole or compound made up of subject and accident, on the one hand, and, on the other, to signify a type of being *per se*. What is more, these distinctions will help in understanding why it is that being is sometimes said to be predicated *substantialiter* of what falls under the categories, whereas at other times it is said that no creature has being said of it *substantialiter*, *per essentiam* or *essentialiter*. Turning now to the question of being as accidental predicate, we shall continue our discussion by looking at the third mode of being listed in *Metaphysics*, V.7. From there we will move on to other texts.

96. *In VII Metaphysic.*, lect. 1, n. 1252.

2. Being as Accidental Predicate

The third mode of "being" distinguished in *Metaphysics*, V.7, is being as what is true. To the question, "Is man an animal?" we reply, "He is" and in so doing we signify that it is true to say that man is an animal. So too, by replying to the question, "Is man a stone?" by "He is not," we signify that it is false to say man is a stone.[97] In this mode, then, to be (*esse*) and is (*est*) signify the composition of a proposition which the intellect makes in judging. This being which is truth is not in the things which exist and which fall under the categories; truth is in the mind, although things may be called true because they are causes of truth in the proper sense (*ratio propria*) of the term.[98] That is, the truth of a mental composition or division, of a judgment of the mind, depends on the way things are: what is composed in the proposition must be composed or together in reality if the proposition is to be true; so, in the negative proposition, what is divided must be apart in reality if the proposition is to be true. We want now to make a rather lengthy citation from St. Thomas in which he compares this second mode of being *per se*, being as what is true, with the first, *ens perfectum*. In the passage we find an interesting statement about being as it pertains to accidental and substantial predication.

It should be noted, however, that this second mode compares to the first as effect to cause. For it is because something is *in rerum natura* that truth or falsity is had in the proposition, something the intellect signifies by means of the verb, *is*, insofar as it is a verbal copula. But, because something which in itself is non-being can be considered by the intellect as a certain being, e.g. negation and the like, a thing is sometimes said to be in this second way and not in the first. For blindness does not have any existence in reality; rather it is a privation of being. Now it is accidental to a thing that something is truly affirmed of it by intellect or word, for things are not related to knowledge but vice versa. The being that a thing has in its own nature is substantial and therefore when we say "Socrates is," if the *is* is taken in the first way it is a substantial predicate, for being is superior to any particular being as animal is to man. If however it is taken in the second way it is an accidental predicate.[99]

97. *In VI Metaphysic.*, lect. 4, n. 1223.   98. *Q. D. de ver.*, q. 1, a. 2, c.

99. "Sciendum est autem quod iste secundum modus comparatur ad primum, sicut effectus ad causam. Ex hoc enim quod aliquid in rerum natura est, sequitur veritas et falsitas in propositione, quam intellectus significat per hoc verbum *est* prout est verbalis copula. Sed quia aliquid quod est in se non ens intellectus considerat ut quoddam ens, sicut negationem et huiusmodi, ideo quandoque dicitur esse de aliquod hoc secundo modo, et non primo. Dicitur enim quod caecitas est secundo modo, ex eo quod vera est propositio, qua dicitur aliquid est caecum; non tamen dicitur quod sit primo modo vera. Nam caecitas non habet aliquod esse in rebus, sed magis est privatio alicuius esse. Accidit autem unicuique rei quod aliquid de ipsa vere affirmetur intellectu vel voce. Nam res non refertur ad scientiam, sed e converso. Et ideo cum dicitur 'Socrates est,' si

(a) "Ens ut Verum" as Accidental Predicate

In the proposition, "Socrates is," the predicate can be considered in two ways. First, as a verbal copula, as sign of a composition made by our minds. That is, it is true that Socrates exists: being in the sense of what is true is had in an operation of our mind. This type of being is accidental to the being enjoyed by things *extra animam*, i.e. the things which are independently of our knowing them. That is why, when the *is* in "Socrates is" is taken to be a sign of mental composition, it is said to be an accidental predicate. It is quite accidental to Socrates that he should provide occasions for the utterance of true propositions. It is not being in the sense of true which constitutes him as a being *in rerum natura*; rather his existence *extra animam* founds the possibility of being in the sense of what is true.[100] It is because any being which falls under the categories can cause truth in our mind that the term is extended to things and we say that whatever is is true since whatever is can be known by our mind. But the truth convertible with being *extra animam* is not truth in the proper sense of the term, but in a secondary sense.[101] Being in the sense of true is only in the mind (*res rationis tantum*).[102] *Is*, then, as the sign of a mental composition signifies a being which is accidental to being *extra animam*.

St. Thomas, in the text quoted above, has drawn our attention to the fact that being in the sense of true is wider in scope than the first mode of being *per se*. He often makes this point. "Whatever is called being in the first mode is being in the second mode, because everything which has natural being in reality can be signified to be in an affirmative proposition, as when we say color is or man is. However, not everything which is being in the second way can be being in the first way."[103] Many things can be said to be in the sense that they figure in true propositions, but they do not for all that amount to something

---

ille *est* primo modo accipiatur, est de praedicato substantiali. Nam ens est superius ad unumquodque entium, sicut animal ad hominem. Si autem accipiatur secundo modo, est de praedicato accidentali."—*In V Metaphysic.*, lect. 9, n. 896.

100. Just as its not being *extra animam* founds the truth of the proposition "Homer is blind." Homer's blindness *is* only in the sense that Homer cannot see. To be blind is to lack a capacity, not to have a capacity of a certain kind.

101. Just as things which are in the sense of *ens ut verum* may be such that they are not being in the sense of those things which, because they exist, are true.

102. *In V Metaphysic.*, lect. 9, n. 897.

103. "Quaecumque ergo dicuntur entia quantum ad primum modum, sunt entia quantum ad secundum modum: quia omne quod habet naturale esse in rebus potest significari per propositionem affirmativam esse, ut cum dicitur: color est vel homo est. Non autem omnia quae sunt entia quantum ad secundum modum, sint entia quantum ad primum. . . ."—*In II Sent.*, d. 34, q. 1, a. 1, sol.

positive in reality. Privations and negations, non-being, can enter into true propositions: but they are not thereby numbered among the things which *aliquid in re ponunt*,[104] and which are being *per se* in the first mode. "Peter is blind" means that he cannot see, which may be perfectly true, but Peter's inability to see is not a positive reality; it is precisely the absence of a certain reality, a privation of something positive. Doubtless there are positive reasons for this inability, but the inability is not there in the way that the damaged organ is—or in the way Paul's ability to see is something real.

If we let this suffice as an indication of what being in the sense of true means, we can turn to a remark lodged in discussions of *ens ut verum* which paves the way to a treatment of our overriding problems. Comparing *ens perfectum* and *ens ut verum*, St. Thomas writes: "Being is predicated differently following on these modes since taken in the first way it is a substantial predicate and pertains to the question, 'what is it?' but according to the second mode it is an accidental predicate, as the Commentator says there [commenting on *Metaph.*, V.7] and pertains to the question, 'Is it?'"[105] This text echoes that already quoted from the commentary on the *Metaphysics*. If we advert to the remarks made above about things predicated *substantialiter*, it is easy to see what is meant. Being *per se*, in the sense of *ens perfectum*, is divided according to modes of predication which reflect modes of being. These modes of being pertain to *ens extra animam* and each mode expresses the whatness of what is according to that mode. Thus, "Socrates is an animal" and "color is a quality" are both examples of substantial predicates. And, again, that true statements can be made about such beings is accidental to them.

Despite this initial intelligibility, there are difficulties which remain. In the commentary on the *Metaphysics*, St. Thomas says that the *is* in "Socrates is" is *de praedicato substantiali* if understood in the first mode of being *per se*.[106] This presents difficulties from the point of view of other remarks of St. Thomas. For example, he writes: "And therefore the Commentator says in [his comments on] the fifth book of the *Metaphysics* that this proposition, 'Socrates is' *is* is an accidental predicate according as it signifies the entity of the thing or the truth of the

104. *De ente et essentia*, cap. 1.
105. "Ens autem secundum utrumque istorum modorum diversimode praedicatur: quia secundum primum modum acceptum est praedicatum substantiale, et pertinet ad quaestionem quid est; sed quantum ad secundum modum, est praedicatum accidentale, ut Commentator ibidem dicit, et pertinet ad quaestionem an est."—*In II Sent.*, d. 34, q. 1, a. 1, sol.
106. *In V Metaphysic.*, lect. 9, n. 896; cf. *In III Sent.*, d. 6, q. 3, a. 2, sol.

proposition."[107] Moreover, the *is* in "Socrates is" is said to pertain to the question *an sit.* What is the significance of this appeal to the questions *an sit* and *quid sit* in discussions of the relation between the first two modes of being *per se*? And what is the significance of appealing to the same questions to discuss *ens extra animam*? Before attempting to resolve these problems, it seems wise to say something about these questions themselves.

(b) The Questions "An Sit" and "Quid Sit"

In order to understand why appeal is made to the question *an sit* both to speak of *ens ut verum* and to speak of the actuality of the essence which is other than the essence itself, we must investigate, albeit briefly, the place in which the question *an sit* is discussed formally as such.

In the *Posterior Analytics*, Aristotle, having in the first book discussed the demonstrative syllogism, turns in the second to a discussion of its principles.[108] These principles are either the middle term or the first indemonstrable propositions. The bulk of the book is concerned with the middle term. Aristotle opens the discussion with the suggestion that a middle term is relevant and required whenever there can be doubt or questioning. Thus, insofar as we can enumerate different questions, we are in effect enumerating different things which can be known (*sciuntur*) since science is acquired through demonstration and thus via a middle term. There seem to be four distinct questions to be asked: does the thing exist, what is it, is it such-and-such, why is it such-and-such. These questions will all have an enunciation or proposition as their answer, but propositions, as has been shown in *On Interpretation*,[109] either add some third thing to the noun or verb or do not. An example of the latter is, "Socrates is"; of the former, "Socrates is white." The questions 'Is it?' and 'What is it?' are answered by "simple" enunciations; 'Is it such-and-such?' and 'Why is it such-and-such?' are answered by enunciations which *in numerum ponunt.*[110] On this basis, the couple *an sit/quid sit* is opposed to *quia sit/propter quid.*

On another basis, the questions 'Is it?' and 'Is it such-and-such?' are opposed to 'What is it?' and 'Why is it such-and-such?' Although 'Is it?' inquires about the *esse simpliciter* of the thing and 'Is it such-and-such?'

---

107. "Et ideo Commentator dicit in V Metaphys. quod ista propositio, 'Socrates est,' est de accidentali praedicato, secundum quod importat entitatem rei, vel veritatem propositionis."—*Quodlib.* II, q. 2, a. 1, c.

108. Cf. *In II Post. Analytic.*, lect. 1, n. 1.

109. *On Interpretation*, 10.19b19–22.   110. *In II Post. Analytic.*, lect. 1, n. 3.

about *esse hoc vel hoc*, in both we are seeking whether some middle can be found or not. This is not what is explicitly asked, of course, but what in effect we are after. Nevertheless, when we know that something is or is such-and-such, there is a mean to be sought. The proof of this is that we don't ask questions about self-evident things. Knowing there is a middle, the questions 'What is it?' and 'Why is it such-and-such?' seek knowledge of what that middle is. Again, one who asks why the sun eclipses is not as such but only concomitantly seeking the middle term of a demonstration.[111] 'Is it?' and 'Is it such-and-such?' agree in asking *whether* there is a middle; 'What is it?' and 'Why is it such-and-such?' agree in asking *what* the middle is.

As has already been indicated, there is an order of precedence between the questions 'Is it?' and 'What is it?'[112] This is made explicit later in the present context. That context must be kept in mind when we read remarks about these two questions. What Aristotle is up to is this. Having pointed out that the middle is the quiddity which, since it is the object of definition, does not seem to be as well the object of demonstration, he argues that the quiddity cannot be demonstrated by convertible terms, nor by division, nor by including in the argument the requirements for definition—all involve a *petitio principii*.[113] After these particular arguments against demonstrating the quiddity, he presents another argument *per rationes communes*.[114] First, he makes this general point: it seems impossible to demonstrate the quiddity because whoever knows what a thing is knows that thing to be. What is not has no whatness. True, we can know what a word means without knowing that an existent thing is named by it. But a demonstration concludes to one thing because it uses a middle which is *per se* one and the conclusion has to be proportionate to the middle. What a man is and the fact that he is differ. Now a demonstration concludes that something is. Hence, to show that something is could only be tantamount to showing what something is if for it to be were the same as what it is. Suppose, then that a demonstration concluded to whatness. Since whatness and existence differ, we would arrive at knowledge of whatness independent of knowledge that such a whatness exists. This can be turned around: the definition which expresses whatness does not tell us that the thing exists. In this the definition of circle does not seem to differ from that of silver mountain.

But can we agree that, since the definition expresses only what a thing is and not the fact that it is, on this showing the phoenix, a silver

---

111. Ibid., n. 6.

113. *In II Post. Analytic.*, lects. 3, 4, 5.

112. Cf. *In I Post. Analytic.*, lect. 2.

114. Ibid., lect. 6, n. 1.

mountain, and what have you can be defined in the same way man can? If we should agree to this, we would be identifying the real definition and the nominal definition.[115] It has recently been argued that St. Thomas does so identify real and nominal definitions.[116] This claim is made, oddly enough, by appealing to the *De ente* where St. Thomas holds that only that has a "what" which *aliquid in re ponat*.[117] We need not be moved by the desire to oppose Aristotle and St. Thomas at all costs to find difficulties here, of course. Only that can have a whatness and therefore be defined, strictly speaking, which exists *in rerum natura*. The definition, however, says nothing of the actual existence of the thing defined. Doesn't it follow then that a judgment of existence will be consequent upon definition rather than prior to it? Yet Aristotle and St. Thomas maintain that until we have answered the question *an sit* we do not raise the question *quid sit*. Doesn't this, in the light of our larger interests, raise another problem? Non-being and privation receive the name "being" because of reference to the question *an sit*, yet of them we do not ask *quid sint*.

The reasons for this stand of Aristotle and St. Thomas must be closely examined. We are told that it is possible to come to know simultaneously that a thing is and what it is.[118] We are told that it is impossible for us to know what a thing is without knowing that it is. The usual case will be this: we can judge that a thing is without knowing

---

115. Ibid., nn. 6–9.

116. Cf. Joseph Owens, art. cit., pp. 6–7. "For St. Thomas, on the other hand, one can know what a phoenix is, or a mountain of gold is, or what an eclipse is, without knowing whether any of these actually exist in the real world."

117. But doesn't St. Thomas also write in the manner suggested by Father Owens? "Omnis autem essentia vel quidditas intelligi potest sine hoc quod aliquid intelligatur de esse suo facto: possum enim intelligere quid est homo vel phoenix et tamen ignorare an esse habeant in rerum natura" (*De ente*, cap. 5). St. Thomas seems to speak of man and phoenix here on an equal footing, as if the phoenix had an essence; moreover, he seems to be saying that we can know the essence while ignoring or being unaware of its actual existence. Now the phoenix is a fictive being and as such, according to the opening chapter of the *De ente*, it cannot have an essence. What are we to make of this example? It can be interpreted in either of two ways. It could be said that St. Thomas was unaware that the phoenix is mythical and that the text could as well speak of man and horse as of man and phoenix. On the other hand, he knew the phoenix is fictive and we can say of him what he once said of Aristotle: *signanter autem utitur hoc exemplo* (*In I Periherm.*, lect. 3, n. 13). The knowledge of whatness at issue then must be interpreted widely so as to include *quid est quod dicitur* or the *interpretatio nominis*. Since the phoenix is fictive this is the only whatness to which it can lay claim. Moreover, since the phoenix is, in a sense, a bird which cannot not exist, since it is indestructible, always arising again from its own ashes, this choice of example has an anti-Anselmian ring to it. But if knowledge of *quid est quod dicitur* does not include knowledge of factual existence, neither does knowledge of quiddity in the sense of essence—with the qualifications we have made in the text.

118. Cf. *In II Post. Analytic.*, lect. 7, n. 5.

what it is. Surely our natural mode of knowing is being described here. Things are denominated from the accidents we perceive, or from some common essential note we grasp.[119] In order to judge that a thing is we must judge in terms of something pertaining to that thing, whether accidental or essential. We can know that men exist because we know that featherless bipeds exist, but this is not to know *what* men are. In other words, we have to know what things are in the sense of knowing some meaning of the term applied to them if we are to judge that they exist; we must have knowledge, not of the *quid est*, but of the *quid est quod dicitur*.[120] Knowing that there are things *in rerum natura* which answer to what the term *man* means, we can go on to ask what they are. It is in this sense alone that, both for Aristotle and St. Thomas, knowledge of whatness presupposes knowledge of existence. For neither man is existence included in whatness.[121] It is ambiguous to say that to know whatness is *thereby* to know existence. If we keep in mind the context of the question *quid sit*, namely that it follows on the question *an sit*, this ambiguity is avoided. It remains forever true that the definition expressing the essence of something *in rerum natura* does not itself affirm that existence: the definition is not a proposition. Moreover, as Aristotle suggests,[122] only the affirmation of existence in terms of essence is fully such: to judge that a thing exists because its accidents are known, or a common essential note is grasped, is to know its existence accidentally or commonly. In that sense, one can maintain that the judgment, "Socrates exists," when it is made in terms of knowledge that Socrates is a rational animal, is a more perfect judgment of existence, indeed the first perfect grasp that this *man*, Socrates, exists.

Why does St. Thomas appeal to the question *an sit* when he is talking of being as true? Both *an sit* and *quia est* ask if something is true.[123] The truth in question is not being as true. Not everything which enters into a true statement answers the question *an sit* in such a way that we can go on to ask what is it? The thing which *aliquid in re ponit* founds in a positive way the truth of a proposition, but privations and even non-being can figure in true statements. Thus, being as true is wider than being *in rerum natura*, and with respect to the latter is something accidental. When, in the *Posteriora*, Aristotle seems to equate sat-

---

119. Ibid., nn. 6–7.
120. Cf. *In I Post. Analytic.*, lect. 2.
121. *Posterior Analytics*, II.7; St. Thomas, lect. 6.
122. 93a28–29: "Thus it follows that the degree of our knowledge of a thing's essential nature is determined by the sense in which we are aware that it exists."
123. Cf. *In II Post. Analytic.*, lect. 1, n. 3.

isfying the question *an sit* and paving the way to the question *quid sit*, it is the context which explains his procedure. Only that answers the question *an sit* which is something positive in reality; indeed the question may be answered in terms of a partial grasp of whatness. In the *Posteriora* it is science which is being discussed, the demonstrative syllogism, and the four questions are examined from the point of view of their relevance for science. *Ens ut verum* can be the concern of logic, and, with many qualifications, of psychology, but it is *ens* as it falls under the categories which interests science. Now when *ens ut verum* is referred to the question *an sit* this is because, even as we would test a notion from the point of view of science and come up with the answer that it *nihil ponit in re*, we express this in a true proposition and thereby confer on the notion being in the sense of what is true. "The phoenix does not exist," or "There are no centaurs *in rerum natura*" are true statements and the phoenix and centaurs are in the sense that they figure in such judgments. "Yes, they are," we might say, when told that centaurs are fictions, and what we mean is that the statement is true.

There *can* be, therefore, a double reference in the answer to the question *an sit*. As St. Thomas says, it can refer to the truth of the proposition or the *entitas rei*.[124] Even when the latter is precluded, the former is possible. It is easy to understand why *ens ut verum* is accidental to *ens reale*, that to be in the former sense is an accidental predicate of things which fall under the categories. It is the teaching of St. Thomas, however, that even when the question *an sit* refers to the *entitas rei*, an accidental predicate is involved. We want now to examine this doctrine and its compatibility with the text quoted above in which we read that when the predicate in "Socrates is" does not refer to *ens ut verum* but to *ens reale*, it is a substantial predicate.

(c) Existence as Accidental Predicate

On the basis of the texts examined earlier, talk of an accidental predicate would bring to mind either the predication of an accident of a subject (e.g. Man is white) or the fact that to affirm Socrates is sitting is accidental to the sedentary Socrates. The doctrine we are now to examine does not fall under either of these headings. "Hence since everything which is outside the essence of a thing is said to be an accident, the existence which pertains to the question, 'Is it?' is an accident."[125] Now, earlier, we said that what is common to every accident is

---

124. *Quodlib.* II, q. 2, a. 1, c.
125. "Unde, cum omne quod est praeter essentiam rei, dicatur accidens; esse quod pertinet ad quaestionem *an est*, est accidens."—ibid.

the fact that it is not of the essence of the subject of which it is predicated. It is that common notion that must be kept firmly in mind now. Earlier, of course, this common notion was invoked only to cover necessary and contingent accidents, both of which were distinguished from what is predicated *per se* in the first mode. How does the predicate in "Socrates is" save the common notion of accident as compared with the things predicated *accidentaliter* which were examined earlier?

There are a number of remarks of St. Thomas which could lead us to think that existence is an accident in the way the property is. The property was said to be caused by the essential principles of the subject. So too substantial existence is "esse resultans ex his quibus integratur, quod proprium est esse suppositi substantiale." [126] St. Thomas often speaks in this way. "Secunda operatio respicit ipsum esse rei, quod quidem resultat ex congregatione principiorum rei in compositis, vel ipsam simplicem naturam rei concomitatur, ut in substantiis simplicibus." [127] And again: "Esse rei, quamvis sit aliud ab ejus essentia, non tamen est intelligendum quod sit aliquod superadditum ad modum accidentis, sed quasi constituitur per principia essentiae." [128] Although property is other than the essence of its subject and follows from the principles of that essence, it is not the act that existence is, nor is existence a property of the essence. It is because the nature is that the property is, but the nature is because existence inheres in, or adheres to, it. [129] Moreover, the nature is a quasi-efficient cause of property, [130] but no nature is the efficient cause of its own existence since the efficient cause imparts an actuality already possessed to its effects. To say that man exists, then, is to say that the nature is, absolutely speaking; to say man is risible is to say the nature is such-and-such. A *fortiori* existence is not an accident like the contingent accidents discussed above.

Thus, although existence is said to save the common notion of accident, insofar as whatever is *praeter essentiam* is an accident, it does not do so in the way predicamental accident, whether *per se* or contingent, does. Thus, St. Thomas writes: "esse est accidens, non quasi per accidens se habens, sed quasi actualitas cuiuslibet substantiae; unde ipse

126. *Quodlib.* IX, q. 2, a. 2.
127. *In Boethii de trin.* (ed. Wyser), q. 5, a. 3.
128. *In IV Metaphysic.*, lect. 2, n. 558.
129. Cf. Gilson, *Being and Some Philosophers*, p. 225, where he seems to reject this terminology. St. Thomas uses both *adhaerere* (*Quodlib.* II, q. 2, a. 1, c.) and *inhaerere* (*Q. D. de pot.*, q. 7, a. 2, ad 7).
130. Cf. *ST*, Ia, q. 77, a. 6, ad 2; Henri Renard, S.J., *The Philosophy of Man* (Milwaukee: 1948), pp. 60–62.

Deus, qui est sua actualitas, est suum esse."[131] If the common notion of accident is thought to be saved only by necessary and contingent accidents, existence is no accident. "Et sic dico quod esse substantiale rei non est accidens, sed actualitas cuiuslibet formae existentis, sive sine materia sive cum materia. Et quia esse est complementum omnium, inde est quod proprius effectus Dei est esse, et nulla causa dat esse nisi inquantum participat operationem divinam; et sic proprie loquendo, non est accidens. Et quod Hilarius dicit, dico quod accidens dicitur large omne quod non est pars essentiae; et sic est esse in rebus creatis, quia in solo Deo esse est eius essentia."[132] St. Thomas accepts the extension of the word accident to include whatever is not of the essence of the thing. This is a common notion and is thereby opposed to the proper notion, the *ratio propria* of the term. Indeed, it is a notion far more common than that which enables us to group necessary and contingent accidents under the one term, accident. These latter are *praeter essentiam* but as well *esse accidentale*. The actuality of the essence, though also *praeter essentiam*, is *esse substantiale*. That is why *esse*, in the sense of substantial existence, is not an accident in the sense of *per accidens se habens*.[133] The only meaning accident has as applied to existence is the sweepingly general one of *praeter essentiam*.

With respect to material things, *existence* means the actual composition of the components of the essence.[134] "Man exists" means that the substantial form and prime matter are *actually* composed. This actuality is not another essential principle; it is not a *tertium quid* composed of the principles.[135] It is the *actual* composition of the essential principles, the actuality of that which is a man. If it were another essential principle it would enter into the definition of the nature and it would be contradictory to say Socrates or man do not exist. The composition of essence and existence, then, is not a composition of the parts of substance, but a composition of substance with that which adheres to or inheres in it as its actuality. This is as true of created spirits as of material creatures. "Si ergo in angelo est compositio sicut ex essentia et esse, non tamen est compositio sicut ex partibus substantiae, sed sicut ex substantia et eo quod adhaeret substantiae."[136]

For a man to be is for a soul and a body actually to be composed. Existence is this actual composition *in rerum natura*. This is not a composition of essence and existence in general, but of this essence and this existence. For Socrates to exist is for an essence of a certain kind

---

131. *Quodlib.* II, q. 2, a. 1, ad 2.   132. *Quodlib.* XII, q. 5, a. 11.
133. *Quodlib.* II, q. 2, a. 1, ad 2; *Q. D. de pot.*, q. 5, a. 4, ad 3.
134. *Q. D. de virtutibus in communi*, a. 11; *Q. D. de anima*, a. 6.
135. Ibid.   136. *Quodlib.* II, q. 2, a. 1, c.

to be actual. It would seem to be for this reason that St. Thomas speaks of existence as following from the principles of the essence, resulting from them. It is not that essence produces its actuality, but rather that the actuality is of this limited kind because of what is actualized. "Man exists" does not assert the composition of human nature and "the act of all acts even of forms," which is the common notion of existence. Rather, it is the composition of *this* nature and *its* actuality. True, this existence falls under the common notion of existence, but it also restricts it. And, when there are many individuals of the same nature, that which individualizes the nature will individualize existence. Existence is not the principle of individuation, but that which is individualized. Existence does not make human nature individual any more than it makes it to be *what* it is.[137]

There has been a tendency recently to see the judgment of existence as something terminal, as if to know that a thing is were somehow the goal of philosophical knowledge. There are several difficulties with such a view, particularly as a statement about metaphysics. First of all, since only singular things exist, there is a tendency to suggest that the term of metaphysics consists in a judgmental descent to the warmth of existent supposita. But no science, and certainly not metaphysics, is as such concerned with the singulars with which we make experiential contact. Secondly and more pertinently, the question *an sit* is a prelude to the further question *quid sit*. Moreover, the proposition which answers the question *an sit* is a tacit admission that there is a middle to be found which will be causative of the existence recognized in the answer to *an sit*. Once we know that something exists, we ask what it is and our question seeks the cause of the existence. What kind of proposition answers the question *an sit*? Should we say, "Socrates exists"? Yes and no. From the scientific point of view, we would be rather concerned with "Man exists," but of course this will be true insofar as we know that some such man as Socrates is. When *Socrates* is taken as the proper name of one who is a *man*, the judgment that Socrates is founds the truth of the judgment that Man is. This latter, as we have just recalled, poses the further problem of seeking the middle term which expresses the cause of man's existence. In other words, the suggestion is that an argument can be formed in which the quiddity will function as middle term. Would the following be such an argument? "Rational animal exists; Man is a rational ani-

---

137. M. Gilson, while alluding to matter as principle of individuation, qualifies this as an Aristotelian doctrine and seems finally to adopt the view that *esse* is the principle of individuation. Indeed, *esse* is invoked to explain why this man is a saint, that man an artist, etc. Cf. *Being and Some Philosophers*, pp. 171–72.

mal; therefore Man exists." Surely this is *not* what is meant. The putative argument comes down to saying that Man is man, which certainly
does not advance our knowledge. No one asks if man is man or, if he
does, he is asking a question that can receive no answer.[138] How in the
world, then, is the quiddity to function as a middle term in an argument concluding to the existence of that of which it is the quiddity?

The mystery is dissipated if we reflect on what permits us to make
an existential judgment. Such a judgment is the attribution of actuality *in rerum natura* to some thing. The thing judged to exist can be
denominated from accidents. If this is the case, we will be unable to
assign the cause of its existence, in the manner under consideration,
because we don't really know that existence save in a *per accidens* manner.[139] However, if something is judged to exist through a grasp of
some essential note then the proof in question is possible. Note that
the proof of an existential judgment, as presently envisaged, is not
sought in the efficient or final cause. Surprisingly enough (at least for
those who conceive of the existential judgment as the affirmation of
the common notion of existence of some inscrutable *X*), the proof of
the existential judgment comes down to a proof of a definition. One
might immediately object that definition or quiddity cannot be proved,
and make reference to the arguments of Aristotle cited above. Precisely, if what is meant is that there is no proof of the proposition
"man is a rational animal." However, the judgment of existence which
answers the question *an sit* is not going to be made in terms of a perfect grasp of quiddity. If it is made in terms of the grasp of a quidditative note, the possibility arises of proving that proposition by appeal to another quidditative note. This presupposes that the thing we
are dealing with is composed.[140] In other words, if we judge that a
thing exists through the grasp of something material in it, its form,
which is the *ratio materiae*, can function as middle term in the proof of
the existential judgment. "Quod quidem est possibile in substantiis
compositis, ut puta si comprehendamus hominem esse per hoc quod
est animal nondum cognitis aliis, quae complent essentiam hominis."[141] The form will be assigned as the cause of the existence of
the matter, this specific form of this kind of matter.[142] The form is the

138. Cf. *In VII Metaphysic.*, lect. 17, nn. 1650–54.

139. Cf. *In II Post. Analytic.*, lect. 7, n. 7; lect. 8, n. 6.

140. Cf. *In VII Metaphysic.*, lect. 17, nn. 1669–71; *In II Post. Analytic.*, lect. 8, n. 3; *In I Post. Analytic.*, lect. 41, n. 8.

141. *In II Post. Analytic.*, lect. 7, n. 6. I have taken the liberty of replacing *rationalis* by *animal* in this text, thereby making it, I think, easier to grasp. Aristotle uses 'animal'.

142. Cf. *In VII Metaphysic.*, lect. 17, n. 1663.

cause of the existence of the matter;[143] to assign the form is to give the *ratio essendi* of the thing which was first known through what is material in it and thereby judged to exist. Such an argument uses the definition through formal cause to give the *propter quid* of the matter through knowledge of which the thing was judged to exist. That is why we read of the definition which is as a conclusion of a demonstration and of the definition which is *propter quid* and differs from the demonstration only in form.[144] The whole quiddity is not demonstrated by such an argument, but the quiddity can be derived from the argument.[145] Although such a demonstration gives the *ratio* or *propter quid* of the matter, this is not a *propter quid* demonstration in the usual sense, that in which a property is shown to belong to a subject because of what that subject is. The proof of the existential judgment does not show existence to be a property of essence; rather it assigns the form as the cause of the existence of the matter, it gives the reason for the existence previously affirmed.

What of the objection, almost certain to arise, that this is "essentialism"? Although it is difficult to know, in every instance of its use,[146] precisely what this term is meant to cover, let us say that the objector feels that Aristotle and St. Thomas are reducing existence to essence, that all the foregoing "demonstration" does is manifest whatness. Neither side of the objection holds. What Aristotle and St. Thomas are doing is assigning the cause of existence. They envisage a situation when a composite is judged to exist; this judgment must have a subject, known in some way, of which existence is affirmed. If "Man exists" stands for "Such-and-such an organized body exists" or, equivalently, "Man is a body organized in such-and-such a way," we seek the cause of what is judged to exist, and the cause precisely of its existence. That cause will be the form. The upshot of the proof is knowledge of what these existent things called men are. We thereby know more perfectly what their existence is: it will be the actual union of this specific form and this matter.

An instructive example of the close link between our knowledge of existence and knowledge of what exists is found in discussion of God's existence. We do not judge that God exists through the grasp of any-

143. Cf. *In II Post. Analytic.*, lect. 7, n. 2; *Q. D. de virtutibus in communi*, a. 11, c.; *Q. D. de anima*, a. 6.

144. Cf. *In II Post Analytic.*, lect. 8, n. 10; *In I Post. Analytic.*, lect. 16, n. 5.

145. ". . . quod quid est potest accipi ex ipsa demonstratione, non potest demonstrari."—*In II Post. Analytic.*, lect. 8, n. 11.

146. Cf. "The Ambiguity of Existential Metaphysics," *Laval théologique et philosophique* 12/1 (1956).

thing pertaining to what He is; if we can conclude to the fact that God exists, we do so from knowledge of his effects. "Unde manifestum est quod sicut nos habemus ad cognoscendum quia est aliquid, ita nos habemus ad cognoscendum quid est." [147] It is this fact which enables us to avoid a difficulty which can arise when we deny, in God, any composition of essence and existence. For then it might seem that since we know God exists and in God essence and existence are one, we know what God is. The flaw in the reasoning is that, although we know God exists, we don't know God's existence.[148] As Aristotle has remarked, "Thus it follows that the degree of our knowledge of a thing's essential nature is determined by the sense in which we are aware that it exists." [149]

3. Being as Substantial Predicate

By way of introduction to the present section, we want to analyze a quodlibetal article [150] to which reference has already been made. From this analysis, several further problems will arise, problems whose solution will enable us to see the ramifications of the doctrine that substantial existence is *praeter essentiam* and is therefore an accidental predicate of any creature.

The quodlibet asks whether the angel is substantially composed of essence and existence. St. Thomas, in the body of the article, begins by noting that one thing can be predicated of another either *essentialiter* or *participative*. We have examined the statement of this distinction earlier. St. Thomas continues:

According to this [distinction] then it must be said that being is predicated essentially of God alone, because the divine existence is subsistent and absolute existence; of no matter what creature it is predicated by way of participation for no creature is its existence but is something having existence. So too God is his goodness; creatures however are called good by way of participation because they have goodness . . . Whenever something is predicated of another by way of participation, there is something there other than that which is participated.[151]

---

147. *In II Post. Analytic.*, lect. 7, n. 7.
148. *ST*, Ia, q. 3, a. 4, ad 2.
149. *Posterior Analytics*, II.8 93a28–29.
150. *Quodlib.* II, q. 2, a. 1.
151. "Secundum ergo hoc dicendum est, quod ens praedicatur de solo Deo *essentialiter*, eo quod esse divinum est esse subsistens et absolutum; de qualibet autem creatura praedicatur *per participationem*: nulla enim creatura est suum esse, sed est habens esse. Sic et Deus dicitur bonus essentialiter, quia *est* ipsa bonitas; creaturae autem dicuntur bona per participationem, quia *habent* bonitatem. . . ."—ibid.

It might appear that predication *essentialiter* and *participative* applied to "being" amounts to a distinction between *esse* and *habens esse*. Yet St. Thomas is speaking of *ens* and doesn't *ens* mean *quod est* or *habens esse?* St. Thomas is saying that God is existence and that creatures, when they exist, have existence. Does he mean that the *ratio entis* as said of God is existence and when said of creatures is *habens esse?* It is certain that *habens esse* exemplifies the complexity which participation is said to involve.

But note that something is participated in either of two ways. In one way, as being of the substance of that which participates in the way genus is participated by the species. Existence is not participated in this way by the creature, for that is of the substance of the thing which enters into its definition. Being, however, is not put in the definition of the creature because it is neither a genus nor difference; hence it is participated as something not of the essence of the thing. That is why the questions 'Is it?' and 'What is it?' differ. And since whatever is outside the essence of the thing is said to be an accident, the existence which answers to the question 'Is it?' is an accident. Hence the Commentator says . . . that this proposition "Socrates is" involves an accidental predicate insofar as it signifies the being of the thing or the truth of the proposition.[152]

That being is participated as something not of the essence of what participates it is indicated by noting that being does not enter into the definition of anything; it does not do so because it is neither genus or difference. Moreover, it seems to be being as it answers the question 'Is it?' which is not a genus. It is easy enough to see that *esse* does not enter into the definition of any creature, but if *ens* here means "existing," we may wonder if that is what *ens* means when it is shown that it cannot be a genus. It is possible, of course, to raise doubts concerning the statement that being does not enter into definitions. Being is that which is first conceived by our mind and that into which every concept is resolved.[153] Doesn't this imply that, in some meaning of the phrase, being enters into the meaning of anything whatsoever? Indeed, doesn't

---

152. "Sed sciendum est, quod aliquid participatur dupliciter. Uno modo quasi existens de substantia participantis, sicut genus participatur a specie. Hoc autem modo esse non participatur a creatura. Id enim est de substantia rei quod cadit in eius definitione. Ens autem non ponitur in definitione creaturae, quia nec est genus nec differentia. Unde participatur sicut aliquid non existens de essentia rei; et ideo alia quaestio est *an est* et *quid est*. Unde cum omne quod est praeter essentiam rei, dicatur accidens; esse quod pertinet ad quaestionem *an est*, est accidens. Et ideo Commentator dicit . . . quod ista propositio, 'Socrates est,' est de accidentali praedicato, secundum quod importat entitatem rei, vel veritatem propositionis."—ibid.

153. *Q. D. de ver.*, q. 1, a. 1, c.

esse enter into the *rationes* of the supreme genera (e.g. substance is that to whose quiddity it belongs not to be in another) and into the definition of essence (that through which and in which the thing has existence)?

> But it is true that this name being, in so far as it signifies the thing to which existence of this kind belongs signifies the essence of the thing and is divided by the ten genera, not univocally however, since existence does not belong to everything in the same way, but to substance *per se* and to the others in other ways.[154]

Insofar as *being* signifies that to which existence belongs, it signifies essence and is the first mode of being *per se* discussed in *Metaphysics*, V.7. This is the being which is divided by the ten categories, but not in the way in which a genus is divided by its species. In other words, being thus understood is not a genus. How does this understanding of being fit into the division with which the quodlibet begins? That is, is being as signifying the essence predicated *essentialiter* or *participative* of what falls under the categories?

Not all of these are relevant questions, of course; moreover the statement of some of them is ambiguous. They seem nevertheless to be the kind of question currently being put. We will deal explicitly with the question of the *ratio entis*, and of being as the subject of metaphysics.

(a) The "Ratio Entis"

The first mode of being *per se* is that which is divided into the ten categories.[155] Being so understood "significat essentiam rei."[156] Being will mean here "what is" (*quod est*), "what has existence" (*quod habet esse, habens esse*). Since being signifies what is, it can be predicated essentially of whatever falls under the categories though not in the same way of everything. Being in this sense, then, does not seem to signify something other than what things are, but precisely what they are. Isn't this why St. Thomas can say "quaelibet natura essentialiter est ens"?[157]

If the being which is predicated *essentialiter* of what falls under the

---

154. "Sed verum est quod hoc nomen ens, secundum quod importat rem cui competit huiusmodi esse, sic significat essentiam rei, et dividitur per decem genera; non tamen univoce, quia non eadem ratione competit omnibus esse: sed substantiae quidem per se, aliis autem aliter."—ibid.

155. Cf. *In V Metaphysic.*, lect. 9, n. 889.

156. *De ente et essentia* (ed. cit.), p. 3, line 12.

157. *Q. D. de ver.*, q. 1, a. 1.

categories means *quod est, habens esse* or *quod habet esse*, is not *esse* part
of the very ratio of the name and doesn't it follow then that *esse* is of
the essence of that of which *ens* is predicated *essentialiter?* Since this is
a consequence we would not want to accept, we must examine how it is
that *esse* is part of the *ratio entis*. The shortest statement of this is: "hoc
vero nomen Ens imponitur ab actu essendi."[158] This remark occurs in
a passage where St. Thomas is discussing what are called the transcen-
dentals. Whatever is is a thing, is one, is good, is true. What does this
mean? The *supposita*, the things denoted by these terms, are the same
but are denominated differently, through different notions or *rationes*. It is the same thing which is a being, a thing, one, etc., although
these terms and the notions signified by them differ. The *suppositum* is
denominated a thing (*res*) from its essence or quiddity; the quiddity is
id a quo nomen imponitur ad significandum. In the case of the term *being*,
the supposit is denominated from its act of existence. Now, although
in the creature its essence is other than its existence, if the term imposed from what it is (*res*) and the term imposed from its existence
(*ens*) did not signify the same thing (though through different *rationes*) they could not be called convertible.[159] That from which the
name being is imposed to signify, i.e. existence, is not part of the essence of that which the name is imposed to signify, i.e. the subject of
existence. "Alio modo esse dicitur actus entis inquantum est ens, idest
quo denominatur aliquid ens actu in rerum natura. Et sic esse non attribuitur nisi rebus ipsis quae in decem generibus continentur; unde
ens a tali esse dictum per decem genera dividitur."[160] *Esse* is attributed
to what is in reality, to things which *aliquid in re ponunt*. That to which
esse is attributed is denominated *ens*; what is named from existence is
the subject of existence. In the case of being, it happens that that from
which the name is imposed to signify is not of the essence of that
which is denominated. That is called a being to which *esse in rerum natura* is attributed, but actually to be in reality is not *what* that which is
named "being" is.

What now of the text reproduced at the beginning of this section?
Ens, we read, is predicated essentially only of God; it is predicated by
way of participation of every creature. Does *ens* here mean existence?
St. Thomas seems to indicate this by pointing out that, unlike God,
who is subsistent existence, every creature is a *habens esse*. Moreover,
the creature is said to participate *esse* and consequently to have *ens*
predicated of it as something not of its essence. Can *ens* in this passage

158. *In IV Metaphysic.*, lect. 2, n. 553.   159. Ibid., nn. 550–52.
160. *Quodlib.* IX, q. 2, a. 2.

mean *quod est*? Or does it only mean *quod est* when being is said essentially of creatures? Or is it rather the case that the *ratio entis* can be viewed in different ways while always being *quod est, habens esse* or *id quod habet esse*? A study of texts indicates that the final possibility is the teaching of St. Thomas.

This can be seen by examining the doctrine that *Qui est* is the most proper name of God. Now *qui est* substitutes another gender for the *quod* in *quod est* and both are equivalent to *ens*.[161] In other words, *being* is the most proper name of God. One reason for this is the very signification of the name. "Non enim significat formam aliquam, sed ipsum esse."[162] Since God's essence is existence, *being* or *He who is* properly names him: "unumquodque enim denominatur a sua forma."[163] Any other name adds to the signification of *being*, in one way or another, but *being* is the most indeterminate of all words, since the term does not signify any determinate mode of existence, but is indeterminate with respect to any mode whatsoever. "Ens autem non dicit quidditatem, sed solum actum essendi . . ."[164] How can *ens*, taken to mean *quod est* or *Qui est*, be said to signify only the act of existing? Doesn't the *ratio* include as well the *quod* or *qui*, the subject of the act? Of course, but St. Thomas's point is that the subject is left wholly undetermined as to what it is; it is denominated solely from the formality of its act, which is existence, and the mode of reception or possession of that act is left wholly indeterminate. Thus, although the *quod* is primarily substance, substance is not signified determinately by *ens*; that is why the term is common to substance and accident. Thus, although the *ratio entis* is composite, one of the components is formal with respect to the other, namely the component which is the *id a quo nomen imponitur ad significandum*, what the grammarian calls the *qualitas* as opposed to the *substantia nominis*.[165] The *id a quo* is what is most formal in the signification of the name; the *id a quo* of *ens* is *esse* and it is from that point of view that *Qui est* or *ens* is the most proper name of God.[166] From the point of view of the *id ad quod nomen imponitur ad significandum*, "Deus" is a more proper name of God than "He who is." It is not, therefore, because *ens* does not have a composite *ratio* that it is the proper name of God; its *ratio* is composed (*quod est* or *qui est*), but that which the name being is imposed to signify is left wholly undetermined as to

161. *In I Sent.*, d. 8, q. 1, a. 1, c.: ". . . hoc nomen 'qui est' vel 'ens' imponitur ab actu essendi."

162. *ST*, Ia, q. 13, a. 11.   163. Ibid.

164. *In I Sent.*, d. 8, q. 4, a. 2, ad 2.

165. Cf. *In III Sent.*, d. 6, q. 1, a. 3; *In I Sent.*, d. 22, q. 1, a. 1, ad 3.

166. *ST*, Ia, q. 13, a. 11, ad 1.

what it is by the *ratio entis*, it is signified only as *quod est* without any indication of what the *quod* is.

That this is the case with *ens* as it is said to be the proper name of God is clear from the cautionary notes St. Thomas introduces. Thus, upon reading that *Qui est* is the most proper name of God, we may think that it escapes the dictum that *omne nomen cum defectu est*[167] as applied to God. But *Qui est* is a defective name: ". . . cum esse creaturae imperfecte repraesentet divinum esse, et hoc nomen qui est imperfecte significat ipsum, quia significat per modum cujusdam concretionis et compositionis; sed adhuc imperfectius significatur per alia nomina . . ."[168] It is the most proper name of God only in the sense that it is the least improper.[169] Could we avoid the composition of the *ratio entis* and say that *Ipsum esse* is the most proper name of God? St. Thomas suggests this in replying to an objection which cites the Boethius of the *De hebdomadibus* to the effect that *ens* is that which participates *esse*. But God is *ens*, ergo, etc. St. Thomas replies: ". . . dicendum quod dictum Boetii intelligitur de illis quibus esse competit per participationem, non per essentiam; quod enim per essentiam est, si vim locutionis attendamus, magis debet dici quod est ipsum esse quam sit id quod est."[170] *Ens* and *esse*, however, like *bonus* and *bonitas* both fall under the community of the remark: "omne nomen cum defectu est quantum ad modum significandi." As St. Thomas points out,[171] a concrete name applied to God (e.g. *ens*) has the advantage of signifying what subsists and the disadvantage of complexity; an abstract name (e.g. *esse*) has the advantage of simplicity but the disadvantage of signifying as a *quo*.

This excursus into the matter of the divine names was committed with a view to explicating the *ratio entis*. It has emerged that *quod est, habens esse* or *quod habet esse* is always the notion signified by the concrete term *ens*. That from which the term is imposed to signify is *esse*. The subject of *esse* is included in the signification of *ens*, but is left wholly undetermined from the point of view of its *modus essendi*. That is why we can say that *ens* signifies only *esse*. If we look to the *id a quo* of this name, we find that it is something other than the thing which is denominated from it, at least in the case of creatures. That is why being is not their proper name; as such it does not manifest *what* they are. In the case of God, the composition of the *ratio entis* is recognized, as following only on our mode of knowing. He is his existence and,

167. *SCG*, I, cap. 30.   168. *In I Sent.*, d. 8, q. 1, a. 1, ad 3.
169. Cf. Cajetan, *In Iam*, q. 13, a. 11, n. 5.
170. *Q. D. de pot.*, q. 7, a. 2, ad 8.   171. *ST*, Ia, q. 13, a. 1, ad 2.

since *ens sumitur ab esse*, it is the proper name of God "quia sic denominatur quasi a propria sua forma."[172] The proper name of the creature will be that which is imposed from his form or quiddity. Nonetheless, because quiddity is included in the signification of *ens*, though indistinctly as to what it is, creatures are signified by being. That is why St. Thomas remarks, in the quodlibetal article, that *ens*, insofar as it implies the subject of existence, signifies the essence of the thing and is divided by the ten genera. Insofar as we consider the *id a quo*, however, being will not signify the essence of creatures but something other than their essence.

Is this interpretation compatible with the discussion of the verb in the *Perihermeneias*? In commenting on Aristotle St. Thomas observes that "nec ipsum *ens* significat rem esse vel non esse. Et hoc est quod dicit, *nihil est*, idest non significat aliquid esse. Etenim hoc maxime videbatur de hoc quod dico *ens*: quia *ens* nihil aliud est quam *quod est*. Et sic videtur et *rem* significare, per hoc quod dico QUOD et *esse* per hoc quod dico EST. Et si quidem haec dictio *ens* significaret *esse* principaliter, sicut significat *rem* quae habet esse, procul dubio significaret aliquid esse."[173] How can this statement be reconciled with those in which *esse* is said to be most formal in the signification of *ens*? The context of this remark makes it clear that the *esse vel non esse* that is not signified by *ens* is that which is signified by the proposition. *Ens* is a term of simple apprehension and, although its *ratio* is complex, it is not complex in the way a proposition is. When something is apprehended as *ens*, it is grasped under the formality of existence. And, though what exists is left wholly undetermined in this apprehension, it is what exists which is being apprehended. The *composition* of the subject and existence is not as such signified by the term *ens*, as if the term meant, "Something exists." "Sed ipsam compositionem, quae importatur in hoc quod dico EST, non principaliter significat, sed consignificat eam inquantum significat *rem* habentem esse. Unde talis consignificatio compositionis non sufficit ad veritatem vel falsitatem: quia compositio in qua consistit veritas et falsitas, non potest intelligi, nisi secundum quod innectit extrema compositionis."[174] The concept of being is not a judgment; it does not signify existence in the way in which the proposition does and, consequently, is neither true nor false. Being is the apprehension of supposita from the point of view of that which is absolutely minimal, namely that they have existence. The thing grasped as subject of existence, as that to which *esse actu in rerum*

172. *Q. D. de pot.*, q. 2, a. 1, c.   173. *In I Periherm.*, lect. 5, n. 20.
174. Ibid.

natura is attributed: this is what is grasped when *ens* is grasped. In this sense, the thing is what is principally signified by *ens*. Yet, in the *ratio entis*, that which is formal, that from which the name is imposed to signify, is existence.

(b) "Ens inquantum Ens"

St. Thomas's remarks on the *ratio entis* must be taken as criteria in assessing current views on the nature of Thomistic metaphysics. This metaphysics, we are told, must be seen as "existential," a quality allegedly manifest in St. Thomas's statements concerning the subject of metaphysics. That subject is designated by the phrase *ens inquantum ens*. Such a phrase would seem to mean being taken precisely as such, so that what would concern us is what pertains to being *per se* and not to being of this or that particular kind. St. Thomas likens this to the relation of genus and species. If we are concerned with the genus as such, we want to determine what belongs to it *per se* and not what belongs to its species as such. Indeed, what is *per se* to the species is *per accidens* to the genus.[175] The existential interpretation of *ens inquantum ens* is: the thing or essence considered precisely as existing. Or it is said, in the *ratio entis*, we can emphasize either the *quod* or the *est*; the former is the essentialist approach, the latter the existential and Thomistic approach. This is a somewhat ambiguous option. If taken to mean that *esse* is what is formal in the signification of *ens*, in the sense of the *id a quo nomen imponitur*, nothing could be truer. If it means that essence is grasped from the vantage point of existence so that *ens* denominates the thing precisely as that to which *esse in rerum natura* is attributed, again nothing could be truer. However, if it means that the concept of being is at once a grasp of essence and the judgment that it exists, it is difficult to see that this is what St. Thomas teaches. Unfortunately, this last interpretation is the one favored by Thomistic existentialists. We have examined the view above[176] and need not repeat the criticisms already made. Suffice it to say now that if *ens* is taken to mean "essence grasped as existing" in such a way as to include a judgment of existence, we are faced with a view at variance with that of St. Thomas—a fact of considerable importance when Thomistic metaphysics is being discussed.

A passage that has provided difficulty for those desirous of finding an "existentialism" in the texts of St. Thomas is found in the commentary on Book Gamma of the *Metaphysics*. Aristotle is arguing that the

---

175. *In IV Metaphysic.*, lect. 1, n. 531.
176. Cf. Part A above of the present chapter.

science concerned with being as being must concern itself with unity as well. What is called a man, a being and one is the same; the terms *man, being* and *one* all designate the same thing.[177] We have already seen that if this were not the case, *ens* and *unum* could not be convertible terms. They both signify the same thing, but from different points of view, through different *rationes*.[178] St. Thomas states Aristotle's second argument in this way.

> Quaecumque duo praedicantur de substantia alicuius rei per se et non per accidens, illa sunt idem secundum rem: sed ita se habent unum et ens, quod praedicantur per se et non secundum accidens de substantia cuiuslibet rei. Substantia enim cuiuslibet rei est unum per se et non secundum accidens. Ens ergo et unum significant idem secundum rem.[179]

A thing has being predicated of it, not because of something added to it (for then the question would arise as to how being is said of that which is added and so to infinity or we stop at that to which being belongs *per se*) but by reason of itself, *per se*. Doesn't this contradict the doctrine that something is denominated *ens* from *esse* which is not *what* it is and in that sense is an accident? In the commentary, St. Thomas cites Avicenna as one who sensed this difficulty. The Arabian held that a thing is a being and one due to something added to it. "Et de ente quidem hoc dicebat, quia in qualibet re quae habet esse ab alio, aliud est esse rei, et substantia sive essentia eius: hoc autem nomen ens significat ipsum esse. Significat igitur (ut videtur) aliquid additum essentiae."[180] It might appear that St. Thomas can only agree with Avicenna. Yet he disagrees and his reason for doing so is extremely important.

> Sed in primo quidem non videtur dixisse recte. Esse enim rei quamvis sit aliud ab eius essentia, non tamen est intelligendum quod sit aliquod superadditum ad modum accidentis, sed quasi constituitur per principia essentiae. Et ideo hoc nomen Ens quod imponitur ab ipso esse, significat idem cum nomine quod imponitur ab ipsa essentia.[181]

Ens is imposed to signify from *esse*; the thing is denominated a being from its existence. However, although *esse* is other than essence it is not another nature but the very actuality of the essence, an actuality which is as it were constituted by the principles of the essence.

---

177. ". . . idem enim est dictum homo et unus homo. Et similiter est idem dictum, ens homo, vel quod est homo: et non demonstratur aliquid alterum cum secundum dictionem replicamus dicendo, est ens homo, et homo, et unus homo."—*In IV Metaphysic.*, lect. 2, n. 550.

178. Ibid., n. 553.
180. Ibid., n. 556.

179. Ibid., n. 554.
181. Ibid., n. 558.

Album means that which has whiteness; the thing is denominated from an act which is other than what it is, is denominated from an accidental nature. But when a thing is called *ens*, it is denominated from the actuality of what it is. The thing is what is denominated and since the *id a quo* is not an accidental nature the thing is not denominated *ens* through some added nature. That is why *ens* like *unum* is predicated *in quid* of that of which it is said.

This same point is made in the commentary on Book X.[182] *Being* does not signify some nature added to the thing thanks to which the thing is called a being. Neither *one* nor *being* signifies some subsistent thing apart from the things of which they are predicated. We do not look for One and Being apart from the things which are one and being. We ask what is it that is one, what is it that is being. There is no unity or being apart from the things which are called one; at least we cannot argue from the unity of the notion said of many to some one thing apart from the many.[183] However, *being* and *one* signify the nature of that of which they are said although they do not signify some nature over and above the things of which they are predicated. It is in this that these common notions differ from accidents.[184] Once again St. Thomas singles out Avicenna for criticism. "Hoc autem non considerans Avicenna posuit quod unum et ens sunt praedicata accidentalia, et quod significant naturam additam supra ea de quibus dicuntur."[185] In both cases the commentator was deceived by the equivocation of the terms involved.

Similiter etiam deceptus est ex aequivocatione entis. Nam ens quod significat compositionem propositionis est praedicatum accidentale, quia compositio fit per intellectum secundum determinatum tempus. Esse autem in hoc tempore vel in illo, est accidentale praedicatum. Sed ens quod dividitur per decem praedicamenta, significat ipsas naturas decem generum secundum quod sunt actu vel potentia.[186]

The being signified by the composition of the proposition is being as true. However, as St. Thomas indicates in the quodlibetal article, we can consider the *is* in *Socrates is* either as sign of the composition made by the mind (*ens ut verum*) or as signifying the entity of the thing. In either sense, he has said there, it is an accidental predicate. To affirm that something exists is to affirm that it exists here and now since the verb signifies with time.[187] *Ens* however, as it is divided into the categories does not assert that anything exists. The natures so divided are

---

182. *In X Metaphysic.*, lect. 4, n. 1276.   183. Ibid., n. 1964.
184. Ibid., n. 1980.   185. Ibid., n. 1981.
186. Ibid., n. 1982.   187. Cf. *In I Periherm.*, lect. 5, nn. 4–5.

denominated from *esse*, they are that to which *esse* is attributed, but it is the nature which is denominated and not its factual existence at any given time. That is why St. Thomas says that *being* signifies these natures according as they are in act or in potency, using the disjunctive both sides of which, though with priority and posteriority, are explained with reference to *esse*. This passage would seem to underline the manner in which *esse* is part of the *ratio entis*. If we say that metaphysics is concerned with things *as existing*, wouldn't we mean in the present? And is any science concerned with something so contingent as that? To think of metaphysics as reaching its term in such judgments as "Socrates is" is to separate oneself rather definitively from the doctrine of St. Thomas.

How can we reconcile St. Thomas's rejection of the view that *ens* is an accidental predicate with his remarks elsewhere that *ens* is an accidental predicate? *Ens* is not an accidental predicate insofar as what is denominated by the term is the subject of existence. *Ens* is an accidental predicate insofar as that from which the name is imposed to signify is *praeter essentiam* in the case of creatures. Since the creature is not that from which he is denominated *ens*, he is said to participate in it. And, as in the case of *lux* in the quodlibetal article, if there is something separate in the sense of subsistent which is *esse*, then this will be called being *essentialiter* and not by way of participation. Compare the following statements.

(1) Socrates est albus,
(2) Socrates est homo,
(3) Socrates est ens.

In (1) *albus* means "id quod habet albedinem." Whiteness is not what Socrates is and therefore Socrates participates in it as not being of his essence. In (2) *homo* means "id quod habet humanitatem." Socrates is not humanity and is said to participate in it, but humanity signifies the very essence of Socrates. In (3) *ens* means "quod habet esse," "habens esse"; Socrates is not *esse* but participates in it. Insofar as he is what has existence, however, the term signifies his essence. Just as *humanity* cannot be predicated of him so neither can *esse*. The concrete terms *homo* and *ens* are both predicated *in quid* of Socrates although the one is imposed from essence and the other from existence.

The doctrine that there is a real composition of essence and existence in every creature does not entail that the *ratio entis* is a proposition. The thing is denominated a being from *esse* which is other than what the thing is, but what the term is imposed to signify is the subject of existence whether actually or potentially composed with existence.

We cannot, then, say that the subject of metaphysics is the thing considered as existing if by that we mean that *ens* is as such the judgment that essence exists. Furthermore, the doctrine that existence is an accidental predicate (and so too *ens*, if we consider the *id a quo nomen imponitur*) is not one that St. Thomas invented but appears in his writing on the authority of others, e.g. Hilary and Avicenna. As he is careful to point out, this must not be understood as if being is predicated of the thing because of some accidental nature added to it. No, being is predicated of the thing *per se* in the sense of not *per aliud*. The thing's substantial existence is not an added nature. And yet, since it is other than the thing's essence it can be called an accident in just that sense, i.e. of what is *praeter essentiam*. What the term *being* signifies, however, is the very essence of which it is predicated: this is *id ad quod nomen imponitur ad significandum*.

Despite the difficulties of his teaching on the predication of being and the apparently contradictory assertions, the text of St. Thomas reveals a complex, subtle and finally consistent doctrine. And, although *esse* is what is most formal in the *ratio entis*, there is no basis for the claim that the subject of metaphysics, as described by St. Thomas, includes *esse* in the way in which this is attained in the judgment.

4. Conclusion

We want to return now to *Metaphysics*, V.7, and indicate, by way of conclusion, the order among the various modes of "being" enumerated there. We saw that St. Thomas looks on Book Delta as ordered to the development of the science of metaphysics and not as a random lexicographical effort that happened to become wedged into this difficult work of Aristotle's. That science considers the *communia* which are predicated not univocally but according to priority and posteriority, that is with controlled equivocation or, in St. Thomas's use of the term, analogically, of their inferiors. In his commentary on Book Delta, St. Thomas will often spell out the order among the various meanings of a common term. He does not do this in commenting on chapter 7, but the order can be manifested without great difficulty.

There is, we have seen, a primary division into being *per se* and being *per accidens*. Being *per accidens* is a whole resulting from the accidental composition of substance and accident (the possible complexities of which we examined). There is, then, an obvious reference of being *per accidens* to the first mode of being *per se*.[188]

188. Cf. *In VI Metaphysic.*, lect. 4, n. 1243, for the reduction of *ens per accidens* and *ens verum* to the being *per se* which is divided into the categories.

Being *per se* is had according to an absolute consideration. We have seen that the predicate of such a proposition as "Socrates is white," the is-white, considered in itself, is *esse accidentale*. In other words, the accident considered in itself is that to which it is proper to be in another. The order among the various kinds of being *per se* in the first mode is something often discussed in the *Metaphysics*. That of which *being* is primarily predicated, that which realizes the *ratio entis* first of all and most properly is substance.

The reference of the second and third modes of being *per se* to the first is clear from the commentary of St. Thomas. Being as true is founded on that which is *in rerum natura*, i.e. the being which is divided into the categories. Moreover, that which is divided into the categories can be or not be, i.e. have *esse* attributed to it actually or potentially. Since there is priority of actuality, the first mode of being *per se* is called *ens perfectum*.

Thus there is a reduction of all modes of being to that which is divided by the categories and in that mode substance has priority over the other categories. Thus this chapter sets the stage for the further developments of the *Metaphysics*. In Book VI, Aristotle removes being *per accidens* and being as true from the concern of this science. Metaphysics will be concerned with the being which, as St. Thomas remarks, "dividitur per decem praedicamenta," and "significat ipsas naturas decem generum secundum quod sunt actu vel potentia."[189]

189. *In X Metaphysic.*, lect. 3, n. 1982.

14

ESSE UT ACTUS INTENSIVUS

In his two books on participation, Father Cornelio Fabro has developed a theory of the way in which *esse* is central to the metaphysics of St. Thomas which, if it sounds somewhat like what has become, for better or ill, a commonplace of recent Thomistic interpretation, nevertheless is established in such a way that, while Fabro's assertions are verbally the same as those made by others, the meaning of the assertions changes in an important way.

La Nozione Metafisica di Partecipazione appeared first in 1938 and a second edition came out in 1950. After an historical survey of the doctrine of participation, Fabro prefaces his interpretation of Aquinas with a treatment of Thomistic realism in the course of which he speaks of the nature of metaphysics. The text from which he begins is the famous article 3 of question 5 of the *Expositio* of the *De trinitate* of Boethius where *abstractio* and *separatio* are employed to speak of the difference between natural science and mathematics, on the one hand, and metaphysics on the other. I do not intend to dwell on Fabro's interpretation of this passage which may be found on pp. 129–135 of his book. Fabro does not wish to deny that formal and total abstraction are involved in establishing the subject of metaphysics; his point would seem to be that more than abstraction is required. "Questa astrazione termina alla ragione di essere; e per il modo secondo il quale avviene quest'astrazione, che ormai possiamo chiamare senz'altro *metafisica*, la ragione di essere è a un tempo la più astratta ed insieme quella che maggiormente ci fa conoscere la realtà quale è in sè" (p. 138). Metaphysics is described as moving from abstract notions back through the phantasm to existent individuals where the equality gained as a result of abstraction is disturbed by the recognition of the inequality of species of the same genus and of individuals of the same species. In short, the mode of being of abstract notions implies diversity and since metaphysics is concerned with being it will comprise this diversity and inequality under the notion of being. For there is a notion of being and it is abstract. "Anche l'atto di essere, che è il termine della riflessione teoretica, e che è detto oggetto della metafisica, in quanto diviene oggetto della considerazione intellettuale, anch'esso è infine una ragione nozionale astratta, anzi, come si diceva, è la ragione più astratta . . ." (p. 139). The notion of being, first grasped by formal abstraction, is the most imperfect and confused imaginable and is had at the outset of the intellectual life. Metaphysical reflection is required to turn this confused and imperfect concept into the one which is richest in representative power (cf. p. 143, n. 1). This metaphysical reflection is described as dialectical. All things agree in having the proper notion of being ("Tutti gli esseri convengono in questo: nell'avere la propria ragione d'essere"; p. 140) yet each being has its proper mode of being. Consequently, "la nozione di essere è intrinsecamente inadequata ad informare la mente una volta per sempre, ma esige di essere esplicitata, *volta per volta*, nell'oggettivazione: onde dal sapere il modo di essere reale di una cosa, non è deducibile, *a priori*, quale sia quello di un'altra cosa, se non in un modo approssimativo ovvero proporzionale" (p. 140).

Exactly how is the most impoverished concept transformed into the richest concept? Fabro suggests that, as the life of intellect proceeds and we become better and better acquainted with the diversity of beings, the concept of being is not so much filled up by way of these determinations as it is recognized to be something which transcends particular modes of being and is not exhausted by them. The concept of being comes to stand for a perfection and formality which is superior to every other formality to which it can be applied. Fabro summarizes his views by enumerating three steps in our understanding of being. First, there is a confused grasp of being by way of formal abstraction which is the starting-point of the intellectual life. Secondly, the proportional notion of being is grasped and this is the subject of metaphysics. Finally, there is the notion of being (*ultima ragione d'Essere*) which is the term of metaphysical induction. This final grasp is of the fulness of actuality, the fulness of intelligibility. In relation to it, all modes of being are seen as restrictions, as degradations, as partial negations of its fulness. The way to this culminating concept is called intensive abstraction by Fabro to oppose it to the extensive abstraction of previous grasps of being. What such intensive abstraction arrives at is a coincidence of conceptual universality and intensity of representation. Fabro indicates that the divine knowledge and even angelic knowledge are spoken of in this way by Aquinas and adds, "A suo modo anche la conoscenza umana tende a realizzare qualcosa di simile nel suo grado supremo ch'è la metafisica."

Fabro returns to this approach to being in *Participation and Causality* which appeared in 1960.[1] Now, however, he is dubious of the crucial role of the text in the *Expositio* of Boethius's *De trinitate*. Judgment is awareness of the factual existence of things (*esse in actu*) and Fabro is critical of the suggestion that the perceptual awareness of factual existence is the keynote of Thomistic metaphysics (Fr., p. 75). This must give way to metaphysical reflexion: "entre la première notion de l'*ens*, à l'aube de la pensée, et la notion technique d'*esse* de la 'resolutio' métaphysique, il y a au moins un double passage. En premier lieu: de la notion initiale confuse d'*ens* en général a la notion méthodologique de l'*ens* comme 'id quod est, quod habet esse' selon une dualité explicite de sujet (*essentia*) et d'acte (*esse*). Aristote s'en tient la, tandis que saint Thomas poursuit jusqu'à la détermination de l'*esse* comme acte ultime transcendantal, qui est l'objet propre et immédiat de la causalité divine" (Fr., p. 79). We must go beyond *esse in actu* to *esse ut actus*, beyond limited acts to the unlimited fulness of being.

Fabro sees the Thomistic synthesis as incorporating what is best in Aristotle and Platonism and the easiest route to an understanding of what he means by *esse ut actus*, *esse* as intensive act, the term of intensive abstraction, is by way of his comparison of Aristotle and Plato.

For Aristotle, *einai* signifies nothing of itself, Fabro says.[2] It takes on meaning only as linked to something which is. That is why Aristotle must think of being as immediately divided by substance and accident. Substance, concrete substance, is one way of being *in actu*, accident is another and apart from these determinations, being means nothing. Aristotle's criticism of Plato is aimed at the reification of abstractions he thought his master guilty of. Humanity does not exist, men do; sickness does not exist, but some men are sick. Forms are that thanks to which something is such-and-such but forms do not themselves subsist. Fabro takes Aristotle to be saying that the locus of reality is not the abstract but the concrete. If we consider the predicable hierarchy, *à la* the tree of Porphyry, it is by descent that we gain the really real. Fabro speaks of this as an intensive conception of the concrete. "L'approfondimento dell'aristotelismo portò presto San Tommaso a quella che abbiamo detta la concezione intensiva del concreto secondo la quale la forma sostanziale è l'atto primo in senso forte, in quanto cioè porta alla materia col proprio atto specifico—p.es. l'anima che da

---

1. *Partecipazione e Causalità* (Torino: 1960); *Participation et Causalité* (Louvain: 1961). It is not the case that one of these is the translation of the other; they are different, though not radically different, versions of the same work. That is why I specify *Fr.* or *It.* in the text.
2. For another view, see Chapter 13 above.

all'uomo la razionalita—tutte le altre formalita che quest'atto pre-
suppone: nell'uomo l'animalita e la corporeita nell'ordine predica-
mentale, la vita, l'intelligenza e l'esse nell'ordine transcendentale . . .
poichè soltanto a questo modo si salva l'unita del reale e quindi la con-
sistenza dell'essere stesso" (It., pp. 328–9; Fr., p. 341). Intensification
is had by proceeding in the direction of the concrete, therefore, and
not in the direction of the abstract. The corollary of this, of course,
would be that to know a thing only as a being is to know the least about
it possible.

The predicable hierarchy just sketched is thought to be a consequence of our peculiar mode of knowing. It does not imply any one-
to-one correspondence between the steps or degrees on its scale and
real beings. There is nothing which is being without being either a
substance or an accident; there is nothing which is merely a substance;
nothing which the generic notion of living thing names just as such,
that is, as concrete, etc. While in some way grounded in the real order,
the predicable hierarchy refers immediately to our imperfect and abstractive manner of knowing sensible things.

Let us assume that, besides the predicable or logical hierarchy,
there is a real or ontological one, a scale which would run from the
least of cosmic substances through man and on to the angelic hierarchy and culminate in God. What is the relation between the predicable and ontological hierarchies? The intriguing thing about Fabro's interpretation of Aquinas is that he wants to put together intensification
and abstraction and, in accomplishing this, he sees an advantage of
Platonism over Aristotelianism. "On peut dire que la forme, en avan-
çant plus loin dans l'abstraction, s'enrichit en même temps et se charge
toujours plus d'être et de perfection d'être. Il s'agit pourtant plutôt
d'une universalité de perfection, que de celle de prédication, et elle ne
pourra être universalité de prédication qu'étant d'abord universalité
de perfection. Le 'prédication intensive' et, par conséquent, l'abstraction intensive, sont les bases de la prédication extensive et de l'abstraction logique" (Fr., p. 201).

This is a crucial point in Fabro's interpretation. There is a predicable scale with being at the top which proceeds downward on the Porphyrian tree toward less and less common terms which nevertheless
express more and more intensive acts. That is why *vivere*, as a mode of
esse, does not leave behind anything expressed by the latter term: it is
a more intensive possession of *esse*. On the other hand, Aquinas,
under the influence of Platonism, sometimes speaks as if the reverse
were true: ". . . esse inter omnes alias divinae bonitatis participa-
tiones, sicut vivere et intelligere et huiusmodi, primum est et quasi

principium aliorum, *praehabens in se omnia praedicta*, secundum quem-
dam modum unita" (*In I Sent.*, d. 8, q. 1, a. 1, c.). Fabro finds here the
basis for saying that *esse* which, in the predicable hierarchy, is the least
of assertions, may be looked upon as precontaining in itself the acts
designated by more concrete terms on the predicable scale. "Mais il
faut admettre que, dans cette dialectique, la 'compréhension et l'extension', par rapport a la 'forme d'être' (*forma essendi*) ne se trouvent
pas en relation inverse, mais qu'elles se réfèrent l'une a l'autre, et que
l'une se fonde sur l'autre" (p. 202). Fabro allows that for "classical
thought" and for logic this is a difficult doctrine for in the metaphysical and dialectical synopsis what has the greatest extension also
has the greatest intension, what can be said of everything tells us the
most about anything. The exact nature of what he thinks he is doing is
clear from his eulogy of Plato: "mais il est certain, néanmoins, que si
dans l'antiquité quelqu'un a compris que le 'mouvement' de la pensée
devait être parallèle et correspondre au 'mouvement' de l'être, et ne
pas seulement être son mirage, c'était Platon" (Fr., p. 202).

The dialectical ascent to *esse* as intensive act, as the summation of all
perfections, is described by Fabro as a kind of "passaggio al limite" (*La
nozione*, p. 169, n.), and clearly *esse* as *perfectio separata* is the intent of
Ipsum esse subsistens as a divine name. But Fabro is not employing *esse ut
actus* simply as a *terminus ad quem* of the metaphysical enterprise. "La
perspective propre à l'analyse métaphysique, c'est que le point de départ et le point d'arrivée coincident effectivement: le départ est l'*esse*
comme acte de l'*ens* et l'arrivée est l'*esse* comme acte des actes et perfection de toutes les perfections. L'*esse* qui est au départ, l'acte le plus
commune, se manifeste à la fin comme acte le plus intense, qui tran-
scende tous les actes et doit les engendrer de l'éternelle et inépuisable
profondeur de sa plénitude" (Fr., p. 252). It is surely difficult to get
hold of the exact nature of the coincidence or identity of starting-
point and point of arrival Fabro insists on. Moreover, *esse ut actus* answers to a concept which is so representationally rich that it includes
within itself all perfections, all determinations of being. In short, for
Fabro, *esse* in the peculiar way that Aquinas speaks of it is a window on
the world which brings everything into view because it signifies the
summation of all perfections. In knowing *esse*, we know everything.

The preceding paragraph has taken on a critical flavor and I want
to continue and conclude critically. First, and repetitively, Fabro tends
to identify the two senses of *ens commune* that Aquinas is at some
pains to keep separate or, if he does not identify the two senses, Fabro
suggests some kind of identity of reference as in the quoted remark
on the coincidence of starting-point and term of metaphysical reflec-

tion. Fabro seems to want to make *esse commune, ens sine adiecto*, the most intensive. "Nec oportet, si dicimus quod Deus est esse tantum, ut in errorem eorum incidamus, qui Deum dixerunt esse illud esse universale quo quaelibet res formaliter est. Hoc enim esse quod Deus est, huius conditionis est ut nulla sibi additio fieri possit: unde per ipsam suam puritatem est esse distinctum ab omni esse . . . Esse autem commune, sicut in intellectu suo non includit aliquam additionem, ita nec includit in intellectu suo aliquam praecisionem additionis; quia si hoc esset, nihil posset intelligi esse in quo super esse aliquid adderetur" (*De ente*, cap. 6). Does *Ipsum esse subsistens* name God via a concept that is so representationally rich that it expresses the totality of all perfections? Obviously not. If it did (a) we would be enjoying the beatific vision and (b) one divine name would suffice. But we require a plurality of divine names precisely in order to approximate the fact that God is the summation of all perfections. Yet every divine name expresses one perfection and excludes others because of the fact that these names first have meaning for us thanks to our knowledge of created perfections. *Esse* is preferred to all other divine names because it does not include in its signification any determinate mode of being: to be wise, to be good, etc. If we set aside these limited modes and retain *esse*, what do we have? "Et hinc remanet tantum in intellectu nostro quia est, et nihil amplius: unde est sicut in quadam confusione" (*In I Sent.*, d. 8, q. 1, a. 1, ad 4). To say of God that He is subsistent *esse* is the safest and best way to speak of Him because it says the least, is most confused, least informative and thereby implies least restriction on the divine being. That what is called *Ipsum esse subsistens* can also be called *Ipsa sapientia, Ipsa iustitia*, etc. involves other names, other concepts: we can say that what *esse* names is all these things, but not that *esse* means all these things.

Further, Fabro's discussion of the important doctrine in lesson 1 of Aquinas's commentary on chapter 5 of the *De divinis nominibus* may be said to involve a kind of essentialism, by which I mean putting a premium on the abstract expression. *Vivere est esse viventibus. Vivere* does not flow from the *esse* of the living thing: it is that *esse. Vivere* does not lie in wait of any further act, *esse*, in order for the living thing to get into the real order. But *vivere*, for Fabro, is read from essence or form—it is the act which follows per se, without intermediary, on the form, *Forma dat esse*: the soul gives being to the living thing. There is no composition of *vivere* and *esse* except logically, abstractly. To prefer the term *esse* to *vivere* in speaking of living things is to prefer confusion to clarity.

Finally, it may be said that Fabro badly describes what he is doing. In his appeal to Plato for an identification of the "movement" of thought and the "movement" of being he suggests that what is first in reality must be first in our discursive thought. The movement of metaphysics is such that it goes from *esse* to *esse* and ends by identifying the logical and real hierarchies. But if Fabro's writings show anything they show (a) that the real hierarchy is not in one-to-one correspondence with the predicable hierarchy and (b) that our starting-point is anything but what is first in reality. What is really first must be sought as a dialectical limit but we don't run to first base if we are already there.

One is conscious, in attempting to reduce to a few fundamental points writings so erudite, nuanced and uneven as Fabro's, that distortions are inevitable. But if inevitable, they are no less unpardonable. I would not be honest with myself if I did not end this brief sketch on a laudatory note. Cornelio Fabro is easily one of the most important, learned and illuminating Thomists on the scene today and there are countless instances of tight and rewarding exegesis as well as daring and provocative synthetic flights in just about anything he does. My central misgiving about his treatment of *esse ut actus intensivus* is that, rather than retaining the proper mode of human understanding, which is multiple, complex, analytic, discursive, as the backdrop against which dialectical efforts to surmount these limitations can be not only corrected but, indeed, understood, he has reduced metaphysics to a dialectic of limits. The result is something like denying the difference between the polygon and the circle because the circle is the dialectical limit of the multiplication to infinity of the sides of the polygon. The fun and the point goes out of such dialectical reductions if the poles are taken really to fuse. What I have in mind can be found on almost every page of Aquinas's commentary on the *De causis* where the Neoplatonic is given new meaning and acceptability by being put into juxtaposition with a more grounded approach to *metaphysicalia*. And, of course, *vice versa*.

15

PHILOSOPHIZING IN FAITH

If it is reasonable to believe in God it nonetheless seems pretty clear that faith has little commerce with the kinds of reasons we as philosophers pursue. This is an odd and puzzling fact, one that we all recognize and yet one we are in constant danger of forgetting. In these remarks I want to dwell briefly on a number of things we all know, hoping to hold your interest not by the bright gleam of the novel so much as by the soothing hues of the familiar.

The very existence of philosophical papers devoted to the question of God's existence suggests an interesting contrast. On the one hand, as philosophers, we may seem to strike the stance of a man on a podium, winding his Ingersoll, waiting for God to put in an appearance, if not on the premises, at least in the conclusion. On the other hand, most of us learned to speak of God in an accepting way at our mother's knee. Our faith is not a consequence of argument or proof, and this is a necessary not a contingent fact. It is not simply that some men have believed almost as long as they have breathed, accepting as true whatever God has revealed of himself, while others, less well brought up, arrived at faith through proofs. No one believes as a result of proofs since this would be a contradiction. It is knowledge that proofs provide and one cannot know and believe the same thing. One who hoped to arrive at faith through demonstrations and proofs would be conceptually confused. But what then is the believing philosopher up to? Is he, when he fashions or defends demonstrations of God's existence, attempting, as Kierkegaard might say, to open up a make-believe, or make-unbelieve, parenthesis in his life?

Let me begin by indicating how one might go about showing that, if faith is reasonable, its reasonableness cannot be sought in formal demonstrations. The effort is against reductionism, against the assumption that there is some single way to establish the reasonableness of assent. The contrary view, the target of the effort, may be summed up in the following maxim: It is immoral to give our assent to a proposition without sufficient evidence. People who make that sort of remark often have religious belief in mind and they would seem to be suggesting that its features are wholly unique. That suggestion in turn invokes a very odd picture of what it is to be a man. It was for that reason that Kierkegaard, through his pseudonym Johannes Climacus, observed that the reason we have forgotten what it means to be a Christian is that we have forgotten what it means to be a man. Cardinal Newman, too, both in the *Oxford University Sermons* and in *The Grammar of Assent*, confronted the claim that reasonableness is a single sort of thing and his response to it can be summarized as follows: it is unreasonable to demand that every instance of human behavior be reasonable in a single sense of that term. Unreasonable because the demand could not possibly be met and it makes no sense to say that we are under an obligation we cannot meet. Ought implies can. Like Kierkegaard, Newman suggests that we take a look at what it is to be a man.

Well, let us take a look. From time to time, we find it necessary to cross a street. By and large, we leave one curb and set out for the opposite one on the basis of a few swift guesses: the light is green, the traffic seems to be responding to the signal, the pavement looks solid, we have often walked down this street before, and so on. We are voting with our feet here, inarticulately, but it could of course be said that, if asked, we might express the proposition that it is now safe to cross the street. Do we really have sufficient evidence to assent to that proposition? Stung perhaps by the enunciation of the maxim that it is immoral to give our assent on insufficient evidence, we might murmur a *mea culpa* and—and what? Well, we could devise procedures that would increase our knowledge of the situation; we could run tests on the pavement, get equipped with a portable radar which would warn of that rare and antic driver, wear a pair of glasses which would correct for sun glare on the signal lights, and many other things.

My summary of Newman's reaction could thus seem to come down to this: while it is by and large impractical to demand total circumspection for every deed, nonetheless, in principle, any deed could meet such demands. Furthermore, we might be told that there is a scale in the affairs of men, and crossing streets is low on it, whereas as we approach the upper rungs it is increasingly necessary to ask for evidence.

But what if the kind of probative procedure, the proving out of propositions, which seems called for by the maxim, is not simply impractical but in principle impossible? We need a story. Once upon a time there was a young lady named Gwendolyn. On a sultry night in June she is drawn to her window by the seductive pluck of a guitar and this proves to be the first in an inexorable chain of events linking her with the importunate strummer. She drops a golden braid, he climbs to her casement, they talk, breathing deeply the while, far into the night. One overcast night some weeks later, Gwendolyn puts down the *Discourse on Method*, stands before her mirror, and knows a gnawing doubt. Does Pablo Baxadors really love her as he says he does? Having let down her hair to Pablo, she decides to do the same with her mother. She is told that her father was once as ardent as Pablo and of course a comparison of her paunchy progenitor with Pablo does little to allay our Gwendolyn's doubt. She wants proof positive that Pablo loves her, so let the comedy begin. She reviews the evidence. Pablo shows up most every night, by full and gibbous moon; he worries the steel strings of his guitar until his fingers look like a North American martyr's. He says he loves her. But how can she know? It is intolerable to Gwendolyn that only her hairdresser should know for sure. How can she prove out Pablo? Well, she makes him take one of those multiple choice tests which appear in *Reader's Digest*. He scores 95. But Gwendolyn knows all about tests. She hires detectives. Leafing through their voluminous reports, she reads that there is no other woman on the other side of town; Pablo has always been where he said he was, at school, at work, at home. She finds recorded there his purchases of the flowers and peanut brittle and spools of dental floss that he regularly sends her. Will her doubts now go away? Why should they? Perhaps the detectives are in Pablo's employ, that cunning boy.

We leave Gwendolyn with her methodical doubt. Such stories are meant to show that the demand for a certain kind of rational basis for a human deed is in fact the introduction of an alien factor. Whatever may emerge from such a procedure, it will never be Pablo's certified love. A proved love is no love. That is the moral of the story. You remember that in the fairy stories it is never the princess who sets our hero those impossible tasks and tests; it is always the mean uncle or the conceptually confused king.

Such stories are reminders of what we always knew. There is no sure-fire one-shot way to speak of the way our language works, of how our deeds are done. We perceive once more how fantastic it is to seek the model of every sentence in "The cat is on the mat," uttered, as the saying goes, in standard circumstances. But of course there are no standard circumstances. I may utter that sentence to locate Flossie, to tell a joke, to translate from the Portuguese, to illustrate internal rhyme or iambic trimeter, etc. To take as standard that use of language whereby we make impersonal descriptive remarks about the world is to be insanely selective; to identify rational behavior and the making of such utterances is to consign 99 percent of what we say and do to outer darkness. But why should we agree that 99 percent of our lives is in principle irrational? Why not take another look at "rational" and see how various and diverse its meanings are. In Newmanian terms, why not observe how irrational it is to demand that rationality always mean what it can only rarely mean?

The point of all this for the philosophy of religion is to show that, once we have loosened up our conception of reasonableness and recognized that it is not and cannot be one thing, well then, assent to religious truths may not seem as odd as at first appears. Were men to articulate the judgments which make up the warp and woof of their lives, the resultant propositions would look no more like "The cat is on the mat" than "Christ died for our sins" does. Nor again is it merely the case that it would take impossibly long to check them out in the standard way. What has too often been taken to be the standard way of checking out propositions simply cannot touch what our fundamental workaday judgments are all about; love and trust and promising to be faithful for a lifetime are not empirical hypotheses which it would be immoral to accept without testing. They are not empirical hypotheses at all. Very few things are, and I mean "few" from the strictly quantitative point of view. To dream of a *mathesis universalis*, a *characteristica generalis*, which would machine-like test any and every proposition is madness, and it is productive of a picture of ourselves which puts not only religion in doubt but just about everything else as well.

This sort of thing is familiar to us all. I think its application to so-called religious language has been by and large good. How very wrong it was of believers to get into the position of assuming that there was a paradigmatic use of language, a univocal procedure of verification, and then to go on as if the Incarnation, the forgiveness of sins and life everlasting were empirical hypotheses which had better be able to stand the test or else.

The story I told earlier had as its moral: a proved love is no love. So too one might say: a proved God is no God. This proposition gains its strength from the nature of faith; it reminds us that no one's faith can be the result of proof, of demonstration, of reason in that sense. Let me recall the way that Johannes Climacus argued that the Incarnation both is and is not an historical event. If there are standard procedures whereby events can be certified as historical, and there are, then it should be historically decidable whether or not a man named Jesus lived at a given time, said such-and-such, was said to do this-and-that, and so forth. But what such testing procedures could not establish is the truth of the claim made by him and about him, namely, that he is the Son of God. The believer and the non-believer have equal access to the purely historical dimension and they could arrive at perfect agreement on that plane. They differ in that the believer holds that they are speaking of the Son of God whereas the non-believer can only say, that is what he called himself, that is what others called him. The truth of the claim cannot be decided by the historical method, nor of course its falsity either. Climacus wants us to see that no contemporary of Christ could have been an eye-witness of the truths believers believe. All kinds of contemporaries of Christ saw and heard, but then, as now, only a few believed. Do those who believe know more facts than those who do not? Not if facts are what the bodily eye can see and the natural reason understand. The vision that can replace faith was not had by the contemporary eye-witnesses of Christ's earthly life. What Climacus is stressing is that faith is a gift, not a natural achievement. It is not something which can be made to emerge by more careful historical research, for example; it does not result from such testing procedures.

What I have been saying up to now is only a complicated way of making the simple point that believing is not knowing, knowing is not believing. Of course we can and do speak of items of knowledge as beliefs; we can and do speak of the knowledge of faith. The contrast of faith and knowledge invokes a very determinate sense of those terms. In the case of religious faith, belief is the acceptance of a proposition as true, not because I understand it, but because God has revealed it and my acceptance of it is linked with my presumed desire for happiness. When this contrast is developed it becomes clear that what I believe I do not understand and what I understand I cannot believe. The application Climacus has made of this contrast is clear: what I can know or understand about the life of Christ is not what I as a believer believe about him. This sounds wholly orthodox and yet it induces a certain uneasiness, if only because it is reminiscent of John Wisdom's parable in his essay "Gods." There, you remember, two men were in utter agreement on the facts concerning a garden but one of them spoke of an invisible gardener to account for the garden and the other refused to do so. Talk of a gardener seemed a gratuitous excursion beyond the facts to the one man though not to the other although neither maintained that the facts were premises from which the gardener emerged as a necessary conclusion. There is as well a word for the uneasiness we feel and the word is fideism.

Let us look again at what Climacus has to say of history and faith. Needless to say, few believers occupy themselves in the search for the historical Jesus. For most of us, our belief encompasses both those truths about Christ which could be decided by the historical method as well as those which could not. That is, I believe that Christ was born on Christmas and involved in my belief are many claims about what anyone at all could have noticed if he were in the right place in Bethlehem at the right time on that night so long ago, but as well such claims as, that baby is God incarnate, that he has come to save us from our sins and reconcile us with the Father. We just don't sort out the merely historical from the truths which escape it. And for a good reason. I want to suggest that there is an asymmetry here that it is fatal to overlook. If one began from the merely historical, one could never conclude to faith. Faith is not the product of historical inquiry. Faith is not a necessary function of, or result of, knowledge. That is the great truth of the reminder. However, if there is no positive transition from knowledge to faith, knowledge can play a negative role, a destructive role, and this precisely because faith is not simply parallel to, above and separate from the historical: it includes it. What I have in mind is this. If someone were to announce that he had, by the historical method, definitively disproved that a man named Christ lived when he is thought to have lived, said what he is thought to have said, etc., his claim has more than historical import. Earlier we adopted the irenic assumption that believer and non-believer were in agreement with respect to the historical facts. Now we assume the opposite. Could this be a matter of indifference to the believer?

Well, yes; certainly in one sense. If I pick up the *South Bend Tribune* and read a story to the effect that Professor Saltpeter has exploded the myth of the historical Jesus I am not likely to cancel dinner, wire Blackwell's for a copy of the book, toss and turn in my bed at night as if my faith were in escrow until I had assessed Saltpeter's arguments. No doubt I would just go on to the sports page and more substantive matters. This is not obscurantism, only healthy common sense. There have been scads of Saltpeters, even in my own limited experience. Until now they have all been shown to have cooked the evidence in one way or another and I simply presume that Saltpeter has done the same. In other words, my reaction suggests, not that there is no need to answer Saltpeter, but that it will be done and done easily. However, if this should not be done, by someone, if the book withstood every critique, if it had been definitively proved that Christ never existed, then I am in trouble. Then I would be in the wholly untenable position of believing to be true what is known to be false. This is so because, in order to believe that Christ is man and God, I have to believe that he was born, walked around, talked, suffered and died, that he rose again from the dead, turned water into wine, was transfigured on Mount Thabor. Notice how that sentence contains in mixture things which are amenable to historical investigation and others which are not. In Kierkegaardian terms, faith presupposes and includes history even though faith cannot be deduced from history. That is what I meant by asymmetry. One can know that the man Christ existed and not believe that he is God incarnate; but one cannot believe in God incarnate and know that the man Christ never existed.

The realization that faith is not a product of knowledge or proof has often led believers to denigrate the classical proofs of God's existence. Indeed, some defenders of the faith seem willing to use any club at all to pummel those venerable syllogisms. I have often marveled at the insouciance with which believers assail the proofs and even go so far as to maintain that no proof of God's existence is possible. They wish, of course, to make an unassailable point. Metaphysics is no more capable of producing faith than history is. No man's religious faith is or could be grounded in proofs. From this it is sometimes concluded that faith is a self-sufficient language-game, that it has no connection with the realm of knowledge. To hold this is what I should mean by fideism. Moreover, as I put it earlier, such a stand seems unaware of the asymmetrical relation between faith and knowledge. That asymmetry had to do, you recall, with the positive and negative roles of reason. A definitive proof of existence of God could not of itself lead on to faith; were one to know with all possible certainty that God exists one would not thereby accept or have to accept what believers believe about God. However, and this is the negative side, if the existence of God could be definitively disproved, this would surely affect faith radically. The believer cannot be in the situation of accepting as true what is known to be false.

It might be doubted that this contradiction is possible. Since those truths which are believed cannot be known to be true, it would seem to follow that they cannot be known to be false either. I believe that there is a trinity of Persons in God because I cannot know it; my inability to know it to be true would seem to exclude the possibility of anyone's knowing it to be false. But of course disputes between Trinitarians and Unitarians take place against the background of the assumption that God exists. Which leads me to suggest this: anything the believer believes implies the proposition that God exists. Thus, if it could be definitively shown that the concept of God is incoherent, that it makes no sense to say that God exists, then this affects faith in much the same way that a definitive disproof of the historical Jesus would.

As it happens, the parallel can be pressed farther. Just as the believer believes both truths of faith and truths accessible to the historical method, so the Christian believes not only what God has revealed of himself but also that God is knowable by man apart from revelation and faith. This is not to say that proofs of God's existence lead on inexorably to the acceptance of what God has revealed to us of himself; it is most certainly not to suggest that the first task of every believer is to occupy himself with proofs of God's existence. Gilson, in *Le philosophe et la théologie*, has dealt sufficiently with that absurd suggestion. Quite obviously, too, that is not the force of the phrase *praeambula fidei*.

We have come back, you see, as sane men must, to St. Thomas Aquinas. The more I reflect on what he has to say on the relationship between faith and knowledge, faith and philosophy, faith and theology, the more convinced I become that he provides us with the distinctions and subtleties we need to maneuver through the vexed matters I have been recalling to your attention. The phrase *praeambula fidei* was introduced to cover those matters which, although they had been revealed by God, need not have been, because in principle they can be known. That there is a God, that there cannot be more than one God, that God is the cause of all else—such truths we have held since childhood along with others like the Trinity and Incarnation. I suggested earlier that truths of faith imply the proposition that God exists and that, moreover, this is a proposition decidable apart from faith. This does not mean that my acceptance of the Trinity and Incarnation would follow from my fashioning a cogent proof of God's existence. It does mean that those truths of faith could not stand if it were definitively disproved that God exists. Is it not here that we find the source of the believer's interest, as believer, in proofs for the existence of God? Of course God can be shown to exist only under some description and the favored one in philosophy has been as ultimate cause. Were such a proof valid and cogent it would demonstrate something that is implied in what the believer believes although it would not give a demonstrative underpinning of his faith as such.

No doubt this is why we often see contrasted the God of the philosophers and the God of the believer. From the point of view of religious faith, what philosophy has managed to say of God must seem exiguous and thin. How much richer is our conception of God when we have accepted what he has revealed to us of himself. This is not to say, of course, that the description under which God is known in philosophical discussions is in conflict with what God has revealed of himself. In the creed we affirm that God is creator of heaven and earth and though, in the context, that connects with a whole network of affirmations undreamt of in philosophy, we nonetheless recognize that the classical proofs are, however inadequately, glosses on the truth that God is creator. That is why we can say that the God of the philosophers and the God of the believer are the same God.

Aquinas, I should say, enables us to retain, without a smidgin of smudging, the distinction between faith and reason and, at the same time, to avoid fideism. A proved God is no God when it is a question of what God has revealed of himself. For the believer to conceive of his faith as some kind of hypothesis which requires testing and certification by supposedly standard procedures is a lamentable confusion. God did not become man in order that men might become philosophers. And yet, involved in our faith is the tenet that, apart from faith, the God who has revealed himself to man, though not as he has revealed himself, can be known by man. It is of importance to the community of believers that some occupy themselves with God as knowable, not because faith requires this but because, should it appear that it can be definitively disproved that God exists, this could not leave our faith undisturbed. You and I, by talent, vocation and predilection, as well as by what must seem to us a good dose of the fortuitous, occupy that occupation. Let me close with a story which may capture some of the flavor of our task.

There was once a boy who loved his father. Among the things the father told his son was that once, long ago, in the war, he had been awarded the purple heart. The boy tells his friends who, looking at the father supine on the porch swing, hoot and jeer and make those obscene noises we associate with little boys. The son does not thereby doubt his father. He jiggles the porch swing and asks where the medal is. Somewhere. Maybe in the attic. Together with his friends the boys ransack the attic. No medal. In the muggy heat the jeers mount to the rafters. They return to the porch. The father says the medal may be in his den. The boy and his friends scour the den. No medal. They return to the father whom the son does not doubt although, for the sake of his friends, he would like to find that medal. Look in my dresser, the father says. While they search, the other boys recall the father's story of a twenty pound northern pike, of being at the Indianapolis 500 the first time A. J. Foyt won it all. The boy does not distrust his father. The medal is not in the dresser. His friends leave, hooting, jeering, making strange gestures. Many years later, his father dead, the boy, now a man, is gathering his father's effects. At the back of the closet he finds an old seersucker robe. Pinned to its lapel is a purple heart. The son unpins it and puts it in his pocket. He is not surprised. He always believed his father.

A strange son? Perhaps, yet very much like us. Antecedently we believe that a proof of God's existence can be fashioned and if we go in search of it this is not because our faith requires it or because others who come to see its cogency would thereby have to believe what God has revealed. Strange sons. Strange quest. And there is a strange phrase that one can find in John of St. Thomas, quoted by Maritain, which sums it up: *philosophandum in fide*.

16

ON BEHALF OF NATURAL THEOLOGY

The Christian philosopher often seems to be insisting that his faith is no impediment to his philosophizing, apologetics having become sheepish apology. How elated some were a few years back when a shift in the philosophical currents suggested that asserting there is a God was no longer an indictable offense. The fact that religious faith got off by being put on roughly the same footing as paranoia and bright-eyed claims that the world had just doubled in size seemed to some believers a small price to pay. It was like finding out that everyone is crazy, the world an asylum and the talk of believers, like that of flat-earthers, an irreducible language game. "So's your old man," so to say.

Natural theology, on the other hand, may seem to be the claim that theism can flourish in the absence of religious belief. If the pagan can come to knowledge of God by considering the things of this world, God's revelation of Himself to man through Christ may seem a mere addition to a happily ongoing situation, gratuitous in several senses of the word. That is, it looks as if men do not *need* any special relevation and, if it is vouchsafed them, it gilds the lily rather than plants the mustard seed. The suggestion that there is salvific knowledge short of faith rightly incenses believers mindful of Paul's dictum, "Sine fide impossibile est placere Deo" (Heb. 11:6). But it is that same Paul who gave what Roman Catholics have long taken to be the Scriptural warrant for Natural Theology, namely,

Invisibilia enim ipsius a creatura mundi per ea, quae facta sunt, intellecta conspiciuntur, sempiterna eius et virtus et divinitas, ut sint inexcusabiles; quia, cum cognovissent Deum, non sicut Deum glorificarunt aut gratias egerunt, sed evanuerunt in cogitationibus suis, et obscuratum est insipiens cor eorum. (Rom. 1:20–21)

How can one maintain both that without faith it is impossible to please God and that since pagans could come to knowledge of the invisible

things of God from an understanding of what He has made, their failure to praise and thank him is without excuse?

In this paper, I shall do several things. First, I shall briefly recall St.
Thomas Aquinas's familiar doctrine that there are two theologies and
his characterization of their essential difference. Second, I shall ask
what would follow if there were no such thing as natural theology.
Third, I shall ask what does in fact follow from the opposite case, i.e.
the truth that natural theology is indeed possible. A few things that
don't follow will also be mentioned. Finally, in a hortatory mood, I
shall suggest that believers stop speaking as if their faith were an impediment to philosophizing, putting them in an anomalous position
vis-à-vis their healthily agnostic colleagues. The grace of faith is the
best thing that ever happened to the human mind and it is culpable of
the believer to act as if the opposite were true.

1. THE TWO THEOLOGIES

Early, middle and late in his writings, St. Thomas speaks of a two-
fold knowledge of God, one that was achieved by pagan philosophers
and which is based on knowledge of material things, another that results from God's revealing Himself to men. Thus, in his commentary
on the *De trinitate* of Boethius (q. 2, a. 2, ed. Decker, p. 87.7–15) and
in that on the *Sentences* of Peter Lombard (prolog., q. 1, a. 1), both
early works, Thomas makes this distinction. So too in the *Summa contra gentiles*, 1, cap. 3, he speaks of two kinds of truths about God. The
one kind in every way exceeds the capacity of the human mind, e.g.
the trinity of Persons in the one divine nature; the other kind is such
that even natural reason can arrive at it, e.g. that God exists, that He is
one, and the like. Finally, the opening discussion of the *Summa theologiae* (Ia, q. 1, a. 1) recalls the distinction.

Thomas has several grounds for asserting with confidence that
there are these two ways of knowing God. The first is the Scriptural
warrant already cited. Thomas takes Paul to be saying that sinful man
can, apart from revelation and by considering the things of this world,
come to knowledge of God. The second basis is the fact, as Thomas
takes it to be, that philosophers have achieved this knowledge. Thomas
holds that Aristotle devised sound proofs for the existence of God.
What is, is possible.

The notion of philosophizing that emerges from such discussions is
this. No matter how arcane and sophisticated a philosophical discussion becomes, it is in principle possible for the philosopher to lead the

discussion back to starting points which are available to any man in virtue of his being human. Philosophical doctrines do not appeal to some special knowledge or insight had by the few, though only a few may succeed in arriving at these doctrines. However chancy arrival at the *terminus ad quem* may be, the *terminus a quo* is where each and every one of us already is. That is why a theology based on natural reason must be able to show how truths about God are derived from truths about the world and depend ultimately on truths no man can gainsay. By contrast, the theology which has as its principles what God has revealed to us about Himself is only ready to take its inferences and conclusions back to starting points in revelation. And since these starting points are held to be true thanks to the grace of faith, only believers are in possession of the principles of theology. Of course the theologian does not confine himself to what has been revealed:

Et ex istis principiis, *non respuens communia principia*, procedit ista scientia; nec habet viam ad ea prodanda, sed solum ad defendendum a contradicentibus. [And from these principles, while not disdaining common principles, this science proceeds; it has no way of proving its starting points but can only defend them against those who contradict them.] (*In I Sent.*, q. 1, a. 3, quaestunc. 2, ad 1)

2. THE NEGATIVE HYPOTHESIS

What would be entailed by the assumption that there could be no natural knowledge of God? Needless to say, the question does not mean: what would be the plight of this believer, Quidam, if he were unable to succeed at natural theology? The vast majority of believers wisely do not bother their heads with natural theology. This is not to say that they are unaware of the way in which human and natural affairs speak of an author. The believer will doubtless wonder in his heart how any man aware of the goods and evils of this life could possibly fail to be aware of God. But this is no claim to sound and cogent proof. The believer does not need such proof. That is not the way he came to be a believer. He would be untroubled by headlines announcing the refutation of the proof from motion.

Quidam, call him a simple believer, is not thereby an obscurantist. For one thing he accepts St. Paul's statement that men can come to knowledge of God from His creation. Furthermore, he is confident that some believers can handle skeptical attacks on talk about God and our ability to know Him, but Quidam, such is his simplicity, would not have at his fingertips distinctions between natural and supernatural knowledge of God, and the like. He believes what God has revealed, what the Church teaches, and that's that.

The negative hypothesis is here taken to mean not that there are some men and some believers who have no natural theology, but that no man, perhaps particularly the believer, can engage in natural theology. Natural theology is a program that cannot be fulfilled. Perhaps it would be held that, due to sin, man's intellect has been so weakened that it is absurd to think that he could attain to knowledge of his creator without special help. Perhaps one mistakenly thinks that natural theology commits one to the view that there is salvific knowledge apart from grace and faith. Whatever the reason for entertaining the negative hypothesis, certain consequences would follow if that hypothesis were true, consequences not in every way desirable.

The first difficulty with the view is that it seems to run afoul of that passage in Romans. Paul is speaking of pagans when he goes on about how they can come to knowledge of the creator from creation. He does not seem to be saying that they might be converted and thereby come to knowledge of God. I suppose one might say that men once had this ability and it has been taken away. But that would seem to make what is called a natural capacity a sort of special gift.

The second difficulty with the view is that it would seem to force the believer to adopt a very stern attitude toward philosophy. It would become his policy that philosophers never have and never will be able to fashion a sound argument for God's existence. As a historian of philosophy, he would be committed to showing (a) that all the proofs that have been fashioned are invalid or unsound or (b) that they arrive at false statements about God. That the Christian is necessarily struck by the distance between what philosophers have said about God and the richness of revelation goes without saying.

The most serious difficulty entailed by the negative hypothesis is that it encourages fideism. That is, it leads believers to maintain that, since nothing counts in favor of theism, nothing counts against it either.

3. THE CONSEQUENCES OF NATURAL THEOLOGY

Now the first thing to be insisted upon about natural theology is this: if it works, it proves the truth of theism, *it does not establish truths of faith*. There are no sound, cogent, knockdown dragout proofs of what is *de fide*. Natural theology is not a program meant to change religious beliefs into knowledge claims. When Thomas distinguishes two kinds of truth about God, they are precisely truths which can be known and truths which can only be held on the basis of authority, that is, believed. There is no suggestion that the latter are to be transformed into the former. Indeed, there is the explicit denial that this is possible. What is *de fide* cannot be known or proved from what everybody naturally knows. The point of Thomas's position is that there are some truths about God which can be known.

Of course this means that some truths about God *which have been* revealed can be known to be true. In Scripture we find both those truths about God which natural reason can know (that He exists, that He is one) as well as, and most importantly, truths about God which no man could possibly attain save by grace and faith. The first sort of revealed truth, what Thomas calls preambles of faith, need not have been revealed, in the sense that they could be held to be true independently of accepting them on God's say-so. And, as is well known, Thomas asks why it is that God should reveal to us, besides truths about Him we could never otherwise attain, truths about Him which are knowable to natural reason, and he finds any number of reasons why it is well that God did as he did (*SCG*, I, cap. 4).

Furthermore, just as natural theology does not have for its purpose turning *de fide* truths into known truths—mysteries into preambles— so too when natural theology is successful it does not provide any grounds for faith in any strict sense of *grounds*. That is, if natural theology succeeds in its initial task, to prove the existence of God, no *de fide* truth follows from this as a consequence. If it did, the *de fide* truth would be transformed into a known truth and, as we have seen, that is not part of the program of natural theology, indeed it is explicitly denied as a possibility.

I insist upon these things because I think that at the heart of much Protestant opposition to the very notion of natural theology is the fear that it amounts to seeing religious belief as a replaceable attitude in this life, as if, by dint of increased knowledge, one could know what one formerly believed. What Thomas calls mysteries of faith, as opposed to preambles of faith, are precisely truths about God which *cannot* be derived from what anybody knows. If I accept the Trinity and Incarnation and the forgiveness of sins and the other articles of faith as true, I do so because God has revealed them and, as long as I live, this can be the only basis for accepting them as true. For Thomas, as I have argued elsewhere, to know and to believe are formally different mental attitudes and it is impossible for the same person simultaneously to know that p and to believe that p. In the case of ordinary beliefs, it may be in principle possible to stop believing p because one has come to know p. In the case of the objects of religious faith, no such transformation is possible in this life. Thus, if natural theology be spoken of as attempting proofs of beliefs, *distinguendum est*. This cannot mean proofs of beliefs in the sense of mysteries of the faith; such an effort would be confused and/or contradictory. Therefore, beliefs that are proved must be beliefs in the ordinary sense of the term. That is, propositions whose truth was accepted on someone's say-so when there is nothing about the content of those propositions which would require that they be accepted on the basis of authority. If believed, they are nonetheless knowable, and thus faith can be replaced by knowing, perhaps as a result of a proof. This means that the content of these propositions is such that their truth and falsity is decidable by reference to what everybody knows.

The truths of faith, the mysteries of faith, are not decidable in that way. One of the fascinations of pagan philosophy for the believer has been to see what, independently of all revelation, men have had to say about God. On what basis do they think that claims about God are true? In what ways do they describe God? However inadequate from the point of view of revelation—which of course is not a criticism of these efforts as philosophical—one can marvel at the similarity between some conclusions of natural theology and some revealed truths. It has not seemed fanciful to our forefathers to maintain that "There is a first unmoved mover" is equivalent to "God exists" and thus coincides with what believers have accepted as true from their mother's knee. You can get an argument on it, but some of our predecessors maintained that in arguing that things other than God are His effects, philosophers were aware of the world as created by God. Certainly some of the things philosophers have said about God are synonymous with what God has revealed about Himself, for example, that God is one, that He is intelligent, that He has a will, and so forth. It was by noticing this that Thomas dubbed some of the things that have been revealed as *praeambula fidei*, to distinguish them from revealed truths which are mysteries.

Once more, it is what may seem to be in the offing when this sort of thing begins that has led to wariness concerning natural theology. If some revealed truths are said to be identical with proved truths and thus one can replace holding those truths on authority by holding them on the basis of argument, where will this sort of thing stop once it has begun? The prospect that the whole of revelation is to be subjected to this sort of testing procedure, to find if it can be seen to follow from what everybody knows, rightly causes concern. But no such prospect is in view by St. Thomas Aquinas when he argues for natural theology. And the reason for that we have already seen. By definition, mysteries of faith are such that their content does not permit of decidability with reference to what everybody knows.

Well, it might be said, it is one thing for a pagan to wonder whether or not there is a God and to try to devise proofs but this is not a proper occupation for the believer. Why not? Because, for the pagan, until the proof is devised, God's existence is unknown and is even perhaps a matter of doubt. Certainly prior to having a proof on the basis of which one might say "I know God exists" he is in a state where he must say, "I don't know that God exists." Now from this it seems to follow that any believer who sets about formulating a proof for the existence of God is in a position of having to say, "I don't know whether God exists." But that seems to amount to a denial of the existence of God or at least a denial of the truth of the proposition "God exists." Fortunately, this is not the case. To believe that God exists is not to know that God exists. The believer can ask himself if the proposition which he holds to be true on God's say-so could be held on some other basis, say that of a proof. While he is pursuing this possibility, he does not cease to hold that the proposition "God exists" is true, though his warrant for its truth is authority, revelation. The denial of "I know God to exist" is not equivalent to a denial of "God exists." The truth of the proposition "God exists" must be held in some way or other, by faith or knowledge. While one cannot hold it to be true by both faith and knowledge at the same time, one need never stop holding it to be true (by faith) while one looks to see if it can be known to be true (by a proof).

It can be seen that natural theology does not provide grounds for or a foundation of faith if "grounds" and "foundation" are taken to mean some basis on which the truth of what is believed can be conclusively established. If we were to grant that the program of natural theology has been achieved beyond the wildest dreams of philosophy, it would still be the case that the natural theologian would be not one whit closer to establishing the truth of the mysteries of faith than he was at the outset.

Nonetheless, if natural theology achieves its goal of proving that God exists and of establishing some of His attributes, this can be used in formulating an argument to show the reasonableness of accepting the mysteries of faith as true. If we think of the totality of revelation as AB, and take A to stand for the *praeambula fidei* and B to stand for the *mysteria fidei*, then we might say: if A can be known to be true, it is reasonable to assume that B is true. If some of the things God has revealed can be seen to be true, it is not unreasonable to say that the other things He has revealed are also true, even if I cannot now see them to be true. Would this argument persuade a non-believer? Hardly. But then we should not think that there is any argument which can transform a non-believer into a believer. To hold this would be to confuse preambles and mysteries. Of course an argument could suffice to turn a non-theist into a theist. But one who has become a theist is not one positive step closer to being a believer. You might say that, if he knows the proposition "God exists" is true, he has one less impediment to accepting "God became incarnate in Jesus" than has the man who thinks "God exists" is false.

Pascal, we remember, held quite correctly that truths of faith cannot be proved to be true. Nonetheless, he sought, in the *pari de Pascal* passage, to formulate an argument to the effect that it is unreasonable not to accept Christianity as true. Whatever we think of the argument, and I think Pascal himself was less than impressed by it, there is nothing inconsistent in trying to formulate it.

If natural theology cannot ground faith in any straightforward and positive sense, what is the motive for seeking it? For Aristotle, the motive would have been simply to know what could be known, to see what knowledge man can achieve of the divine. Our question becomes interesting when it is put to the believer. Why should the believer trouble himself about such things as proofs for the existence of God, the problem of evil, and so on? He has no need of a proof to decide the truth of "God exists." He does not have a problem of evil in any standard sense. It is not God who is in the dock, so far as the believer is concerned. He is more likely to have the problem of good. Why should so many blessings and graces come his way, sinner that he is? What need does he have of natural theology?

We have seen that it will not do to say he seeks it in order to have a way of persuading non-believers of the truth of Christianity. Such an aspiration would bespeak a confusion about what faith is. We have also seen that it does not make any sense to say that the believer needs natural theology as a basis for his faith. Since that just about exhausts the possibilities, it can look as if the whole enterprise of natural theology is otiose and ought to be allowed to slink silently into a richly deserved obscurity. I did not become a believer as a result of a fifty drachma course in natural theology. I became aware of my faith in the same way that I became aware that, generally speaking, I speak prose. The fact is that no one became a believer *as the result of an argument*. Of course God could use the occasion of philosophizing to give one the grace of faith, but then He can use any occasion He wishes. What felt need does natural theology fill?

The first justification of natural theology is the same one it had for Aristotle and the pagan philosophers. Man's inquiring mind is a gift of God and it is right that he should use it. Not all knowledge is sought because it has some practical or utilitarian value; some knowledge is its own excuse. Natural theology, as the culminating task of metaphysics as Thomas understands it, is as well the culminating task of speculative philosophy. To establish the truth of the proposition "God exists" is desirable in and of itself. (And of course if *per impossibile* the contradictory of that proposition were true, it would be good to know that.) As Romans 1:20–21 suggests, this speculative truth indirectly implies practical consequences and one who does not draw them is without excuse.

But for the believer the chief importance of natural theology is that it functions as a reminder that faith bears on truth and that it is reasonable to believe. Looking backward, so to speak, he can see the way natural theology is subordinated to the theology based on Sacred Scripture, he sees a continuum and he sees compatibility between natural knowledge and revealed knowledge. This is not a reductionism. Perhaps we see the point more easily in the negative mode. Nothing known can be in conflict with what is believed. This is the believer's policy and it is a profound sign of the reasonableness of faith. But the positive side of this is that known truths are compatible with revealed *de fide* truths. God is the source of the faculty whereby we arrive at known truths, God is the source of revelation. It would be an abomination to suggest that God could be in conflict with Himself. The believer thus sees that if his mind has been rendered captive, his keeper is the truth. He does not accept what God has revealed because he thinks it absurd, irrational, nonsense, but because it is the truth.

This is why the believer is more likely to ask how natural knowledge is compatible with belief rather than the other way around.[1] The truth that God has revealed is the measure, not the measured. In reflecting on believed truths, furthermore, some believers will generate what is called theology. That is, they may ask what several revealed truths entail by way of a consequence. They may ask what a believed truth in conjunction with a known truth entails. Here there is a faith seeking understanding, a deeper penetration of what God has proposed for our acceptance. As Bonaventure suggested the *intellectus* and *scientia* involved here are as much gifts as acquisitions.

It has often been noticed that believers show more interest in things

---

1. ". . . e converso philosophia sit ad metas fidei redigenda." *In Boethii de trin.*, q. 2, a. 3, p. 95.13.

like proofs for the existence of God than do non-believers. From the perspective of faith, strictly philosophical matters take on an interest and significance that the "pure" philosopher cannot be expected to see. Philosophy, natural theology, looked at through the eye of a believer like Thomas Aquinas, suggested a prelude or preamble to faith, not that one can qua philosopher make the step into faith on some natural basis, but rather that, from the perspective of the faith, there is a marvelous hanging together of things. However inadequate they may be from the perspective of faith, the truths about God gained by philosophers are seen to be compatible with those which God has revealed. Indeed, some of these *praeambula fidei* show up in revelation itself.

Motivated by the desire to show that what is given us by the *lumen fidei* must be compatible with what we learn through the *lumen naturalis rationis*, the believer becomes interested in philosophy itself. As a believer, he wants to show that all God's works are compatible with one another, but of course qua philosopher he will not appeal to that policy as to what commends what he has to say philosophically. A noteworthy feature of a believer like Thomas, is the confidence he has in the power of human reason. This is motivated by his faith. To regard reason as solely a source of error, as a capacity incapable of achieving its end, would be, for Thomas Aquinas, an insult to God. But, as we have seen, this does not prevent him from saying that philosophy must be measured by faith.

Does Thomas, in speaking so confidently of the range of reason, overlook the consequences of sin? Does he take too sunny a view as to what men could do apart from the influence of grace and faith? I don't think so. "If the only way open to us for the knowledge of God were solely that of the reason, the human race would remain in the blackest shadows of ignorance" (*SCG*, I, cap. 4). This suggests our final consideration.

4. THE ADVANTAGES OF THE BELIEVER IN MATTERS PHILOSOPHICAL

I said at the outset that it is wrong of the believer to act as if his faith were an impediment to philosophizing. There are a number of considerations which can serve to remind us what a blessing for philosophy itself the faith is. First of all, on the practical side, a consideration of the decalogue suggested to someone like Thomas that many of these precepts stating what is never compatible with the ideal of human perfection are such that they could be known by natural reason alone. Indeed, in Thomistic terms, it looks as if precepts of Natural Law have been revealed. But Natural Law is made up of first principles in the practical order. How extraordinary that God should find it fitting to inform man explicitly of such basic truths.

The case of God's existence is somewhat different, in that this is not a starting point, but a point of arrival. Nonetheless, God saw fit to reveal to men truths that men could in principle arrive at without divine help.

The clear implication of these two examples is that, because of man's sinful condition, he has been rendered so weak that even first principles of practical reason have to be reinforced by a divine reminder. As for proofs of God's existence, Thomas Aquinas paints a very bleak picture of what life would be like if men had only their natural reason to rely on. Clearly he means natural reason in its present, i.e. sinful, condition.

From this I conclude that, apart from the light and reinforcement it receives from a setting of grace and faith, natural reason is a feeble reed indeed on which to have to rely. In its Christian state, natural reason is more likely to be able to achieve its own ends. This is the sort of thing that Jacques Maritain and Etienne Gilson and others were discussing in the early thirties, the problem of Christian Philosophy. Philosophizing as an activity carried on by a believer is better able to achieve philosophical ends. This is what I meant when I said earlier that faith is the best thing that ever happened to the human mind.

To have mentioned that old discussion of Christian Philosophy is all I dare do now. The pursuit of that topic would carry us very far afield. I want to end by citing what I take to be a Thomistic version of Plantinga's wish to make articles of faith basic propositions. In discussing the certitude of faith, Thomas writes,

Magis enim fidelis et firmius assentit his quae sunt fidei quam etiam primis principiis rationis. [The believer more intensively and firmly assents to those things which are of faith than even to the first principles of reason.] (*In I Sent.*, q. 1, a. 3, sol. 3)

The warrant for the truth of faith is God himself, whereas the warrant for the truth of reason is God only indirectly. That is why, if *per impossibile*, there were a real conflict between faith and reason, the believer would stick with his faith. But of course what he believes is that no such conflict is really possible.

17

CAN GOD BE NAMED BY US?

In asking whether God can be named by us, whether he comes within the reach, if not the grasp, of our language, Thomas Aquinas is posing a question, the answer to which is surely decisive for theology, both philosophical and scriptural.[1] Of course, the very asking of the question seems to beg it, unless such referring to God as the question appears to do falls short of naming him or unless the context in which the question occurs minimizes its apparently mendicant nature.

The context is the first part of the *Summa theologiae*, and it is question 13 of that part which takes up the topic of the names of God. Since God has been the subject of discussion throughout the preceding twelve questions, we might think that the concerns of question 13 are tardily introduced. Should not problems associated with talking about God preface the *Summa*? Does not my subtitle, by suggesting that we are concerned with matters on the threshold of philosophy of religion, implicitly criticize the order of the *Summa*? Surely to establish, if it can be done, that God can indeed be spoken of by us, is to issue a charter for a discipline rather than to accomplish one of its internal and subsequent tasks.

It is only with trepidation that one casts doubt on the order of the *Summa theologiae*. It has long been regarded as the very paradigm of a well-ordered set of problems and questions ranging over a unified subject matter. Such works as the *Isagoge* of John of St. Thomas display the interlocking architecture of the work, an architecture so transparent that, though the *Summa* was left unfinished by Thomas, it was easily completed by cannibalizing other writings of the saint for discussions of the remaining topics.[2] Not that there is any real need

---

1. The very first question asked in the *Summa theologiae* is whether, over and above what philosophy can tell us about God, there is need for another doctrine. See *ST*, Ia, q. 1, a. 1. Another and thorough comparison of the two theologies is found in Thomas's exposition of the *De trinitate* of Boethius, q. 5, a. 4.

2. The *Supplementum* of the *Summa theologiae* contains this posthumous completion

for a work such as John of St. Thomas's. The *Summa* itself wears the structure of its bones very near the skin, and Thomas is at pains to connect discussions and to indicate why this problem is taken up before that, and so on. What justification does Thomas offer for the apparent postponement of an issue that seems to demand settlement prior to doing theology? Let us glance at what goes on prior to the discussion of the divine names.

Question 1 of the first part is methodological, concerning itself with the nature and scope of sacred doctrine. Indeed, articles 9 and 10 discuss aspects of the language of Scripture, its largely symbolic, or metaphorical, character, and the fact that, in interpreting it, we must recognize a plurality of senses of the narrative. Question 2 is the well-known discussion of the existence of God, with its elaboration of the *quinque viae*.[3]

> Once we know *that* something exists, there remains to consider *how* it exists, with an eye to knowing *what* it is. Because we are unable to know what God is, but can only know what he is not, we can consider not how he is but how he is not. First then we must consider how he is not; second, how he is known by us; third, how he is named.

This is the prologue to question 3 and it suggests that questions 3–11 form a unit, since question 12 asks how God can be known by us and question 13 asks how he is named. The suite of questions (3–11) Thomas depicts as concerned with the way God does not exist takes up the following attributes: God's simplicity, his perfection, his goodness, his infinity, the way he exists in creatures, his immutability, eternity, and unity.

When Thomas turns from all this to ask how God can be known and named by us, it might be said that he is now intent on raising questions as to what the earlier considerations involved, that these earlier considerations provide him with a body of data to which he can refer for concrete examples in undertaking to discuss the general problems of God's knowability and nameability. In short, we could say

---

of its plan. John of St. Thomas, a seventeenth-century Spaniard, has been a great influence on Thomists of our time, notably Jacques Maritain and Charles De Koninck. His *Isagoge ad D. Thomae theologiam*, a remarkable précis of the *Summa theologiae*, is found in his *Cursus theologicus* (Paris: 1931), vol. 1, pp. 143–219. There is a French translation, *Introduction à la théologie de saint Thomas* (Paris: 1928), by M.-Benoît Lavaud.

3. As a believer, Thomas accepts as true the proposition 'God exists'. What need is there then of proof? If one *knows* God exists, can one still *believe* it? These and allied questions are much discussed by Thomas. See my *Saint Thomas Aquinas* (Boston: 1979; Notre Dame: 1981), pp. 145–69, and Chapter 10 above.

that, on Thomistic principles, we must first know something before we can reflect on the nature of knowledge.[4] From that perspective, we would seek in questions 12 and 13, not some establishment of the transcendental possibility of knowing and naming God, but the relatively more modest effort to reflect on acknowledged instances of knowing and naming, with an eye to characterizing them generally.

This possible explanation for the place of questions 12 and 13, while not without merit, is nonetheless not what we find Thomas offering.

Because in the foregoing we have considered how God is in himself, it remains to ask how he is in our knowledge, that is, how he is known from creatures.[5]

It is as if the discussion is moving from how God is not to how God is (not) known by us and, thus, from a discussion of negations which, however much they depend on reference to things other than God for their meaning—as immutability requires mutability for its meaning—point to how it is with God, whether or not there are any creatures—moving from that to a discussion of negations which bear on created activity, namely our knowing. If this contrast seems obscure, it is one to which we shall be returning.

What now of our opening difficulties? There are 119 questions in the first part of the *Summa theologiae*, and question 13 can thus be called early. Nonetheless, when we consider its contents—can God be talked about by us?—it seems to be a question that should have been posed at the outset. Now one reason it might have been postponed is that theology, in the more-than-philosophical sense of the term, presupposes faith, and the theologian, as believer, accepts as true what God has revealed of himself, and this entails that he accept the meaningfulness of Scripture. Beyond that, the proofs of God's existence in question 2, tracing the way God can come to be known (as opposed to believed) to exist, as well as the subsequent discussion of negative divine attributes, are a necessary prelude to discussing our knowing and naming God. It is as if we must first know and name God if our knowing and naming God are to constitute a thematic subject. Use precedes mention, and that seems reasonable. Taxonomically, God's knowability and nameability are not divine attributes in the same way that immutability, eternity, unity, etc. are.[6]

---

4. See *ST*, Ia, q. 54, a. 3.   5. This is the prologue to q. 12.
6. See John of St. Thomas, p. 152.

I

The philosophy of religion, in recent years and in countries where English is the native tongue, has turned on the question whether meaningful language about God is possible. We find what might be called the charter of this discipline in its Thomistic form in the following passage.

In reply I say that, as Aristotle said, vocal sounds are signs of concepts and concepts are likenesses of things and thus it is clear that vocal sounds are referred to the things to be signified by way of the mind's conception of them. Thus it is that, to the degree a thing can be intellectually known by us, it can be named by us. But it has been shown earlier that in this life God cannot be seen by us in his essence but rather is known by us from creatures, according to the relation of principle and by way of excellence and remotion. So it is, then, that he can be named by us from creatures.[7]

This passage, the body of the article,[8] is a fair sample of Thomas's style in the *Summa*, and perhaps it will no longer be considered exiguous simply because its syllogistic structure leaps to the eye. The basic argument is this:

(1) We name things as we know them.
(2) God is known from creatures.
(3) God is named from creatures.

Brooding over this argument is a theory of meaning borrowed from Aristotle. I propose to say something of this Aristotelian background in order to cast light on the first premise and, in the light of this, having discussed the second premise briefly, to examine anew the conclusion, drawing on points made in subsequent articles of question 13.

The portion of the quoted text that recalls the Aristotelian theory of meaning reads as follows.

Voces sunt signa intellectuum, et intellectus sunt rerum similitudines. Et sic patet quod voces referentur ad res significandas mediante conceptione intellectus.

---

7. *ST*, Ia, q. 13, a. 1.
8. The structure of an article of the *Summa* mimics more or less as closet drama the public exchanges that were the medieval quodlibetal and disputed questions. A thesis is proposed as answer to a question and followed by a numbered series of supporting arguments, after which the *Sed contra est* turns the discussion by citing an authority to the contrary. The body of the article, ritualistically begun with the words *Respondeo dicendum quod*, argues for the contrary of the initial thesis and is followed by numbered replies to the arguments introduced in support of the initial thesis. Thomas's own view is to be found in the body of the article and in the replies to objections—those initial supporting arguments now seen as threatening the answer Thomas favors.

Vocal sounds are signs of concepts and concepts are likenesses of things. Thus it is clear that vocal sounds are referred to the things to be signified through the medium of an intellectual conception.

The passage of Aristotle to which reference is made is found in *On Interpretation*; here it is in the Latin version Thomas used in commenting on that work.

Sunt ergo ea quae sunt in voce earum quae sunt in anima passionum notae: et ea quae scribuntur, corum quae sunt in voce. Et quemadmodum nec litterae eaedem omnibus, sic nec eaedem voces: quorum autem hae primorum primo notae sunt, eaedem passiones animae sunt; et quorum hae similitudines, res etiam eaedem.[9]

Spoken words are the symbols of mental experience and written words are the symbols of spoken words. Just as all men have not the same writing, so all men have not the same speech sounds, but the mental experiences, which these directly symbolize, are the same for all, as also are those things of which our experiences are the image.

That Aristotle distinguishes vocal sounds from script is not an idle complication, since it enables him to set up a proportionality. As writing is to speech, so speech is to thought. The similar relation is that of being a symbol of. English translators render the Greek *symbola* as "symbols"; the Latin text has *notae*, and Thomas's paraphrase in the *Summa* employs *signa*. A sign is something which leads on to knowledge of something other than itself; in that sense, knowledge by signs is discursive and, Thomas adds, our signs are perceptible because our knowledge is discursive, taking its rise from sensible things.[10] Thus, writing perceived as writing brings to mind the spoken language. Similarly, speech makes known what is in the speaker's mind.

It is just here, of course, that this account of meaningful vocal sounds comes under criticism. Is it in fact true that speech draws our attention to the speaker's ideas? The term in question is, in the Greek, *pathēmata tēs psychēs*, in Latin, *passiones animae*, in English, affections of the soul. Thomas, in the *Summa*, uses *intellectus*, not in the sense of the faculty of the soul (that sense occurs at the very end of Ia, q. 13, a. 1, c.), but in the sense of what is understood. Now this we have rendered by 'concept'. What is understood, concepts, are said to be likenesses of things. We have, then, a triad: *vox—intellectus—res*. The vocal sound is the sign of the concept, and the concept is a likeness of things. Is it the fact that the concept is a likeness of, representative of, some thing or things that prevents the discourse initiated by the vocal sound from

9. *On Interpretation*, 16a3–8. The English is from the Oxford translation of Edgehill.
10. *Q. D. de ver.*, q. 9, a. 4, ad 4; *ST*, IIIa, q. 60, a. 4.

terminating in the mind of the speaker? Is there some reason why the concept is not called a *sign* of reality? If it were, the proportionality could become a veritable parlay.

Script : speech :: speech : concept :: concept : thing. And, the relation of signifying being transitive, the detour through the mind, as it would then be, might not attract the same kind of criticism as is attracted by the suggestion that signification terminates in the thought of the speaker. The familiar criticism springs from the theory's suggestion that meanings are mine, personal, private, and this does not square with the public and common character of language.

Needless to say, were one to try to drop out any mention of mental activity in explaining significant vocal sound, offering perhaps the view that a vocal sound has meaning insofar as it refers to some thing, one would be confronted with the equally familiar difficulty that words like 'centaur' and 'nothing' and 'and' do not seem to have any thing or object to which they refer.[11] Indeed, such a view of significant speech encounters difficulties as soon as it is applied to anything other than proper names.

But the fact that other accounts of the meaning of significant speech encounter difficulties is no defense of the theory Thomas accepts. Nowadays, both of the views mentioned, dubbed the ideational and referential views, have been put aside in favor of a fresh start, and there have been attempts to read Thomas on naming God in the light of these latter-day developments.[12] Laudable as such efforts are, my intention here is to proceed on a more historical and pedestrian plane. Does Thomas hold that vocal sounds signify concepts and not things, concepts and things, or things and not concepts? The last can be ruled out, though what he has to say of proper names comes closest to realizing that option. What Thomas does hold is that vocal sounds signify concepts immediately and things mediately. A first reason for holding this is drawn from common nouns.

For it is not possible that they should signify things immediately, as is evident from their very mode of signifying; for this name 'man' signifies human nature in abstraction from singulars. Hence it cannot be that it signifies a singular man immediately, which is why Platonists held that it signified the separate Idea of man. But since for Aristotle this does not really subsist as abstract, but is only in the human mind, it was necessary for Aristotle to say that vo-

---

11. See Mortimer Adler, *Some Questions about Language* (LaSalle, Ill.: 1976).
12. See William P. Alston, *Philosophy of Language* (Englewood Cliffs, N.J.: 1964). On less historical discussions of such matters, see Patrick J. Sherry, "Analogy Today," *Philosophy* 51 (1976), pp. 431–46, as well as his "Analogy Reviewed," *Philosophy* 51 (1976), pp. 337–45.

cal sounds signify the conceptions of the mind immediately and, via them, things.[13]

A second reason, drawn from the context of naming God, is the fact that while many divine attributes signify the absolutely simple God, they are nonetheless not synonyms. How can they fail to be synonymous if they mean or signify the same thing? 'Horse' and 'man' can be said to be nonsynonymous because they signify different things, but the divine attributes 'merciful' and 'just' cannot fail of synonymy because they signify different things. It is because divine attributes refer to the divine substance by way of diverse conceptions that they are not synonymous.[14]

Of these two arguments on behalf of the claim that a word does not directly signify an existent thing, the first, that drawn from universality, is the more accessible. Moreover, it suggests a way of avoiding misunderstandings about the way concepts are likenesses of things. The concept cannot be thought of as a sort of snapshot of a thing, since things are singular and the concept does not include singular notes. This is clear enough in the case of the accounts of common nouns. 'Man' does not receive an account that mentions what is peculiar to Democritus or Plato. That is what Thomas meant when he called our intellectual knowledge abstractive. He does not at all mean that the mind plucks from reality what is given there as it is plucked, a point Geach has made.[15] But are there not concepts answering to such definite descriptions as "the cup I am holding in my hand now" and "the one and only heavyweight champion of the world"? We could express the meaning of 'man' by "the animal endowed with reason" but that would not make it a definite description in the sense intended—a phrase that picks out a singular as such. Definite descriptions cannot function as the meaning of any name except, of course, a proper name, and this does not provide an account of the common terms included in the description.[16] We need definite descriptions because there is nothing in the world, outside the mind, that answers to common names as common. But this seems to lock immediate signification even more firmly to existence in the mind. To say that our words mean things as they are understood would seem to entail that being-understood is a component of the meaning of any term, and this is

13. *In I Periherm.*, lect. 2, n. 5. This has been translated by Jean Oesterle: *On Interpretation: Commentary by St. Thomas and Cajetan* (Milwaukee: 1962).

14. *Q. D. de pot.*, q. 7, a. 6.

15. Peter Geach, *Mental Acts* (New York: 1957), pp. 130–31.

16. See *Q. D. de ver.*, q. 2, a. 1, ad 11.

absurd. While the terms 'concept' and 'thinking' may plausibly be said to signify mental activity, it is clearly ridiculous to suggest that 'horse' and 'avalanche' do.

Before seeing how Thomas avoids so silly a result, let us reflect on the significance he finds in the fact that, in *On Interpretation*, Aristotle calls the vocal sound the sign of the concept, whereas he says the concept is a likeness of the thing. Ackrill, in his scolding donnish manner, swiftly interprets this as if it were an utterance of the village idiot: "Aristotle probably calls them likenesses of things because he is thinking of images and it is natural to think of the (visual) image of a cat as a picture or likeness of a cat. But the inadequacy of this as an account or explanation of thought is notorious."[17] Later he sees that the point is that vocal sounds are conventionally, by human institution, signs of concepts, whereas concepts are naturally concepts of the things conceived. But he is apparently so out of sympathy with the text and its author that he gets lost in an irrelevant digression on the possible material for axe handles and ends by remarking that one will find in Plato's *Cratylus* a brilliant discussion of the question whether language is conventional or natural. His reader suspects that if Ackrill is this unhelpful on the first pages of his commentary, he will not prove a very illuminating guide in what follows. But surely the fact that vocal sounds differ among men, though their ability to think does not, is deserving of more attention. To say that thoughts are likenesses of things is a way of making the point that, while we come to expect a diversity of language among men—it is said that there are four thousand different languages in use on earth now—we persist in thinking that translation is possible, that men can make themselves understood. Furthermore, when we consider that a sign functions in a discursive fashion—it being known, it leads on to knowledge of something else[18]—the concept might be refused the appellation 'sign', at least initially, in order to draw attention to the fact that concepts are not first known and then draw the mind to something else. If the concept is a sign, it is a sign of a different sort than script and vocal sounds are.[19]

If the vocal sound signifies what is understood, it will be in discussions of the object of understanding that the answer to our question

---

17. *Aristotle's Categories and De Interpretatione*, trans. J. L. Ackrill (Oxford: 1963), p. 113.

18. *ST*, IIIa, q. 60, a. 4.

19. See John of St. Thomas, *Cursus philosophicus Thomisticus*, ed. Reiser, 3 vols. (Turin: 1930), vol. 1, pp. 646–722, esp. pp. 702–7.

should be found, viz., does signification terminate in the thinking process as what is signified? Understanding, unlike the chopping done with Ackrill's axe, is an immanent activity. If it does not terminate outside, what is its object? What is understanding an understanding of? Thomas lists four possibilities: the thing (*res*) understood, the intelligible species whereby the intellect is actualized, the act of understanding, and the conception of the intellect.

Quae quidem conceptio a tribus praedictis differt. A *re* quidem *intellecta*, quia res intellecta est interdum extra intellectum, conceptio autem intellectus non est nisi in intellectu; et iterum conceptio intellectus ordinatur ad rem intellectam sicut ad finem: propter hoc enim intellectus conceptionem rei in se format ut rem intellectam cognoscat. Differt autem *a specie intelligibili*: nam species intelligibilis, qua fit intellectus in actu, consideratur ut principium actionis intellectus, cum omne agens agat secundum quod est in actu; actu autem fit per aliquam formam, quam oportet esse actionis principium. Differt autem *ab actione intellectus*: quia praedicta conceptio consideratur ut terminus actionis, et quasi quoddam per ipsam constitutum. Intellectus enim sua actione format rei definitionem, vel etiam propositionem affirmativam seu negativam. Haec autem conceptio intellectus in nobis proprie *verbum* dicitur: hoc enim est quod verbo exteriori significatur: vox enim exterior neque significat ipsum intellectum, neque speciem intelligiblem, neque actum intellectus, sed intellectus conceptionem qua mediante refertur ad rem.[20]

This conception differs from the foregoing three. (1) From the thing understood, because that is sometimes outside the mind whereas the conception of the intellect is in the intellect; again, the conception of the intellect is ordered to the thing understood as to its end: it is in order to know the thing understood that the intellect forms a concept of it. (2) It differs from the intelligible species, for the intelligible species, thanks to which the intellect is in act, is considered to be the principle of the intellect's action, since every agent acts insofar as it is in act; it is made to be in act thanks to form, the principle of action. (3) It differs from the activity of intellect, because the concept is the term of activity and, as it were, constituted by it. For the intellect by its activity forms a definition of the thing, or affirmative or negative propositions. This conception of the intellect within us is properly called a word, and this it is that the external word signifies. The external word does not signify the intellect, nor the intelligible species nor the activity of intellect, but the conception of the intellect mediated by which it is referred to things.

This passage suggests the complexity of Thomas's account of the object of knowing. It is clear that there can be no crude identification of the meaning of the vocal sound and "affections of the soul," where that phrase might be taken to mean psychological activity, let alone the individual's psychological activity. The distinction between agent

20. *Q. D. de pot.*, q. 8, a. 1.

and passive intellect is in play here. The passive intellect—the *tabula rasa*—is a potency which is actuated by the intelligible species, sometimes called the impressed species, thanks to the agent intellect which illumines the sense image or phantasm. Actuated by the species as form, the intellect generates the activity of thinking which, as immanent act, terminates in the conception formed by it. It is this conception, exemplified by the definition formed by mind, that is signified by the exterior word, the vocal sound. Definitions are unlikely to be thought of as personal or private. Definition can be understood as the account given when the meaning of the word is sought, the *logos* of the opening definitions of the *Categories*, the *ratio nominis* of Thomas.[21] When one gives an account of a word, he doubtless must have in mind what he is expressing, but he is not as such (at least always and necessarily) expressing what he has in mind. Very well. But is not Thomas committed to the view that the conception of intellect, as the immanent term of the activity of understanding, *exists in the mind*, and is not the conception the meaning or significate of the spoken word, so that it must follow that, for Thomas, the meaning of any word is something that exists in the mind?

The question is best considered by reverting to its association with universality. The meaning of a common noun cannot be a singular as such. 'Man' does not *mean* Socrates or Plato. No more, we should say, does it mean some mental existent. Hence, as Thomas observed,[22] the Platonic view that there must be something distinct from singulars and from the concepts of our mind which can serve as the meaning of the common name. It is as if such objects, Ideas, receive names common to singulars as their proper names. Thomas's view is developed with reference to the following.

(1) Man is white.
(2) Man is rational.
(3) Man is a species.

Human nature can be considered in three ways. It can be considered as such—*natura absolute considerata*—and when it is, only that is truly predicated of it which is a component part. Thus, in (2), 'rational' pertains to human nature as such because that nature is 'rational animal'. From this point of view, neither singularity nor plurality pertains to the nature: "Hence if it is asked whether this nature so considered is

---

21. See my *The Logic of Analogy* (The Hague: 1961).
22. See note 13 above.

one or many neither should be granted because both are outside the concept of humanity although both can befall it."[23] If uniqueness were of the nature of humanity, it could not be multiplied in Socrates and Plato; if plurality were of the essence of humanity, it could not be one as it is in Socrates. Now the same sort of distinction is invoked when it is asked if human nature exists. Existence is not of the essence of humanity, and when it does exist, existence is an accidental predicate of the nature. And just as it is the fact that the nature is sometimes many and sometimes one that leads to the recognition that unity and plurality are accidental to the nature, so the fact that the nature sometimes exists in the mind and sometimes in singulars leads to the recognition that existence of either kind is accidental to it. Nor should we, as Adler appears to do,[24] speak of a third kind of existence, that enjoyed by the nature as absolutely considered.

This nature, however, has a twofold existence, and following on either accidents befall the nature; it even has a manifold existence in singulars because of the diversity of singulars. And yet neither kind of existence should be said to pertain to the nature according to the first consideration of it, namely, the absolute consideration. For it is false to say that the essence of man, as man, exists in this singular, since, if to exist in this singular belonged to man as man, it would never exist except in that singular; so too if it were of the essence of man not to be in this singular it would never be in it. The truth is that man as man does not exist in this singular or that, or in the soul. Thus it is clear that the nature of man absolutely considered abstracts from both kinds of existence, although it does not make precision from them.[25]

(1) and (3) above express truths which depend on one or the other kind of existence. If (1) is true, this is because some man is white, while (3) is true because human nature is predicable of many numerically distinct things. "To be predicable of many" (universality) is not part of the nature of man nor of the meaning of 'man' as if from "Man is a species" and "Socrates is a man" we could infer "Socrates is a species." To be universal is something that happens to a nature as it is known by us, just as to be white is something accidental to the nature as it is found in such individuals as Socrates. The meanings of common nouns do not include, as a constituent or component, "existing in the mind." No more does the meaning of 'man' include the traits

23. *De ente et essentia*, ed. Roland-Gosselin (Paris: 1948), chap. 3, p. 24, lines 10–13. There is an English translation and superb commentary by Joseph Bobik, *Aquinas on Being and Essence* (Notre Dame: 1965).

24. Adler, pp. 92–97.

25. *De ente et essentia*, p. 25, line 9–p. 26, line 10.

of singular existents. This prompts a further essential consideration.

When the common name is said to signify immediately the conception of the intellect and mediately the thing, this cannot be taken to say that thanks to its immediate meaning the common name *names* something. If naming is taken to be the application of the common name to a singular (as in "Socrates is a man"), then of course for the name to have a meaning is not thereby for it to name something. Indeed, it was just to underscore this that the distinction between *significatio* and *suppositio* was made. The universal nature was said to be, following Aristotle, *aptum natum praedicari de multis*: to be predicable, to be applicable to singulars. But the application or predication of the common name to/of the singulars which are placed under it (*supposita*), is expressed in a proposition which is either true or false. The meaningful name is not of itself true or false except in an extended sense. The proper name, Thomas quotes others as saying, is such that its meaning and supposition are identical.[26] That does not mean, of course, that proper names are as such true or false.

A final word on *similitudo*. Things are said to be similar which share a form, though not in exactly the same way (if they did, we might call them equal). Now, the nature signified by the common name is found in singulars along with other things. The formal aspect of things, conceived by the mind in abstraction from material or individuating characteristics, is predicable of those singulars as its supposits. It is this formal link that may be taken to underlie talk of *similitudo*, *assimilatio*, and *repraesentatio*.[27] To inquire after likeness in some crude sense between conception and thing is no more fruitful than to inquire after it when the poem or dovecote are said to be expressions or likenesses of what their makers had in mind. The former claim is no more (or less) obscure than the latter, but he who looks for pictures in the poet's mind to correspond to the rhythms of his lines probably needs jokes explained to him too.

These few remarks about the theory of meaning invoked by Thomas at the outset of what we have called a charter text for philosophy of religion have been aimed at a single difficulty that has been found with it, a difficulty which is perhaps losing some of its force as a philosophical dogma.[28] The reader will not need to be told that the theory confronts a host of other difficulties. But, of course, difficulties are

---

26. *ST*, IIIa, q. 39, a. 1, and Ia, q. 39, a. 4, ad 1.

27. A recent discussion of this can be found in "Being and Being Known," in Wilfrid Sellars, *Science, Perception, and Reality* (New York: 1963), pp. 41–59.

28. See Zeno Vendler, *Res Cogitans* (Ithaca: 1972).

not refutations. Let us turn now to the argument which presupposes the theory of meaning we have been discussing.

II

God's nameability is a problem for Thomas because of the following assumptions. First, human intellection, presupposing as it does sense experience, has as its connatural object the nature or quiddity of sensible reality.[29] Second, the intellect's dependence on the senses is not merely genetic but constant. Natures which exist in material singulars are grasped intellectually in an immaterial way. By this is meant that the mind's concepts do not include singular and individuating notes; the nature is conceived as formal, as apt to be found in many. But the nature of a material thing can only be grasped truly and completely when it is known as existing in particulars. Particulars are grasped through sense and imagination. Thus there is a continuing reliance on the senses if the intellect is to have adequate knowledge of its commensurate or connatural object.[30] Third, God is not a material object.[31] Fourth, obliquely and by extrapolation from its connatural object, the human mind can gain some knowledge of immaterial things. Finally, the obliquity and indirection of our knowledge of God will be reflected in the way we talk about him, including the meaning of the names attributed to him.

Philosophy of religion continues to betray its origin (or rebirth) as a response to positivist attacks on the meaningfulness of religious language. Whatever the vagaries and ultimate fate of the principle of verification, the attack touched a nerve. If there was in the attack an apparent confusion of meaning and truth, there was also a sense that the use of our language to talk about God distorts and stretches it beyond its normal range. The agnostic or atheist, thinking himself in possession of a standard and paradigmatic use of language, often the language of physical science, which is itself a language only in an extended sense of the term, easily finds human talk about God out of order. But the sense of inadequacy, of the poverty of human language, is felt far more acutely by the believer. Certainly Thomas Aquinas exhibits no tendency to suggest that everything is in order with our talk about God. Such talk is easily misunderstood; the believer may come to think of God as a thing among things, accessible

29. *ST*, Ia, q. 12, a. 4.
31. Ibid., q. 3, a. 1.

30. Ibid., q. 84, a. 7.

and nameable much as anything else is. From the very outset of the *Summa*, Thomas reminds us again and again that we are unable to know what God is, that the divine nature so far exceeds the capacity of the human mind that we must settle for knowing what God is not rather than what he is.[32]

This conviction scarcely reduces him to silence, however. One might even find in the *Summa* a matter-of-factness in discussing things divine that seems presumptuous. Our topic, the nameability of God, would, if pursued in its amplitude, lead beyond the considerations in the treatise on God as one, to those Thomas develops in discussing the manifestly theological topics of the Trinity and Incarnation.[33] None of these treatments suggests to the casual reader, a writer in the grips of negative theology. However imperfect human language is to express the divine, Thomas does not counsel silence.

The second premise of the argument in our charter text is, in its entirety, this: "It was shown above that God cannot in this life be seen in his essence but is known by us from creatures according to the relation of principle and by way of excellence and remotion."[34] The three-fold distinction is an abiding feature of Thomas's thought and permits us to speak of three kinds of divine attribute: negative, relative, and affirmative. Our earlier remarks about the characterization of questions 3–11 suggest that in them Thomas is concerned with negative attributes. (Actually, this turns out to be not wholly true because of questions 5 and 6 which deal with the good in general and the goodness of God, respectively.) It is certainly the case that articles 2–7 of question 13 turn on the other two kinds of divine attribute. When, in article 2, Thomas asks if any name is said of God *substantialiter*, he is, in effect, asking if there is not a kind of attribute which is neither negative nor relative. Having assured himself that there is, he asks in article 3 whether all such attributes are metaphorical and argues that they are not. Article 4 argues that such attributes are many but not synonymous, for reasons we have touched on. Article 5 is the famous claim that the affirmative attributes are names analogically common to God and creatures, which (article 6) are said first of creatures, from one point of view, and first of God, from another. Article 7 discusses relative attributes. Articles 8 and 9 discuss the name 'God' with particular reference to the question whether it is a proper name. Article

32. Thomas often confronts the following objection: we can know the existence of God insofar as we know that He exists; in God, nature and existence are identical; therefore, we can know the divine nature. See, e.g., *ST*, Ia, q. 3, a. 4, ad 2.

33. See, e.g., ibid., q. 39, and IIIa, q. 16.

34. *ST*, Ia, q. 13, a. 1.

11 discusses 'He who is' as the most proper name of God and a final article asks whether, given the simplicity of God, it is possible to form affirmative propositions (with their suggestion of complexity: "God is P") about God.

I mention the wider setting in order not to mislead the reader as to the adequacy of the few remarks to follow. It is the affirmative, as opposed to the negative and relative, divine attributes that are said to be analogically common to God and creature. We shall examine this doctrine which, while in many ways familiar, is not always understood, with a particular eye to seeing the role of negativity in the affirmative attributes.

III

It is what I have called affirmative attributes that Thomas says may be predicated of God *substantialiter*, that is, may be taken to express, not simply what he is not, by removing some characteristic from him, nor what he is in relation to something else or, more accurately, that something is related to him, but the divine nature or substance itself, however inadequately. The examples of this kind of attribute that Thomas gives are 'good' and 'wise'. When God is said to be wise, the sense of the claim is *not simply* that God is the cause of created wisdom or that he is unlike things which lack cognition. Rather, 'wise' is taken to express, inadequately to be sure, what God is: "Therefore, it must be said, on the contrary, that names of this sort signify the divine substance and are predicated of God substantially, but are deficient in the way they represent him." [35] Now this claim seems to contradict his reiterated remark that it is impossible to know what God is and that we can know only what God is not. In explicating what he means, Thomas repeats that God is known from his creatures, and thus God is knowable only to the degree that creatures manifest or represent what he is. Some perfections found in creatures are such that they can be thought of as in God, though in a manner that escapes our comprehension. The preexistence of perfections in God is grounded in (a) the fact that he is the cause of creatures and that the perfection of the effect must in some way preexist in the cause, and (b) that God is the summation of perfections. Names signifying perfections found in creatures can signify the divine nature insofar as those created perfections manifest or represent their source.

35. Ibid., a. 2.

When therefore it is said, 'God is good', the sense is not, 'God is the cause of goodness', or, 'God is not evil', but the sense is 'that which we call goodness in creatures preexists in God' and this indeed in a higher way.[36]

In order to get some understanding of this, we must take into account the distinction Thomas introduced in article 1 between a perfection and its mode. There he exemplifies the contrast by noting the difference between such concrete and abstract terms as 'white' and 'whiteness'. Of these, he wants to say that they signify the same thing (*res significata*), that is, the same quality or accidental form, but in different ways (*modi significandi*). The concrete term signifies a *quod*, the perfection in a subsistent, so that the account of 'white' would be 'that which has whiteness' (*habens albedinem*), whereas the account of 'whiteness' would be 'that whereby something is white', in short, a *quo*. Now if every name is either concrete or abstract, no name seems appropriate to God. Names which signify a subsistent thing imply composition, and God is simple; names which signify the simple perfection do not signify it as subsisting. As Thomas says elsewhere, "omne nomen cum defectu est quantum ad modum significandi," every name is defective with respect to its mode of signifying when applied to God.[37] When this realization is applied to the affirmative divine attributes, the threefold *viae* deriving from Pseudo-Dionysius can be illustrated in the following way.[38]

(1) God is wise.
(2) God is not wise.
(3) God is wisdom.

The way of affirmation, (1), does not compare to the way of negation, (2), as its contradictory, because what is affirmed is the perfection (*res significata*) and what is denied is the mode (*modus significandi*). This same terminology is employed to express the doctrine of the analogically common name.

The briefest comparison Thomas gives of univocal, equivocal, and analogous names is this: when things are named univocally, the same name signifies the same perfection in the same way; when things are named equivocally, the same name signifies quite different perfections; when things are named analogically, the same name signifies the same perfection in different ways.[39] That is, a name predicated

36. Ibid.
37. *SCG*, I, chap. 30.
38. *In I Sent.*, d. 2, q. 1, a. 3, and d. 3, q. 1, a. 3.
39. Ibid., d. 22, q. 1, a. 3, ad 2: "Ad secundum dicendum quod aliter dividitur

analogically of many has the same *res significata* but different *modi significandi*. The familiar example is 'healthy' as it occurs in:

(4) Pluto is healthy.
(5) Alpo is healthy.
(6) Urine is healthy.

'Healthy', being a concrete term, will have as its account 'that which has health.' As signifying that, it is of course predicated univocally of Pluto, Fido, and Bowser. Insofar as the name is predicated analogically, as in (4)–(6), we can take "———— health" as a meaning frame in which the *res significata* is given and the blank is to be filled in with different *modi significandi*.[40] In the example, the modes are, respectively, "subject of . . . ," "cause of . . . ," and "sign of. . . ." Filling in the blank with any of these gives us an account, meaning, or *ratio* of the term. It can be seen why the accounts or *rationes* so constructed are said to be partly the same (same *res significata*) and partly diverse (diverse *modi significandi*).[41]

Beyond this, the doctrine of the analogous name requires that one account of the name be privileged, the *ratio propria*, which will be found in only one of the analogates, of which accordingly the analogous name is said *per prius*: "When something is said analogically of many, it is found according to its proper meaning in one of them alone from which the others are denominated."[42] In short, there is an order of priority and posteriority among the many meanings of an analogous term such that one of its meanings is required in order to grasp the others. Thus, when urine is said to be healthy, what is meant is that it is a sign of health in the subject of health. The analogous name not only has a plurality of meanings which are partly the same and partly different, but one of those meanings is primary and the other(s) secondary.

The second-order vocabulary that is generated by analyzing the example of 'healthy' (*res significata, modus significandi, ratio propria*, etc.) is what Thomas means by a logical vocabulary and to say that the doctrine of analogous names is a logical one means only that this second-

---

aequivocum, analogum et univocum. Aequivocum enim dividitur secundum res significatas, univocum vero dividitur secundum diversa differentias, sed analogum dividitur secundum diversos modos."

40. The abstract form of the term enters into the account of the concrete form and vice versa, underscoring the fact that the perfection is never grasped independently of some mode.

41. *ST*, Ia, q. 13, a. 5.

42. Ibid., q. 16, a. 6.

order account of it is logical; it does not mean that analogous names *signify* accidents accruing to names as they are known by us.[43]

When Thomas says that the affirmative divine attributes consist of names that are analogically common to God and creature, it is the foregoing doctrine he has in mind, and we are meant to compare

(7) Socrates is wise

and

(1) God is wise.

in such a way that we see that the adjectival name 'wise' signifies the same perfection (*res significata*) but in different ways (*modi significandi*). Now Socrates has wisdom, meaning that the subsistent entity Socrates possesses an accidental quality whereby he grasps cognitively the order of things. The *res significata* here, awareness of order (*sapientis est ordinare*), is taken to be distinguishable from the mode of having it peculiar to humans, i.e., as an accident distinct from substance, something acquired that can be lost, and so forth. (2) above is the denial, in God, of this way of having wisdom, and the denials are familiar from question 3 where Thomas discussed the divine simplicity. In the standard case of the analogous name, we should be able to produce another mode of signifying to replace the one being denied. As is notorious, we cannot do this in the case of the divine wisdom. All we can say, on the model of Ia, q. 13, a. 2, is 'that which we call wisdom in creatures preexists in God and in a higher way'. That higher way is expressible only by negating the lower, creaturely way, and the *via eminentiae*, (3), is, as it were, the affirmation of this denial, or, better, a *negatio negationis*. To say that God *is* wisdom is also modally defective, as is clear from what was said earlier about concrete and abstract terms.

The key to the affirmative divine attributes lies in the intelligibility of the claim that perfections found in a limited way in creatures are thinkable while negating those creaturely limitations.[44] If it is not easy

---

43. See *The Logic of Analogy*, pp. 166–69. For another view, see J. M. Ramirez, *Opera omnia*, vol. 2, *De Analogia* (Madrid: 1972), pp. 1675–88. The view of analogy presented in the text of this chapter, however solidly grounded in the texts, is not universally held by students of Aquinas. Battista Mondin, *The Principle of Analogy in Protestant and Catholic Theology* (The Hague: 1963), accepts it. An excellent book, B. Montagnes, *La doctrine de l'analogie de l'être d'après saint Thomas d'Aquin* (Louvain: 1963), pursues the matter chronologically and finds many of the most vexing texts to be early formulations later abandoned by Thomas. Even if true, this would not relieve us of the necessity of understanding the various formulations, not least in order to assess Montagnes's interpretation.

44. See Alistair McKinnon, *Falsification and Belief* (The Hague: 1970).

to grasp what is being affirmed when this is said to be possible, it is hard to know why its possibility is so often swiftly denied. Thomas on occasion suggests thought-experiments on qualities such as whiteness, arguing that, apart from its being received in and multiplied by subjects, we could imagine it as unique. Are not the Platonic things-in-themselves products of such a projection? For that matter, the difficulty is present in the contrast of 'white' and 'whiteness'. When the abstract and concrete term are said to signify the same perfection in different ways, that perfection is never grasped independently of those modes. In any case, the real problem of perfections themselves is one of truth rather than meaning.

A further feature of the deficiency of the affirmative divine attributes, one that underlies Thomas's query as to their possible synonymy, is precisely their plurality. When God is called good, wise, just, etc., these predicates are not synonymous, because different accounts are given of each, and the accounts differ because they are imposed from different perfections found in creatures.[45] But these many names do not refer to any plurality or complexity when affirmed of God, though how perfections which are diverse in creatures can be one simple thing we cannot know.

This must suffice to show that Thomas's distinction of affirmative attributes from negative and relative ones does not mean that the emphasis is any less on deficiency and inadequacy on the part of our knowing and naming.

IV

While the short Thomistic answer to our titular question might seem to be, "Yes, but analogically," we have seen that analogy is invoked only in the discussion of affirmative attributes. The negative and relative attributes have their own difficulties, to be sure. One might wonder if the name 'God' itself is caught by one of the categories of divine attribute. In article 10 of question 13, Thomas discusses univocal and analogical uses of the name 'God' and that already makes it clear that 'God' is not a proper name according to Thomas since, in order to be univocal or equivocal, a name must be shared, common. But while he holds that 'God' is an appellative rather than a proper name, Thomas, in discussing the Trinity, indicates that in some ways 'God' is like a proper name.[46] It is just because any adequate discussion

---

45. *ST*, Ia, q. 13, a. 4.   46. Ibid., q. 39, a. 4, ad 1.

of whether 'God' is a proper name would necessitate introducing the philosophical distinctions made in the difficult context of Thomas's discussion of the Trinity of Persons in God that I do not enter into it here. One can appreciate the subtleties required to move intelligibly among predications true of the divine nature and those true of a divine person. Things get even more complicated in the discussion of the Incarnate God. If Christ died for our sins, did God die? Indeed, was God born in Bethlehem? The ascription of predicates to Christ in virtue of his humanity or in virtue of his divinity calls for a niceness of distinction and precision of language that cannot fail to attract the interest of the philosopher. Of course, it was not to titillate the philosophical mind that Thomas generated such linguistic precisions as he did, but in order to get as clear as he could about what God had revealed to man. There is perhaps no better way to realize the ineffability of God.

18

THE ANALOGY OF NAMES IS A LOGICAL DOCTRINE

In his commentary on the *Sentences*, asking *Utrum omnia sint vera veritate increata*, St. Thomas fashions the following argument.

Videtur quod omnia sint vera una veritate quae est veritas increata . . . verum dicitur analogice de illis in quibus est veritas, sicut sanitas de omnibus sanis. Sed una est sanitas numero a qua denominatur animal sanum, sicut subjectum ejus, et medicina sana, sicut causa ejus, et urina sana, sicut signum ejus. Ergo videtur quod una sit veritas qua omnia dicuntur vera.[1]

The things called, analogically, healthy are denominated from numerically one form; therefore, since several things are called true analogically they must be denominated from numerically one form.

The reply to this argument has long been of particular interest to students of St. Thomas's doctrine on analogous names, not least because it provides the underlying framework of Cajetan's division of analogy, in his *De nominum analogia*, into analogy of inequality, analogy of attribution (or proportion) and analogy of proper proportionality. Of these three kinds of analogous name, the first is not an analogous name, Cajetan assures us. Not a very propitious beginning, we might think: there are three kinds of analogous name and the first kind isn't analogous at all. Cajetan's procedure becomes intelligible when we see that he has mistakenly read St. Thomas's unraveling of the argument quoted above as if it provided a threefold division of analogous names. Well, doesn't it?

Ad primum igitur dicendum quod aliquid dicitur secundum analogiam triplicter: vel *secundum intentionem tantum, et non secundum esse*; et hoc est quando una intentio refertur ad plura per prius et posterius, quae tamen non habet esse nisi in uno; sicut intentio sanitatis refertur ad animal, urinam et dietam diversimode, secundum prius et posterius; non tamen secundum diversum

---

1. *In I Sent.*, d. 19, q. 5, a. 2, obj. 1.

esse, quia esse sanitatis non est nisi in animali. Vel *secundum esse et non secundum intentionem*; et hoc contingit quando plura parificantur in intentione alicujus communis, sed illud commune non habet esse unius rationis in omnibus, sicut omnia corpora parificantur in intentione corporeitatis. Unde Logicus, qui considerat intentiones tantum, dicit, hoc nomen corpus de omnibus corporibus univoce praedicari: sed esse hujus naturae non est ejusdem rationis in corporibus corruptibilibus et incorruptibilibus. Unde quantum ad metaphysicum et naturalem, qui considerant res secundum suum esse, nec hoc nomen, corpus, nec aliquid aliud dicitur univoce de corruptibilibus et incorruptibilibus . . . Vel *secundum intentionem et secundum esse*; et hoc est quando neque parificatur in intentione communi, neque in esse; sicut ens dicitur de substantia et accidente; et de talibus oportet quod natura communis habeat aliquod esse in unoquoque eorum de quibus dicitur, sed differens secundum rationem majoris vel minoris perfectionis. Et similiter dico, quod veritas, et bonitas, et omnia hujusmodi dicuntur analogice de Deo et creaturis. Unde oportet quod secundum suum esse omnia haec in Deo sint, et in creaturis secundum rationem majoris perfectionis et minoris; ex quo sequitur, cum non possint esse secundum esse utrobique, quod sint diversae veritates.[2]

The second member of this division is Cajetan's analogy of inequality, the first his analogy of attribution and the third his analogy of proportionality. With respect to the second member of the division, it seems clear that it is not a type of analogous name. "Body" predicated of celestial and terrestrial bodies with the meaning "three dimensional matter-form composite" is a univocal term. Should we fashion meanings more appropriate to celestial and terrestrial bodies, meanings which express the putative difference in their matters, "body," with these new meanings, would not be univocally predicated of celestial and terrestrial bodies. The judgment that a term is predicated univocally of many is based on its having one meaning, *ratio* or account, as said of each of them. Whether or not that *ratio* is adequate, proportioned, to the things spoken of does not affect the definition of the univocal term. The common, generic term is often taken to exhibit what St. Thomas has in mind here. "Animal" with the meaning or *ratio* "living body endowed with sensation" is univocally predicated of man and brute. A *ratio* less inadequate of man would add "rational" to the above account, but of course that would not be a new meaning of "animal." One satisfied with the abstract, with the conceptual equalizing (*parificantur in intentione*) which is the boon and bane of human knowing, need have only a limited vocabulary whose terms range univocally over quite unequal things. *Omnia animalia sunt aequaliter animal sed non aequalia animalia.*

Important and fascinating as this second member of St. Thomas's

2. Ibid., ad 1.

division, it is the first and third members which must concern us here. How would the untutored eye interpret the difference between an analogy *secundum intentionem tantum et non secundum esse*, on the one hand, and, on the other, analogy *secundum intentionem et secundum esse*? First, some sense of what "analogy" means would be sought, and what better meaning than unequal, ranked, ordered arrangement? Opposed to analogy is equalization, *parificatio*, while analogy is spoken of in terms of prior and posterior, more and less. Ranking is either real or intentional. If our neophyte took analogy or inequality on the intentional level to mean the ordering of a plurality of *rationes* signified by the same term, he would have in hand the concept of an analogous name. Would he not then conclude that what St. Thomas is saying is this: sometimes the denominating form of the analogous name is in only one of the analogates, is numerically one, and sometimes it is in all of the analogates. And what would follow from this? The traditional claim has been that the consequence is that there are two kinds of analogous name, but surely the straightforward implication is that, since an analogous name sometimes is found with one situation *secundum esse* and sometimes with another, the *secundum esse* situations are accidental to what is meant by analogous name. If some men are white and some men are black, black and white are accidental to what it is to be a man. The first objection, quoted above, now appears for the fallacy it is. A far cruder version of it would be this: triangle is said univocally of all triangles just as animal is said univocally of all animals; the differences which divide the species of animal are drawn from substantial form; it would seem therefore that the differences which divide the species of triangle are drawn from substantial form. St. Thomas's treatment of the argument which would move from the fact that both "healthy" and "true" are predicated analogically to the conclusion that the set of things named healthy must be identical to the set of things named true makes it clear that our ability to recognize that a term is being used analogously does not of itself involve the assertion that the denominating form exists in all or only one of the analogates.

In a parallel text (*ST*, Ia, q. 16, a. 6, c.), St. Thomas prefaces his discussion with definitions of univocal and analogous term: (a) "Quando aliquid praedicatur univoce de multis, illud in quolibet eorum secundum propriam rationem invenitur, sicut *animal* in qualibet specie animalis"; (b) "Sed quando aliquid dicitur analogice de multis, illud invenitur secundum propriam rationem in uno eorum tantum, a quo alia denominantur." As is his wont, St. Thomas immediately illustrates what he means by an analogous name with the example of "healthy."

Cajetan, in his commentary on this passage, refuses to accept the description of analogy St. Thomas has given. It is clear that Cajetan thinks that in the case of a genuinely analogous name the *ratio propria* is found in each of the analogates and that, of course, is what St. Thomas has said is peculiar to univocity.[3] After showing how "healthy" is an analogous term, St. Thomas has added this: "Et quamvis sanitas non sit in medicina neque in urina, tamen in utroque est aliquid per quod hoc quidem facit, illud autem significat sanitatem." Only the animal is denominated healthy from a form or quality intrinsic to it which is the denominating form of the word "healthy." Now, if that remark were identical to the claim that, when a term is predicated analogously of many, it is predicated according to its *ratio propria* of one of them alone, we could understand Cajetan's consternation. Something which happens to be true of things called healthy analogously would have been built right into the definition of what it means for things to be named analogically. But of course whether or not the denominating form, e.g. *sanitas* or *veritas*, exists in each of the analogates of *sanum* and *verum* is not the point at issue when it is said that the analogous name is predicated according to its *ratio propria* of only one of the analogates. To see this, we must be clear about the second-order or logical vocabulary St. Thomas employs to set forth the character of the second intention analogy.

There is no better starting point than the example of "healthy." Needless to say, being univocal, equivocal or analogous is not something which attaches to a word independently of how it is used. If we think of the recurrent term "healthy" in such assertions as "Fido is healthy" and "Bowser is healthy," we would say that the term has the same meaning or account in its two occurrences. In short, it is there a univocal term. "Healthy" exemplifies analogy when we have in mind its occurrences in the following assertions: Fido is healthy; medicine is healthy; urine is healthy. We cannot give exactly the same account, meaning or *ratio* in explaining these occurrences of the common term. By the same token, it seems excessive to suggest that we have utterly different meanings of "healthy" in these uses. So it is that we say that the analogous name has meanings which are partly the same, partly different. In what does the sameness consist? The obvious candidate is what we have called the denominating form, that is, in the privileged example, health. St. Thomas sometimes suggests that a common notion, a *ratio communis*, of the analogous name can be formed. Clearly, this will not be like the common notion which answers to a

---

3. Cf. Cajetan, *In Iam Summae theologiae*, q. 16, a. 6, nn. 3, 5 et 6.

generic term. The *ratio communis entis*, we remember, is said to be *habens esse* or *id quod habet esse*. *Esse*, of course, is *id a quo nomen ens imponitur*. So too health is that from which the term healthy is imposed. On the model of the common notion of "being" we could thus fashion a common notion of "healthy": *habens sanitatem*. I have suggested elsewhere that it is advisable to think of this as the possibility of a *ratio* rather than a *ratio*. That is, *habens* in *habens esse* is a blank or variable whose fillers or values will differ. Now, as will be recognized, the second-order or logical label for what I am calling the denominating form is *res significata* and the logical label for what fills in the blank or is a value for the variable in the *ratio communis* is a *modus significandi*. We can now set forth the way in which "healthy" enables us to formulate the logical doctrine of analogical meaning.

The *ratio communis sani* will be *habens sanitatem* or "health." Various modes of signifying health can fill in the blank and constitute different meanings or *rationes*. They are: subject of, cause of and sign of. As said of Fido, "healthy" has the meaning "subject of health." As said of medicine, "healthy" has the meaning "cause of health." As said of urine, "healthy" has the meaning "sign of health." Thus, St. Thomas will say that a term used analogously signifies the same *res significata* but has different *modi significandi*. Not just any way of signifying the denominating form is constitutive of the *ratio propria* of the term in question. Rather, one way of filling in the blank, one combination of *modus* and *res*, is understood to be primary. The meaning "healthy" has as said of Fido, namely, "subject of health," is the *ratio propria* of the term, and insofar as it has other meanings, "cause of healthy" or "sign of health," these depend upon the first meaning, since we understand cause of health in the subject of health or sign of health in the subject of health. This is what is meant when it is said that the analogous name is said according to its *ratio propria* of one of the analogates alone. This is universally true of every example of an analogous term St. Thomas mentions. It is not peculiar to "healthy." How odd it would be if the standard example of an analogous name were systematically misleading. It is of course true that in the example of "healthy" as analogous name, the *res significata* is found in only one of the analogates whereas in many names common to God and creatures the *res significata* is found in both analogates. But this has nothing to do with the claim that the analogous name is said according to its *ratio propria* of only one of the analogates.

When the parallel texts of *Summa theologiae*, Ia, q. 16, a. 6, and *In I Sent.*, d. 19, q. 5, a. 2, ad 1, are placed side by side and allowed to cast light on one another, it becomes quite clear that our ability to recognize a term as analogous is independent of any assertion as to whether or not the *res significata* is intrinsic to all the analogates. Furthermore, it seems that when we do judge that the *res significata* is an intrinsic form in each of the analogates or, on the contrary, judge that it is an intrinsic form of only one of the analogates, we are not thereby adding to what is meant by an analogous name. That is, these further judgments do not seem to me to be productive of types of analogous term.

A sign of the rightness of this conclusion is found in the way St. Thomas speaks of names analogously common to God and creatures. In article 2 of question 13 of the *Prima pars* of the *Summa theologiae*, he seems to allow that this analogy could be understood in the case, say, of "wise," if the meaning of the term as predicated of God were "cause of human wisdom." The usual account of an analogous term could be given: the *res significata* would be wisdom, and a secondary meaning would be cause of wisdom. If he rejects this it is because he does not think that all we mean to say when we call God wise is that He is the cause of created wisdom. His point, therefore, bears on the content of the concept, of the first intention. The wisdom of creatures is what we first know and talk about and, given the meaning of the term as applied to men, we are denominating them from a quality they possess. Our mode of signifying created or human wisdom thus involves an acquired quality, distinct from essence. Insofar as the *res significata*, wisdom, can be removed from modal constraints, we can fashion a meaning of the term such that, as predicated of God, it can express the divine wisdom without the suggestion that the divine wisdom is an accident distinct from essence. Thus, the creature is called wise from an intrinsic form and God is called wise because of what He is. The *res significata* of the name "wise" said analogically of God and creature is found in both analogates. If it is the same *res significata*, as it is, it is not the same in the sense of numerically one, existing in only one of the analogates. This assertion is based on what we mean when we call Socrates wise and what we mean when we call God wise; that is, it is based on the *content* of the *rationes* or meanings of the term. When we say the name is analogous, we are speaking of a relation between the *rationes* of the term; that is, are saying that the *res significata* of the term is signified in different ways and that one way of signifying the *res* is primary, the *ratio propria*. In names analogously common to God and creature, as in all other analogous names, the *ratio propria* is found in only one of the analogates. Since we name things as we know them, it is clear that according to the order of imposition of the name it first means created wisdom. We have no direct or immediate cognitive access to God but must know him through or by means of what we know of creatures. Created wisdom is an acquired characteristic whereby all things are referred to what is really primary or first. Let us imagine that something like that is the *ratio sapientis*. If we affirm "wise" of God, we have in mind the *res significata*; if we deny "wise" of God, it is because we know His wisdom cannot be an acquired characteristic, an accident distinct from His essence. Employing the *via eminentiae*, we fashion a *ratio* by saying that the *res significata*, wisdom, exists in God in a way we cannot comprehend, as one with His essence and other perfections. Thus, there is clearly a dependence in the order of naming on the meaning of the term as it is predicated of creatures, but the meaning the term has as said of God does not express dependence on creatures. The divine wisdom is not dependent on created wisdom, however much our knowledge of and talk about divine wisdom depends on our knowledge of and talk about created wisdom.

When we affirm that the analogy of names is from first to last a logical doctrine in the writings of St. Thomas, we are understanding logic in the way St. Thomas himself does. The second intentions which are the concern of logic attach to first intentions. The differences between the things called healthy analogously and God and creature as named analogously which give rise to Cajetan's mistaken division are differences, not between them as named analogously, but are differences drawn from the content of the first intentions or *rationes*. Since this is so, such differences are not productive of types of analogous name. The many *rationes* analogously signified by "healthy," "being" and by "true," "wise" and other names common to God and creature, are, as analogous terms, in every way the same. The same second-level or logical account of what is meant by an analogous term applies to them all. When we are speaking of a particular analogous term, we identify its *res significata* and *modi significandi* and the *rationes* constructed of these. On the level of first intentions, on the level of the content of these *rationes*, many differences unaccounted for in the observation that the term in question is analogous will come to the fore and occupy our attention. If such differences were constitutive of types or kinds of analogous name, our list of types would threaten to become infinite. But the basic mistake would be to confuse the logical and real orders, the second and first intentional. When it is a question of analogous names, the distinction of analogy into attribution and proper proportionality is as inappropriate as a distinction of genus into mathematical and natural. Of course this is not to say that the difference between mathematics and natural science is unimportant. No more does what has been argued here question the importance of the fact that, in names common to God and creature the perfection talked about is found in both. To end on a hermeneutic note. Any interpretation of what St. Thomas means by analogous names must make sense of the fact that the Angelic Doctor almost always illustrates this doctrine by appeal to the example of "healthy." An interpretation which must insist that the example does not illustrate what is being talked about is to that degree suspect and unlikely to be in tune with the thought of St. Thomas.

19

APROPOS OF ART AND CONNATURALITY

Owing, doubtless, to the bifurcated influence of contemporary thought, which is engaged on the one hand in bloodless analysis and on the other in an impassioned, voluntaristic emphasis on the nonintellectual, Thomists have of late been talking a great deal about connatural knowledge. Indeed, in the encyclical *Humani Generis*, Pope Pius XII has seen in connatural knowledge a refutation of the claim that Scholastic thought does not pay sufficient attention to the role appetite plays in knowledge.

Never has Christian philosophy denied the usefulness and efficacy of good dispositions of soul for perceiving and embracing moral and religious truths. In fact, it has always taught that the lack of these dispositions of good will can be the reason why the intellect, influenced by the passions and evil inclinations, can be so obscured that it cannot see clearly. Indeed St. Thomas holds that the intellect can in some way perceive higher goods of the moral order, whether natural or supernatural, inasmuch as it experiences a certain "connaturality" with these goods, whether this "connaturality" be purely natural or the result of grace; and it is clear how much even this somewhat obscure perception can help the reason in its investigations.[1]

In what follows, we will first examine the meaning of connatural knowledge in the moral order and then St. Thomas's use of the term "connatural" in other contexts. Then we will try to see why, if the notion of affective connaturality is to be extended to the realm of art, one must distinguish between the habit of art and poetic knowledge, as Maritain has done.

1. A. C. Cotter, S.J., *The Encyclical "Humani Generis," with a Commentary* (Weston: 1951), par. 34, pp. 37–39.

1. JUDGMENT AND CONNATURALITY

In the three texts of St. Thomas Aquinas most often referred to when the question of connatural knowledge arises, we find him talking about judgment as the act of the wise man. There are two kinds of wisdom and consequently two kinds of judgment. With regard to what is to be done, there are two judgments which are relevant. The one is that which can be given by one who possesses moral science; such a man can judge about virtuous acts even if he himself does not possess virtue. Of this man, we would say that he has a cognitive grasp of ethical matters and judges *per modum cognitionis*. Another type of judgment in moral matters is that made by the virtuous man who may or may not have learned moral science. When he judges what is to be done, he is involved in a more than cognitive way, since he is inclined toward what ought to be done by the virtues he possesses. His judgment, accordingly, is one *per modum inclinationis*.[2]

It is this second kind of judgment that St. Thomas, in another text,[3] calls a judgment which is based on a connaturality with the things which are to be judged. The first kind of judgment, that *per modum cognitionis*, is correct because of a perfect use of reason. The rectitude of the judgment based on connaturality is due to something other than intellect. It must be kept in mind that the act of judging is always an act of intellect;[4] it is not that something other than the intellect makes the judgment when connaturality is spoken of, but that the rectitude of the intellect's judgment must be due to something outside the intellect itself.

The emphasis in the above-mentioned texts is on practical wisdom, and what is alluded to as connaturality is brought out quite clearly by St. Thomas in his analyses of the judgment of prudence which is

2. "Dicendum quod cum iudicium ad sapientiam pertineat, secundum duplicem modum iudicandi, dupliciter sapientia accipitur. Contingit enim aliquem iudicare uno modo per modum inclinationis, sicut qui habet habitum virtutis, recte iudicat de his quae sunt secundum virtutem agenda, inquantum ad illa inclinatur; unde et in X Ethic. dicitur quod virtuosus est mensura et regula humanorum actuum. Alio modo per modum cognitionis, sicut aliquis instructus in scientia morali posset iudicare de actibus virtutis etiam si virtutem non haberet."—*ST*, Ia, q. 1, a. 6, ad 3.

3. "Dicendum quod sicut supra dictum est sapientia importat quamdam rectitudinem iudicii secundum rationes divinas. Rectitudo autem iudicii potest contingere dupliciter: uno modo, secundum perfectum usum rationis; alio modo, propter connaturalitatem quamdam ad ea de quibus iam est iudicandum. Sicut de his quae ad castitatem pertinent, per rationis inquisitionem recte iudicat ille qui didicit scientiam moralem; sed per quamdam connaturalitatem ad ipsa recte iudicat de eis ille qui habet habitum castitatis."—ibid., IIaIIae, q. 45, a. 2.

4. Ibid.

sapientia viro.[5] Prudence is an intellectual virtue, *recta ratio agibilium.* Unlike science, prudence is concerned with contingent and variable things in their very contingency and variability, with what ought to be done here and now in these particular circumstances. The prudential syllogism has for its major a rather universal proposition, one grasped in a purely cognitive way, *intra limites intellectus;*[6] for example, the goods of another ought to be returned. What prudence must do is see particular circumstances in the light of this common principle. The common principles which serve as the major of prudential syllogisms may be drawn from the diligent inquisition of moral science or may be something absolutely of natural law. However it is had, what is of present interest in the reasoning of prudence is the minor. How will prudence judge in this particular case when it is a question, say, of this borrowed book, whose permanent possession would be a great good? One can accept the universal statement that what belongs to another should be returned; in an ethics class one may find it relatively easy, within the confines of a fictive case, to apply the principles to "particular" circumstances. But now, here and now, what is the person's judgment about returning this borrowed book? He is involved in the judgment of the here and now, and the history of his past actions enters into the reckoning, the kind of person he is. *Qualis unusquisque est, talis finis ei videtur.*[7] The judgment of the particular circumstances, the minor of the operative syllogism, depends for its rectitude on the appetitive condition of the person who is to act. The judgment is *extra limites intellectus* in the sense that the appetite influences the judgment of reason. What is required here and now is not theoretical truth but the practical truth which is goodness.[8]

The truth of the speculative intellect is quite in keeping with the movement of the intellect relatively to things. The intellect is said to be true insofar as it is in conformity with reality, and the properly cognitive mode consists in the assimilation of things to the intellect. The intellect receives things, not in the manner in which they exist in themselves, but rather in its own immaterial mode. In order for a material thing to be known intellectually it must be separated from the mode belonging to it as it exists; that is, from its materiality and consequent singularity. Intellectual knowledge is abstractive, immaterial, universal. Appetite, on the other hand, tends towards things as they are in themselves. We love things for what they are and as they are

5. Prov. 10:23. Cf. *ST*, IaIIae, q. 47, a. 2, ad 1.
6. Cf. Cajetan, *In IamIIae*, q. 58, a. 5.   7. Ibid., n. 8.
8. *Q. D. de virtutibus in communi*, a. 6, ad 5.

in themselves. For this reason we could say that the mode of appetite is more existential than that of intellect.[9] Now, something of this conformity with things as they are in themselves, of this existential mode, is present in the notion of the practical truth of the prudential judgment.

Prudence is an intellectual virtue, but a virtue of the practical intellect which seeks knowledge in order to operate. Since prudence is concerned with human affairs, it is to the end of man that it directs individual actions; as is always the case when something is to be done, the end is the principle.[10] The end of man is something which is given, for it follows on the nature of man. This end is something which is known naturally.[11] The considerations of prudence, its judgments and its command, must presuppose this end and the rectification of appetite relatively to this end.

Consequently, it is requisite for prudence, which is right reason about things to be done, that man be well disposed with regard to ends; and this depends on the rectitude of his appetite. Therefore, for prudence there is need of moral virtue, which rectifies the appetite.[12]

It is because the intellect cannot conform to the particularity and contingency of singulars that the judgment of prudence cannot be true with speculative truth. But it is precisely singulars which must be judged when it is a question of commanding an action here and now. From the point of view of cognition, only opinion could be had about singular contingents as singular and contingent. And yet I must make the right decision. The rectitude of my judgment, accordingly, must depend upon something other than intellect.

On the other hand, the truth of the practical intellect depends on conformity with right appetite. This conformity has no place in necessary matters, which

---

9. *In de divinis nominibus*, cap. 2, lect. 4: "Tertius modus habendi est, quod doctus est ista quae dixit ex quadam inspiratione diviniore, quam communiter fit multis; non solum discens, sed et patiens divina, idest non solum divinorum scientiam in intellectu accipiens, sed etiam diligendo, eis unitum est per affectum. Passio enim magis ad appetitum quam ad cognitionem pertinere videtur, quia cognita sunt in cognoscente secundum modum cognoscentis et non secundum modum rerum cognitarum, sed appetitus movet ad res, secundum modum quo in seipsis sunt, et sic ad ipsas res quodammodo afficitur. Sicut autem aliquid virtuosus, ex habitu virtutis quam habet in affectu, perficitur ad recte iudicandum de his quae ad virtutem illam pertinent, ita qui afficitur ad divina, accipit divinitus rectum iudicium de rebus divinis."
10. *Nicomachean Ethics*, 1151a16.   11. *ST*, IIaIIae, q. 47, a. 6.
12. "Et ideo ad prudentiam, quae est recta ratio agibilium, requiritur quod homo sit bene dispositus circa fines; quod quidem est per appetitum rectum. Et ideo ad prudentiam requiritur moralis virtus, per quam fit appetitus rectus."—ibid., IaIIae, q. 57, a. 4.

are not effected by the human will, but only in contingent matters which can be effected by us . . .[13]

The truth of the prudential judgment depends upon rectified appetite, appetite determined to the end or good. And since appetite, as we mentioned above, moves towards things as they are in themselves, as they exist, appetite assimilates one to what is desired; one becomes like what one loves, is connatural with it. It is precisely this connaturality which is characteristic of appetite that makes the prudential judgment, which depends upon appetite, a judgment by connaturality or inclination. Moral science, because its consideration of *agibilia* does not entail appetite,[14] judges *per modum cognitionis*. It is precisely the influence of appetite on the prudential judgment of *agibilia* which makes this judgment one *per connaturalitatem*.

2. VIRTUE AND APPETITE

The judgment through connaturality, as it figures in the texts cited, is such because of a special dependence on appetite. Why is it that the influence of appetite on the object of intellect makes the judgment connatural? If this is not answered, we shall encounter great difficulties when we find St. Thomas speaking of the habit of principles as proceeding *per modum naturae*. An even greater difficulty arises when we read that the habitus of geometry induces a kind of connaturality with the geometrical. If we speak of connaturality in these last two cases, we are clearly not speaking of affective knowledge. It is therefore imperative that we examine the scope of the term "connatural" in St. Thomas if we are to avoid calling the most perfectly scientific knowledge affective.

In Aristotle's *Ethics*,[15] one reads that moral virtue is more certain

13. "Veritas autem intellectus practici accipitur per conformitatem ad appetitum rectum. Quae quidem conformitas in necessariis locum non habet, quae voluntate non fiunt; sed solum in contingentibus quae possunt a nobis fieri . . ."—ibid., a. 5, ad 3. Cf. Cajetan, in loc., n. 4.

14. *In VI Ethic.*, lect. 7, n. 1200: "Omnia ergo de quibus hic fit mentio intantum sunt species prudentiae, inquantum non in ratione sola consistunt, sed habent aliquid in appetitu. Inquantum enim sunt in sola ratione, dicuntur quaedam scientiae practicae, scilicet ethica, oeconomica et politica."

15. *Nicomachean Ethics*, 1106b10. Cf. *In II Ethic.*, lect. 6, n. 315: "Sed virtus est certior omni arte, et etiam melior, sicut et natura. Virtus enim moralis agit inclinando determinate ad unum sicut et natura. Nam consuetudo in naturam vertitur. Operatio autem artis est secundum rationem, quae se habet ad diversa. Unde certior est virtus quam ars, sicut et natura." Cf. *Q. D. de ver.*, q. 10, a. 10, ad 9.

than science. The reason given is that moral virtue inclines in the
same way as nature does; that is, by determining the appetite to one
object. Virtue is generated by accustoming the appetite to a certain
mode of operation by repeated acts; this custom becomes a second
nature which determines the appetite to one object.[16] Far from settling
anything, this raises a series of questions. The intellect, too, is the subject of habits, of second natures; and because of these, the intellect is
determined to one. Is not "determination to one" what distinguishes
science from opinion?

First of all, we must ask what meaning of certitude is at play in the
remark that moral virtue is more certain than art or science. This is a
puzzling phrase because certitude is something we should tend to re-
strict to reason and science. *Moral* is derived from the Latin *mos*,
which has a twofold signification. Sometimes it signifies custom; sometimes it signifies a natural or quasi-natural inclination to do something. "Now *moral* virtue is so called from *mos* in the sense of a natural
or quasi-natural inclination to do some particular action."[17] This second meaning of *mos* is, of course, close to the first, for custom is a second nature and gives an inclination similar to that of nature. What is
more, the inclination spoken of belongs most properly to appetite.[18]
With regard to certitude, it is well to recall the distinction St. Thomas
makes between certitude *simpliciter* and certitude *secundum quid*. The
first, absolute certitude, is taken from the cause of the certitude; certitude in this sense has degrees insofar as its causes are more or less
determined. Certitude *secundum quid* is that taken from the part of the
subject, and in this sense that is most certain which is most perfectly
proportioned to the intellect.[19] This distinction is reducible to another
St. Thomas makes, that between the motive for adhering to a truth
and the evidence of the truth. Evidence gives certitude *secundum
quid*.[20]

What seems to emerge, then, is this: Moral virtue is said to be more
certain than art and science because it gives a more perfect determination to one. Why is this? It is nature in the sense given in Aristotle's
Physics which is first of all a principle of determination to one.[21] And,

16. *Q. D. de virtutibus in communi*, a. 9.

17. *ST*, IaIIae, q. 58, a. 1: "Dicitur autem virtus moralis a more, secundum quod
mos significat quamdam inclinationem naturalem, vel quasi naturalem, ad aliquid
agendum."

18. Ibid.: "Manifestum est autem quod inclinatio ad actum proprie convenit ap-
petitivae virtuti, cuius est movere omnes potentias ad agendum."

19. *ST*, IIaIIae, q. 4, a. 8.   20. *Q. D. de ver.*, q. 14, a. 1, ad 7.

21. *Q. D. de malo*, q. 6, a. 1.

in the *Physics*, nature, which always operates in one way, is distinguished from the principle of rational acts.[22] Reason is said to be *ad opposita* and not *ad unum*,[23] even when it is the subject of habits. For example, the physician in knowing health knows its opposite, sickness. The explanation of the *ad opposita* is based on a difference between intellect and will already mentioned and indicates why will better saves the *ratio naturae*. It is because intellect receives things in its own mode that oppositions in things do not preclude intellect's possessing opposites. Appetite, on the other hand, relates to things as they exist, and in existence the presence of one thing *eo ipso* excludes its opposite. Thus appetite is more *ad unum*.[24] A further indication that will is more like nature than is intellect is found in the fact that the former moves as an efficient cause and the latter as a formal cause.[25] That nature is an efficient cause is seen in its *ratio propria*.[26]

What we have already seen in the analogy of the name *nature* can also be seen by an analysis of the analogous name *virtue*. The definition of virtue given by Aristotle in the second book of the *Ethics*[27] is "that which makes the one having it good and renders his operation good." Given the recurrence of "good" in the definition, as well as the fact that good is the object of appetite, it is difficult to see how we can speak of intellectual virtues. In addressing himself to the difficulty, St. Thomas points out that the reference to the good required for virtue can be either formal or material.[28] A potency is formally related to the good when it bears on it precisely as good, something only appetite can do. A power can be related to the good materially when it bears on a good but not under the formality of goodness. Thus, those habits which have appetite as their subject, or which depend on appetite, are most properly virtues. Those habits, on the other hand, which are neither in appetite nor dependent upon it, can refer materially to the good and be, in a certain sense, virtues. With this as background, St. Thomas goes on to discuss intellectual virtues.

Both the speculative and practical intellect can be perfected by habits in two ways: first, absolutely and as such, insofar as their acts precede will and move it in the line of formal causality; secondly, insofar as their acts follow on appetite as commanded and elicited by it. Hab-

---

22. *In II Physic.*, lect. 13 (ed. Pirotta), n. 503.

23. *In IX Metaphysic.*, lect. 2, nn. 1789–93. An examination of the difference between intellect and will considered *ad opposita* can be seen in our "A Note on the Kierkegaardian Either/Or," *Laval théologique et philosophique* 8/2 (1952), pp. 230–42.

24. *Q. D. de caritate*, a. 6, ad 8.   25. *ST*, IaIIae, q. 9, a. 1, ad 3.

26. *In II Physic.*, lect. 1, n. 294. *In V Metaphysic.*, lect. 5, n. 810.

27. *Nicomachean Ethics*, II.5.   28. *Q. D. de virtutibus in communi*, a. 7.

its generated by acts of the first kind are less properly virtues, since they do not bear on the good formally as such. *Intellectus*, science, wisdom, and art are virtues in this sense.[29] These habits only render the subject capable of operating in a certain fashion; there is no disposition of appetite relative to the good which is consequent on the possession of these habits. In the classical phrase, they make one *potens* but not *volens*.

Those habits of the speculative and practical intellect which follow on the will are more truly virtues, for by them one is made not only capable of acting correctly but also willing to. St. Thomas shows what he means by analyzing faith and prudence.

By faith, the intellect operates *per modum naturae*, and intellect is not moved by its proper object as in the case of science. Rather, in faith, one assents "through a choice of the will turning to one side rather than the other."[30] Will enters into the very specification of the object of faith, and not merely in the line of efficient causality.[31] John of St. Thomas has written some very illuminating pages on the role the will plays in the assent of faith. The will, he says, can add nothing to the apprehension of the object, to its evidence; but it can render it pleasing. Moved by the will (under the influence of grace, of course) determining its object, the intellect assents to the truths of faith because they are pleasing.[32] *Nemo credit, nisi volens.*

Prudence, a virtue of the practical intellect, does not depend upon

---

29. Ibid.: "Dicitur enim aliquis intelligens vel sciens secundum quod eius intellectus perfectus est ad cognoscendum verum; quod quidem est bonum intellectus. Et licet istud verum possit esse volitum, prout homo vult intelligere verum; non tamen quantum ad hoc perficiuntur habitus praedicti. Non enim ex hoc quod homo habet scientiam, efficitur volens considerare verum, sed solummodo potens; unde et ipsa veri consideratio non est scientia inquantum est volita, sed secundum quod directe tendit in objectum."

30. *ST*, IIaIIae, q. 1, a. 4: ". . . per quamdam electionem voluntarie declinans in unam partem magis quam in aliam."

31. *Q. D. de virtutibus in communi*, a. 7: "Unde voluntas imperat intellectui, credendo, non solum ad actum exequendum, sed quantum ad determinationem obiecti: quia ex imperio voluntatis in determinatum creditum intellectus assentit; sicut et in determinatum medium a ratione, concupiscibilis per temperantiam tendit."

32. John of St. Thomas, *Cursus theologicus, In IIamIIae, De Fide*, disp. 3, a. 7, n. 758 (Collectio Lavallensis, p. 203): "Respondetur enim voluntatem non addere aliquid objecto ex parte veritatis ut possit sufficienter movere quod alias de se non poterat, sed addere aliquid ex parte convenientiae, quia in quod movet voluntas repraesentatur ut conveniens ipsi voluntati, et ex hoc movetur intellectus ad assentiendum illi non quia visum sed quia placens et conveniens. Unde licet objectum obscure propositum non sit sufficiens ad movendum convincendo et necessitando intellectum, est tamen sufficiens ad movendum ad assensum voluntarium: voluntas movendo intellectum reddit illum dispositum ut sit mobilis ab illo objecto, obscuro quoad veritatem, apparente autem quoad convenientiam et complacentiam (saepe enim nobis placent res cognitae in confuso et in obscuro)."

the will for the determination of its object but only for its end. Given the will's ordination to the end of man, prudence seeks the means of attaining this end. We have already seen its dependence on moral virtue in making its judgment.

An indication of the difference between faith and prudence on the one hand and *intellectus*, science, wisdom, and art on the other can be seen in the fact that a man does not lose the habit of science by not knowing certain truths which pertain to that habit. In the case of faith, however, while faith remains, one cannot believe anything contrary to faith. The reason given is that science inclines *per modum rationis*, whereas faith inclines *per modum naturae*.[33]

These different habits participate in the *ratio virtutis*, then, in this order: first, moral virtues; then such intellectual habits as faith and prudence; and finally and least properly, *intellectus*, science, wisdom, and art. So, too, with regard to the way in which they imitate nature and incline *per modum naturae*. The same order obtains. Appetite takes priority over intellect in imitating nature; and habits which have appetite as subject or which depend in a special way upon appetite will incline *per modum naturae* more properly than purely intellectual habits.

In the light of this, it should no longer surprise us to find St. Thomas using the notion of connaturality in speaking of knowledge which is in no way affective. *Connatural* means "in accord with nature"; and since *nature* means many things, so too will *connatural*. Thus in speaking of geometry, St. Thomas says that, once one possesses the science, its objects become as it were connatural to the intellect.[34] One might object that St. Thomas is here placing under connaturality what he elsewhere divides against it. Such an objection assumes that *connatural* has only one meaning for St. Thomas; namely, affective knowledge. It is because the habit of geometry is a second nature that its objects become connatural to intellect. One must simply avoid identifying *connaturality* in such a context with the meaning that the same term has in the texts we discussed at the beginning of this paper. And, of course,

33. *In III Sent.*, d. 23, q. 3, a. 3, sol. 2, ad 2: ". . . dicendum quod habitus scientiae inclinat ad scibilia per modum rationis. Ideo potest habens habitum scientiae aliqua ignorare quae ad habitum illum pertinent. Sed habitus fidei cum non rationi innitatur, inclinat per modum naturae, sicut et habitus moralium et sicut habitus principiorum; et ideo quamdiu manet, nihil contra fidem credit." Cf. *ST*, IIaIIae, q. 1, a. 4, ad 3.

34. *In VII Ethic.*, lect. 3, n. 1344: "Secundum exemplum est de pueris quando primo addiscunt, qui coniungunt sermones quos ore proferunt sed nondum eos sciunt, ita scilicet quod mente intelligant. Ad hoc enim requiritur quod illa quae homo audit fiant ei quasi connaturalia, propter perfectam impressionem ipsorum in intellectum: ad quod homo indiget tempore in quo intellectus per multiplices meditationes firmetur in eo quod accepit."

it is knowledge through affective connaturality that most Thomists have in mind when they speak of connaturality.

What are the advantages and disadvantages of knowledge by affective connaturality with the object? In the practical order, we can see that, for better or worse, the condition of appetite exercises a decisive role in the operative syllogism. *Qualis unusquisque est, talis finis ei videtur.* In the theoretical order, custom, connaturality, reason led by appetite, is indispensable at the outset of the intellectual life—and an abiding danger as well. At first, one assents to the truth *quia placens* or because one believes in his master.[35] In either case, appetite enters into the very specification of the object of intellect. But the intellect should eventually proceed *per modum rationis* and assent because of the evidence of the object proposed. The danger of custom in the intellectual life is pointed out by Aristotle at the end of the second book of the *Metaphysics*.[36] One may *want* the poets cited as authorities or one may *want* a mathematical procedure in metaphysics because one finds these familiar and pleasing.

When things are beyond the comprehension of our intellects, affective connaturality assumes a new and awesome importance. We have seen in the remarks of St. Thomas and John of St. Thomas the role which the will plays in the assent of faith. The evidence of its proper object being insufficient to bring about the assent of intellect, the will moved by grace prompts assent. This assent is not absurd, as Kierkegaard thought, for the intellect could not assent in this fashion to something which contradicts what it knows with certitude. So, too, in the gift of wisdom, the influence of the will perfected by charity proportions divine things to the intellect, makes it connatural with them, so that one judges sapientially, referring everything to God.

3. THE VIRTUE OF ART

Our analysis of texts has indicated somewhat precisely the role the will plays in connatural knowledge. We will now go on to see why the notion of judgment by affective connaturality or inclination does not apply to the habit of art.

A virtue, we have seen, is a quality which makes the one having it good and renders his operation good; or, as it is also expressed, that which gives not only the ability, but also the inclination to act well. It is

---

35. *In Boethii de trin.*, lect. 1, q. 1, a. 1.   36. *In II Metaphysic.*, lect. 5.

the central position of good as the object of virtue which led St. Thomas to distinguish between virtues properly so called and those habits which are less properly virtues. There is no question here of judging their respective worth, dignity, or desirability. Rather, it is a matter of unequal participation in the *ratio virtutis*. In analogous names, that which most properly saves the *ratio nominis* is not always the most perfect *in re*.[37] Now, since the good enters in a very special way into the *ratio* signified by the name virtue, and since goodness is the proper object of appetite, those habits will most properly be called virtues which have appetite as their subject or which depend in a special way upon appetite. The intellectual virtues of faith and prudence were seen to depend upon appetite as preceding the proper act of reason, and thus they were said to be properly virtues. Of the acquired virtues, *intellectus*, science, wisdom, habits of the speculative intellect, and art, a habit of the practical intellect, were said to be least properly virtues. The will can move these virtues as an efficient cause insofar as their objects are included under the common notion of the good; but these four habits are of themselves only materially related to the good.[38]

What is of interest here, of course, is that art is aligned with the habits of the speculative intellect rather than with prudence when it is a question of how art saves the *ratio virtutis*.[39] Art does not make the one possessing it a good man; it merely makes him capable of judging correctly what ought to be done if the artifact is to be good. *Perfectio artis consistit in iudicando*.[40] In order that a man *use* art well, his appetite must be rectified by moral virtues.[41] Just as in the case of the speculative habits, it does not matter whether the artist is angry, sad, or elated when he operates; the artifact can still be well made. The vices of the artist are no less vices, but they do not necessarily affect his art. An indication of the fact that the perfection of art is in the judgment is the frequently quoted remark of Aristotle that the artist who intentionally makes a mistake is better than one who does so unintentionally; in prudence, however, it is less wrong to err unintentionally than intentionally.[42] Since judgment is properly of intellect, then, it would appear that art is more intellectual than prudence. Not depending on appetite as does prudence, art does not rely on the rec-

---

37. *SCG*, I, cap. 34; *Q. D. de virtutibus in communi*, a. 7, in fine.
38. *Q. D. de virtutibus in communi*, a. 7.   39. *ST*, IaIIae, q. 57, a. 3.
40. Ibid., IIaIIae, q. 47, a. 8.   41. Ibid., IaIIae, q. 57, a. 3, ad 2.
42. Ibid., a. 4. Cf. ibid., IIaIIae, q. 47, a. 8.

tification of appetite relatively to the end of man. Moral virtues are necessary for the good use of art, but that is all.[43] This is but another indication of art's affinity with the habits of the speculative intellect.

Thus far it would seem that connaturality, an intrinsic dependence upon appetite, has nothing to do with art any more than it has with the habit of first principles or science. And yet to settle for this would seem to be an overlooking of the rather important fact that art is a virtue of the practical intellect. And the practical intellect, unlike the speculative intellect, does not seek knowledge for its own sake but with a view to operation. And, whether the operation is doing or making, the role of the will would seem to be somewhat more central than in speculative knowledge. What is more, St. Thomas tells us that art is true with practical truth, and practical truth is the intellect's conformity with rectified appetite.[44]

On the one hand, St. Thomas had said that art, like science and wisdom, is not dependent upon the rectification of appetite. On the other, he applies the notion of practical truth, conformity with rectified appetite, to art. How can these two affirmations possibly be reconciled?

Cajetan, in commenting on the article in question, devotes the bulk of his treatment to art and practical truth. What distinguishes the practical from the speculative, he argues, is not knowledge but the fact that the former directs.[45] The truth of the direction of the practical intellect must always depend upon rectified appetite. However, Cajetan would distinguish between two meanings of rectified appetite in order to maintain the difference between art and prudence. The truth of the direction of the practical intellect *in agibilibus* is dependent upon conformity with appetite rectified with regard to man's end. The truth of the direction of the practical intellect in matters of art, on the other hand, is dependent upon appetite rectified relatively to the end of art.[46] Cajetan warns the novice in these matters not to confuse the truth of the direction of art with the use of art. Direction and use coincide in the production of the artifact, but they remain formally distinct.[47]

43. Ibid., IaIIae, q. 57, a. 1.   44. Ibid., a. 5, ad 3.
45. *In IamIIae*, q. 57, a. 5, n. 2.   46. Ibid., n. 3.
47. Ibid., n. 4: "Adverte namque coincidentiam usus cum directione in arte: et vide quare apparet quod veritas huiusmodi spectet ad usum, et non ad artem. Quamvis enim usus et directio in arte coincidant, distinguuntur tamen saltem ratione: et arti convenit directionis veritas, non ratione usus, sed ratione propriae naturae, quae nata est dirigere non nisi determinata ad directionem ab appetitu recto. In virtutibus autem speculativis, solum usus invenitur pendens ab appetitu."

The difficulty that arises yet again is: What manner of rectification of appetite is required by art? In prudence, this rectification is had by the possession of the moral virtues, having appetite as their subject. Cajetan has made clear that it is not the moral virtues which give the rectification of appetite that art requires. Does this last kind of rectification require virtues? If not, why speak of rectification? If so, what precisely are these virtues supposed to be? Perhaps a glance at the artistic process as described by St. Thomas will dissipate these difficulties.

St. Thomas distinguishes three steps in the actual direction of art.[48] Presupposed by this actual direction are a great many things, of course: the knowledge the artist might have, his experience of life, and so on. But in the actual direction there would be first of all the *intentio finis*, reason proposing to the will the artifact to be made. The next step, the *excogitatio formae*, is the judging of the means necessary to realize the proposed end. It is here, as we have seen, that the perfection of art lies. Now, the question we are asking is, Since the judgment of the means will be true by practical truth—that is, in conformity with rectified appetite—what is required on the part of appetite for this rectification? We have already seen that it does not require the rectification had by means of the moral virtues.[49]

The end of art is contained in the exemplar idea which is present in the mind of the artist. The end of art, unlike that of man as man, is not had *in affectu* as by the moral virtues.[50] The judgment of the means of attaining the opus, then, is not dependent on the condition of the appetite as is the judgment of prudence. St. Thomas's solution of our difficulty is succinct and simple. The will does not require any habitus to perfect it and relate it to the end proposed by art.[51] The appetite does not need any virtues to bring it more surely under the control of art; the judgment of art, therefore, is not affected by appetite. This is why St. Thomas places art with the speculative virtues

48. *Q. D. de ver.*, q. 4, a. 1.

49. John of St. Thomas, *Cursus theologicus, In IamIIae*, disp. 16, a. 4: "Sed tamen ista regulatio artis in actibus differt a regulatione morali, quia moralis est secundum legem impositam actibus liberis, et juxta rationis dispositionem ad recte agendum, artificiosa vero est dispositio objecti omnino independens a rectitudine et intentione voluntatis aut a lege recte vivendi, sed solum rem ipsam intelligendam aut cognoscendam vel operandam in se rectificans juxta finem artis, non ut rectificetur arbitrium operantis."

50. *Q. D. de ver.*, q. 5, a. 1.

51. *ST*, IaIIae, q. 58, a. 5, ad 2: "Dicendum quod principia artificialium non diiudicantur a nobis bene vel male secundum dispositionem appetitus nostri, sicut fines, qui sunt moralium principia, sed solum per considerationem rationis. Et ideo ars non requirit virtutem perficientem appetitum, sicut requirit prudentia."

and not with prudence; and this is also why we cannot say that the judgment of art is one by affective connaturality.

4. POETIC KNOWLEDGE AND CONNATURALITY

Although no one has maintained that the judgment of art is connatural, it has been held that poetic knowledge—as opposed to, and presupposed by, art—is a type of connatural knowledge. In a paper already lengthy, it would not do to attempt an analysis of these views. Ours will be the much less ambitious task of seeking in the metaphor, the proper instrument of the poet, evidence of connatural knowledge.

If, as we have tried to show, the judgment of the means of realizing the idea, which is the proper act of the virtue of art, does not lend itself to the notion of connaturality, it seems that the creative or exemplar idea does. One can be said to judge connaturally when appetite moves the mind in the order of formal causality, coloring and influencing that which specifies the intellect: when *affectus transit in conditionem obiecti.*[52] When a truth which is above the comprehension of the intellect is presented for assent, the will, under the influence of grace, can render the truth, not evident or intelligible, but pleasing. The consequent assent of the intellect is due to a specifying activity of appetite. Could one derive from this the general rule that whenever a connection is not sufficient to move the intellect in the proper line of evidence and truth, appetite can formally influence the judgment by rendering the connection pleasing?

Poetry is said by St. Thomas[53] to be concerned with things which do not have sufficient intelligibility to force the assent of the intellect. It is because of the lack of truth and cogency that poetry is said to need metaphors in order to seduce reason into assenting. This last remark may be a sign of something which had preceded the poem in the experience of the poet. When one reads *Dover Beach*, he is presented with a judgment on man's relation to the universe. Without hazarding an exegesis of the poem, it could be said that the net conclusion is that one's beloved is the sole refuge in a deluding, malevolent, even irrational, universe. Stated as baldly as this, the idea is not much, but of course that is not how Arnold presents the idea. Appeal is not made directly or solely to the mind; rather, the images and rhythms of the

52. Cf. John of St. Thomas, *Cursus theologicus, In IIamIIae, De donis* (Collectio Lavallensis), disp. 18, a. 4, n. 584.

53. *In I Sent.*, prolog., a. 5; *ST*, IaIIae, q. 101, a. 2, ad 2.

lines get into our viscera and emotions, and the "argument" is rendered pleasing and acceptable. If we accept *Dover Beach* it is not *quia verum est* but rather *quia placens*.

This is hardly revolutionary. Neither does it seem forced to say that Arnold, by writing the poem, is allowing us to share in a way he once looked at things. And, just as our experience in reading his poem is not an exercise in pure reason, neither, we can surmise, was the experience which the poem conveys a totally rational one. (One could say "more than rational"; but this phrase seems to signify something other than a quantitative "more," as if what were meant is "better than rational" or suprarational. Poetry may be more human than science, but it is for all that *infima doctrina*.)

If one takes a rather broad view of metaphor as a seeing of things in terms of other things, one might imagine the poet finding a pleasant *collatio* (later to be expressed in metaphor) to which his intellect can assent. The likening of his love to a rose surely does not appear to the poet as something charged with intelligibility, and yet, in the very confusion of the comparison, there is something which appetite can transform into something pleasant. The expressed metaphor would be a result, presumably, of the judgment of the virtue of art. How best express the collation which has been rendered pleasant? The answer to this question, it would appear, is found in a rational search for the best verbal expression for the previous confused connection in the poet's mind.

It would seem that it is something like this that is intended when poetic knowledge is spoken of in terms of affective connaturality. We have seen that, if one is desirous of applying such connaturality to the realm of art, one must attach it to something other than the virtue of art. Perhaps some such appetitive connaturality is involved in the knowledge of the poet; nevertheless, there would seem to be a more profound and more traditional way of speaking of the knowledge of the poet as connatural, this time using the term to signify something other than the influence of appetite on the judgment of intellect. One thinks of the phrase, *poetae nascuntur*; poets are born, not made. If it is true that a poet is born such, that his physical make-up (not to be understood superficially) and his imagination are especially apt for finding surprising similitudes among things, then his knowledge would be connatural in a much more basic sense of the term. Is this why Aristotle speaks[54] of a gift for finding metaphors, an inborn gift

54. *Poetics*, 1459a5.

(*ingenium*), not to be learned, following on the very nature of this man who is a poet?

Whichever of these two ways of extending the notion of connaturality to poetic knowledge is chosen, it is certain that there is no place for affective connaturality in speaking of the direction by the virtue of art. Whatever the explanation of it, it is delightfully true that the poet can come upon the world in a grain of sand and render this collation, if not less unlikely, nevertheless pleasing and cogent.

20

MARITAIN AND POETIC KNOWLEDGE

It could be said that the philosophy of art has had as little influence on its ostensible subject as the philosophy of science has had on its. Thus it is noteworthy that Jacques Maritain's reflections on art and poetry, spanning his long active career, not only were inspired by a profound involvement with art and artists but also influenced artists who reflected upon their own efforts. To cite a single instance, Flannery O'Connor, in the letters collected by Sally Fitzgerald under the title *The Habit of Being*, often acknowledges her debt to *Art and Scholasticism*.

What precisely was it that O'Connor learned from Maritain? It seems that the basic lesson was that art is not self-expression:

Also to have sympathy for any character, you have to put a good deal of yourself in him. But to say that any complete denudation of the author occurs in the successful work is, according to me, a romantic exaggeration. A great part of the art of it is precisely in seeing that this does not happen. Maritain says that to produce a work of art requires "the constant attention of the purified mind," and the business of the purified mind in this case is to see that those elements of the personality that don't bear on the subject at hand are excluded. Stories don't lie when left to themselves. Everything has to be subordinated to a whole which is not you. Any story I reveal myself completely in will be a bad story.[1]

Art is a virtue of the practical intellect whose end is the *bonum operis*, the good of the artifact. This notion that Maritain got from Thomas Aquinas who got it from Aristotle came to Flannery O'Connor like a fresh wind. It both confirmed her own hunch and influenced her later work. But the passage she puts in quotation marks is one that any student of Maritain will recognize as what is most distinctive about the great French Catholic philosopher's views on artistic knowledge.

Maritain once said that he would prefer to be seen as a Paleo-Thomist rather than a Neo-Thomist. He was immersed in the thought

1. *The Habit of Being*, ed. Sally Fitzgerald (New York: 1979), p. 105.

of his master—*Vae mihi si non thomistizavero*—but like all genuine disciples he was a creative follower, extending the insights he found into areas undreamt of by his mentor. This is nowhere more evident than in the uses to which Maritain put the concept of judgment by connaturality which he had found in Thomas. His analogical prolongation of the concept of connatural knowledge from its Thomistic setting into the realm of poetic knowledge provides not only a topic central to Maritain's aesthetics but also a good test case of his style of creative Thomism.

In what follows, I shall recall the Thomistic doctrine, developing it in the settings St. Thomas himself did, and then go on to consider Maritain's extension of connatural knowledge to poetry, emphasizing first how the analogy limps and then its essential fruitfulness. My first task entails some rather technical discussions but in pursuing it I will keep technical language and scholarly documentation to a minimum. A basic way of pursuing the second task would be to trace the chronological development of Maritain's thoughts on the matter, singling out the persistent strands, drawing attention to aspects which emerge only gradually and late. This will not be my way here. Rather, assuming without proving the essential unity and consistency of Maritain's thought on this matter, I shall blend a number of sources with an eye to giving the strongest possible presentation of his thought.

In the first question of the First Part of the *Summa theologiae*, where St. Thomas is setting forth his conception of theology, the question arises as to whether or not theology can be characterized as wisdom. The third objection in article 6 suggests that theology cannot be called a wisdom because it is acquired by means of study whereas wisdom is an infused gift of the Holy Ghost. Thomas's reply to this objection caught Maritain's eye and planted a seed that was to bear an immense fruit.

Since judgment pertains to wisdom, wisdom will vary as types of judgment vary. In one way, a person judges by way of inclination, as one who has the habit of virtue rightly judges those things which are to be done according to that virtue, insofar as he is inclined to them; that is why it is said in *Nicomachean Ethics*, X, that the virtuous man is a rule and measure of human actions. In another manner, by way of knowledge, as someone instructed in moral science can judge the acts of virtue even if he does not have the virtue.[2]

As is well known, the *Summa theologiae* was intended to be an introductory work but, since the neophyte in theology is supposed already to

2. *ST*, Ia, q. 1, a. 6, ad 3.

be a philosopher, preliminary discussions of theological issues always ride on brief reminders of what is already known from philosophical study. The remarks Thomas here makes concerning the judgment of the virtuous man and the judgment of the man learned in moral matters, the moral philosopher, are meant to remind his reader of what he will have learned from the study of such works as Aristotle's *Nicomachean Ethics*. Let us recall some of those presuppositions.

The reader of the *Nicomachean Ethics* is not someone on the threshold of the moral life; he comes to this work of philosophical reflection against the background of his personal history of action. Human action, by definition, is rational behavior, so moral philosophy presupposes an experience which has a cognitive component. Any man who acts knows what he is doing; he acts consciously. But this is not to say that he has a theory of action. Does he need the kind of reflection moral philosophy constitutes in order to act well? Surely not. Moral philosophy is not a necessity for good human action. On the contrary, it could be argued that unless there were instances of good human actions, moral philosophy would have no empirical base on which to begin. It would be an odd claim that one without three credits of ethics is prevented from becoming a good man. "One does not become good by philosophizing," Aristotle points out. And, in the passage cited by Thomas in the quotation above, Aristotle observes that with respect to human actions the virtuous man is a rule and measure. The moral philosopher is guided in his reflections by noticing the way good men behave.

Moral action involves judgments both as to what is the perfection or good of the human agent and as to how this good can be achieved in fleeting and changing circumstances. However, it is another tenet of Aristotle's that most men are bad. The fact that every human person after a certain age is willy-nilly engaged in the moral life does not entail that everyone is acting well. This suggests something of a paradox. If we should select a human agent at random—it might be oneself— then, if Aristotle is right, the statistical probability is that we will have selected a bad man. Nonetheless, the agent we have chosen should be such that, besides that in him which explains why he is going wrong, there is also some intimation of what really constitutes his good.

Moral philosophy, as practiced by Aristotle, is the effort to sort out the judgments latent in human action and to appraise and assess them in the light of principles which are also latent in human action. The aim of moral philosophy is not simply to arrive at theoretical knowledge of human action, but to provide guidelines which will enable the agent to act well in the future. Moral philosophy thus appears as reflection on the level of generality which takes its rise from particular human actions and seeks to close the circuit by being helpful to future human actions. This is what is meant by calling it practical knowledge. Its ultimate aim is the perfection not of the mind, but of action, choices, decisions.

On the assumption that "happiness" is a term everyone will accept as designating the point of acting at all, Aristotle would argue that most men seek their happiness or fulfillment where it cannot really be found. Once true happiness has been clarified, the moral philosopher is in possession of his most powerful tool for determining the kinds of action which are conducive to or destructive of human happiness, and he can give general advice on that basis. It is the generality of moral philosophy which is its *grandeur et misère*. Clarification of what we ought to do is an achievement but, being general, it does not immediately apply to the singular circumstances in which we must act. True, the moral philosopher can develop cases, tell stories of typical human acts, but these are meant to range over many instances and there remains the problem of application. Moral philosophy cannot itself close the circuit mentioned earlier.

The judgment of the moral philosopher is a purely cognitive one; it does not as such engage his subjectivity. This is why, as Thomas points out, he can speak of virtues even when he does not possess them. It is the recognition that the judgment which is embedded in the singular act is not a purely cognitive one which leads to the distinction between two kinds of judgment. By moral upbringing, by the study of moral philosophy, or even without it, I act in the light of more or less articulate notions of what one ought to do in circumstances of a given kind. What happens when my action is not in conformity with my knowledge? Let us say that I know I should be temperate in the consumption of alcohol, I may even be a poet of temperance, and yet, alas, I overindulge and later feel remorse. My defective action does not seem to be a cognitive defect. Yet, when I overindulge, I *decide* to do so, I *judge* that it is good for me to have another drink here and now. Knowledge is in conflict with knowledge, judgment with judgment. The singular judgment or decision will be in conformity with the principle when the good expressed by the principle is *my* good, when my appetite is inclined to it habitually. That is why Thomas speaks of the singular moral judgment as true by conformity with rectified appetite: that is, with the appetitive orientation to the true good. If I am appetitively inclined to what is not my true good, my purely cognitive recognition of the true good cannot be efficacious in action.

Perhaps this will suffice as a gloss on the passage from the *Summa theologiae*. Any singular moral judgment is a judgment by way of inclination and it will be a good one if I am inclined to what is my true good. If we ask advice of a good man who is not also a moral philosopher his answer, after reflection, is likely to take the form, "Well, what I would do is. . . ." That is, he puts himself in our shoes and judges in accordance with his steady orientation to the true good. The advice of the moral philosopher, on the other hand, does not depend on his own moral condition.

The judgment by appetitive inclination or, as it may also be dubbed, affective connaturality, has its natural habitat in the analysis of singular moral decisions. Thomas himself extended it to discussions of the assent of faith as well as to judgments of the Gift of Wisdom. In the primary instance, will or appetite has a steady inclination to the true good, thanks to the possession of habits of virtue. That is why the virtuous man is the measure in human action. In the assent of faith, unless the will, prompted by grace, moves the intellect, there will be no assent. So too judgments made under the influence of the Gift of Wisdom presuppose an appetitive orientation. Nowhere does Thomas apply this sort of talk to the realm of art.

Thomas has good reasons for not speaking of a judgment by way of inclination or affective connaturality in the case of art. Prudence or practical wisdom is the virtue of the practical intellect, thanks to which a person judges well as to what will make his actions, and himself, good, and this judgment, in order to be efficacious, depends upon the possession of moral virtues, that is, on a steady appetitive orientation to the true good. The aim of prudence is to make the human agent good. Art, on the other hand, is a virtue of the practical intellect whose aim is the good or perfection of the thing made. Prudence is concerned with doing (the *agibile*) and art with making (the *factibile*). In *Art and Scholasticism*, chapter 3, Maritain develops this contrast.

Art, which rules Making and not Doing, stands therefore outside the human sphere; it has an end, rules, values, which are not those of man, but those of the work to be produced. This work is everything for Art: there is for Art but one law—the exigencies and the good of the work.[3]

The sequel to this passage may very well be what Flannery O'Connor found so liberating in Maritain's presentation.

3. *Art and Scholasticism and The Frontiers of Poetry*, trans. Joseph W. Evans (Notre Dame: 1974), p. 9; hereafter cited parenthetically in the text as *A and S*.

Hence the tyrannical and absorbing power of Art, and also its astonishing power of soothing; it delivers one from the human; it establishes the *artifex*—artist or artisan—in a world apart, closed, limited, absolute, in which he puts the energy and intelligence of his manhood at the service of a thing which he makes. This is true of all art; the ennui of living and willing ceases at the door of the workshop. (*A and S*, 9)

Maritain is here being guided closely by St. Thomas Aquinas. In speaking of art as a virtue (*recta ratio faciendorum*), Thomas stresses the independence of art from the condition of the appetite of the maker: it is not his good but the good of the work that is in view. An artist is not praised as artist because of his appetitive condition but rather because the work he makes is good.[4] This leads Thomas to see an affinity between art and the speculative virtues. The aim of the latter is truth and a mathematical argument is assessed without reference to the moral character of the mathematician. Summarizing this, Thomas introduces, almost as an aside, an extremely important point. The intellectual virtues and art are *capacities* to do something well, whether arriving at the truth or producing good artifacts—but they do not insure the good *use* of those capacities. In order for the artist to use well the art that he has, he must be in possession of moral virtues which perfect his will.

The tradition in which Maritain moves sees the capacity of the artist to produce good artifacts as independent of his moral condition. There is no intrinsic dependence of art on moral virtue any more than there is an intrinsic dependence of geometry on the moral character of the geometer or for that matter of moral philosophy on the appetitive condition of the moral philosopher. In prudence or practical wisdom there is such an intrinsic dependence; this virtue simply cannot be had if the person's appetite is not steadily oriented to the true good. Thus Thomas will say that prudence gives both capacity and use. The suggestion is that theoretical knowledge and art are amoral.

If the judgment of the artist were to be one by way of affective connaturality, then the appetite of the artist must be in some way in conflict with the good of the artifact; he needs moral virtues to bring his appetite under control and thereby make the many particular judgments he must make in order to effect the artifact. But Thomas Aquinas, on whom Maritain is relying, does not see this to be the case. The judgment of the artist as he proceeds in his work is not intrinsically dependent on virtues which steadily orient his appetite to the

4. *ST*, IaIIae, q. 57, a. 3: "Non enim pertinet ad laudem artificis, inquantum artifex est, qua voluntate opus faciat; sed quale sit opus quod facit."

good of the artifact. From this it follows that the judgment of the artist cannot be described as proceeding by way of affective connaturality. No more could one describe the judgments of the geometer or of the moral philosopher as being instances of judgments by way of affective connaturality.

From a narrow exegetical point of view, then, one would have to say that the thought of Thomas Aquinas provides Maritain no basis for speaking of poetic knowledge as an instance of affective connaturality; on the contrary, it impedes him from doing so. Any student of Maritain will know that on many occasions he was confronted with criticisms of this sort when someone would point out to him that the texts in Thomas on which he sought to rely did not sustain the use to which he wished to put them. This was true in political philosophy, philosophy of science, his discussions of degrees of practical knowing and so forth. As often as not, the critics were right. Maritain was working from texts of Thomas, not merely providing glosses on them, although sometimes he himself seemed imperfectly aware of this. What he had to say of art and morality, which has a good Thomistic base, provided him with the opening through which he went on to speak of creative intuition as involving affective connaturality. He thereby extended the Thomistic notion of affective connaturality in a way that does not conflict with his master but which surely goes beyond him.

The distinction Thomas makes between capacity (*facultas*) and use and his claim that speculative virtues and art give only a capacity and not the inclination to use it well is in many ways a puzzling one. On the one hand, it underwrites the obvious fact that a good geometer may not be a good man; on the other hand, it seems to invite the almost excessive divorce of art from human life of the kind we see in the passage from *Art and Scholasticism* quoted earlier. There is something unsavory in the suggestion that one has a choice between being a good artist or a good geometer, on the one hand, and a good man, on the other. Furthermore, to do geometry or to write a poem would seem to be instances of human actions and these, we argued earlier, are by definition moral. How can some human activities escape the net of morality if human actions are as such moral? One is reminded of Yeats's poem "The Choice."

> The intellect of man is forced to choose
> Perfection of the life or of the work
> And if it take the second must refuse
> A heavenly mansion, raging in the dark.

If we begin with the speculative sciences, a way to resolve this difficulty suggests itself. Elsewhere, I have discussed this matter in conjunction with Maritain's notion of Christian Philosophy.[5] Doing geometry is a human act and as such is subject to moral appraisal. Let us imagine a mathematician, in his office, at his blackboard, chalking his way toward a proof hitherto unknown to men. He achieves it. On the basis of this we can say that he is a good geometer. Why does that not entail that he is a good man? Well, let us say that, while he works, his assistant who was leaning out the window, fell and, dangling precariously by his fingertips, is shouting for help and the geometer ignores him. No achievement in geometry is going to override the misfortune of the assistant who loses his grip and plummets to his death as the geometer turns from his blackboard crying "Eureka."

The skill or capacity of the geometer is put to use in a context which provides ways of appraising what he is doing which are moral not mathematical. It is the same activity which gets him good grades as a geometer and bad grades as a man. A more morally sensitive geometer does not, on that score, get good grades as a geometer, but rather as a human being. And the moral considerations always take priority; they are overriding. At the wake, the geometer cannot justify what he did, or failed to do, by sketching for the widow the proof he was writing on the blackboard the day her husband fluttered down seven stories and became a lifeless, messy asterisk on the parking lot below. Thus the *use* of his capacity is in the moral order and for the assessment of that the usual moral considerations obtain, including the doctrine of prudential judgments by way of affective connaturality.

This is the sort of consideration we find Maritain undertaking in the final chapter of *Art and Scholasticism* in which he discusses art and morality: "Because it exists in man and because its good is not the good of man, art is subject in its exercise to an extrinsic control, imposed in the name of a higher end which is the beatitude of the living being in whom it resides" (*A and S*, 71). The little book *The Responsibility of the Artist*[6] is a later and more thorough discussion of the same matter. What has been said of the geometer may be said of the shoemaker or sonneteer. Sketching an undraped model in a public park at

5. Cf. *One Hundred Years of Thomism*, ed. Victor Brezik, C.S.B. (Houston: 1981), pp. 63–73.

6. Jacques Maritain, *The Responsibility of the Artist* (New York: 1972), hereafter cited parenthetically in the text as *RA*. In Maritain's *The Range of Reason*, one finds essays on artistic judgment and on knowledge through connaturality. See also Rafael-Tomas Caldera, *Le jugement par inclination chez Saint Thomas d'Aquin* (Paris: 1980).

noonday would require a justification of the artist other than the result on canvas, or at least would have, in a saner day. Taking samples of human skin with a sharp knife in the subway cannot be justified by the artist's claim that he is in search of more realistic pigments. The contralto ought to pay her bills and high notes are not enough. And so on. The artist is a human being and the common moral demands on human beings apply to him. These demands may dictate that he not practice his art in certain circumstances.

All that is true enough, but it is scarcely interesting. At least it would not be if there were not artists who have wished to fashion a morality controlled by the good of the work alone, with everything else resolutely subordinated to it. Maritain's discussion of Art for Art's Sake, in the book just mentioned, relies heavily on his personal knowledge of such artists as Cocteau and his readings in others such as Wilde. He knows that artists have often devised a pseudo-morality, requiring great self-abnegation, even asceticism, and a ruthless treatment of others, in order to accomplish the ends of their art. They are a facet of that phenomenon Kierkegaard calls the aesthete. The Kierkegaardian aesthete is not necessarily an artist in the usual sense—he may be a hedonist. But hedonism too makes its demands lest one become jaded. There must be a rotation of crops to stave off boredom and to retain some novelty in the constantly repeated activity.

This shadow morality, while it does not question the distinctions Maritain has taken from Aquinas, modifies them subtly. An artist can take the end of his art as his supreme good in the way the poem of Yeats suggests. Morally evil action will then be justified as providing experience important for the production of an artifact. Wilde, noting that the poet must depict both good and evil, saw justification for the claim that he must *be* good and evil.

None of this takes us to the center of Maritain's contention that poetic knowledge involves affective connaturality. But it is the way to the center. The morally good use of the capacity the virtue of art provides is extrinsic to art as such; it merely places it in the wider human moral context in which art is exercised and enables us to make a two-fold assessment of it, intrinsic as art, extrinsic as moral. Maritain wants to argue for more than an extrinsic or *per accidens* connection of morality and poetic knowledge:

A moral poison which warps in the long run the power of vision will finally, through an indirect repercussion, warp artistic creativity—though perhaps this poison will have stimulated or sensitized it for a time. At long last the work always *avows*. When it is a question of great poets, this kind of avowal does not prevent the work from being great and treasurable, yet it points to some soft spot in this greatness. (*RA*, 93)

There is a refreshing lack of moralizing in Maritain's discussion of the relationship between art and morality. He is not interested in denying that men who are reprehensible human beings nonetheless produce works of art of undeniable excellence. Yet he is attracted by the view that the morally good person will be a better artist for that very fact.

This can mean at least two things, as we have already seen. It can mean that artistic activity is engaged in by a human being and thus comes under a moral assessment as well as an aesthetic one. The discipline required of the artist is itself a moral achievement and can indeed form part of a network of practices which make up his way of life. Maritain will regard this as a shadow morality if the good of the artifact is taken to be the supreme good of the artist as man as well as artist. The undeniable discipline and restraint and asceticism in such a life may be such that ordinary moral demands, being seen as conflicting with the good of the work, are ruthlessly set aside.

But there is a sunnier possibility. Maritain feels, and that is when the moral virtues, while retaining their orientation to the human end, *also* facilitate the achievement of the ends of art. And then, speaking of the artist's affinity with his subject matter, Maritain suggests that a parallel can be drawn between art and contemplation. The contemplative enters into affective union with God and this affectivity supplies a kind of cognitive object, a type of knowledge. *Amor transit in conditionem objecti*, as John of St. Thomas put it: the appetitive relation between lover and beloved itself becomes thematic. Here we have the basis for Maritain's prolongation of the notion of affective connaturality to poetic knowledge.

We have also reached the point where Maritain's use of the notion of affective connaturality in speaking of poetic knowledge touches on his use of intuition for the same purpose. Increasingly, his interest turned to the preconceptual or non-conceptual knowledge out of which the fashioning knowledge of the artist arises, the sense of the world and of reality which precedes the constructive work. *Creative Intuition in Art and Poetry*, perhaps the most important single work in aesthetics Maritain ever wrote, is precisely devoted to this. To pursue Maritain's treatment of intuition, however, is beyond the scope of this modest paper.

The text in Aquinas from which Maritain begins, with its distinction between the judgment of the moral philosopher and the judgment of the moral agent, suggests a contrast in aesthetics that Maritain did not draw, namely that between criticism or theory, on the one hand, and practice or production, on the other. The working artist does not require a theory of art any more than every human agent must have an articulated moral theory. The dependence of criticism on art also emerges from pursuing this parallel. Just as the moral philosopher must presuppose the existence of good men and be guided by them as he develops his theory, so too criticism and aesthetic theory are parasitic on the existence of artifacts. Given the artifact and the ostensible good intended, the critic can then assess how well and to what degree the artist has achieved the end he set himself. Finally, just as moral theory has what use it has when it is returned to the order of singular actions from which it took its rise, so criticism and aesthetic theory are ultimately justified by the way they enhance our appreciation and understanding of art.

Maritain went in a different direction from the passage in question, a direction which finally led him to the view summarized in this way:

Let me add that the highest form of knowledge through inclination or congeniality is provided by that kind of presence of the one within the other which is proper to love. If the novelist is the God of his characters, why could he not love them with a redeeming love? We are told (it is irrational, but it is a fact), that Bernanos could not help *praying for his characters*. When a novelist has this kind of love even for his most hateful characters, then he knows them, through inclination, in the truest possible way, and the risk of being contaminated by them still exists for him, I think, but to a lesser degree than ever. (*RA*, 114)

A novelist's way of seeing his characters, their hopes and dreams, their actions, his vision of life, in short—is that what Maritain is drawing our attention to? There are many things which go into the way an artist, or anyone, sees the world. The novelist, whatever his vision, must struggle to be true to it, to enable his reader to *see* in Conrad's sense or, in the Hemingway sense, to write *truly* of it. As for the artist's vision, apart from its metabolic, psychological, genetic or other accidental components, there seems room as well for an influence of moral character. Maritain has suggested a number of ways in which the artist's moral character can influence his art. His position remains tantalizingly vague. That may be one of its attractions. Who today will dare to carry on the line of investigation Maritain opened up?

Index of Names and Topics

Index of Texts of St. Thomas Aquinas